PERSONS IN RELATION

PERSONS IN RELATION

AN ESSAY ON THE TRINITY AND ONTOLOGY

NAJIB GEORGE AWAD

Fortress Press
Minneapolis

PERSONS IN RELATION
An Essay on the Trinity and Ontology

Copyright © 2014 Fortress Press. All rights reserved. Except for brief quotations in critical articles or reviews, no part of this book may be reproduced in any manner without prior written permission from the publisher. Visit http://www.augsburgfortress.org/copyrights/ or write to Permissions, Augsburg Fortress, Box 1209, Minneapolis, MN 55440.

Cover image: Detail from Cotton Faustina Manuscript, 13th c. (Source: Wikimedia).

Cover design: Erica Rieck

Library of Congress Cataloging-in-Publication Data
ISBN: 978-1-4514-8037-5
eBook ISBN: 978-1-4514-8425-0

The paper used in this publication meets the minimum requirements of American National Standard for Information Sciences — Permanence of Paper for Printed Library Materials, ANSI Z329.48-1984.

Manufactured in the U.S.A.

This book was produced using PressBooks.com, and PDF rendering was done by PrinceXML.

To
*Jouhayna, Hala, Ziad, Zainah, George, Najib Jr., and Samira—
my beloved, striving family in Syria, our destroyed homeland,
whose love, support, and belief in me embrace me wherever I am*

CONTENTS

Preface ... ix
Introduction ... 1

Part I. The Roots: Theology and the Question of Self in Modernity

1. The Modernist Condition ... 19
2. Theological Conditioning? ... 35

Part II. The Challenge: Trinitarian Theology and/in Postmodernity

3. The Postmodernist Conditioning ... 97
4. The "Trinity" and the Evaluation of the Theological Re-Conditioning Ambition ... 141

Part III. The Proposal: Trinitarian Theology and Postmodernity: In Correlation?

5. Correlation and/as Hierarchism, or What We Do Not Need ... 203
6. Correlation beyond Hierarchism ... 239
7. Perichoresis of "Person" and "Relation" and Trinitarian Theology ... 259
8. Correlation as Relationship Model in/with the World ... 291

Conclusion: When Theology Stands in History ... 303
Bibliography ... 309
Index of Names ... 333
Index of Subjects ... 337

PREFACE

The idea of writing this book goes back to 2005. At that time, I finished writing my doctoral dissertation on the personal individuation of the Holy Spirit (published later as *God Without a Face? On the Personal Individuation of the Holy Spirit*, [Tübingen: Mohr Siebeck, 2011]). In order to pursue my doctoral research, I delved deeply and extensively into the doctrine of the Trinity in modern, medieval, and patristic eras alike. I realized from that intellectual journey the profound relevance and connectedness of the doctrine of the Trinity to the entire spectrum of Christian theology. I also perceived from my broad reading of the literature on trinitarian theology, especially the contemporary ones, that the doctrine of the Trinity is undoubtedly center-stage on the theological and philosophical scene in our postmodern age.

Be that as it may, I decided to take my study of trinitarian theology further, into the realm of the key anthropological and conceptual notions of "personhood" and "relationality." The result was this book, which attempts to think about how trinitarian theologians of the modern and postmodern eras interacted with, and were shaped by, other modernist and postmodernist forms of inquiry. Postmodernity is thus the main context of this endeavor, and the notions of "personhood" and "relationality" are its primary subject.

Between 2005, when I started developing this project, and 2009, when I finished its first draft, many people contributed to my research process and made the production of this book a real possibility. I am deeply indebted to the Langham Trust, especially Dr. Chris Wright, and to its sister trust, John Stott Ministries, for generously offering me a one-year scholarship to pursue this project in a proper research center at the Yale Divinity School. Without this generous grant, I would have not been able to achieve my goal.

My sincere gratitude and appreciation go also to Yale Divinity School, personified in Prof. Miroslav Volf, who kindly invited me during the academic year of 2008–09 to visit Yale and pursue research for one year as a Visiting Fellow in his Yale Center for Faith and Culture. Professor Volf offered me all the support and help I needed to sharpen my arguments and carefully assess my claims in this book. Professor Volf's invitation enabled me to enjoy the massive available resources in the Yale Divinity School's library, and Yale University's Sterling Library, which supplied me with all the literature I needed to complete my work.

I also convey my profound and unstinting gratitude to the Overseas Ministries Study Center (OMSC) and its ex-Director, Dr. Jonathan Bonk. I cannot find enough words to thank Jonathan for his incredibly generous offer of a free-of-charge residence at the center, which nicely sheltered me during my stay in New Haven. During my time at OMSC, Dr. Bonk was steadily supportive and encouraging to me and my project in ways I cannot even begin to praise.

My gratitude goes also to certain individuals, without the help of whom this project would have not seen the light. I am deeply indebted to the dear Professor Emeritus, David Kelsey, with whom I enjoyed discussing my project while I was at Yale. Professor Kelsey offered me and my project a considerable portion of his precious time. His remarks, critiques, and corrections played a substantial role in shaping the manuscript's form, as well as the arguments and claims I made therein. His challenging questions have consistently inspired me to dig deeper and elaborate more thoroughly.

My sincere thanks go also to Prof. Dr. Hans-Peter Grosshans of Münster University. Professor Grosshans kindly and patiently read through the entire manuscript and provided me with valuable suggestions that have made the text more solidly and systematically constructed.

I also extend my thanks and perpetual appreciation to Dr. Terry Wright, who proofread the very first draft of the text before I submitted to Fortress Press and improved its English and who also prepared the indexes to the published version of the text. This is not the first manuscript Terry has proofread for me and helped prepare for publication. In this, he was helpful as always.

I am, most of all, grateful beyond words to Fortress Press for paying attention to my text and showing willingness to publish it. I sincerely thank every member of their team, who in their highly professional and impressively meticulous work, helped make the dream of producing this volume in its final form come true. My gratitude goes especially to Michael Gibson and Lisa Gruenisen for their professional and careful editing. Without their valuable comments and advice I would not have been able to solidify and crystalize my arguments, particularly in the second chapter.

To all these persons and institutions I am in much debt and endless gratitude. If there is valuable knowledge in this book, it must be attributed to their help, assessments, corrections, and suggestions. If, on the other hand, there are still gaps and weaknesses despite their impressive contributions, the responsibility lies solely on my shoulders.

Hartford Seminary, Connecticut
December 2013

Introduction

I. Between the Church and Historical Context

The Christian church acknowledges its historical and contextual nature, and it commits itself to the call of imaging God's people in every historical era, as well as to be the servant of those who exist with the community of the triune God in the same, current living context. It believes that the gospel of its Lord and Savior, Jesus Christ, is a witness addressed to the world as a message that is substantially shaped by historical language and contextual, cultural bearings. Catholic theologian Piet Schoonenberg eloquently expressed the rootedness of the church and its theological discourse in people's living and thinking contexts when he said that "theology stands in history, not in eternity," and therefore those among the "theologians who thought that they wrote for all times show, through that very fact, that they were historically conditioned."[1] Throughout its long history, the church has always acknowledged that, as the community of God, it is called by its Lord and Master to become a religious community *in* history and *for* history at the same time. Everything the church believes in, or declares as its theological thinking, is an intellectual and spiritual discourse that is related to a specific historical and cultural context, and it should at least be spelled out in a language relevant and coherent to the life-setting in which this theological message is brought about.[2]

This historical and contextual nature of the church of Christ and its message—let alone the historical reality of the life of Jesus of Nazareth—has

---

1. Piet Schonnenberg, S.J., *Man and Sin: A Theological Review*, trans. Jospeh Donceel, S.J. (Notre Dame: University of Notre Dame Press, 1965), 192. Kathryn Tanner is not far from the truth when she argues, probably along the same lines, that it is questionable whether "Christians have a self-sustaining society and culture of their own, which can be marked off rather sharply from others." Kathryn Tanner, *Theories of Culture: A New Agenda for Theology* (Minneapolis: Fortress Press, 1997), 96.

2. Graham Ward finds in this orientation toward history and context *the* core reason and the main significance of developing Christian apologetics. Far from circling around reflexivity, Ward argues that apologetics "orientates theological discourse towards a specific cultural and historical negotiation concerning public truth." "Without the orientation of Christian apologetics toward the world," Ward continues, "the theological task is merely an exercise in navel-gazing." Graham Ward, "Barth, Hegel and the Possibility of Christian Apologetics," in *Conversing with Barth*, ed. John C. McDowell and Mike Higton (Aldershot, UK and Burlington, VT: Ashgate, 2004), 53–67, 53.

made Christian theologians throughout history unquestionably sensitive to the intellectual and cultural context in which they exist and develop, all the while assessing, with the help of this setting's multifaceted means and methods, their theological thinking. Some theologians consider themselves revolutionary spokespersons of God's truth *for* or *before* the historical and intellectual context of their age. Others consider themselves prophetic theologians of God's truth *against* the historical and intellectual context, in which the church is called to challenge the prevailing culture by means of the gospel message. Yet others consider themselves theologians *of* history and context, who seek to interpret human experience and questions from a certain relational and interactive approach, drawing on the frameworks of meaning from within the context.

Be that as it may, it is natural, and even expected, to realize from studying the history of thought that Christian theology has always been part of the discussion on, and thinking about, each intellectual era's interpretation of the constitutive notions of human identity, notions such as "self," "person," and "relation." When the Platonic, dualistic view of reality was popular in the ancient, dominantly Greco-Roman world, various theologians developed an anthropological hermeneutics that speaks about personhood as an embodied soul containing in itself the conflicting elements of good and evil. Inspired by Origen of Alexandria, many fathers during the first Christian centuries believed that the selfhood, or personhood, of the human lies in an external objective reality, which is absolutely good in nature and elevates the human to an ontological level above all other existing species in the hierarchy of God's creatures.

When, on the other hand, in the Middle Ages Aristotle's opposition to Plato's dualism caught the attention of leading thinkers, the church's theologians, most notably Thomas Aquinas, conceded that the human soul belongs to the existing world and that it is not to be distinguished from the physical body by means such as hierarchical order or ontological existence. The goal of this emphasis on the body-soul unity was to give a metaphysical and intellectual value to the notion of "subsistence" besides the notion of "essence," especially in relation to the inquiry on the proper method of knowing. The core idea was showing that the self, or the personal substance, of the human being lies not only in *what* this self is but also in *how* this self is what it is.

Later on, when the modernist stress on the intellectual and the rational aspects of the existing subject dominantly characterized the Enlightenment's understanding of personhood and self, theologians became totally involved in thinking, negatively or positively, about the Boethian understanding of "person" as "an individual substance with a rational nature." Many of them used and considered it as both the referential definition for understanding personhood in (and as) God, as well as in (and as) the human. The same manner of interaction or involvement in the intellectual discussion of the surrounding context clearly continues in today's theology too. With the escalating emphasis, in our so-called "postmodern" or "late-modern" intellectual context, on notions such as "personhood," "relationship," "participation," "event," "movement," "narrative," and so on, today's theologians are also reevaluating, and rapidly revising, Christian theology's previous understanding of "personhood" and "relationality" within the framework of the doctrine of God and theological anthropology. In this gradually broadening endeavor, theologians aspire to occupy leading positions in today's intellectual context by means of reinterpreting reality and understanding existence from different points of departure and distinguished inquiries.

It is quite essential for the role of the Christian church in the world that theologians are responsibly aware of the necessity of their involvement in the contemporary context's intellectual discussions. Theologians are to be commended and encouraged further about their conspicuous willingness to participate with secular and non-Christian intellectuals in their occupation with reunderstanding and reassessing the traditional hermeneutics of the notions of "self," "subject," "personhood," and "relation." By opting to participate, theologians are confessing before the world that producing a contextually relevant theological hermeneutics is part of their academic and religious cause, and not something that diverts theology away from its main mission. Having said that, the more crucial and important question before any theologian in today's context is this: How is theology, as an ecclesial reflection, supposed to execute this involvement, and what kind of contribution should it make to the running discussion on these notions? In other words, in their attempt at interacting with other thinkers in today's intellectual context, theologians find themselves confronted with the question of how they can relate to the present intellectual context without compromising the core message of the Christian faith; or how, that is, they should relate the content of the Christian texts to the context(s) of today's world, without either letting the text authoritatively dictate the context, or allowing the context exploitatively to twist the claims of the text.

It is by virtue of this very historical-contextual nature of the church's involvement in the surrounding intellectual space, and not in spite of such a nature, that the question of the proper relation between theology and culture was first raised in the history of Christianity. The inquiry about the appropriate form of such a relation is even more obviously demanded, and more tangibly required, within the context of the modernity-postmodernity curve that we are witnessing in our era. The primary direction of Christian theology at the edge of this new human intellectual turn, as Diogenes Allen correctly notes, is either accepting "the principles and outlooks of the modern world and [minimizing] the distinctive content and basis of Christian doctrines, or [retaining] Christian doctrines verbally while isolating them from the present day and, in effect, [remaining] pre-modern."[3]

II. But, What Relationship with Context?

It is inevitable, in today's theological scholarship, to address these questions: What is the appropriate relationship(s) between Christian faith and the historical context in which it exists? What kind of relationship should Christian faith have with philosophy, culture, reason, and, in the postmodern age, with the applied sciences? More challenging still, should theology be a follower, or a leader, of other disciplines of knowledge? Should theology justify, or rather challenge, human secular/nonreligious thought from the angle of the belief in an absolute external reality called God? Should Christian theology try to prove itself *the* criterion for understanding truth, or should it rather merely make do with gaining the intellectual context's recognition of it as one hermeneutical tool among many equal others? Should theology unreservedly and unconditionally adopt the rational axioms and cultural convictions that are prevalent in its historical context, or should it rather criticize this context and its constituents unreservedly and indistinguishably? Or, more specifically, should theology succumb to the contemporary criterion of validity, which, as Ingolf Dalferth shows, appears to be only allowing "a market of possibilities of meaning and sense, from which we choose according to our own individual wishes and needs, but not from the perspective of truth and untruth"? Should theology, as Dalferth continues, become just a religious language that is merely expressive of an extreme relativistic form of belief, where each man has his own god and each woman her own goddess, and where for every life situation there is a theological discourse that justifies and promotes its appropriate deity?[4]

In this systematic-contextual study, I endeavor to tackle these questions by tracing a particular model of a relationship between theology and the contemporary intellectual context of postmodernity. I attempt to show the

3. Diogenes Allen, *Christian Belief in a Postmodern World: The Full Wealth of Conviction* (Louisville: Westminster/John Knox, 1989), 7. Italics are mine.

4. Ingolf U. Dalferth, "Time for God's Presence," in *The Future of Theology: Essays in Honor of Jürgen Moltmann*, ed. M. Volf, C. Krieg, and T. Kucharz (Grand Rapids and Cambridge: Eerdmans, 1996), 127–41, 137.

negative aspects and consequences of relating theology to the intellectual context of postmodernity without first discerning each side's particular nature and allowing each one to contribute to this relationship by means of its own distinction from, and sometimes contradiction of, the other. What I offer here is not a contextual theology, or a theology of contextuality, in the crude sense of the word. It is rather a systematic analysis and assessment of how theology attempts to relate to its postmodernist context, and the ramifications of the relational choices it makes on Christian faith.

What motivates my study is my increasing realization that in the recent scholarly arena there is a noticeably rapid spread and publicity of some contemporary theological discourses, which one can safely call "postmodern theologies." Though versatile and far from monolithic in claims and conclusions, these theologies seem to disclose a common, collective concern: they all demonstrate a Christian intellectual endeavor to invest in various contemporary, dominant, and popular rationales, and epistemological hermeneutics and notions, and appropriate them to the theological, doctrinal discourse on God and his triune nature. The promoters of such an appropriation are seemingly zealous about redeeming theology and retrieving the role and influence theology once had; yet this was denied during the age of modernity. They are trying to overcome all the constraints imposed on theology by the Enlightenment, by convincing the world that theology can prove its validity and regain its legitimacy in the eyes of the nonreligious, atheist, and secular surrounding culture, if only given a chance. These theologians, in addition, argue that theology before any other side must be held accountable for the depreciation and marginalization it suffered in modernity. For, instead of becoming good news for the modern human of that era, Christian faith became one of the representatives of the unreasonable, meaningless heritage of the irrational, premodern past. Aiming at sheer survival regardless of the consequences, these postmodernist theologians argue, theology in modernity decided to adopt unreservedly all the dominant and prevailing key concepts and epistemological rules of inquiry in this context and to apply them slavishly to its interpretation of God's reality. This eventually forced the Christian church sometimes to pay the high price of turning its theology from a discourse on God *for* and *before* the historical context into a discourse about the historical context itself, into a historical story about the human *for* and *before* his or her free, autonomous existence and perfection. The striving for survival and recognition-gaining led the church to twist its discourse into an anthropocentric rather than a theocentric one.

Against this old history of submission to modernity, numerous theologians in the postmodern era aim at retrieving theology's central place and claiming its referential validity one more time in the general intellectual and cultural context. In this, they are reacting bluntly against the modernist trends of theology, and postulate instead that theology should, and can, be reliably referential in, and relevant to, the contemporary forms and rules of intellectual inquiry. In the worst-case scenarios, and even if it is no longer feasible to consider theology the "first and best" discourse available, theology can still be plausibly construed as a valid hermeneutical discourse among many other equally reliable ones, and it should be neither undermined nor marginalized in comparison with them.

Such postmodernist theological trends are at bottom discourses that are different in character and thinking strategies from the theological discourses we had in modernity. They set before their eyes the task of remembering today's intellectual context of theology's equal validity, and they highlight the authenticity of its intellectual particularity in relation to other available contextual discourses. Their efforts stand as a serious warning against any remaining conventional, modernist allegation that theology cannot contribute uniquely to the postmodern world because: 1) it is just one old-fashioned form of thought among some surviving others, with which the world today has benevolently to coexist, yet is not obliged to use. 2) Since what theology offers can be stated and gleaned in an even more efficient and coherent intellectual manner by other intellectual discourses, theology can then be dispensed with and replaced. Against such allegations, many postmodernist theologians claim that only the theological rules of intellectual inquiry and interpretation can help today's world-context to read coherently and authentically the nature of human existence. The Christian hermeneutics of notions like "future," "hope," "love," "trinity," "relationality," "personhood," "redemption," "eschatology," "charity," "otherness," and so on, enables humanity to glean new webs of meaning and encounter unique readings and expressions of reality about itself and creation. In postmodernity, many theologians believe that theology needs only to show the contemporary intellectual context that Christian belief in God is essentially nothing but a special linguistic reflection on the possibility of human progress and human self-actualization. The Christian discourse on God is the tool needed to formulate new intellectual discourses that exceed and overcome the ideological and oppressive discourses that prevailed in modernity.

It is within this broad context of the relation between theology and its contemporary (modernist and postmodernist) intellectual inquiries that I attempt to examine the validity of contemporary theology's understanding of "personhood" and "relationality." I intend to do this by examining the role that postmodernist theologians and other thinkers bestow upon the notions of "personhood" and "relationality" in the theological and nontheological reasoning on both the human and the divine natures. Pursuing this examination immediately places the doctrine of the Trinity at the center of my study and makes it the key subject of my analyses and arguments. Why the doctrine of the Trinity rather than any other teaching from the storehouse of Christian faith? Because, first, I follow the theological approach which emphasizes that the doctrine of the Trinity is *the* content and the foundation of any intellectual discourse or theological interpretation of Christian faith. And, secondly, because one cannot ignore or undermine the strongly renewed interest in the concept of the Trinity, let alone the Christian doctrinal hermeneutics of the Trinity, in today's intellectual arena. Christoph Schwöbel draws our attention to this intensive interest in the Trinity by pointing to the growing realization in today's context of the central relevance of the primary idea of "Trinity" or the notion of "triadic reality." There is a noteworthy admittance today, as Schwöbel notes, that the idea of "Trinity" is not only relevant in relation to entire subjects that are constitutive of the whole project of Christian theology, but is also equally relevant to the other social and scientific areas of knowledge in general.[5]

Having stated the above, it is not my intention here to study the relation of theology to the surrounding intellectual condition from the dimension of the doctrine of the Trinity per se. I would pursue my study, rather, from the perspective of two specific notions that are conceptually inherent to the content of the doctrine of the Trinity and enjoy a central place in this doctrine's terminological package. I will focus on the trinitarian hermeneutics of "personhood" and "relationality" and see how some key modernist and postmodernist trinitarian theologians deal with these two notions.

III. "Personhood" and "Relationality" as a Contextual-Conceptual Framework

But why study the relation between theology and other intellectual forms of inquiry specifically in relation to "personhood" and "relationality," rather than in the light of other notions? If the claim that "what we and our institutions are

---

5. Christoph Schwöbel, "The Renaissance of Trinitarian Theology: Reasons, Problems and Tasks," in *Trinitarian Theology Today: Essays on Divine Being and Act*, ed. C. Schwöbel (Edinburgh: T. & T. Clark, 1995), 1–30. "In being relevant for the main doctrinal topics, trinitarian theology also reflects the interface these topics have with non-theological forms of inquiry" (2).

is largely a matter of persons in relationship"[6] is correct, then even the rational, philosophical, and theological reasoning per se, and not only the institutions that practice it, is also reflective of, and founded on, an understanding of "person" and "relation." It is founded on these notions to such an extent that the attention they enjoy in the research arena even underlies the relationship between theology and any existent intellectual context. In principle, every thought-form is expressive of someone making an intellectual, experiential, sensual, or physical connection with someone or something else. So, every form of existence *in* or existence *with* is formed by two components: personal identity and relational connection. In this elementary presumption, I side with many other philosophers of religion and theologians who believe that the concepts of "person," "personality," "relation," and "relationality" represent the central focus for theological and philosophical reflections[7] on God and humanity alike. The inquiry about the meaning of personhood, as Schwöbel states, similarly dominates a wide spectrum of recent public issues. These issues extend "from the ethics of genetic technology and medical research and practice to the debates about the character of legal responsibility and very practical issues of penal reform."[8]

In this study, I aim to tackle questions such as: How should theologians evaluate and implement some contemporary notions of "personhood," "selfhood," and "relationality" in the light of the Christian trinitarian doctrine of God? Should theology adopt, or rather reject unqualifiedly the prevailing intellectual understanding of these notions in today's intellectual arena? Or should it instead exceed the two previous options of either "following" or "standing over against" other forms of intellectual inquiry, with these two options' dangerous extremism, toward another more convenient form of interaction with, and relatedness to, its historical, intellectual context? The validity and necessity of raising these questions today stem, as I will argue in this study, from a recent problematic submission and subordination of the trinitarian hermeneutics of God to the contextually and anthropologically centered interpretations of "personhood," "selfhood," and "relationality." I will argue that there is today an emphatic adoption of a postmodern obsession with certain interpretations of "personhood," "selfhood," "communal/relational existence,"

---

6. Colin E. Gunton, *The Promise of Trinitarian Theology*, 2nd ed. (Edinburgh: T. & T. Clark, 1997), 83.

7. C. Schwöbel, "Editorial Introduction," in *Persons, Divine and Human: King's College Essays in Theological Anthropology*, ed. Colin Gunton and Christoph Schwöbel (Edinburgh: T. & T. Clark, 1999), 1. Schwöbel attributes the pioneering anticipation of the coming to age of this focus to John R. Illingworth, *Personality—Human and Divine* (London and New York: Macmillan, 1894).

8. Schwöbel, "Editorial Introduction," 6–7.

and "otherness" as well as an uncritical, and even sweeping, incorporation of them into the Christian theology of God. I will show that this is the case especially in the theologians' adoption of a contemporary postmodernist tendency to pursue a total identification of "personhood" and "relationality," to collapse ontology into epistemology, and to reduce "substance" or "being" to mere "subsistence" or "existence."

It is well known that these two notions, "personhood" and "relationality," are inherently central to the Christian discourse on God the Trinity, and they are no less constitutive of the other doctrinal interpretations of the Christian faith's components, such as Christology, pneumatology, soteriology, ecclesiology, and eschatology. Although the history of doctrine clearly discloses that these two notions always had a central place in Christian pedagogy, it is not far from truth to say that they occupy a much more central place, and they continue playing an indelibly foundational role in the postmodernist theological thinking about God and the God-creation relationship. They still enjoy this significance simply and primarily because these two notions occupy an equally central place in the postmodernist, nontheological context of the intellectual inquiry on the human self and the human-world relationship. In order, therefore, to perceive postmodernity's recent impact on theological reasoning, and to understand the negative impact of some theologians' obsession with overcoming modernity and breaking out of its preconditioning boundaries with the help of postmodernist intellectual tools, I will study how some recent theological trends invest the postmodern understanding of "personhood" and "relationality" in the doctrine of the Trinity. I will argue that this investment distorts the integrity and balance of the biblical and creedal theology of God and presents an inappropriate ontology that cannot be unreservedly or uncritically adopted by Christian thought. I will show how in this investment the notion of "personhood" was conceptually collapsed into the notion of "relationship" in such a way that turns God, and eventually the human person as well, into mere event or mere relational movements, that is, into a mere idealist network of activities. Instead of a balanced theo-logical ontology that maintains a distinction between God's personhood and God's relations—a lack of this distinction suggests separation between God's personal identity and God's relationships—there are postmodern theological trends, which I will point at, that propagate an ontology in which "personhood" means merely "relationality" or relational events: personhood connotes "being a relationship," rather than "being *in* relationship." I will show that such a reductionist ontology distorts the infinity of God's being by turning God from a wholly-other being into a conceptual expression of an anthropological, ideal form of existence. It equally denies God's personal mystery by turning the divine Trinity into a mere linguistic expression of humanity's searched-for state of "openness to otherness."

Be that as it may, the core issue this study discusses—insofar as the question of the relation of theology and other intellectual forms of inquiry is concerned—will not be whether theology should or should not develop a hermeneutics of "personhood" and "relationality" by the help, and in the light, of the available, prevailing intellectual rules of inquiry that are offered by other disciplines. It is rather whether or not every understanding of "personhood" and "relationality" that is offered by other discourses in today's context is congenial with the Christian doctrinal teaching on the triune God and on the human being within the framework of God's relation with creation. Within the dialogue between theology and other intellectual forms of inquiry, the case this study essentially aims to argue is the necessity of maintaining and revalidating a theological ontology that distinguishes (not separates) "personhood" from "relationality," God from humanity's communion with God, and God's personal being from God's relational presence with the human being. The importance of such ontology, as Colin Gunton correctly notes, lies in admitting the necessity of rooting the concern about relating theology to culture, and about renewing Christianity in relation to the external surrounding context. This cannot be achieved except by the aid of a theology of personhood and relationality that prevents conflating theology and every rational element definitive of a specific, historical, and narrow cultural context into each other.[9] I will explain this necessary distinction between theology and context, which Gunton points at, by talking about the importance of the ontological differentiation between "personhood" and "relationality"—the differentiation, that is, which both modernist and postmodernist theological trends fail to maintain.

I attempt to argue for this failure by displaying modernist and postmodernist theologies that are not principally different from each other in the way they treat "personhood" and "relationality" within the context of the doctrine of the triune God in general, and the theological understanding of the human self in particular. My argument will reveal that I do not principally agree with the general claim that "there exist in the Western tradition two distinct, sometimes overlapping, views of the person, one of them believed almost everywhere, but wrong; the other neglected but right."[10] Instead, my discussion will state that the spectrum of the notions of "personhood" and

---

9. Ibid., 22–23.

10. Gunton, *The Promise of Trinitarian Theology*, 83. Gunton speaks specifically about Descartes' individualistic view of personhood, on one side, and about the relational view of personhood that,

"relationality" in modernity and postmodernity is much more multifaceted and complicated than a "black-and-white" framework suggests. Nevertheless, my study will also suggest that what some postmodernist theologies emphasize and rely on are trends for which earlier modernist thinking on selfhood and subjectivity, both theological and philosophical, paved the way. The conflation of "personhood" with "relationality," and the reduction of "three persons" into three "relational movements," are not pure postmodernist inventions. The seeds of these tendencies are actually sown in the soil of the modernist theological and philosophical interpretations of "selfhood," "subjectivity," and "individualism." These interpretations pave the way for, rather than stand over and against, the postmodernist reduction of God's being and the human self into a mere process of relational movement or a collection of communal activities. Eventually, this culminates in the reduction of the triune God's divine persons into mere movements of relationality, the existential reenactment and imitation of which the human is called for in order to be his or her full self. This reduction invites me to believe that the inconvenient relationship which theology found itself trapped in with modernity witnesses its ultimate extension and bears its ripest fruits in postmodernity.

IV. This Study's Structure

This study is divided into three main parts. The first part is titled "The Roots," and it deals with the relation between trinitarian theology and some of the intellectual forms of inquiry that are related to the notions of "self" and "personhood" in the context of modernity. It maps what I believe to be the roots of the main theological and philosophical hermeneutics of "personhood," "selfhood," and "relationality," which we see scholars entertaining and emphasizing in postmodernity. I start with an analysis of Boethius' understanding of "person" and then trace the interpretation of this Boethian understanding in the philosophy of transcendent subjectivism. After this, I discuss its implementation in the ontology of subjectivity and personhood that characterize major theological discourses on the relationship between God and humanity in modernity. I view how Paul Tillich and Karl Barth interact with this modernist understanding of selfhood and subjectivity, and how they deal with its anthropocentric connotations. I examine whether their discourses on God counter and challenge, or follow and succumb to the modernist criterial

---

according to Gunton, finds its beginning in the philosophy of people like Macmurray and Coleridge, on another.

rules of inquiry and understanding. I show that though these theologians depart in their theological projects from challenging their contemporary intellectual era, their ultimate conclusions, thought-forms, and methods of interpretation in essence do not go beyond the boundaries of reasoning that were delineated and certified by the modernist context. By pointing at the argument, methods, and intellectual implications of the theological discourses of Tillich and Barth, I attempt to show the shortcomings of the theological reasoning related to the modernist context, which ensues later in postmodernity, though it takes different forms and pertains to other dimensions.

In the second part of the study, which is titled "The Challenge," I demonstrate how the inappropriate relation that theology constructed within modernity's intellectual context continues within, but does not substantially transform, the postmodernist context. Instead of liberating theology from a blind subjection to other forms of inquiry by means of launching a balanced and mutually influential relationship with other forms of inquiry in today's context, there is a tendency among theologians today either to 1) continue the borrowing-following strategy by adopting postmodernity's popular rules of inquiry and unreservedly applying them to theological reasoning, or to 2) jump to an opposite reactionary extreme by endeavoring to prove that postmodernity is from beginning to end theologically conditioned (in reaction to the modernist demand from theology to prove that it is from beginning to end "rational"). I argue that either stance expresses an inappropriate attitude toward other forms of inquiry and reflects a secondary and useless role for theology in today's world.

After setting the general framework of this interaction between theology and postmodernism, I study specifically how trinitarian theology deals with the postmodernist centralization of "relationality" and "otherness" in opposition to the modernist centralization of "individuality" and "self-centeredness." I argue that instead of examining the validity of these notions' postmodernist trends in interpretation, there are trinitarian theologians who unquestionably borrow these interpretations and apply them to the trinitarian doctrine of God. By doing this, they reduce God to the linguistic expression of an idealist image of relationality, in accordance with which the human is called to live in order to be his or her real self. Against this phenomenon, I refer back to the Christian tradition, and specifically to Thomas Aquinas's theology of "relation" and "participation," from which I borrow what I deem to be a balanced interpretation of "relationality" that can correct both recent hermeneutics of "relationship" and "otherness," and a contemporary obsession that turns the doctrine of the triune God into a discourse on relational ontology.

If theology wants to free itself from the chains of modernity's rules of intellectual inquiry and contribute positively and uniquely to today's arena of knowledge, then theology should examine the one-sided postmodernist emphasis on "relationality" and "otherness" by means of the hermeneutics of the relation between "person" and "relation," and "being" and "existence," which we find in the doctrine of the Trinity. It should not turn this doctrine into a discourse that reflects a specific reduction of "personhood" into mere "relationality," and of "being" into mere "existence," that is dominant today. Theology should not allow this if it wants to maintain the particularity of the theological rationale that underpins the Christian understanding of the triune God.

In the third part of the study, "The Proposal," I suggest "correlation" as a model of interaction between theology and secular forms of intellectual inquiry. I argue that "correlationality" is a more appropriate relational model to express the link between the notions of "relationship" and "personality" in the Christian doctrine of the Trinity. Since the notion of "correlation" is widely and intensively used in modern theological and philosophical scholarship, I start this part with a chapter on the notion of "correlation" that, in my view, theology should avoid and even criticize. As examples of an investment into such an inappropriate correlation in today's trinitarian theology, I outline the proposals of David Tracy, Gordon Kaufman, and Mark Taylor. I argue that their models of correlation do not take sufficiently into consideration the particularity and integrity of theological scholarship, but tend, rather, to transform theology into a form of inquiry that primarily proves itself congenial with the contextual and rational presumptions, and rules of thought, that are already dominant in today's intellectual arena. As an alternative to this form of correlation, I point in the following chapter to the correlational model of relationality proposed by Francis Watson and Hans Frei. I see in their understanding of the relationship between theology and other forms of inquiry, as well as between the theological fields of research, a model of correlation that exceeds any form of hierarchism or subordination.

In the last two chapters of the book, I take the search for a proper correlation between theology and other forms of inquiry back to the specific issue of the notions of "personhood" and "relationality" in the particular context of the doctrine of the triune God. I suggest here that the trinitarian theologies of Jürgen Moltmann and, more emphatically, Wolfhart Pannenberg, as reliable and balanced understandings of the relationship between "person" and "relation" on one side, and between "unity" and "particularity" on the other. In Pannenberg's theology, in particular, this understanding is based on a "unity-in-self-distinction" model of correlation, which is similar to what Watson and Frei suggest when they speak about a nonhierarchical relationship between theology and other forms of intellectual inquiry. After I outline the trinitarian thinking of Moltmann and Pannenberg, I end the study with a chapter on how these two theologians implement their trinitarian logic of "unity-in-self-distinction" in their understanding of the relationship between theology and other fields within the general scholarly context of reasoning. I propose their implementation as a reliable model that theology today can follow in its attempt at interacting with other forms of intellectual inquiry in the postmodern context.

I hope the reader will be able to perceive that this study presents two layers of inquiry: a general one on the relationship between theology and other intellectual forms of inquiry (theologizing on the relation of theology to the context), and a more specific one, which functions as a case study, on the relationship between trinitarian theology and the main hermeneutical trends regarding "self," "personhood," "relationship," and "otherness" (reshaping the theology-context relation from a trinitarian perspective and by means of trinitarian notions). It is a combination of systematic, analytical, and critical assessment, and of the construction of trinitarian hermeneutics of relationality, by means of looking at some major segments from the history of contemporary theologies of God and humanity on one side, and the history of philosophical anthropology in the modern age on another. It is not a comprehensive display of that history of thought, and not a detailed commentary on its theological and philosophical milestones. It is a selective display of what I believe to be major stations on the way toward situating theology's relationship with contextual forms of intellectual inquiry within a framework of questions on the meaning of "selfhood," "personhood," and "relationality."

This stated, it is my hope that this study will invite today's theologians to explore more acutely and critically Christian theology's role in today's context, and to examine whether the strategies of thinking and interpretation we use to do theology today are fairly expressive of the particular nature and claims of Christian faith or not. More specifically, I call for doing this examination in relation to the contemporarily developed Christian understanding of the triune God and its ambition of making an impact on, and becoming a referential criterion for, understanding human existence and nature in today's context. The doctrine of the Trinity can undoubtedly transform our understanding of the meaning of "selfhood" and "otherness," and can take human thinking beyond the limits and mistakes of any contextually limited and one-sided mindset. But it can do this only when it correlates with other nontheological hermeneutics of human nature and selfhood in a nonhierarchical, nonsubordinationist mode of relationality. It can do this when it reflects theology's uniqueness and maintains its integrity, and when it does this with the aid of a relationship-hermeneutics based on the "unity-in-self-differentiation" correlation between the three divine persons in the eternal Godhead.

PART I

The Roots: Theology and the Question of Self in Modernity

1

The Modernist Condition

I. The Questions of Personhood and Self in Perspective

The inquiry about the theological and philosophical meaning of the notion of "person/personhood" is undoubtedly far more sophisticated, challenging, and demanding than any inquiry on this notion within the general, anthropological contexts, where one would, for instance, only ask "why *Homo sapiens* is 'person' and other animals are not?"[1] When it comes to the inquiry on the conceptual connotations of the idea of "personhood," as Alistair McFadyen correctly notes, "It is rarely as easy to give a good answer as it is to raise a good question."[2] I believe there are three reasons for this difficulty.

1. Philological Difficulty

The first reason is philological. The word "person" as such is not clearly monolithic in meaning or conception, neither in today's scholarship nor in antiquity's. From the time of the Stoics and the Presocratic philosophers onwards, the term was linguistically used in a variety of ways and was applied to various contexts of constructive scholarly discourses. Each one of these linguistic spheres and scientific settings generates numerous meanings and presume equally versatile connotations for the term "person"—even if the perennial reading of the history of thought may invite the reader to conjecture that the moral connotations of the concept of "person" seem to be the only common, combining constituent between all the various, extractable meanings and definitions. And, even if this possibility justifies the conclusion that it is these moral connotations alone that bestow upon the concept of "person" a prominent combining and interdisciplinary role between fields likes bioethics,

---

1. Brain Garrett, "Person," in *Routledge Encyclopedia of Philosophy*, ed. Edward Craig (London & New York: Routledge, 1998), 7:319.

2. Alistair I. McFadyen, *The Call to Personhood: A Christian Theory of the Individual in Social Relationships* (Cambridge: Cambridge University Press, 1990), p. 1.

law, political science, philosophy, and theology,[3] this does not exempt the one who examines this notion from paying attention to such a variety of meanings and miscellaneous usages of the word "person" in the discourses of the different relevant disciplines.[4]

2. PHILOSOPHICAL DIFFICULTY

The second reason is philosophical. At an early stage of the age of modernity, philosophers and scholars established that personhood cannot designate any clear-cut distinction that can be ascribed exclusively to the human race. Scientific explorations and empirical observations led scholars of the modern age to establish that there is a continuity, rather than substantial ontological difference, between *Homo sapiens* and other species on earth. It was the realization of the possibility of such continuity rather than difference, for instance, between humans and animals, as John Brooke reminds us, that motivated Charles Darwin's study of the origin of species, tracing their evolution and dissolving, eventually, any serious divide between them.[5]

Today, science is far more advanced than in the time of Darwin, and we can go way beyond the frontiers that the latter reached in terms of understanding nature and its species' evolution. This advancement, nevertheless—and instead of challenging Darwin's and the modernist belief in the continuity between humans and animals—affirms this continuity more inarguably than ever before and leaves the belief in human ontological uniqueness and superiority on noticeably shaky ground.[6] Modernist philosophers from the eighteenth century onwards also adopted an early edition

---

3. Thus argues Niel H. Gregersen in "Varieties of Personhood: Mapping the Issues," in *The Human Person in Science and Theology*, ed. N. H. Gregersen, W. B. Drees, and U. Görman (Grand Rapids: Eerdmans, 2000), 1–17, 1. On the centrality of morality and practices in discerning the meaning of personhood, see John F. Crosby, *Selfhood of Human Person* (Washington, DC: Catholic University of America Press, 1996), 9–40, and Karol Wojtyla, "Human Nature as the Basis of Ethical Formation," in *Person and Community: Selected Essays*, ed. Karol Wojtyla, trans. Theresa Sandok (New York: Peter Lang, 1993), 95–100.

4. Paul Ricoeur eloquently points to the same heterogeneity in the character of the notion of "person," yet in different terms, when he states that "the notion of person is determined by means of the predicates that we ascribe to it . . . the person is thus in the position of a logical subject in relation to the predicates that are ascribed to it." Paul Ricoeur, *Oneself as Another*, trans. Kathleen Blamey (Chicago and London: University of Chicago Press, 1994), 35–39.

5. John Hedly Brooke, "Science and the Self: What Difference Did Darwin Make?" in *The Evolution of Rationality: Interdisciplinary Essays in Honor of J. Wentzel van Huyssteen*, ed. F. LeRon Shults (Grand Rapids and Cambridge: Eerdmans, 2006), pp. 253–73, 254.

of this conviction about the indistinguishability of the human being and, in the light of it, developed a reductionist philosophy of human identity, which states, according to Peter Hick, that the human is just "an animal, or nothing but a bundle of experiences or electrical impulses in the brain."[7] Philosophers such as Kant, Hume, Diderot, Herder, and others also acknowledged the biological and behavioral similarities between humans and animals, and even conceded that human psychological and physical functions could be understood via studying and analyzing those of animals.[8]

One, however, should notice here that these modernist thinkers differ from the postmodernists of today in their (the modernists') reluctance to pinpoint unique features that distinguish humans from animals, or to single out personhood as the unique defining particularity of the human race. They realize such difference is strictly specified in human mental or cognitive capacities. According to the modernist reason-centered philosophers, what makes human beings different and unique, first and foremost, is their cognitive function, which demonstrates itself in self-realization, moral law development, representation, reflection, the ability to abstract, and in the communication and accumulation of knowledge.[9] Even the patron of evolution, Charles Darwin, recognized certain intellectual capacities that are to be exclusively ascribed to the human race. This mental distinction for him is detected in one unique

---

6. See on this, for instance, Nancy R. Howell, "The Importance of Being Chimpanzee," *Theology and Science*, ½ (2003): 179–91. Howell shows that the latest genetic research has proven a 98.4% genetic similarity between humans and the chimpanzee. This percentage drives scientists rapidly to group chimpanzees and their species as "*hominids*," the term, Howell says, "once reserved for humans and human ancestors" (180). Charles Taylor gives an interesting example about this trend of thought, which attempts to prove an existence of "self" or "sense of selfhood" in animals: "I remember an experiment designed to show that chimps too have a 'sense of self': an animal with 'a paint mark' on its face, seeing itself in the mirror, reached with its paws to its own face to clean it. It somehow recognized that this mirror image was of its own body": Charles Taylor, *Sources of Self: The Making of the Modern Identity* (Cambridge, MA: Harvard University Press, 1989), 32, citing from C. G. Gallup Jr., "Chimpanzees: Self-Recognition," in *Science*, June 6, 1983, 86–87.

7. Peter Hick, "One or Two? A Historical Survey of an Aspect of Personhood," *Evangelical Quarterly* 1, no. 77 (2005): 35–45, 38. Hick offers a brief but valuable sketch of the development of the notion of personhood and the changes it faced since it was reflected upon in the Presocratic period. Hick argues that the definition of self as an intellectual reality rather than an expression of belonging to the whole, to all that is, is the outcome of the unfortunate Platonic search for a metanarrative of all that is and of Plato's rejection of relativism. Plato's monism, Hick believes, marked the deadly turn to plurality and change in understanding the self (ibid., 38ff.).

8. Aaron Garrett, "Human Nature," in *The Cambridge Companion to Eighteenth Century Philosophy*, ed. Knud Haakonssen (New York: Cambridge University Press, 2006), 1:161–77.

9. Ibid., 164.

human element, namely the religious orientation, about which Darwin opines the following:

> The feeling of religious devotion is a highly complex one, consisting of love, complete submission to an exalted and mysterious superior, a strong sense of dependence, fear, reverence, gratitude, hope for future, and perhaps other elements. No being could experience so complex an emotion until advanced in his intellectual and moral faculties to at least a moderately high level.[10]

It is not my intention here to research the notion of "personhood" in the light of the discussion about human-animal similarities and differences; however, I do want to show that one of the main complications of inquiring about personhood lies in the difficulty of stating clearly what "human" means and what "human personhood" designates in particular.

3. THEOLOGICAL DIFFICULTY

The third reason for the complication of the inquiry about the meaning of "personhood" is basically theological in nature, and it is what I am primarily concerned about in this study. Christian faith believes that everything pertinent to the human being and existence, personhood included, is meaningless unless it is understood on the basis of belief in God. This claim as such is deemed problematic and rationally unreliable in the intellectual, dominantly atheistic context of modernity. As a result of the modernist disenchantment position toward religiosity and the concept of deity in principle, theology found itself harshly criticized by the modernist rationale when it insisted on considering God and God's self-disclosure a criterion for any truth-claim or method of understanding, including those related to the interpretation of the notions of "personhood" and "self." As a matter of fact, such a theistic criterion was not only challenging, even puzzling, to some modernist thinkers in general; it also created challenges to other theological forms of inquiry, especially the theological hermeneutics of the triunity of God, which is in fact the foundation of the hermeneutics of Christianity's understanding of personhood.

In Christianity, the foundation of the meaning of "person" lies primarily in the theological understanding of the nature and identity of the God of Jesus

---

10. Charles Darwin, *The Descent of Man and Selection in Relation to Sex* (London: Murray, 1906), 146, and Brooke, "Science and Self: What Difference Did Darwin Make?," 260.

Christ, who is biblically and doctrinally triune in being and in dynamic and relational existence. The personhood of God is threefold because God's very self, not only God's actions, is trinitarian in nature: Father, Son, and Spirit. One of the crucial, challenging facts expressive of this trinitarian personhood is that although the Spirit and the Son both reveal to us the personal nature of God's Being as equally "God from God"—consubstantial with the Father—they do not represent a totally identical form of personhood in God because, despite their ontological oneness, they are distinct in existence and in personal identity. The challenging, difficult issue here is that their distinction is not that one is to be considered "person" while the other is not, or that one is a revelation of God's personhood while the other is just a secondary testifier to this revelation, and never personally a revealer of God's identity. Rather, they equally reveal God's personhood in the very way by which each *is particularly and differently* a "person." More complicated still is the fact that one of these two persons has a timely, corporeal personhood, that is, the Son, whose incarnation and humanity as Jesus Christ are constitutive of his being, while the other, namely the Holy Spirit, by her very nature, has not.

If, therefore, the previously mentioned, biological understanding of personal identity can by any means duplicate the complication, it would be by means of possible attention to the noticeable difficulty of speaking (in relation to the Father, Son, and Holy Spirit) in rational and plausible terms about an alleged personhood, such as, for instance, the personhood of the Holy Spirit whose nature substantially and conceptually transcends physical being-ness.[11] This inarguably makes the theological endeavor for understanding personhood in the light of a belief in a God who has a personal identity of a *triune*, rather than a *monos*, nature the more difficult and tricky task, especially if we take into consideration the wider, general difficulties that originated from use of the concept of "person" in the theology of the Trinity throughout the history of Christian doctrine, and particularly during the age of modernity.

Keeping these three complications in mind, I will begin this first chapter by looking at the understanding of the concept of "person" in its wider philosophical and anthropological framework within the intellectual context of modernity. I will do this by examining specific modernist trends in the notions of "personhood" and "self." Second, I will present two major theological approaches that developed a theology of God in interaction with the modernist trends of thought about personhood. One is mainly existence-oriented, while

---

11. For a brief introduction on the physical theory of personhood, see B. Garrett, "Personal Identity," in *Routledge Encyclopedia of Philosophy*, 7:307–8.

the other is revelation-centered. I will argue that these two options are only echo-variations of the modernist, nontheological understanding of "self" and "personhood," rather than attempts to transcend or challenge such understanding. In his essay on human nature, Aaron Garrett claims that "in the end, the battle between reason and 'above' reason which had raged throughout the eighteenth century was won by reason and a uniquely strong assertion of it: Hegelian absolute knowledge."[12] I shall be trying to show in the ensuing sections that in its attempt to offer a plausible understanding of the notions of "self" and "personhood" *from* the context of the doctrine of God, theology in modernity could not confront and deal with the challenging difficulties of the battle to which Garrett points. Instead, theology lost this battle and ended up succumbing to "reason" and endeavoring time and again to prove its intellectual allegiance and loyalty to the rules of the new winner.

II. "Individual" or "Particular": Which Is Boethius' Concern?

In an article titled "Varieties of Personhood: Mapping the Issue," Niels Gregersen takes us back to the ancient interaction between Christian theology and Greek philosophy in an attempt to detect in this interaction the roots of the modernist concept of "personhood." Gregersen points out that the habit of defining "personhood" by means of the human rational capacity and restricting it to human cognitive activities already finds traces in the Stoic tradition. The Stoics spoke about personhood simply as the "role" that is played, or the "outlook" that is demonstrated or imaged by each individual in her societal presence or embodiment. With the Roman philosopher Cicero, Gregersen continues, the Stoic notion of personhood survived in the following centuries, yet this reason-centeredness is now overindividualized and accompanied by a consideration of human moral actions as inherent to the person's *what*, while the human rational ones are inherent to the person's *who*. "Person," accordingly, connoted a rational, individual being who acts particularly "as a moral subject [who is] accountable for his or her deeds."[13]

Gregersen afterwards suggests that the first serious attempt at developing a fully structured understanding of "personhood" in Western Christianity was offered in the writings of the philosopher and theologian Boethius. Boethius developed this interpretation, according to Gregersen, specifically in his *A Treatise Against Eutyches and Nestorius*. In his study of this text, Stephen Hipp surmises that in the definition of "personhood" that Boethius offers, we attain

---

12. A. Garrett, "Human Nature," 680.
13. Gregersen, "Varieties of Personhood: Mapping the Issues," 8.

for the first time "a formal speculative definition of the term [person]," as well as the "culmination in the genesis of the concept of 'person,' and the point of departure for its seminal future in the West."[14] Personhood for Boethius, as Niel Gregersen explains, is mainly "the capacity for rational discernment [that is] present in an individual human being."[15]

Both Gregersen and Hipp believe that despite his awareness that the dimensions of communion and mutual contact ought to be reckoned with for understanding "personhood," Boethius mainly focuses on the public roles of personhood as demonstrations of an *individual* substance. This focus on individuality, Gregersen and Hipp contend, passed through the centuries to the modernist Western understanding of "personhood" and caused problems for the intellectual context of that era. For, despite the fact that the theological interpretation of "personhood" that one finds in the writings of other church fathers—mainly the Cappadocian fathers—maintained strict attention to the notions of "communion" and "relationality" in the hermeneutics of "personhood" (especially in the context of the theological discussions on the triune God), Western modernity selectively inherited from Christian theology the Boethian focus on rationality and individualism, and left behind the Cappadocians' attention to relationality, particularity, and otherness. This argument notwithstanding, the question that one should still ask is the following: Is the modernist adoption of an emphasis on individualism and rationality, heavily invested in Boethius' classical definition of "person," expressive of an accurate understanding of Boethius' own hermeneutics of "personhood"?

In his significant study of the notion of "person" in Boethius and other traditions in Christian history, Stephen Hipp argues that there is a substantial conceptual link between Boethius' definition of "person" and his understanding of the notion of "nature." Hipp affirms that this link is indispensable for conducting subtle considerations about Boethius' classical definition of "personhood." Hipp argues that, following Aristotle's *Metaphysics*, Boethius jots down four meanings to the notion of "nature," the fourth of which specifically refers to the idea of "particularity" and construes it as one of the defining elements of the states of being-ness and of being a substance. "Nature," Boethius says, has more than one meaning. Yet, one can still generally say, according to him, that nature "belongs to those things which, since they exist, can in some way be apprehended [as well as the inapprehensibles (e.g., God)] by the

---

14. Stephen A. Hipp, *"Person" in Christian Tradition and the Conception of Saint Albert the Great* (Münster: Druckhaus Aschendorff, 2001), 79.

15. Gregersen, "Varieties of Personhood: Mapping the Issues," 8–9.

intellect." Nature, in other words, is the specific difference that gives a defining predication of any existing thing.[16] Therefore, Boethius' suggestion means that one cannot just be made *of* a nature. One should also exist *as* and *in* nature as well.

Understanding this emphasis on "in nature" is necessary for perceiving Boethius' reliance on Aristotle's metaphysics of "nature" in his (Boethius') endeavor to define "person." This conceptual reliance, nonetheless, cannot be apprehended apart from the context of Boethius' critical assessment of Eutyches' Christology. In his thinking about "personhood," Boethius has in mind the Eutychian claim that while Christ or the divine *Logos* in eternity is *of* two natures, human and divine, he does not exist as them or does not subsist *in* them both after the incarnation.[17] The incarnate *Logos* in, or as, Jesus Christ, Eutyches concludes, must then be of one nature and one personhood. This means that the divine *Logos* takes merely a figurative human form, but not a substantial human personhood.

In his interaction with such Christological logic, Boethius rejects Eutyches' interpretation of the *Logos*' humanity, because he believes that its logic is based upon the philosophical assumption that two different natures can constitute together the substance of something, without both equally or similarly acquiring a concrete form of existence. There are, that is, natures that exist beyond, or even without, any concrete substance, any form of existence, or ultimately any personal presence. In the case of Eutyches' Christology, Boethius finds such a philosophical background expressed in the claim that the *Logos* has a human nature, yet he does not subsist in a human personhood, but only in a divine one. And, since the nature and the personhood are one and the same thing, according to Eutyches, it is better, from this perspective, to speak about the *one, single* nature and person of the *Logos* after the incarnation. Boethius concedes that the human nature's presence in the incarnate is not necessarily denied in this view. Yet Boethius criticizes this understanding by opining that the human nature, according to this logic, instead exists in Christ via his divine personhood, without needing a concrete form of subsistence of its own (that

---

16. Hipp, *"Person" in Christian Tradition and the Conception of Saint Albert the Great*, 101; and Boethius, "A Treatise Against Eutyches and Nestorius," in *Boethius, the Theological Tractates, the Consolation of Philosophy*, ed. H. F. Stewart, E. K. Rand, and S. J. Tester (Cambridge, MA: Harvard University Press/London: Heinemann, 1973), 1: 5–60 (77–81). The other three are: 1) "nature belongs to those things which, since they exist, can in some way be apprehended by the intellect"; 2) "nature is either that which is able to act or be acted upon" 3); "nature is a *per se* and non-accidental principle of movement" (ibid., 1:100–101).

17. Boethius, "A Treatise Against Eutyches and Nestorius," the introduction, 1–15.

is, the human nature exists *within* the divine nature that is incarnate as human). In such a Christology, Boethius concludes, we have here what can be possibly described as the "religious withering of humanity."[18]

Boethius rejects Eutyches' Christological logic primarily because it does not in his opinion present a proper understanding of the relationship between "substance" and "existence," or "nature" and "personhood." Though he is as strongly critical of the Nestorians' claim of the existence of two persons that are representative of the two natures in Christ as the Eutychians are, Boethius does not support the philosophical understanding of the relation between "nature" and "substance" that underlies the Eutychian logic. Against Eutyches' claim that nature can *be* without concrete subsistence, Boethius argues that every nature exists in a concrete form of subsistence, whether this subsistence was corporeal (bodies) or incorporeal (substances) in form. Why does every nature exist or subsist? Because nature, according to Boethius, is "either that which can act or that which can be acted upon."[19] Action indicates concrete existence, for the substance that has a certain nature must subsist in order to act, or in order for its actions to reflect its nature's predicates. But is nature confined only to corporeal bodies? Boethius says it is not. Nature exists in corporeal as well as incorporeal bodies, because nature is "the principle of movement per se, and [it is] not accidental."[20] This is not to mean that what applies to the relation of nature to its existence in corporeal entities applies completely to nature's existence in incorporeal ones. What, for instance, applies to the human (corporeal) in this regard does not apply to God (incorporeal). Boethius takes this logic to the arena of Christology to argue that in the God-human relationship, the relation of nature to existence is different from the same relation in the case of the divine-human natures in Jesus Christ. In the first, there is a nature that exists in corporeal form (human), which is related to another nature that exists in incorporeal reality (God). In the second, nevertheless, we have two natures,

---

18. C. FitzSimons Allison, *The Cruelty of Heresy: An Affirmation of Christian Orthodoxy* (New York: Morehouse, 1992), chapter 8. For some classic literature on Monophysitism within the framework of the councils' history see, for example, Leo Donald Davis, S.J., *The First Seven Ecumenical Councils (325-787): Their History and Theology* (Collegeville, MN: Liturgical/Michael Glazier, 1983); H. M. Percival, *The Seven Ecumenical Councils, from a Select Library of Nicene and Post-Nicene Fathers* (Grand Rapids: Eerdmans, 1979), vol. 14; W. H. C. Frend, *The Rise of the Monophysite Movement: Chapters in the History of the Church in the Fifth and Sixth Centuries* (Cambridge: Cambridge University Press, 1972); and Roberta C. Chesnut, *Three Monophysite Christologies: Severus of Antioch, Philoxenus of Mabbug and Jacob of Sarug* (London: Oxford University Press, 1976).

19. Boethius, "A Treatise Against Eutyches and Nestorius," I.25.

20. Ibid., I.40-45.

divine and human, that are not only related to each other, but each also is related to its particular corporeal existence and action.

Be that as it may, nature for Boethius is inherent to the subsistence of its substance, and is not concealed behind this subsistence. Rather, this subsistence is what makes the thing its particular being and what bestows upon the thing its distinction as a substance with a particular form of existence. "Nature" becomes intelligible by means of the particular form of its existing substance. This form of the substance's existence not only reveals the substance's predicates, but also defines the substance's nature in its individuation.

It is upon this meaning of "nature"—which Hipp believes Boethius derives from Aristotle's four meanings of "nature"—that Boethius develops his definition of "personhood." Before looking at this definition in Boethius' writing, let me briefly visit Aristotle's *Metaphysics* and read his understanding of the relationship between "substance," "form," and "existence."

In his attempt to answer whether or not only sensible substances exist, Aristotle states that "absurd is the [Platonic] doctrine that there are certain entities apart from those in the sensible universe, and that these are the same as sensible things except in that the former are eternal and the latter perishable."[21] Substances, in other words, cannot, in Aristotle's opinion, exist without forms and without being sensible. Forms are not related to substances by means of intermediaries. They are rather immediately predicative of their substances. Why? Because, says Aristotle, "if there are intermediate objects of sense and sensations, clearly there will also be intermediate animals between the ideal animals and the perishable animals";[22] the thing, that is, which Aristotle believes to be impossible.

Does this mean that the sensible forms *are* the substance they represent, as if they are its nature? Aristotle thinks that this is far from being the case. It just means that the first principles, which are the constituents of something and the generators of what this thing is in nature, can be perceived from this thing's forms and sensible elements. This is just an epistemological and not an ontological relationship. Knowing the nature of the substance via its forms and sensible elements does not mean that these latter are constitutive or exhaustively definitive of the nature of this substance: "to judge from these arguments [i.e., that are related to the forms' and elements' observation and examination] the first principles will *not* be the genera of things."[23]

---

21. Aristotle, *Metaphysics, I–IX*, trans. Hugh Tredennick (Cambridge, MA: Harvard University Press/London: Heinemann, 1975), III.2.997b.20–21.
22. Ibid., III.2.997b.24ff.

One may sense here a possibility of solely focusing on individuality, by means of reading Aristotle as linking to an organic extent the substances and their specific forms. This possibility becomes plausible when one focuses on Aristotle's attention to particularity at the expense of his emphasis on universality. Aristotle knows that this might be gleaned from a face-value reading of his emphasis that the substance exists in and as its form. Therefore, he states that he is not turning individuals into first principles, but rather maintaining that "the first principle and cause must be apart from the things of which it is a principle, and must be able to exist when separated from them." "If this is a sufficient reason," Aristotle continues, "it is the more sufficient that universal concepts should rather be considered to be principles . . ."[24] Aristotle is here neither denying the universal character of the substance's nature, nor this nature's substantiation in individual, particular forms. Yet, more crucially, he avoids stressing one of these two poles at the expense of the other. Intelligibility *and* sensibility, Aristotle states, should both be maintained as equally constitutive of the substance's knowledge.[25]

This explains why for Aristotle "one" does not always connote oneness in number, or at least not always strictly so. This is Aristotle's other way for showing that stressing the presence of the nature in the substance's sensible form is not a negation of universality because it is not an affirmation of individuality. If oneness here does not mean "numerical oneness," it does not then defend individuality, because, for Aristotle, "'numerically one' and 'individual' are identical in meaning."[26] The form of the substances is inherent to the substance's existence not because it individualizes or images it as a numerically single isolated entity. Far from this, the form defines the substance's nature in the sense of reflecting it in its particular, concrete existence. The elements that form the substance's existence are as substantial as their substance's nature. This is why they predicate its nature as such.

---

23. Ibid., III.3.998b.3. Italic is mine. Even if we considered the *genera*, which we infer *from* the form and the sensible elements, a first principle, this does not make the forms a *first* principle for Aristotle because "the definition by *genera* will be different from that which tells us of what *parts* a thing is composed" (ibid., III.3.998b.5).

24. Ibid., III.3.999a.20.

25. "If nothing exists apart from individual things, nothing will be intelligible; everything will be sensible, and there will be no knowledge of anything . . . nor again will anything be eternal or immovable, since sensible things are all perishable and in motion. Again, if nothing is eternal, even generation is impossible; for there must be something which becomes something i.e. out of which something is generated, and of this series the ultimate term must be ingenerated" (ibid., III.4.999b.1–4).

26. Ibid., III.4.1000a.9–10.

In the light of the previous understanding, one can notice that oneness for Aristotle can also mean "oneness in kind," not in number. This makes his speech on oneness and particularity in relation to "substance" and "subsistence" a discourse on the meaning of "individuation," not on the centrality of "individuality." The idea of "individuation" is what underlies Aristotle's saying "if the substance of each thing is one in no accidental sense, and similarly is of its very nature something which *is*—then there are just as many species of Being as of Unity."[27] There is in this attention to "one of a kind" an acknowledgment of difference in terms of "otherness," as well as an attempt to show that the otherness of the substance that expresses its privation subsists or hypostatically stands (i.e., exists firmly, stably, and durably) in a substantial manner in the concrete form of existence, which this substance takes. Without this existence, the privation of the substance is reduced to mere numerical oneness or individuality.

This Aristotelian attention to the particularity or individuation of every substance (which lies in its subsistence in particular forms of existence) is the backdrop of Boethius' understanding of the relation between the nature and its personal form of existence (i.e., *hypostasis* or *substratum*). It shapes the track of Boethius' focus on the category of "particularity" and points ultimately to its central role in his philosophical and theological discourse on personhood in relation to both the triune God and the human species. "Person" designates the thing that makes the human, in his or her individuation, a being in comparison to, and contrast with, other beings. "Person" cannot designate so unless the meaning of "substance" in relation to it circles around particularity; around, that is, what makes the personhood its distinctive subsistence. This meaning of "substance" (i.e., "the specific difference that gives form to anything") is, in Boethius' thought, the "substrate of person"—what carries personhood, what makes it possible and firmly, stably, and durably existent.[28] "Personhood," as viewed from the perspective of this definition of "substance," cannot, then, be predicated to universals, because this would be contrary to the factor of particularity. Particulars, Boethius says, "are those which are never predicated of other things." In such things, he continues, the term "person cannot anywhere be predicated of universals, but only of particulars and individuals; for there is no person of man or animal or a genus; only Cicero, Plato, or other single individuals are single persons named."[29] By being ascribed to individuals and not universals, "person" is properly expressive of itself. It is its own substance.

---

27. Ibid., IV.2.1004a.8–9.
28. Boethius, "A Treatise Against Eutyches and Nestorius," II.5–10 (83).
29. Ibid., II.45–50 (85).

Therefore, the definition of "person" that properly expresses substantiality in terms of particularity should be "an individual substance of a rational nature."[30]

The previously exposed logic in Boethius' text not only explains why for Boethius "person" can only be predicated of particulars and individuals, and not of universals.[31] More importantly and crucially still, and contrary to what Hipp thinks, this explains, in my conviction, why Boethius incorporates the concept of "individuality" into his definition of person.[32] If "person" can only be designative of particulars because it is reflective of what makes the thing its distinctive substantial form, then speaking about individuality as inherent to personhood makes sense as an expression of a "one-of-a-kind" form of distinction. Individuality in this view indicates *individuation* and "one-of-a-kindness," and not singularity or any ontological or existential monistic sense of self-enclosure. Modernity's big fault was in taking Boethius' understanding of "individuality" into a dead end when it separated this notion from Boethius' understanding of "nature" as a designation of particularity and uniqueness, and linked it unwittingly to a notion of metaphysical "rationality" that indicates self-awareness and self-contemplation. Stephen Hipp correctly notes that "individual" in Boethius' definition is married to "substance," and not to "reason" or "rationality."[33] Individuality designates the being's personal individuation and particularity, and not of an individual, single being that is rationally self-sufficient and subsistently self-oriented. This latter meaning was imposed on the Boethian definition and led ultimately to the opposing of "personhood" to "selfhood": to be a "self" meant to be fully and individually a self-contained being, and not a substance in a particular, unique form of personal subsistence.

Stephen Hipp makes a very valuable contribution to the explanation of Boethius' usage of "individual" in his attention to the crucial relation between Boethius' previous definition of "person" and his central insight that "essences can indeed be universals, but they 'sub-stand' in individuals and particulars alone."[34] In the intellectual context of modernity, this claim was inappropriately rephrased into "essence that '*subsists*' in individuals." This is a dangerous

---

30. Ibid., III.5 (85).

31. Hipp, *"Person" in Christian Tradition and the Conception of Saint Albert the Great*, p. 106.

32. Ibid., 107. "The concept of individuality intended by Boethius when defining 'person' as an 'individual' is not easy to determine, not only because of the extreme difficulty in distinguishing his own opinion from that of the author from whom he borrows the notion, but also because of the different and apparently contending theories his analysis brings into discussion."

33. Ibid., 108.

34. Ibid., 111.

reading, or misreading, of Boethius' thinking because it indicates that substantiality is restricted to, and conditioned by, singularity and closed oneness. Whereas "the essence *sub-stands* in individuals and particulars alone" means that the essence qualifies, and gains, an existence that has a particular form, rather than hides or remains concealed behind its particular form of existence.

III. The Traces of Boethius' Legacy in Modernity

In its core, the Boethian notion of personhood states, as Hipp accurately notes too, that "'subsistence' . . . is undetachable from the notions of 'being', 'substance' and 'essence' (broadly understood)," and individuation, in relation to the triune God or the human being, similarly results in "substantiality" and not in "singularity" or "rationality," in the first place.[35] The modernist intellectual context failed, so it seems, to notice the strong link between "particularity" and "individuality" in Boethius' definition of "person," because in modernity there was a tendency to segregate "existence" from "being" and "substance" from "subsistence" according to an "either-or" reasoning strategy (which I will point to when I speak about the impact of Fichte on modernity). This "either-or" criterion led eventually to a division between speaking about the self as "personal and relational" on one hand, and speaking about it as "rational and individual" on another.

From the Enlightenment onwards, both theology and the Western secular, intellectual context associated "personhood" with the common interpretation of the notions of "self" and "subject," which reflect in its content nothing other than the aforementioned one-sided misreading of the Boethian definition of "person" as "an individual subject of rational nature."[36] Instead of maintaining the distinction between the inner nature of being and its concrete existence—which characterizes the original meaning of the oldest Greek patristic term that is designative of "personhood," namely "*hypostasis*," which Boethius also used—"essence" and "existence" were conceptually separated from each other on the basis of the belief that the patristic term "*hypostasis*" per se

---

35. Ibid., 111–12, 116–17.

36. Peter Hick and C. Webb believe that Boethius' "*persona est naturae rationabilis individua substantia*" should rather be interpreted as "the essence of human nature is a specific expression of the rational order of things," which would eventually show that the Western stress on "individuality" and "rationality" by the help of Boethius' definition is not quite congenial with the thinking of the latter's Aristotelian, medieval figure. See Hick, "One or Two? A Historical Survey of an Aspect of Personhood," 41; and C. C. Webb, *God and Personality* (London: Allen & Unwin, 1919), 47.

originally designated "individual/singular subject," and had nothing to do with the subsistence of this subject.

Instead of highlighting "individuation," the modernist thought-form shifted Boethius' definition into an invitation for centralizing "individualism." The logic behind this shift becomes even clearer when we look at it from the modernist one-sided concern about "selfhood" as "inwardness," and specifically as *rational* inwardness. By default, individuation has to do with one's presence with and before others, because it designates the thing that makes this one person his or her unique and different self *in relation to and in comparison with* others. Individuation, therefore, does not help when the point of departure in understanding one's self is a narrow attention to his individual, intrinsic structure of awareness. The attention needs instead to be paid to individualism as a more appropriate expression of *the* inner rational constituent of the human self.

Charles Taylor is one of those who persuasively pave the way for this conclusion when he invites us to see the influence of Plato's notion of "self-mastery" on Western modernist thinking. It was Plato, Taylor argues, who gave to the modernist context the conviction that "reason is at one and the same time a power to see things aright and a condition of self-possession. To be rational is truly to be master of oneself."[37] In Plato's imagination of the ideal human being-ness and selfhood, singleness and rationalism were totally identified and conditioned by each other in the form of conditioning self-awareness, and even defining it, by means of an understanding of the mind as a "unitary space," which alone enables the human to reach into "the state of maximum unity with oneself."[38]

Apart from Plato's "self-mastery" notion, Taylor continues, the modernist interpretation of "selfhood" as an expression of interiority that lies in individualism and rationalism could have never developed.[39] This notion

---

37. Taylor, *Sources of Self*, 116 (115–26). Taylor finds this mainly in Plato's *Republic*.

38. Taylor, *Sources of Self*, 119. Taylor associates this thinking with the Platonic speech about the soldiers of the Republic who aspire to becoming self-sufficient, single agents among others, and points to the derivation of this description in the image of warriors in Homer's writings. The Homeric warriors now represent those single individuals who represent the image of the great hero, whose heroic identity lies in himself, despite the god's empowering of him (e.g., like Achilles). The Homeric warrior is a single, self-aware person, great by virtue of his very own single self (ibid., 118–19). Taylor, however, equally points to a difference between Plato's Republicans and Homer's warriors, in that Plato considers the disposition of the soul more crucial than external success. For Plato, reason's central place in one's self-awareness makes itself apparent in the fact that "the truly, wise, just—and thus happy—person is disinterested in the world of power," that usually relevant to the life of warriors and their passion for glory (ibid., 120–21).

arrived to the modernist mind, as Taylor ably shows, via Augustine's attention to self-reflexivity and consideration of it as part of the human orientation to God, and through Descartes' twisting of this Augustinian thinking by means of centralizing the self's inward reflexivity in the individual's cognitive mastery ordering of his inner ideas.[40] In Descartes' "*cogito ergo sum*" axiom, Plato's association of the centrality of reason, along with the notions of "order," "giving reason," and "giving an account," reaches its ultimate end. It is one of the major factors that encouraged the adoption of Boethius' definition of "person" and invited its interpretation in the way described here. Boethius' Aristotelian attention to individuation was in modernity baptized with the Platonic emphasis on rational self-mastery and self-awareness, eventually turning individualism and rationalism into *the* main constituents of human selfhood. The specific outcome of this shift that concerns me here is the ensuing modernist dichotomization of "the state of being personal" (i.e., dependent on relations with others: subsistence) and "the state of being an individual subject" (i.e., self-sufficient, fully in/as yourself: substance), which I will discuss in the following chapter.

39. Ibid., 120.
40. Ibid., 127–58ff.

2

Theological Conditioning?

1. The Notion of "Self" and the Modernist Theology of God

In this chapter, I endeavor to show that theology responded to the modernist emphasis on understanding "self" and "personhood" as expressive of an individual, rational subject (e.g., Descartes, Kant, Locke, Hume, Nietzsche, etc.[1]) by speaking about God as an ideal, criterial definition of the state of being a dynamic and relational subject. Theologians stressed that God is not an individual being, self-enclosed and isolated in his own atemporal world. God is rather a relational subject, who is open to the other and who is not an isolated self. One should not here mistakenly think that this counterargument is the originating source of the conviction that appeared in the last quarter of the twentieth century, which states that the Trinity is an expression of a sheer state of absolute relationality. This last conviction, as I will discuss in the ensuing part, was shaped by a postmodernist total rejection of the notion of "transcendental self," along with its alternative one-sided transcendentalization of the notion of "being-toward-another."

The previous claim that God is a relational being is not yet a theological total rejection of the modernist notion of "self." It is rather an attempt to marry the notions of "individual" and "relational," which are opposed to each other in the modernist context, first by understanding "self" as an expression of a single entity in a state of flux, and, secondly, by rejecting the claim that the notion of "relational personhood" does not have in its definition a recognizable place for the idea of individuality. Noticeable here is that the attempt to marry "relational" with "individual" in the theological reasoning about God (and God's relation to the human) stands shoulder-to-shoulder with

---

[1]. For critical analyses and assessments of this understanding of selfhood in the literature of modernist thinkers, see Charles Taylor, *Sources of the Self: The Making of the Modern Identity* (Cambridge, MA: Harvard University Press, 1989), 127–210; and Robert C. Solomon, *Continental Philosophy Since 1750: The Rise and Fall of the Self* (Oxford: Oxford University Press, 1988), 7:23–72.

a parallel concern about importing the notion of "infinite" (which is basic in the doctrine of God) into the notion of the "self's" circle of discussion and interpretation. This attempt represents willingness to incorporate into the philosophical knowledge of human nature the ideas of "transcendence" and "mystery," which are central to the religious hermeneutics of "being" and "existence." The purpose of this incorporation is to show that the self can be fully itself, or can be fully its own being, when its relational mode of existence does not obscure, but rather reveals or unmasks, the infinite dynamicity of its particular (individual) character and existence.

Needless to say, this theological attempt to incorporate the notions of "infinite" and "mystery" into the discussion about "personhood" and "self" was a response to a major philosophical contrasting in modernity of the notion of the "infinite" with the notion of "relational." The belief in the incommensurability of the notions of "relational personhood" and "infinity" has a very important metaphysical background that is related to the dissociation of the metaphysical, religious concepts of "transcendence," "infinity," and "beyond-ness"—concepts usually used in relation to the divine—from the relational and personal dimensions of the historico-experiential forms of existence and being-ness, which were central to the modernist philosophical discourse about the human reality, starting from Descartes and Kant, and culminating in Fichte. Among these philosophers, it is Fichte who ultimately believes that the possibility of knowledge about God is rationally impossible because the realm of rational thinking is sharply separated from the metaphysical realm of the concept of God. The impact of Fichte's belief on theological thinking in the context of modernity is immeasurable. Therefore I now turn to his thinking.

1. J. G. FICHTE ON GOD'S KNOWABILITY AND BEING

Essentially, Fichte argues that "thought" is a totally inadequate concept for the idea of Deity. In a nominalist fashion, he rather stresses that God's being can never be known through, or in, any allegedly historical revelatory means.[2]

---

2. J. G. Fichte, *Attempt to a Critique of All Revelations* (Cambridge: Cambridge University Press, 1970). For a good analysis of Fichte's view of God's knowability, see Eberhard Jüngel, *God as the Mystery of the World: On the Foundation of the Theology of the Crucified One in the Dispute between Theism and Atheism*, trans. Darrel L. Guder (Grand Rapids: Eerdmans, 1991), 128–41. For a remarkably educating narration of the conflict between revelation and reason in eighteenth-century continental philosophy, read Maria Rosa Antognazza, "Revealed Religion: The Continental European Debate," in *The Cambridge History of Eighteenth-Century Philosophy*, ed. Knud Haakonssen (New York: Cambridge University Press, 2006), II:666–82. In a relatively more positive appraisal of revelation, as Antognazza points out, Lessing finds a

Fichte's separation of the idea of God from the realm of knowledge demonstrates the following. First, it shows that the prior logic, which underpins Fichte's thought, as Frederick Copleston realizes, is an "either-or" rule of reasoning. Fichte believes that in their thinking and reasoning, philosophers must make a choice between the opposite intellectual claims and forms of inquiry. For having two or more options means that these different options are in essence mutually exclusive and they cannot all be simultaneously true. Fichte was convinced that it is not possible to opt for a synthesis that can possibly take away the opposition between the available options by the aid of a plausible logical reconciliatory combination. The attempt of some philosophers (e.g., Kant) to offer in their philosophical reasoning middle-ground forms of interpretation or logical hypotheses, and to resort to speculative compromises, in order to water down the tension between any two opposites, is not a track that leads to consistency in philosophical reasoning, according to Fichte.[3]

The second dimension that Fichte's separation between "thought" and Deity demonstrates is his application of the aforementioned "either-or" reasoning rule to his interpretation of the notions of "essence/being" and "existence." Fichte believes that the proper option the philosopher should opt for is "the idealist, analytical" and not "the dogmatic, propositional" approach to the relationship between different claims, for the former is the authentic representation of the concern about, and the attention to, the self and the ego in their absolute, moral self-actualization.[4] This conviction explains Fichte's realizable emphasis on "essence" over "existence"; so much so sometimes, that the idea of "infinite Being" in his writings about religion and God almost reductively designates that which is by no means existentially, or even rationally, accessible. In the light of this conviction, Fichte views Christian religion as that religious phenomenon which speaks about a God who is transcendentally emancipated from the realms of reason. Christianity is, therefore, only valid and meaningful outside the realm of philosophy, because it is a discourse designed more relevantly for the heart than for cognitive understanding. Christianity, Fichte believes, talks to the soul, not to the mind; it feeds the emotions, and leaves reason in grave hunger.

---

valuable cognitive role for revelation when he considers its analogues to education and claims that revelation's aim is "to facilitate the development of human potentials, progressing through different phases in accord with the degree of development of the subjects to which it is directed" (ibid., II:676).

3. Frederick Copleston, *A History of Philosophy: Fichte to Nietzsche* (London: Burns & Oates, 1963), VII:39.

4. Fichte, *Attempt to a Critique of All Revelations*, 39.

On the other hand, Fichte thinks that if philosophy would supposedly make a space for the idea of God within its boundaries, it would first turn the Christian personal and relational God into an idealist expression of the idea of "infiniteness," though a *moral* version of "infiniteness" this time. God, that is, has to be seen as "a changeless, necessary Being, who is the ultimate cause of all that happens in the world," and also the one that shapes human moral life.[5] Nothing makes this view clearer in Fichte's thinking than what he writes on the form of the philosophically proper "religion" in his paper, *Public Religion of the Present Age*. Rather than founding religion on any form of revelatory encounter with a reality that meets humanity from without, Fichte defines religion in this text as "an inward consciousness, and indeed a wholly self-sufficiency and self-comprehending consciousness."[6] The ego, for Fichte, does not need to leap at all outside itself toward an opposite other in order to be what it is meant to be as a full self.[7]

Does this mean that religion (as essentially the comprehension and feeling of the infinite and the striving for the supersensual) should disappear because it no longer has a valid place in the world? When he observes human life and ponders the values that people reflect in their social, familial, and personal connections, Fichte realizes that the form of religiosity that yearns for the infinite "still exists whether recognized or not, and [humanity's] capacity still exists for attaining a full and conscious being."[8] From this daily-life observation, Fichte concludes that true religiosity is not outward but inward in nature, and God is not what interacts with humanity as a revealed, communicable reality. God is an expression of the ideal, transcendent perfection that humanity

---

5. Ibid., 76.

6. Fichte, "Public Religion of the Present Age," in *The Popular Works of Johann Gottlieb Fichte*, 4th ed., trans. William Smith (London: Tuebner & Co., 1889), 257–70, 258–59. Fichte believes that one of the immensely negative impacts of this revelation-based religiosity appears in politics and governing systems: "The fear of Gods was an excellent resource for an imperfect Government; it was a convenient thing to watch the doings of the Subjects through the eyes of the Divinity, where the Government either could not or would not exercise this surveillance itself; the Judge was spared the exercise of his own sagacity and penetration, when, by threats of relentless damnation, he could induce the accused to communicate to him willingly the information he desired to possess; and the Evil Spirit performed, without reward, the services for which, at later times, Judges and Police had to be paid" (260).

7. This is the conviction that Paul Tillich quite accurately criticized: "the subjective idealism of philosophers like Fichte is unable to reach the world of contents unless the ego makes an irrational leap into its opposite, the non-ego." Tillich, *Systematic Theology* (Chicago: University of Chicago Press, 1967), 1:171. Tillich is not even criticizing Fichte's subjectivism from a theological, but a purely ontological, approach to the question of Being as basically a question about the human as such, an approach that does not in fact place Tillich against Fichte in terms of approach and method.

8. Fichte, "Public Religion of the Present Age," 261–63.

inhibits by aspiring innately at "pure morality." By pondering the infinite and cognizing the transcendent, humanity is neither approaching, nor is being approached by a divine disclosure of a self-existing Being. The human person is only striving to comprehend the absolute law of duty, to feel it living within herself. Can she capture truly how her earthly life is immersed with fulfillment by virtue of the divine? She cannot, because the divine is infinite and beyond the possibility of any human rational embrace.[9] The more the human person surrenders to the attempt of identifying with the eternal law that lies within herself, the higher she is elevated above time as such.[10] The human person would bridge the gap with the divine by elevating above finiteness and uniting with absoluteness and infinity. The human person would achieve this when she dives into an intrinsic strife for seeing the "whole infinite universal Being," who lies, in Fichte's words, within her very own self.[11]

2. THE IMPOSSIBILITY OF REVELATION

Fichte takes the previous view further when he develops his understanding of the notion of "revelation" in *Attempt at a Critique of All Revelations*. There, Fichte argues that "revelation," as an expression of God's close presence and relational character, is by no means epistemologically reliable, and it cannot rationally characterize infinite being-ness. The only condition wherein the idea of revelation can make philosophical sense is when its content is congenial with the human need of moral self-fulfillment. Echoing Kant's conviction that God cannot be perceived except as a rational postulate that is necessary for practical reason,[12] Fichte states that revelation cannot be the tool for disclosing God per se, for God by default is beyond any thesis-antithesis, ego and non-ego, or logic of perception. The idea of "God" speaks about a Being whose nature consists of no distinction between subject and object, "I" and "other." Though we can form expressions about this idea in our mind, God in essence is the inconceivable. Similarly to Kant, Fichte maintains that God's existence is not impossible after all. Yet having a God that is intimate to finite existence, and perceivable by the human mind, is impossible. God, Fichte says, is the idea that ought only to remain an idea and not to become a relatable reality.[13] God must be this, or there is no place for the idea of God in philosophy. There

---

9. Ibid., 265.
10. Ibid., 267.
11. Ibid., 267.
12. See for example Immanuel Kant, *Critique of Pure Reason*, trans. J. M. D. Meiklejohn (New York: Prometheus, 1990), 4–5.

is no middle-ground alternative to appeal to: either "God" is the name of the infinite and the unknown, or "God" is something known; thus "God" is not the name of the divine infinite Being. It is on the basis of this separation of "infinite being" from "relational existence" that Fichte distinguishes between "empirically conditional faith," under which comes revelation, and "purely rational faith," under which comes the idea of God.[14]

Fichte repeats the same logic in his speech about God's personal being. For Fichte, "person" is an expression of an individual psychological awareness of the self. It is an expression of a finite state of self-consciousness. It designates something that is relative in essence and spatio-temporal in extension: within the boundaries of the visible alone. Be that as it may, God cannot be "person" and cannot have personal nature. Far from being able to speak about God's being, we can only speak about the meaning of existence, which "God" ideally and referentially images before us as "moral law." In human reason and life, God does not take the image of "person," but appears as an action; as a moral action, as the criterial action of morality per se. For Fichte, as David Coffey notes, "if God were infinite, He would not be a person. [For] self-consciousness always presupposes the existence of another, from whom one distinguishes oneself, thus becoming conscious of self. Therefore, if God were a person He could be neither infinite nor the creator of all things."[15] Coffey is correct in showing that Fichte's understanding of personhood in relation to God was an imposition of certain anthropomorphic views of personhood on God's being. God is different from the human whose personal existence lies in a substantial need for relatedness to a different other. The human cannot be a *subject* except in relatedness to another, and, more specifically, in relatedness to a spiritual other. This is not the case with God. God is not by definition a subject that is related to an absolute spiritual other in order to acquire subjecthood. God is rather *this* absolute spiritual other: God is absolute subject. God is the fount of all subjectivity.

---

13. Copleston, *A History of Philosophy*, VII:79. See also Jüngel, *God as the Mystery of the World*, 138. According to Jüngel, Fichte distinguishes God's activity from the schema of thinking about them, rendering God as such a pure activity (139). Jüngel interprets this in congruence with his understanding of God's revelation from without, not against it. This may support Jüngel's conviction that "God's Being is in becoming." I wonder how this concurs with Fichte's basic segregation of metaphysics from existence, and how Jüngel's interpretation is correctly a reflection of Fichte's attempt at a critique to revelation rather than a support to it.

14. Fichte, *Attempt at a Critique of All Revelation*, 157ff.

15. David Coffey, *Deus Trinitas: The Doctrine of the Triune God* (New York: Oxford University Press, 1999), 69, 75.

II. Theology, Existence with/in God, and the Human Self

Against this segregation of "infinite essence" from "relational existence" came existence-oriented theology's—and later on, revelation-centered theology's—strong argument that the concept of "relational personhood" is the missing key point in the anthropology of the eighteenth and nineteenth centuries. In this section, I will look first at the understanding of "relationality" and "personhood" in the proposals of existence-oriented theology, leaving the study of the same notions in the proposal of revelation-centered theology to the following one. On the side of existence-oriented theology, Paul Tillich is worth studying as a major theological figure in the twentieth century who represents an influential voice in this approach. His theology is very important for showing us how, in his emphasis on relationality and existence in relation to God, theologians can sometimes undermine God's being and divine self for the sake of humans. In the ensuing pages, I will show that this is detectable in the prioritization of the state of "ultimate concern" over the being of the subject, with whom such an ultimate concern is interactively held, in the theology of Paul Tillich.

1. Paul Tillich and the Centrality of "Ultimate Concern" for Self-Fulfillment

Paul Tillich is one of the main twentieth-century theologians who argue that the human self is constituted by means of correlation with an "other." His ontological stress on correlation, as Bernard Martin argues, appears in its utmost clarity in his well-known saying: "The self without a world is empty; the world without a self is dead."[16] Tillich defines ontological being-ness as ultimately the "subject-object" correlation: it is basically self-relatedness or self-centeredness. He further believes that "correlation" lies at the base of any ontology,[17] and not only epistemology, almost echoing thereby the trend of thought that understands "oneness" or "unity of being" as merely a state of "existing with" or "existing as," and he locates it strictly in the historical "ciphers" of the existing world.[18]

Theology, in Tillich's view, must not speak about "the situation of the individual as individual and not the situation of the group as group."[19] Theology

---

16. Bernard Martin, *Tillich's Doctrine of Man* (Digswell Place, UK: James Nisbet, 1966), 85.
17. Ibid., 83–86.
18. Karl Jaspers, for example, once said, "To me, unity is realized only in the historic form that makes possible, and calls for, an endless variety of other historic forms." Jaspers, *Philosophical Faith and Revelation* (London: Collins, 1967), 137.

is neither about the one or the many, nor about how they exist together or how they are known. Theology is also not about "man before God" or "God before man," nor is it about "God before creation" or "creation before God." Theology is about the *correlation* between them: the relation called "God-man," the relation named "God-creation." Theology, moreover, is a state of interaction *with* the correlation called "God-man," as this latter is interpreted by us in a specific "situation." Theology is a correlational thinking about the correlation between the subject of knowledge (i.e., the "God-man" relation, in this case) and the situation: a correlational concern about the correlation between two related facts and their specific situations.[20] This correlational nature of theology stems, for Tillich, from the fact that the task of theology as the function of the church is to satisfy the purposes of proclaiming the truth of faith and of making this truth proclaimable for and in every generation.[21] Theology is this correlation that happens between these two concerns on one hand, and the outcome of the interpretation of the correlation between them on another.[22] Theology, in other words, is not a discourse or a set of doctrines. It is an *event*. Theology *happens*, because it is both the state of correlating with an event of correlation that is already taking place between two realities, and the defining situation of the two realities' existence. Theology, so to speak, is a "*course*," not really a "dis-course."

Tillich believes that the substance of any theology is twofold: the form and the content. While the form has to do with the correlation that takes place between the message and the situation, and what existential and categorical features this correlation images, the content is the core of the message; it is what makes this message "religious" rather than something else. Tillich calls the core or the content of the religious message "ultimate concern." It is the central term in Tillich's writings. It expresses the essence of the correlation between the human and the divine. "Ultimate," he states, designates the transcendental in the religious experience, while "concern" designates the existential therein.[23]

---

19. Tillich, *Systematic Theology*, 1:4.

20. Crucial to keep in mind here is that "situation" for Tillich does not designate the conditions or states wherein individuals and groups live, but rather the forms of thinking they use to understand and express these conditions and states of existence (ibid., 1:3–4). When, then, we speak about "modernity," "premodernity," or "postmodernity," what is meant are the forms of hermeneutics and thinking that are used by people to express and interpret their living conditions in various historical and cultural eras.

21. Ibid., 1:3.

22. The same, for example, applies to preaching. A good sermon is not just conducting or performing a successful speech, nor is it just presenting profound and persuasively argued content. The sermon "happens" when a correlation between the speech and the content, between the message and its transmission, takes place.

Combining these two together is the correlation that happens between the "transcendental" and the "existential," which takes place by means of both. Neither of these two poles can actually exist, nor can it "be," without the other. The "ultimate" cannot appear in itself apart from being known by virtue of the "concern" about knowing it. Theology, Tillich conjectures, is "theological" when its object is the religious experience and when "ultimate concern" is the core of this experience. This does not mean, however, that the "ultimate" per se can be the subject of theology and that "the *concern* about the ultimate" is just a secondary, subordinate element. The "ultimate" is a theological subject only insofar as it is a matter of ultimate concern for the human.[24] Apart from the realm of our concern, the ultimate is not part of a correlation that can be perceived by the human. Be that as it may, since form and content are mutually inclusive, and since correlation is the method and the foundation of the theological inquiry about everything, the ultimate or the transcendental is not the subject of theology except in its role as one side in the correlation between the transcendental and the concern about it. "Ultimate concern" is "that which determines our being or non-being." It is what defines "the whole of human reality, the structure, the meaning, and the aim of existence." The "ultimate," Tillich opines, matters insofar as it is part of *our* concern about being or nonbeing, about our whole reality.[25]

Tillich gleans from this understanding of theology's nature that theology's primary task is to "deal with the meaning of being *for us*."[26] It is supposed to explore the correlation that takes place between "the ultimate in us" and our concern about the impact of this latter on our being. It does not do this in a crudely neutral objectifying manner. It does it, rather, correlatively: the theologian does not only observe and analyze a correlation taking place before her. She actually correlates with the occurring correlation, as if she is involved in it. In this sense, the theologian's attitude is supposed to be existential in nature, theology's focal attention should be existence per se—insofar as this existence is reflective of correlationality—and, finally, theology's function should be correlating with the reality of existence—insofar as this existence is the existential situation of the ultimate concern. If all forms of knowledge lie in co-relation, then the theologian reflects in his theology a correlation with the correlational nature of any known reality in existence. By means of this, the theologian is involved in the very "ultimate concern" he or she interprets.

23. Tillich, *Systematic Theology*, 1:11–12.
24. Ibid., 1:12.
25. Ibid., 1:14.
26. Ibid., 1:22. Italics are mine.

Without this involvement, the concern would not be a "concern" but its lack, its absence. And this would turn theology into the study of the "ultimate" per se. Tillich would not want this to happen, because he believes that the ultimate is not meaningful for us, not even theologically, apart from our concern about it. Theology, therefore, is destined to be a study of the "ultimate's" correlation with the "concern about it," and the theologian is one who interprets this correlation as someone concerned—as if, that is, "the state of ultimate concern" is definitive ultimately of the theologian's self per se. This means that theology's task is to show *how* "ultimacy" is always under the canopy of our existential situation. It is supposed to explicate how "ultimacy" is a proper *answer* to our existential condition. Theology, in conclusion, as Tillich suggests, is "answering theology." "It must answer the questions implied in the general human and the special historical situation."[27]

It is of immeasurable significance to notice and keep in mind that in his theological project, Tillich ascribes to the studied situation the role of questioning, and to the theological message the role of answering. He actually *restricts* the role of questioning to the situation and *confines* to the theological message the role of answering. As one delves deeper into his theological system, it becomes apparent that Tillich's correlation is not fully correlational, as a matter of fact. Situations and theology are not easily compartmentalized in their respective roles of questioning and answering: Is there a time when the message asks and not only answers, and the situation answers and not only asks? Is there a "situation-message" correlation that is expressive of a proportionate relation between asking and answering as two roles played by, and two characteristics predicated of, each side of the "situation-message" interaction?

The sketch of Tillich's principal understanding of the nature and task of theology helps us apprehend his views on God and God's knowability. In his book, *The Dynamics of Faith*, Tillich touches upon the identity of "God" in the context of his theological understanding of the nature and dynamics of faith. Contextualizing the doctrine of God within the boundaries of faith makes sense in the light of Tillich's definition of faith as "the state of being ultimately concerned," which is characterized by "total surrender to the subject of ultimate concern."[28] The idea of "total surrender" logically presupposes someone or something to which the believer is supposed to surrender. It presupposes an otherness that is signified by the word "God." So, Tillich concludes, it is

---

27. Ibid., 1:31.
28. Paul Tillich, *The Dynamics of Faith* (New York: Harper & Brothers, 1957), 1, 3.

incumbent on the theological hermeneutics of faith to ask what in the idea of God constitutes divinity.[29]

What, in other words, makes God "the divine other," to whom we ultimately direct our concern about the "ultimate concern," and in whom we find the object of faith present? Tillich answers that what carries the quality of divinity are the elements of "unconditional and ultimacy." In other words, faith is not an "ultimate concern" unless it acknowledges that God is this "other" who represents the objective in the ultimate concern's "subjective-objective" correlation. This "subjective-objective" state of faith becomes an "ultimate concern," says Tillich, only in the presence of another ultimate entity, toward which the human concern must be directed. The finite human cannot transcend the subjective-objective scheme without having the infinite as a reality in itself. False ultimacy, which lies in claiming infinity without having it, Tillich believes, would not enable the finite to transcend the mentioned scheme.[30] God, for Tillich, is not then a mere postulate that is necessary for the human reasoning. God is a self-existing reality that represents the objective infinite in the state of "ultimate concern." God is not an element within the subject's existential acts of personality. God is the object that stands over against the subject in a total correlation that ultimately transcends the scheme between them.

It is one of Tillich's main claims in his theological system that "the language of faith is the language of symbols," and "the fundamental symbol of our ultimate concern is God."[31] Yet this is not, according to Tillich, to allow us to conclude that God per se is a symbol. God, instead, is by default beyond any form of existence: "the ultimate" that directs the human concern beyond any finitude and limitation and makes the human transcend them. To treat God as a symbolic expression means for Tillich that God is turned into mere object.[32] Though God is represented as the "objective" of the state of ultimate concern (i.e., of faith), that is, as the ultimate *of* the concern, God per se is not an "object" for study or analysis that lies outside the realm of correlation. This is also why Tillich would not accept considering God as a "person," because this would negate God's infinity and absoluteness.[33]

---

29. Ibid., 3.
30. Ibid., 11.
31. Ibid., 45.
32. Tillich, *Systematic Theology*, 1:172.
33. Ibid., 1:245. "Personal God does not mean that God is a person. It means that God is the ground of everything personal and that he carries within himself the ontological power of personality."

This conviction explains why Tillich argues that any ontological inquiry about God's being and existence is meaningless, and then postulates that theology should focus, instead, on the epistemological investigation of faith. For Tillich, the task of theology is not proving God's existence, nor does it limit the content of faith, or the theologization on faith, to God's existence or nature. These concerns that are ontological in nature are hardly fruitful in theological reasoning. Why? Because, as David Kelsey points out, ontology for Tillich cannot *describe* the infinite, which encounters the finite in the ultimate concern's correlation that takes place as an act of revelation. "Ontological analysis," Kelsey continues, "can show why men quest for a kind of ontological healing, and it can show how such healing might take place in revelatory occurrences, but it cannot describe the 'transcendent' reality that does this healing."[34] The ontological analysis cannot state anything about the transcendent reality that lies beyond the finite. Ontology cannot "yield the doctrine of God,"[35] and no philosophical doctrine of God based on ontology, concludes Kelsey, need be developed and "none can be."[36]

The previous discussion brings us to Tillich's understanding of God's knowability, which reflects his removal from "theology as a question about who God is" to "theology as a question about who God is *in our mind*." David Kelsey pinpoints such a shift when he notes Tillich's adoption of a religious epistemology from some of the thirteenth century's theological discourses. This adoption states that knowing the ultimate principles is expressive of God's innate presence in the human mind. Kelsey detects Tillich's adoption of this logic in the latter's saying that reason's depth "is not another field of reason which could progressively be discovered and expressed, but is that which is expressed through every rational expression. It could be called . . . 'being-itself' which is manifest in the *logos* of being."[37] The depth of human reason, in other words, lies in nothing other than the reality of God. God is inherently constitutive of the human's deepest realms of self-awareness.

Now, if the ultimate only makes sense to us when it makes itself constitutive of the depth of our selves, and is only "infinite other" for us strictly insofar as it is the center of self-consciousness that is acquired by our ultimate concern, what does "revelation" stand for? Is there a place for revelation in

---

34. David H. Kelsey, *The Fabric of Paul Tillich's Theology* (New Haven and London: Yale University Press, 1967), 51 (51–88).

35. Ibid., 52, citing from Tillich, *Systematic Theology*, 1:243.

36. Kelsey, *Fabric of Paul Tillich's Theology*, 61.

37. Ibid., 65, citing from Tillich's *Systematic Theology*, 1:79. Kelsey points to the application of this logic to Tillich's pneumatology in volume 3 of his systematics.

Tillich's system, and does revelation connote an act of self-disclosure that is exerted by God to make the divine personal, relational self known? We begin to touch upon the core of Tillich's answers to these questions when we start with his interpretation of the occurrence of revelation; more specifically, his view on when revelation *is* "revelation." Tillich believes that the core of revelation lies in the preparedness for its happening in human religion and culture. There is no revelation apart from the situation of existence that turns a certain thing or an event into a "revelation" of an ultimate concern. "There is no revelation unless there is someone who receives it as revelation." Why? Because "the act of reception is part of the event itself."[38] The interpretation of the event is what makes it revelatory of some specific state of ultimacy. It does not make the event revelatory of an ultimate Being, but rather revelatory of a "state of ultimacy." For, this interpretation is a theological apprehension of our reception of the concern about the ultimate, and is not an interpretation of our apprehension of the ultimate reality per se. For Tillich, the ultimate as such, as I showed earlier, is not ultimate in existence unless it is an ultimate in and for our concern. Unless, that is, we realize that it is the depth of our real reasoning.

When, then, does revelation happen, according to Tillich? Revelation *happens* when we interpret our reception of certain events in existence as reflective of the ultimate concern and as responsive to our inquiry about ultimacy. Revelation happens only when a certain historical activity enables the person to correlate her existential situation with the ground and depth of her own being.[39] An activity becomes "revelation" when it reveals a transformative power that makes the human "aware of Being's wholeness in the ecstatic depth of human reason."[40] Revelation, in other words, is the name of every event wherein someone comes to terms with what discloses before the human the depth of existence in general, and the depth of his own being as someone who exists in a specific situation. Revelation is basically "the manifestation of what concerns us ultimately."[41] What is manifested becomes an ultimate concern to us not because it is a mysterious self-existing reality relating to us from without, but because it represents the ground of our own being, of our own self. Because revelation *is* correlation, "revelation is not real without the receiving side, and

---

38. Tillich, *Systematic Theology*, 1:35.

39. See Nancy C. Ring, *Doctrine within the Dialectic of Subjectivity and Objectivity: A Critical Study of the Positions of Paul Tillich and Bernard Lonergan* (San Francisco: Mellen Research University Press, 1991), 161–64, 171–72.

40. Thus John Charles Cooper, *The "Spiritual Presence" in the Theology of Paul Tillich: Tillich's Use of St. Paul* (Macon, GA: Mercer University Press, 1997), 57.

41. Tillich, *Systematic Theology*, 1:110.

it is not real without the giving side."[42] Both the receiving and the giving sides *are* because they correlate, and because what they represent—that is, the receiver is the "concern" and the giver is the "ultimate"—are the two components of a correlation.

If theology is an interpretation of the manifestation of correlation between the human ultimate concern and existing being's situation, and if revelation is "revelation" when it demonstrates to the human that this correlation is the ground of being, where and what is God, according to this theology? In part II of the first volume of *Systematic Theology*, Tillich speaks about God departing from an ontological question about "Being" in general and about the human self in particular. The structure of this part indicates that Tillich is interpreting a correlation between "Being" and "God." It is important to note that Tillich considers the first side of this correlation to be the one that raises the questions, whereas the second is the one who is supposed to answer them. Tillich believes that God becomes meaningful in relation to the inquiry about Being when it is seen as an answer to the inquiry about human finitude in particular.[43] But why finitude and not infinity? Is not infinity more definitive of God's Being? For Tillich, the basic question is an inquiry about finitude because the human, first and foremost, is the center of all the possibilities and levels of knowing. The human, and not the infinite, is the inquiry.[44]

Again, we have here an echo of Fichte's belief that the human is a question unto himself and that the ontological fulfillment (answer) of human being lies in self-awareness. The question of being is ultimately a question about the human and the structures of each human being's relation with existence. This self-awareness reflects self-centeredness and complete individualization. In this self-centered individualization, or individual self-centeredness, lies the personhood of the human being, according to Tillich.[45] The human becomes "person" when his ego becomes a question unto itself, and when this inquiry builds an awareness of the subject-object, human-world structure of being that is ontologically *a priori* to human being.

If the human self-awareness that lies in self-centered individualization is the basic question or the inquiry of inquiries in relation to Being, finitude should by all means be the foundation of God's role in Tillich's theological system. The infinite as a notion has not really any role within this system other than providing directions to the elements of self-awareness.[46] By means

---

42. Ibid., 1:111.
43. Ibid., 1:166. "It is the finitude of being which drives us to the question of God."
44. Ibid., 1:168.
45. Ibid., 1:175ff.

of human awareness of finitude, a person realizes that the infinite is inherent to the sphere of finite awareness. Thus the infinite is apriorically postulated before the process of self-awareness begins.[47] God, so it seems, is one of the means of human self-awareness and the self-fulfillment processes. This is its role and its nature. God is not the Creator of this self in the sense of being its *archē* or originating Cause. God is one of the means of the re-creation of the self—one of the mediums of the identification of the self's essentiality with its actuality, its actions with its potentials.

What is the "triune God," then, in this reasoning system? It follows from the previous Tillichian view that the "triune God" is not a notion designative of the essence or existence of the divine reality, with which we correlate, and with which we construe the ground of our ultimate concern. Within this logical framework, God is in the first place beyond essence and existence, and everything God *is* is inherent to and expressive of our ultimate concern.[48] "The Trinity," therefore, is one of the theological linguistic expressions from the history of doctrine that speaks about the ideal correlation between "the individual" and "the universal." It speaks in triadic terms about the state of concern that lays its roots in the human self and of which the human acquires an awareness via the correlation between the self's situation and the ultimate concern's condition. The three in the divine Godhead, eventually, are no longer "three persons" but merely "three *principles*." Again, Tillich's rejection of speaking about "person" and "existence" in relation to God explains his alteration of "persons" into "principles": we cannot claim three real persons in the Trinity because this will turn God into an object among other objects, which means God ceases to be God.[49]

The "Trinity" is, for Tillich, a symbol that attempts to express this reality, which all religions universally speak about as "the Ground of Being, the power of Being, Being itself." Tillich ascertains that this trinitarian language not only finds traces in the history of Christian doctrine, but also appears in the general history of religions' numerous versions of triadic expressions. The Christian trinitarian language, however, is the most pertinent to the human ultimate concern because it speaks about the infinite (Father) who became finite (Son), and who in his own being (as the ground of the correlation of the infinite with the finite) expresses the real image of life (Spirit) in the human self. God is the

46. Ibid., 1:190. They just "direct the mind to experience its own unlimited potentialities, but they do not establish the existence of an infinite being."
47. Ibid., 1:206.
48. Ibid., 1:228.
49. R. Allen Killen, *The Ontological Theology of Paul Tillich* (Kampen: Kok, 1956), 114–15.

ground of life, and the Trinity *is* the moments within the process of the divine life. Within this context of the ground of life, instead of "Father," Tillich now speaks about "the abyss of the divine"; instead of "Son," he speaks about "the fullness of the content of the abyss"; and instead of "Spirit," he speaks about "the actualization of the power and fullness of the content."[50]

Why does Tillich not consider the Trinity the definition of God's relational nature or as the nature that makes God able to relate? Because he believes that the ground of relationality cannot be a side in the relationship as such. It is what grounds the relationship and makes it be; it is not one of its poles.[51] This understanding explains why theology for Tillich is not about the relationship between God and the human or about God's triune personal nature. God is not a partner, let alone a personal one, in a relationship. God is the *a priori* notion that names the correlation between oneness and particularity, which lies at the foundation of the human's awareness of his or her ultimately concerned self. From this perspective, one can realize that "the triune God" connotes the ground that makes correlation possible between the state of self-awareness and the state of ultimate concern. The "Trinity" is a linguistic expression of the identification of *who* the human is and *how* she exists.

The culmination of Tillich's interpretation of the trinitarian personhood of the divine self is section four of the third volume of his *Systematic Theology*, which is titled "The Trinitarian Symbols." By the time Tillich reaches this stage of his *magnum opus*, he has already established that God in his theological system is this "ultimate concern" that is inherent to human nature and innate to the self's awareness of its self-centeredness and individuality. So, the speech on the Trinity is a further elaboration on the attempt to find the most appropriate symbols for postulating this understanding and displaying its correlational nature. Such a point of departure drives Tillich to an investigation of the development of trinitarian language as a general human phenomenon from the history of human religious awareness, rather than inviting him to construct a plausible hermeneutics of a deity that is trinitarian in nature and identity.

Tillich argues that the correlation and the tension between the universal and the particular, and the tension their correlation generates, require a symbolic language that can maintain the two poles of the tension in balanced and consistent interaction. Here the triadic language finds a role and value in Tillich's analytical investigation. The language of "Father, Son, and Holy Spirit," as Tillich concludes, is the most appropriate linguistic tool that is

---

50. Tillich, *Systematic Theology*, 1:250–51.
51. Ibid., 1:271.

available to Christianity for speaking in a plausible manner about the universality of the ultimate concern and the particularity of life situated-ness on one side, and about the absolute dimensions of self-awareness and the concrete existential forms it takes in every historical situation on the other.[52]

The doctrine of the Trinity plays this role, Tillich says, because it is a dialectical language about this tension between the absolute and the concrete in its various correlational forms. It is not really a language about the being and identity of God, but rather a symbolic expression of "God as ground, God as form and God as act."[53] This triadic language of "ground, form, and act" corresponds with the human's self-perception by means of aspects that are pertinent to human life. The language of "Father" is an answer to the inquiry on "human finitude"; the one of "Christ" answers the inquiry on "human estrangement"; and the one of "Holy Spirit" answers the inquiry on "life's ambiguities."[54]

One can summarize Tillich's theology of God in its trinitarian language as an interpretation of the threefold nature of the ultimate concern in the human self. It is a hermeneutics that endeavors to speak correlationally about the correlation between the absolute and the concrete, between finitude and infinity, and between self-awareness and the life-situation that are constitutive of the human ultimate concern. Only from the context of this hermeneutics can the Trinity as symbolic language about "the self-manifestation of the Divine life to man"[55] be a meaningful statement, and the "Trinity" a useful idea for human existence, according to Tillich.

2. THE OUTCOMES OF THE THEOLOGY OF EXISTENCE ON TRINITARIAN THEOLOGY

The previous analysis of Paul Tillich's understanding of the role of theology in relation to human self-awareness shows that in Tillich's thought we have a theology that actually follows the modernist rules of cognitive investigation and modernity's anthropocentric forms of inquiry. Tillich's strong concern about relationality and correlation leads him eventually to subordinate theology's

---

52. Ibid., 3:283. "In the first consideration we have found that the more the ultimacy of our ultimate concern is emphasized, the more the religious need for a concrete manifestation of the divine develops, and that the tension between the absolute and the concrete elements in the idea of God drives toward the establishment of divine figures between God and man."
53. Ibid., 3:284.
54. Ibid., 3:286.
55. Ibid., 3:294.

creedal speech on the nature of the infinite Being who correlates with human ultimate concern, and upon whose being the human understands her own human nature, to a philosophical, anthropocentric, one-sided interpretation of the event of correlation per se. This is evident from Tillich's tendency to view God's revelation more as a *response* than a question to human inquiry, and as one that serves one's own awareness of the ultimate concern. On the other hand, while Tillich does not mind speaking about "transcendental" as constitutive of rational, correlational knowledge, he reduces this transcendental to the name of the ideal image of an ultimate concern that basically enjoys a relational nature. His focus on "ultimate concern," as Calvin Schrag notes, leads him to believe that God as the *name* of the ultimate concern cannot be construed as a "being," "not even as a being in the sense of highest being."[56] "Beyond-ness" or infinity, then, is conceptually restricted to the territory of "(cor)relation," and "particularity" to the territory of "singularity." Instead of maintaining the Christian doctrinal belief that "God has personhood" and treating God as a Being in, as well as beyond, any static form of relationality, Tillich subjected the doctrinal understanding of "person" itself to a dominant modernist "either-or" dichotomistic form of inquiry: *Either* person means "a state of being relationally beyond itself," *or* it means "a single individual in a state of self-recognition."

Eventually, instead of launching a correlational dialogue between the Christian belief that God is a *triune relational* reality in relationship with the world, and the modernist conviction that human personhood lies in individual, rational self-awareness and self-fulfillment, a proposal such as the one displayed above amounts to an implicit denial of the belief that God is three *persons*.[57] It inevitably collapses "personal individuation" (which is constitutive of the doctrinal claim of three *hypostases* in God[58]) into the idea of "correlative flux of self-realization." It also replaces the doctrine of the Trinity by an "idealist monism" and, eventually, distorts the ontological basis of the theological understanding of "person" that lies in the triune personal particularity of

---

56. Calvin O. Schrag, *The Self after Postmodernity* (New Haven and London: Yale University Press, 1997), 136–37.

57. Something that C. Webb, at the beginning of the twentieth century, has already warned about: Webb, *God and Personality*, 62.

58. In patristic trinitarian theology, the idea of "personal individuation/particularity" is constitutive of how the Greek church fathers understood the technical term "*hypostasis*" when they used it to speak about the three persons in God, Father, Son, and Holy Spirit, in distinction from the one essence/nature (*ousia*). On the dimension of "personal individuation" in the understanding of the notion of "hypostasis," see Najib G. Awad, *God Without a Face? On the Personal Individuation of the Holy Spirit* (Tübingen: Mohr Siebeck, 2011).

"Father, Son, and Spirit." We have instead an inappropriate importation of a strong monistic view of a dynamic and ever-changing self-actualization by means of a correlation with an ultimate concern into the territory of theological inquiry.

Far from being really a corrector or a dialogue-partner, such an outcome reveals theology's *surrender* to modernity's reduction of the meaning of "self" into mere "self-sufficient, self-enclosed subject." It inevitably indicates that theology could not challenge the Enlightenment's deistic belief that God is a supreme "watchmaker" who put the world together and left it to run on its own. God here is reduced to a mere notion that connotes a mute, transcendental, noncommunal, and abstract infinity. "Personhood" is denied to deity here, because "person" is deemed an expression of openness to others; this openness, that is, is considered a threat to "infinity" because it undermines, according to this modernist view, the fact that the infinite should be an absolute, eternal, self-enclosed mind.[59] There is no place for a personal trinitarian identity involving the existence of three divine persons in a dynamic life of self-distinction together and with the world.

There is no chance for such a trinitarian form of identity to contribute anything whatsoever to the understanding of human self and personal being-ness that occupied the intellectual atmosphere of the modern era. Instead, the reduction of the theological doctrine of divine, infinite Being of God is what concurs in its ultimate extent with construing the human self an expression of a single, individual, rational being. A modern worldview shaped by Newtonian,[60] Cartesian,[61] Kantian, Fichtean, and Darwinian anthropocentrism can only

---

59. See Wolfhart Pannenberg, *An Introduction to Systematic Theology* (Grand Rapids: Eerdmans, 1991), 33ff.

60. In his writings on God and Christ, Isaac Newton defends God's absolute transcendence and aloofness by emphasizing that God's substance is unspeakable and unknown, we only know its attributes, never its being: "[W]e have ideas of [God's] attributes, but what the real substance of anything, we know not. In bodies, we see only their figures and colors. We hear only the sounds. We touch only their outward surfaces, we smell only the smells, and taste the savors; but their inward substances are not to be known either by our senses, or by any reflex act of our minds less, then, have we any idea of the substance of God." Isaac Newton, *Principia*, trans. Andrew Motte and Florian Cajori (Berkeley: University of California Press, 1960), 546. Instead of a loving, dynamic, and relational God, Newton emphasized that deity lies in domination, lordship, infinity, absoluteness, and static perfection. And, when he takes this understanding to the Trinity, Newton's understanding of "Father, Son, and Spirit" expresses an allegiance to Arianism. On this, and on Newton's influence on seventeenth-century English trinitarian theology, see Brian D. Spinks, "Trinitarian Belief and Worship: A Historical Case," in *God's Life in Trinity*, ed. M. Volf and M. Welker (Minneapolis: Fortress Press, 2006), 211–22.

61. In his exposition of the history of the notion of selfhood in modernity, Charles Taylor points at Descartes' centralization of "self" in a state of rational, inwardness expressive of self-assertiveness and

tolerate, if at all, an infinitely single deity, static and transcendent in nature, mute and indifferent to other beings, and isolated in existence, because only then this Deity's "infinity" can be true.[62] It can only tolerate such a contribution from religion to the secular thinking on the human self because, in the first place, it believes in alienation, rather than reconciliation, between the "particular" and the "universal," and construes this alienation inherent to the human moral strife of self-maintenance. This was Hegel's criticism of Kant's moral philosophy, when the former realizes in the latter's thinking a tendency to clash subjectivity with objectivity, opposing thereby the universal to the particular and making the first the "master" and the second the "slave/mastered." This is also the same critique that Mark Taylor, in his own words, insightfully rearticulates against Kant's thinking when he says "even the purist moral striving [i.e., in its Kantian version] leads to a continued self-alienation: particularity set against universality, inclination against obligation, desire against duty, passion against reason, self against self."[63] In the second place, consequentially, such a worldview does not allow for any link in anthropology between the state of "being actively relational" and the state of "being absolutely your self." In order to allow any space whatsoever to theology in thinking about the human self, therefore, it requires first converting "God" from "triune, relational person" to a "monad" or individual, absolute mind or notion of infinity. It is natural within this deistic, reductionist framework to see

argues that by means of this notion of selfhood Descartes paves the way for the denial of any association of God with the human inner self in any form of relationality. God no longer appears, Taylor explains, "at the very roots of the self, closer than my own eye . . . the Cartesian proof is no longer a search for an encounter with God within. It is no longer the way to an experience of everything in God. Rather what I now meet is myself: I achieve a clarity and a fullness of self-presence that was lacking before." Taylor, *Sources of the Self*, 157 (143–58).

62. Principal to modernity's understanding of "infinity" here is Descartes' definition of "infinite" as that which is "unreachable through the method [of cognitive reasoning]" or "incomprehensible to objective science," and his belief that "[for infinity] to be true idea, it cannot be grasped at all, since the impossibility of being grasped is contained in the formal definition of the infinite." Descartes, "Fifth Reply," 2:253. See also a serious contemporary criticism of Descartes' understanding of "infinity" in most of Jean-Luc Marion's writings, for instance, "The Idea of God," in *The Cambridge History of Seventeenth-Century Philosophy*, ed. Daniel Garber and Michael Ayers (Cambridge: Cambridge University Press, 1997–98), 1; Marion, *On Descartes' Metaphysical Prism*, trans. Jeffrey L. Kosky (Chicago: University of Chicago Press, 1999); and Marion, "The Essential Incoherence of Descartes' Definition of Divinity," in *Essays on Descartes' Meditations*, ed. Amélie Oksenberg Rorty (Berkeley: University of California Press, 1986), 317–30. For a classical theological critique of Descartes' understanding of infinity in God, read the still-valuable assessment in Jüngel, *God as Mystery of World*.

63. Mark C. Taylor, *Deconstructing Theology* (New York: Crossroad/Chico, CA: Scholars, 1982), 8 (1–22), citing Hegel's critique of Kant from his paper, "Spirit of Christianity," 214–15.

theologians like Schleiermacher and Tillich (and even Barth to a certain extent, as we will see) stating that there is no theological necessity in considering God as *three persons* or even triune personhood in his very nature, and departing instead from a modernist wish of assuming that God by default is "as far beyond being a person as the infinite is beyond the finite."[64]

The existence-oriented theological proposals of people like Schleiermacher and Tillich miss an important dimension of the concept of "person," and of the wholeness of "self," when it undermines the fact that the very theological notion of personhood offered by the doctrine of the Trinity contains a proper hermeneutics about how the particular and the universal can combine in noncontradictory fashion.[65] Schleiermacher and Tillich fail to realize that the defect in the modernist notion of "self" can be solved by paying attention to the characteristic of "beyond-ness" as it is understood in the context of the doctrinal definition of the trinitarian personhood of God *in se*. The absence of the dimension of "beyond-ness," as it is defined from the trinitarian personhood of God, from the modernist concept of "self" is what produces one-sided, narrow views of personhood that seem threatening to theological discourse on God's infinity, as well as imposing a superficial asymmetry between "personal" and "individual" on the general understanding of human self in anthropology.

Instead of associating "infinity" or "beyond-ness" with the notions of "particularity" and "distinction," the absence of the dimension of "beyond-ness" from the modernist understanding of "self" turns particularity in the personal being of the human into a static definition of one's own self-enclosure, so that "personhood" becomes a static mode of identity, and the self becomes a static mode of appearance, instead of a personal nature that is particularly *beyond* as well as *in* its existential setting. This in turn laid very negative side-effects on the theological reasoning of the modern age itself, when it distorted the theological understanding of the personhood *of* God as well as of the personhood *in* God, and sacrifices the Trinity for an abstract, ideal image of oneness. Eventually, God became an individual *Deus* or a self-contained absolute Spirit or Mind.

III. Karl Barth, God's Wholly Otherness, and the Notion of "Self"

In response to the problematic solution to the dichotomy between individuality and relationality in the modernist notion of "self," which I pointed to at the

---

64. G. L. Prestige, *God in Patristic Thought* (London: SPCK, 1981), 265.

65. Ibid., 90–97.

beginning of the chapter, Christian theology produced another existential and experience-oriented proposal, in which "personhood" means first and foremost openness to the world and relatedness to creation. The main example in the twentieth century of the emphasis on this specific concept of "personhood" in the context of the interaction between theology and modernist forms of inquiry on the human self is Karl Barth's challenge of modernist anthropocentrism by means of a revelation-based doctrine of God. Here we see a theologian who, by emphasizing a notion of relationship that is derived from God's relation to the world, tries to reconcile the universal and infinite with the particular and finite. We have a theologian arguing 1) that theology can masterfully show that the individuality of the person is realized and actualized *in* communion with others, not in separation from them, and 2) that "being-your-self" and "being-in-relation-with" are two sides of the same subject: they are the self in its personal, as well as individual, totality. Whether Barth succeeded in his cause or not is to be shown in the following pages.

1. BARTH'S THEOLOGICAL PERSONALITY

Before delving into the ocean of Karl Barth's dense and deep theological thinking, let me share some thoughts on Barth the theologian. There are numerous theologians who stood, like Paul Tillich, on the riverbank of theologians' attempt to interact with modernity's search for the meaning of selfhood, as well as to satisfy the requirements of the modernist forms of inquiry. (One can count here also Schleiermacher, Brunner, Rahner, Lonergan, etc.) To the contrary, on the riverbank of the theological attempt to challenge modernity by theological forms of inquiry, as well as to assess the modernist thinking from the vantage point of God's truth, Karl Barth is so influential and able a theologian as to almost occupy the scene alone. I do not mean by saying this that Barth's theological discourse is from A to Z perfectly accurate and unbeatable, while the discourses of the other theologians who stand on the opposite side of the stream are mostly full of gaps. I am basically pointing to Barth's attitude toward theology in itself before shedding light on his attitude toward other forms of scientific reasoning. I am departing in my study of some parts of Barth's exhaustive theological contribution from a view of his thinking about the role that theology should play in the world.[66]

66. This is why my presentation is not a systematic analysis of the development of Barth's overall theological thought in its chronological or textual order in his *Church Dogmatics*. My purpose here is just to visit sporadically some parts of Barth's theological chapters in various volumes of mainly his *Church Dogmatics*, in such a way that will serve the purpose of my argument. So, for those Barthian scholars who expect me to walk in their shoes and develop a comprehensive, systematic reading of Barth's complete

Karl Barth, as his writings show, is a theologian par excellence. For him, life and knowledge and existence in all their forms are just chapters in the theological story of God's relationship with the human. Therefore, in every word he writes or says, he presents himself as a theologian who is not ready by any means to put his theological mind in the service of the world's rules of reasoning and judging. Doing this means for him snatching the world from the book or the narrative it belongs to: God's story with humanity and God's salvific purpose to creation. Putting theology at the service of the world would not benefit the world, because it would be serving a malformed world, a world that is not itself; a world that is yet in need of God's redemption and re-creation. The world is truly "world" or truly the world that God created when its story and condition are a chapter in the narrative and proclamation of God's being and actions (theology).

This is basically why Barth is not a theologian who is ready to submit theology as a form of inquiry and knowledge to the service of the questions and rules of cognition of other secular forms of inquiry. Theology for Barth is not the means of knowledge, it is the criterion; is not the slave of truth-perception, it is the master. When this master exceeds itself as a master and takes the form, or plays the role, of servant sometimes (out of dialectic-logical necessity[67]), it does not do this in order to understand itself and acquire self-fulfillment. Theology plays the "servant" only for and in the church, not in the service of the rules and conditions of the world.[68] Therefore, theology, for Barth, need not be "rationalized." Rather, "reason," whatever meaning this term

literature and to echo, eventually, their own interpretation of this literature, I must say that my study is not going to follow this track.

67. I am one of those who do believe that Barth's theology is not truly free after all from Hegelian influences, despite the fact that Barth himself was adamantly antagonistic toward Hegel's philosophical project. Dialectical logic seems to be inevitably shaping Barth's thought and reasoning, as one can see in his understanding of the Trinity, but also in his understanding of salvation and Christology, as I will show in the ensuing paragraphs. I have elaborated on the traces of Hegelian influence on Barth's trinitarian thinking in *God Without a Face?* On the Hegelian dialectical idealism's influence on trinitarian theology in the twentieth century, see Richard Robert, "Barth on Time," in *Karl Barth—Studies in His Theological Method*, ed. Stephen Sykes (Oxford: Oxford University Press, 1979), ch. 4; Rolf Ahlers, *The Community of Freedom: Barth and the Presuppositionless Theology* (New York: Peter Lang, 1989); Samuel M. Powell, *The Trinity in German Thought* (Cambridge: Cambridge University Press, 2001); Eberhard Jüngel, *God as the Mystery of the World: On the Foundation of the Theology of the Crucified One in Dispute between Theism and Atheism* (Edinburgh: T. & T. Clark, 1983).

68. This is why being a church dogmatician means for Barth, as John Webster notes, dedicating the theologian's serious attention to, and conducting a mutual conversation with, "the theologians of the church's past" first and foremost. John Webster, "'There Is No Past in the Church, So There Is No Past in Theology': Barth on the History of Modern Protestant Theology," in *Conversing with Barth*, 14–39,

may connote, needs instead to be baptized with theological water in order to become truly "rational."

The above observation on Barth is what the late Colin Gunton eloquently highlights in his introduction to the new edition of Barth's *Protestant Theology in the Nineteenth Century*. Gunton notes how Barth theologizes the history of thought, turning modernist thinking into a history of ideas that is "yet resolutely theological"[69] in content. Gunton then shows how Barth uses theological criteria to judge the validity of human reasoning in general. Barth's treating of philosophers as if they are theologians was considered by some scholars as an example of how one may sometimes allow one's theological prejudices to mislead in the reading of others' thinking.[70] Yet, some other scholars argue that even when doing this, Barth is able to understand some major philosophers (e.g., Immanuel Kant) far better than their own colleagues.[71] In between these two extremes stands Colin Gunton with his attention to Barth's serious consideration of the hermeneutical nature of thought and its contextual framework. "To treat philosophers as theologians," states Gunton, "is [for Barth] to treat them as belonging in the same tradition of thought as that to which Barth himself belonged."[72] Barth reads the philosophers of modernity seriously, aiming at hearing what they actually say, without, however, surrendering the difference between theology and philosophy for the sake of such listening. It is my belief, however, that Gunton here is more reflective of

14–15. Webster's is a valuable bibliography of the composition and publication of Barth's *Protestant Theology*.

69. Colin Gunton, "Introduction," in *Protestant Theology in the Nineteenth Century*, xv–xx.

70. This is what Jean Rohls, for example, charges Barth with: "[S]ince Barth . . . conceives the writing of the history of theology as a theological task, modern Protestant theology is judged on the basis of Barth's own standpoint." J. Rohls, *Protestantische Theologie de Neuzeit I: Die Voraussetzungen und das 19 Jahrhundert* (Tübingen: Mohr, 1997), xix. M. Chapman also critiques Barth's approach by saying that therein "theology was isolated from a history identified with the meaningless slaughter of the fields of Flanders; it was consequently robbed of apologetic potential, except perhaps as a silent witness to the faith of all human constructs." M. Chapman, *Ernst Tröltsch and Liberal Theology: Religion and Cultural Synthesis in Wilhelmine Germany* (Oxford: Oxford University Press, 2001), 186.

71. Gunton, "Introduction," xvi. Also, Claude Welch may be a good example of those who hold such a strongly supportive opinion about Barth's approach. He states, for example, that Barth's *Protestant Theology* is "a book of great power and insight, and within its limits the most provocative of all the works one could cite." Claude Welch, *Protestant Thought in the Nineteenth Century: 1799–1870* (New Haven: Yale University Press, 1972), 1:8.

72. Gunton, "Introduction," xvii. John Webster also stands on the same side with Gunton and states that "Barth did his work [i.e., *Protestant Theology*] . . . out of a pervasive sense of participation in a common history with the theology of the recent and more distant past. He was, quiet simply, no iconoclast." Webster, "'There Is No Past in the Church, So There Is No Past in Theology,'" 22.

his own character as a theologian than of Barth's. The concern about launching an "open dialogue with philosophy . . . by the affirmation of difference"[73] seems to me a charitable attitude more expressive of the Barthian Gunton, rather than of Karl Barth himself.[74] In his own particular, sometimes furious manner, Barth listens seriously to the philosophers in order to show from the theological stage he stands on that they are in fact false prophets of anthropocentrism, who speak with their mouth about God while in their heart they are actually talking about the human being

At any rate, perceiving this attack against anthropocentrism is indispensable if one wants truly to apprehend Karl Barth's understanding of the relationship between theology and secular forms of inquiry in modernity. It is even the more significant for understanding Barth's views on selfhood and personhood (divine and human) in relation to the Trinity and to human beings. In order to analyze this attack against anthropocentrism, I will start with Barth's *Protestant Theology in the Nineteenth Century*, before I move to his *Church Dogmatics*. What I am not doing in this section on Barth, however, is the following: 1) I am not making a study of the development of Barth's thinking. I do not look at all Barth's writings, neither in their chronological, nor in their intellectual sequence. I only pick up his above-mentioned two major works, because they serve the concern of my chapter. 2) I am also not making a systematic analysis of the relationship between the interpretations that Barth offers to the various doctrines of faith in his multivolume *magnum opus*. I visit specific sections therein that are related to his interpretation of human and divine self, which I believe to be demonstrative of Barth's theological attitude toward the dominant notions of self and personhood in modernity. Out of this reading, I will see what relationship Barth constructs between theology and nontheological forms of inquiry.

In his essay on Barth as a historian of theology, John Webster makes the following intriguing claim:

> It is precisely as he struggles to come to terms with the dominant figures of modern theology that Barth shows himself, in very

---

73. Gunton, "Introduction," xvii.
74. I concur with Christoph Schwöbel when in his foreword to Colin Gunton's posthumously published course lectures on Karl Barth (Colin Gunton, *The Barth Lectures*, ed. Paul H. Brazier [London: T. & T. Clark/Continuum, 2007], ix–xxiv) he states that Gunton's treatment of Barth "is always enthusiastic, even when it is enthusiastically critical" (xxiii). This is what I too experienced as I attended Gunton's course lectures on Barth in 2001—an educational experience with a unique theologian that I will remember all my life.

important aspects, as a thoroughly modern theologian, taking up modernity's questions even when he turns inside out the answers developed with such skill by his forbears and, above all, feeling responsible for shouldering (not evading or dismissing) its tasks as a responsible participant in its history.[75]

In the following study of Barth's thinking as a theologian who stands within the boundaries of modernity, I will examine whether or not, in this very same attempt to shoulder modernity's theologians—even if this meant, as Webster states, turning inside out the answers they developed—Barth's proposal is more appropriate than those of these other theologians, or if it actually falls with them into almost the same trap. Do Barth's method and thought-form really reflect a theology that speaks strictly "from faith to faith," and do they indicate Barth's successful adherence to his conviction that theology "has no role to play vis-à-vis the 'secular or pagan' realm of thought"?[76]

2. BARTH ON MODERNIST ANTHROPOCENTRICISM: THE FRAMEWORK

The beginning of Barth's understanding of the relationship between theology and other forms of inquiry lies in his answer to the question: What does it mean to study the history of theology, and how should we develop a proper understanding of its subject matter? Barth's answer to this question can never be clearer:

> even as an object of historical consideration, theology demands theological perception, theological thought and theological involvement . . . it is a *condition sine qua non* of the success of our understanding that it should be approached theologically, in accordance with its subject-matter.[77]

What does it mean to study theology? It means to perceive theology theologically; to understand "the understanding of theology" as itself a theological notion. It means to think about the act of perceiving, to perceive

---

75. Webster, "'There Is No Past in the Church, So There Is No Past in Theology,'" 16.
76. Graham Ward, "Barth, Hegel and the Possibility of Christian Apologetics," in *Conversing with Barth*," 54, citing from Karl Barth, *Church Dogmatics*, ed. and trans. G. W. Bromiley and T. F. Torrance (Edinburgh: T. & T. Clark, 1961), I/1, 4–5.
77. Barth, *Protestant Theology in Nineteenth Century*, 1.

perception as such, as a theological event. How is one able to do this? By engaging in the theological inquiry as a *theologian*; that is, as someone who already defines himself by intellectual characteristics that are derived from the subject matter. It is something like answering the question "how do I learn to swim?" by saying "by swimming," by jumping into the sea itself and moving there *as if* I am a swimmer and know how to swim already. The "as if" here is necessary to grasp Barth's logic. Barth believes that the theologian would never be able to capture the subject matter of theology.

Yet the one who studies the subject matter of theology should delve into this task by thinking, perceiving, and studying *as if* one is already a theologian, as if one is already inside the circle of the subject matter of theology. One should jump into that sea and perform *as if* one is a swimmer already, simply because one will never be fully a swimmer. One will always be *as if* a swimmer, because the deepest depth of this sea is always beyond one's diving capacities. The focal emphasis here is that we understand the subject matter of theology *only* from within; only when we act *as if* we are theologians; only when we think and perceive *as if* we are theologians.[78] This *as if* finds indirect traces through Barth's *Church Dogmatics* quite often, for example, when he speaks about theology as a procedural task that is always "on its way"; when he speaks about the judge who acts *as if* he is judged; the "yes" that seems *as if* a "no"; the God who relates to his creatures *as if* Father, Son, and Spirit; and the human sinner who lives *as if* a complete self in the likeness of Christ without getting there except eschatologically and never historically.

How do we acquire a proper theological knowledge of the historical understanding of theology's subject matter? Barth says: only when we ourselves are taken up by the subject matter of theology; only when our understanding becomes an answer to an Other's action that encounters us as a question from without.[79] Notice here Barth's overturning of Tillich's "question-answer" axiom. Here, the human answers rather than questions. The human's role is to respond, to be challenged, to be encountered. Theology is a human attempt to respond to God, not the human quest for meaning by searching for God.

---

78. This is extractible, for example, from Barth's claim that theology is essentially a human appropriation of the Word of God, and this appropriation is constantly questionable because it is by nature fallible and stands in need of criticism and correction, of critical amendment and repetition. See Karl Barth, *Church Dogmatics*, ed. and trans. G. W. Bromiley and T. F. Torrance (Edinburgh: T. & T. Clark, 1936–77), I/1, 14, and G. Ward, "Barth, Hegel and the Possibility of Christian Apologetics," 58.

79. Barth, *Protestant Theology in Nineteenth Century*, 2. "We know history only when something happens in us and for us, perhaps even happens against us; we know it only when an event concerns us, so concerns us that we are there, that we participate in it" (1).

Barth certainly concedes that theology asks questions *about* God. Yet he would not permit any human condition to question God himself. To the contrary, the subject matter of theology (God) questions theology and theologian alike, and through them God also questions existence. Theology itself, Barth insists, should be subjected to questioning and skepticism because it is a human activity. Yet theology should be questioned *theologically*, from within the truth of God itself, and should be questioned only by theologians who are already fully submerged in the waters of theology, and only from the vantage point of its subject matter.

Does theology question its understanding of its subject matter in a vacuum? Barth insists that theology is of a historical nature and it questions itself within a spatio-temporal context. This is not to say that the historical context shapes theology's self-questioning or re-conditions its answers. By questioning itself, instead, theology also questions its presence and existence and their components (time, space, life-settings, and so on) and contexts. Theology's self-questioning is an inquiry that happens in human history, but also is conducted *about* this history as well. Theology questions human history not by virtue of its own prerogatives, but because of the truth of its subject matter. God is the Lord of theology, says Barth; therefore, it is the obligation of theology to remind history, by means of questioning it, that it is "meant to bear witness to the truth of God, not to [human] achievements."[80] Does modernity stick to this witnessing duty? No, it does not. And because modernity divinizes humanity instead of God, Barth contends that it demands theological interrogation. In his *Protestant Theology in the Nineteenth Century*, Barth gives his explanation of why theology must question modernity.

Barth argues that the beginning of the anthropocentric sin of modernity starts from what is known in the history of science as "the Copernican Revolution." According to Barth, instead of opening human eyes to one's humility and finitude, and making humanity realize that absolute value lies in God and not in nature, the Copernican revolution drove humanity to believe that it is greater than had so far been realized in the history of thought. Instead of perceiving the greatness of the Creator behind the discovered world, humanity claimed what was discovered and known to itself: the world became *its* world,[81] the territory of *its* self, *its* self-confidence, the sphere of *its* self-fulfillment.[82]

---

80. Ibid., 3, 8.
81. Ibid., 24. "Once again man . . . began to be conscious . . . of a capacity for thinking which was reasonable to no other authority than himself" (25).

For Barth, the geocentrism of premodernity was not essentially altered by heliocentrism in modernity, but ultimately by anthropocentrism. The more the human knowledge about the world and the universe expanded, the stronger the human feeling of self-confidence and of autonomy became. Instead of realizing the greatness of the Creator behind the discovered world, the human claimed what was discovered and known to himself: the world became *his* world,[83] the territory of *his* self, *his* self-confidence, the sphere of *his* self-fulfillment. The human discovered now that she is capable of knowing and doing; of knowing how to know and how to do and of actualizing this knowledge and action in the existing world. Modernity names the arena of "all-conquering, absolute man, who expressed himself also and with special effect in [the] field of human activity." The human is active, no longer passive; free, no longer dominated; referential, no longer follower: the human "no longer had an emperor."[84] The field of human activity is no longer dominated by super-powers; no longer dictated by absolutes. It is the human's field; under the rule of the human alone and only. "The ultimate reality to be reckoned with in man," therefore, as Thomas Hobbes says in his *Leviathan*, is now the human's "instinct to preserve himself and enjoy his life accordingly," as well as the realization that the force the human needs to achieve this instinctive goal lies inside people themselves, as John Locke says in *Two Treatises on Civil Government*.[85]

Within this anthropocentric sphere, Barth recognizes an attempt to make humanity's self-awareness the most superior element in existence and turn God into merely one of the ideal images of this self-awareness. But, if God is related to human self-awareness as its ideal figure, then commonality, and not difference, must be emphasized between the human and the divine. And,

82. Ibid., 39–40. "The ultimate reality to be reckoned with in man," therefore, as Thomas Hobbes says in his *Leviathan*, is now the human's "instinct to preserve himself and enjoy his life accordingly," as well as the realization that the force humanity needs to achieve this instinctive goal lies inside people themselves, as John Locke says in *Two Treatises on Civil Government*. See for further details Thomas Hobbes, *Leviathan*, ed. Richard Tuck (Cambridge and New York: Cambridge University Press, 1996); and John Locke, *Two Treatises of Government and a Letter Concerning Toleration*, ed. Ian Shapiro (New Haven: Yale University Press, 2003).

83. Barth, *Protestant Theology in Nineteenth Century*, 24. "Once again man . . . began to be conscious . . . of a capacity for thinking which was reasonable to no other authority than himself" (25).

84. Ibid., 27. Barth thinks that the French Revolution was not what destroyed the empirical old order in Europe. Such order had already been broken inwardly inside the mind of the European. This revolution was just the inevitable, necessary effect (28).

85. Ibid., 39–40. See for further details Thomas Hobbes, *Leviathan*, ed. Richard Tuck (Cambridge and New York: Cambridge University Press, 1996); and John Locke, *Two Treatises of Government and a Letter Concerning Toleration*, ed. Ian Shapiro (New Haven: Yale University Press, 2003).

if there is any distinction between God and humanity, it would not be seen in terms of essence or content, but only in terms of degree: "God is spirit, man is spirit too. God is mighty and so is man. God is wise and benevolent, and so is man. But [man] is all these things, of course, infinitely *less perfectly* than God."[86] Belief in God is still acknowledged in human life, yet not for its own sake or value. It is maintained as a useful hypothesis, to which the human can resort whenever she needs to find an explanation for the evil conditions of the world. "Believing in God," according to Barth, means in modernity understanding the human self in all its dimensions of expressivity, and "obeying and knowing God's will" means clearly and correctly understanding ourselves and the world. By means of this, Barth notes, the human in modernity believed that he "finds the theodicy he was seeking and together with it the anthropodicy he was more truly seeking."[87]

Barth argues that by turning God into just the name of one of the voices of human reason itself, humanity contradicts its very own wish to actually hear the voice of truth from a source that lies outside itself. God is reduced irreparably into an intrinsic echo of humanity's very own voice, so that instead of moving beyond one's self-limitation, humanity dives further into the mud of this limitation, dragging God down to the dark bottom. What humanity missed by this is the possibility of *becoming* other than its limitations, which lies in the wholly otherness of God. The difference between God and humanity that lies in the former's infinity and otherness could have salvaged humanity from its slavery under the yoke of "sameness," and the static, fixed and almost dead "is-ness." Barth comments that when Ludwig Feuerbach speaks about God as humanity's projection of its own wishful thinking and ideal aspirations,[88] he does not, then, challenge theology, but rather the anthropocentrism of modernity. It is the mind of the modernist age, not the church, that rejected first and foremost the otherness of God and his difference from humanity in essence, claiming instead a total identification between them, with simple difference in terms of degree. It was modernity that turned God into one of the elements of human self-awareness and self-projection.

In order to understand Barth's reading of how anthropocentrism challenged theology in modernity, we need to trace the answers he gives to the following questions: "[W]hat was the attitude of the man of the eighteenth century to the subject-matter of theology? What did it mean for him? . . .

---

86. Barth, *Protestant Theology in Nineteenth Century*, 60.

87. Ibid., 60–62.

88. Ludwig Feuerbach, *The Essence of Christianity*, trans. George Eliot (Buffalo, NY: Prometheus, 1989).

what did men make of this subject-matter? What form did it take under their hands?"[89] Barth answers these questions by affirming that the subject matter of theology (as with all other forms of knowledge) was not exempted from the imposition of human absolutism on its content. The human turned the knowledge of God into a fixed experience within the boundaries of human reason and capabilities alone. Knowing God, Barth notes, designated human absolute omnipotence: the human is now in control of every existing thing, not only the universe and human being, but also God.[90] Rather than a reality that encounters the human from without her finite realm of being-ness and existence, God is now fully humanized and transformed into a human experience of self-realization that is inwardly perceived.[91] Barth points at four phenomena in the modern age, which he construed as demonstrative of this humanization of the reality of God: 1) politics, 2) moral and societal life, 3) intellectual and scientific knowledge, and 4) the human self.[92] Among the four domains, Barth's analysis of domain number two, which is related to human moral inwardness and social individualism, is the one that is most pertinent to my study in this chapter. I will therefore focus on it in the ensuing paragraphs.

Barth detects the traces of the modernist turn to the individual, inner self in the reduction of theology (if not of Christianity altogether) into an individualistic, inwardly affair that works in the service of the human's self-awareness and self-fulfillment. "God" is treated here as the ultimate inner expression that drives the human inwardly to take only one's own self seriously over against everything else that is extrinsic to it and different from it. Barth calls this a theologically constructed transformation into absolute individualism. He opines that "individualization means the enthronement of man . . . means that this man, the man who I feel myself to be, is given authority to be the secret outside God. Individualization means making inward . . . of what is external, objective to man, by which it is . . . eaten up and digested, made into something within man."[93] Here, "authority over things outside God" does not express a perception of God's otherness or God's extrinsic relationship to what is other than the divine. God's objective otherness is already eaten up, and God is already made into something within the human. If,

---

89. Barth, *Protestant Theology in the Nineteenth Century*, 67.

90. Ibid., 69. "The man of the eighteenth century approaches even Christianity with belief in the omnipotence of human capability. Now he believes he can experience and know even the essence of Christianity as the omnipotence of human capability."

91. Ibid., 70.

92. Ibid., 71ff.

93. Ibid., 99.

therefore, God is inwardly inherent to human self-awareness as an element of human absoluteness, "everything outside God" is meant to point to what lies extrinsically outside the boundaries of human absoluteness. In other words, Christianity is reduced in modernity into a religious discourse on the relation between the human's self-awareness and the existing world, which is external to one's absolute being-ness. It is not a discourse on the human in relation to God.

Be that as it may, the subject matter of theology, as Barth concludes, is no longer God as a reality opposite the human, but the human's struggle to conquer in the battle of discovering one's self or discovering the ultimate reality that lies within this self. Theology is no longer "*theo-logos*," but pietism. The fight of the original pietist, Barth says, is the following: "[H]e wants to have Christianity, he wants to believe, but belief . . . for him means taking Christianity seriously from the perspective and by the criterion of taking himself seriously, incorporating it into the kingdom of man, and consequently means the interiorization and resultant abolition of the confrontation between man and Christianity . . ."[94]

One of the main examples of this interiorization attitude, according to Barth, is the modernist speech about the incarnation. This doctrine challenges the pietist because it claims that the Word of God has become flesh in an external, objective human person called Jesus Christ, who is historically distant from the individual of today. This claim is as such a challenge to individualism and interiorization, because it forces the pietist, who takes Christian faith seriously and aims at preserving it, to look outside her own self; to extend beyond her inwardness and self-boundaries. The outcome of this challenge, Barth continues, is very negative and unfortunate: as God's eternal otherness was denied before, the external historical otherness of the incarnate word, Jesus Christ, is now similarly denied. Instead of going toward the incarnate Lord in

---

94. Ibid., 100. For a comprehensive and meticulous study of Barth's debate with the pietists of his age, read Eberhard Busch, *Karl Barth & the Pietists: The Young Karl Barth's Critique of Pietism and Its Response*, trans. Daniel W. Blösch (Downers Grove, IL: InterVarsity, 2004). Busch draws our attention in a thought-provoking manner to the firsthand knowledge of pietism, which Barth acquires from his family background. This is how Busch eloquently points this out: "[T]he *background* of Barth's critique of pietism has crucial significance not the least because it considerably relativizes if not refutes this objection to his *critique of pietism*. For this early history shows that pietism was not foreign to his background but was very familiar to him so that he got to know it in the best light in the environment in which he was first at home. And even more it shows that for years, stretching up to Barth's first theological writings, pietism was one of the experiences that had a positive influence on him and that he consciously affirmed. He knew it not only from the outside with the eyes of the enemy but also from the inside with the eyes of a friend" (9).

himself, the pietist of modernity pulls the incarnate down into the swamp of human subjectivist, experiential inner feelings. What is now believed to be the true meaning of the incarnation, as Barth realizes, is the pietist's conviction that "the real birth of Christ is in our hearts; his real and saving death is that which we have to accomplish ourselves, his real resurrection is his triumph in us as those who believe in Him."[95]

In this form of Christianity, everything is interiorized and brought right into the circle of one's own self-fulfillment. Other people's communion with the individual is as such insignificant. The otherness of the others need no longer disturb the individual self by its presence or relatedness. It can, nevertheless, find a space in the individual's life insofar as the individual can find the same components that are inherent to the other already innate to his own self. The drastic impact of this attitude lies in its transforming impacts on theology: rather than a theological speech about God who speaks to me and with me, we will have a theological discourse on God who speaks *in* me, speaks *as* me, and even speaks *me*. Within this total identification of theology's subject matter with self-awareness, it is an inevitable conclusion that in modernity "the renewal of life possible to men was to be understood as the realization of Christianity, or the realization of Christianity was to be understood as a renewal of life possible to men."[96]

In order to understand the logic that led Barth to emphasize the centrality and wholly otherness of God in opposition to anthropocentrism, and if we want to perceive why Barth believed that the truth of God is the only corrective to the serious shortcomings of modernism, we need to visit shortly G. W. F. Hegel's dialectical philosophy. There, we find a thought-form that is prominently present and undeniably detected in Barth's writings.

In an attempt at analyzing the foundations of Hegel's dialectical thinking (which lies in his reevaluation of the cosmological, teleological, and ontological proofs[97] of the existence of God), Mark Taylor points to Hegel's departure

---

95. Barth, *Protestant Theology in the Nineteenth Century*, 101. Barth convincingly argues a few lines down that the notion of "verbal inspiration" may very possibly express the same individualization and interiorization of the incarnation. This notion, Barth says, "was not so much a care of man being open to the Bible as of the Bible having to be open to man at any price; . . . in short, this Biblicism also . . . was an act of the concern for relationship to the present . . ."

96. Ibid., 91.

97. These proofs represent arguments for the existence of God that have been developed by various philosophers, theologians, and scientists throughout the Western history of thought. Such attempts at finding logical arguments for the existence of God go back to Plato and Aristotle in antiquity, Anselm of Canterbury and Thomas Aquinas in the Middle Ages, up to Descartes, Kant, Hume, Nietzsche, Richard Swinburne, and Alvin Plantinga in the modern ages. For some literature on these evidences, see, for

from Kant's undermining of the cosmological argument's cognitive validity.[98] According to Taylor, Hegel observes in Kant's analytical thinking an inversion of the proper relation between the "contingent/finite" and "the absolutely necessary/infinite," which the cosmological argument traditionally depicts. This inversion occurs when Kant renders the finite and the infinite, and contingency and necessity, mutually exclusive and opposed. This opposition is now perceived from a bottom-up, world-God process of cognition: from the contingency of the world and its finiteness up to God and his infinite necessity. Hegel saw in this analytical interpretation of the cosmological argument a logical subordination of the infinite to the finite and a controlling of the infinite by the finite's conditions and existence.[99] Against the Kantian analytical boxing of the infinite within the boundaries of the finite, Hegel argues that the dialectical understanding of the relationship between the infinite and the finite proves that because the finite, by the default of its contingency, is "*inherently* dependent and self-contradictory," its being, its being its "self," "necessarily entails the being of . . . its opposite or the absolutely necessary/infinite."[100]

It is not my intention to delve deeper into Hegel's appraisal of the analytical understanding of the cosmological argument or into Taylor's significant reading of it. I invoke Hegel's logic here to ground my conviction that a similar logic and concern is the driving force behind Karl Barth's theological reasoning on the relationship between God and humanity. Barth, like Hegel, and certainly like Kierkegaard, wants to show the dependence of the contingent, finite human on the necessary/infinite God, and to invert the Kantian inversion of the relationship between the finite and the infinite. Barth wants even to exceed both Hegel and Kierkegaard in absolutely stressing the *complete* and one-way reliance of humanity on God. If Hegel would ultimately reconcile the finite with the infinite by discovering the infinite as a moment within the dialectic process of the finite's self-realization or actualization, and if Kierkegaard would

example, Richard Swinburne, *The Existence of God*, 2nd ed. (Oxford and New York: Oxford University Press, 2004); Dennis Bonnette, *Aquinas' Proofs of God's Existence: St. Thomas Aquinas on "The Per Accidens Necessarily Implies the Per Se"* (The Hague: Martinus Nijhoff, 1972); Karl Barth, *Anselm: Fides Quaerens Intellectum: Anselm's Proof of the Existence of God in the Context of His Theological Scheme* (Eugene, OR: Wipf & Stock, 1975); and James L. Mackie, *The Miracle of Theism: Arguments for and Against the Existence of God* (Oxford and New York: Clarendon, 1982).

98. See for example Kant's argument in Immanuel Kant, *The One Possible Basis for a Demonstration of the Existence of God*, trans. Gordon Treash (Lincoln: University of Nebraska Press, 1994).

99. Taylor, *Deconstructing Theology*, 28 (23–44). Taylor reads from W. G. F. Hegel, *Lectures on the Philosophy of Religion*, trans. E. P. Spiers and J. B. Sanderson (New York: Humanities Press, 1968).

100. Taylor, *Deconstructing Theology*, 28ff.

maintain a paradoxical differentiation between the infinite and the finite by means of a similar location of the infinite, though "wholly other," within the realm of the finite's self-individualization, Barth would exceed both thinkers[101] by stressing that the opposition between the finite and the infinite is not just a logical necessity that serves the self-actualization of the finite. The opposition is a fundamental indication of 1) God's complete otherness as a divine, infinite, transcendent self: it is an opposition that is definitive of God and not of the human, and 2) the fact that the human's *archē*, history, and destiny lie only in the hands of God. God as the *Lord*, *Creator*, and *Perfector* of human existence makes the human exist and be. Instead of a movement from the finite to the infinite, Barth adopts Hegel's dialectical movement from the infinite to the finite, yet without concluding that "the being of the finite is not only its being, but is also the being of the infinite."[102]

3. BARTH'S THEOLOGICAL DECONSTRUCTION OF ANTHROPOCENTRICISM: THE ARGUMENT

Why does Barth believe that the infinite does not need the finite at all, but that the infinite is necessary to the finite? A possible answer to this question that is relevant to my discussion here is offered in IV/3.1 of Barth's *Church Dogmatics*. There, under section 70, titled "The Falsehood and Condemnation of Man," Barth states that the human obsession with self-assertion lies at bottom with humanity's contingency and humanity's need for God's salvation. When we look at Jesus Christ's mission, crucifixion, and resurrection, and discern the

---

101. I do not agree with Graham Ward's claim that Barth's theological method brings together Hegel and Kierkegaard in a "creative tension": "Barth forges a theological method that brings together, in a creative tension, the synchronic dialectic of Kierkegaard's 'infinite qualitative difference' with the diachronic dialectic of Hegel's 'possibility that the truth might be history' and that theology's knowledge 'was only possible in the form of a strict obedience to the self-movement of truth, and therefore as a knowledge which was itself moved.'" Ward, "Barth, Hegel and the Possibility of Christian Apologetics," 63. I do not find Ward's claim convincing, not only because tension is a "tension" no matter how creative it was, but also because I believe that Barth attempted to exceed both thinkers' dialectic by emphasizing the wholly otherness of God *in*, and not in spite of, his relationship with Creation. Nevertheless, one can still argue that Barth's method is more Hegelian than Kierkegaardian in character.

102. Taylor, *Deconstructing Theology*, 29, and Hegel, *Lectures on the Philosophy of Religion*, 3:254. Barth definitely rejects Hegelian and dialectical interpretations of the teleological argument. He would strongly refuse to deem God an immanent, structural principle that directs the universe from within, or one that is inherent to the human individual as a necessary condition of her subjective actuality. God is the Lord of the human future that lies always ahead and confronts the human from without his or her natural life procession or intersubjective actualization.

identity of the one to whom Christ came as God's reconciliation, we do not see a human self like the one that modernity triumphantly and idealistically speaks about (the perfect creature, in whose self-assertion and self-fulfillment lie the ultimate value of existence). We see, instead, the sinning human person, who is under the rule of "falsehood" that necessarily, Barth says, puts the human on the inescapable track of condemnation.[103]

How do we come to this knowledge of humanity's sinful condition? Barth thinks that we get this knowledge of God encountering the human condition in the revelation of Jesus Christ. Why can the human not recognize this falsehood alone apart from its disclosure in the encounter with Jesus Christ? Falsehood, according to Barth, is the human state of denial that makes us lie to ourselves and think that being away from God and breaking with the covenant is what grants us freedom and self-fulfillment. In other words, anthropocentrism, for Barth, is the technical name of humanity's sinful condition as someone chained to a false understanding of the meaning of human being-ness.[104]

Noteworthy is the dialectical logic that Barth's consecutive elaboration on human falsehood demonstrates, especially when he argues that rather than separating humanity from God, sinfulness or falsehood actually proves that humanity cannot break free from God. The human can only sin, can only be in a state of falsehood, over and against the truth and over and against God. "Even in his untruth," Barth dialectically affirms, "[the human] can live *only* by the truth of God.[105] The human is dialectically destined to be related to God, for only the opposite of human falsehood "unmasks him as a liar."[106]

In this very section of volume IV, Barth states that his logic here is far from dialectical in nature. For, contrary to dialectical thinking, according to Barth, he believes that the human is not openly and hospitably welcoming his opposite infinite and willingly facing his falsehood via interaction with this opposite. Far from this dialectical positivity, Bart affirms that the human faces God's truth with negativity, in that he rejects this truth and "advances against it his untruth."[107] Barth's claim notwithstanding, it is my belief that Barth in

---

103. Barth, *Church Dogmatics* IV/3.1, §.70.1.309.

104. Ibid., IV/3.1, 372–74. It is my belief that in Barth's understanding of falsehood one can detect a borrowing of Nietzsche's definition of falsehood when he says: "not wishing to see something which one sees, not wishing so to see something as one sees it: that is what I call falsehood . . . the commonest falsehood is that by which one deceives one's self." Nietzsche, *The Antichrist: An Essay Towards a Criticism of Christianity*, trans. Thomas Common (Mineola, NY: Dover, 2004), §.55.

105. Barth, *Church Dogmatics* IV/3.1, 374.

106. Ibid., IV/3.1, 375.

107. Ibid., IV/3.1, 375.

his argument is only reversing and revising the dialectical logic, rather than exceeding its boundaries or replacing it altogether. His attention to the human rejection of God's truth waters down indeed any Hegelian-like dialectical rule of interdependence, that is, as the human needs the divine to acquire awareness of her falsehood, the divine, in turn, relies on the human falsehood to be fully the divine's absolute truthful self. Barth strongly and accurately negates this mutual-dependence dimension in the dialectical logic he follows. He rightly emphasizes, instead, God's wholly otherness and absolute lordship over the human. He places the truth of God over against the human inner apprehension and cognition. His from-without approach to truth is a proper corrector to modernity's anthropocentric reduction of truth into an innate, subjectivist, and circular process of reasoning that generates a closed circle of self-awareness. Barth explicitly opines that truth, in the first instance

> does not address us; it contradicts us and demands our contradiction . . . it would certainly not be the truth if it did not have the tendency and power to pierce that obscurity, to penetrate that first aspect, to change us and therefore to open us to itself . . . things gained in this easy and self-evident way . . . would be distinguished . . . by the fact that they would entail no unmasking of man, no exposure of him as a liar, and therefore no summoning of him to a knowledge of the grace of God, to faith and obedience.[108]

God's lordship and wholly otherness lie in the fact that, despite human falsehood, God's truth *strikes* the human, reaches her whether she succumbs to it or not, and makes the human aware of her falsehood whether she approves it or not. God's wholly otherness appears in the human's inability to resist God's truth detection and exposition of her falsehood and lying. It also appears in the summoning of the human out of falsehood and in making her confess God's truth in obedience and service. Absent from Barth's speech about this relation between God's truth and the human is the dimension of mutual interaction, which should not always necessarily mean reciprocal dependence, but rather communion and correspondence. Instead of correspondence, Barth prefers to stress submission and surrender.[109] The human cannot actually be herself, Barth says, if the truth did not strike her with its sovereignty and absoluteness. If God's

---

108. Ibid., IV/3.1, 377.
109. Ibid., IV/3.1, 376.

relation to the human was otherwise, this latter would not be who she is as creature.[110]

Barth conjectures that the gravity of human falsehood lies in the fact that this falsehood is no mere moral problem, but, rather, a deeply spiritual and humanly substantial one. This gravity appears primarily in the human desire to avoid encountering the truth that God proclaims in Jesus Christ's witness.[111] More crucially still, the gravity of the human evasion of truth does not consist, for Barth, in disengagement with, or dissociation from, relation with God. It rather lies in human cunning and the malicious attempt at twisting God's truth according to human convictions and self-centered purposes.

The falseness of the human appears especially, therefore, where earnestness, respectability, and devotedness to truth stand in their most impressive form.[112] In this earnestness and devotedness, human falsehood seeks nothing but to transform the truth of God in Jesus Christ by separating the truth from the testifier to the truth, Jesus Christ, who personifies truth in his own self. It eventually narrows down truth into the merely human, cognitively inaccurate discourse on the God-human relationship.[113] Why does the human seek to segregate the truth from its testifier? Because the human is not happy with the fact that Jesus Christ does not represent a triumphal super-human, but the man of the cross; not a man of self-fulfillment, but a man of self-denial; not a man of self-assertion, but a man of sacrifice. Jesus Christ, as the truth of God over against human sinfulness, is a threat to the human's false anthropocentricism. The Christ-centered truth is the enemy of human-centered falsehood. If human falsehood is so powerful and influential over the human self, the only hope for the human to be saved from falsehood—that is, to be herself—lies in a reality beyond her; outside the boundaries of her sin. And, since this other reality, without which the human cannot even live her falsehood, is God's truth in Jesus Christ, the real road of human self-fulfillment (i.e., redemption and salvation) begins from and ends with God's action and will.

At this stage, I can say that Barth's path of encountering modernity's anthropocentricism, as I display it here, first starts with describing the world's condition, and second, shows what it is in the midst of this condition that prevents the human from salvaging herself from self-estrangement and reaching the stage of self-fulfillment. The ensuing step in his interaction with

---

110. Ibid., IV/3.1, 376. "[The human] would not be who he is if the promise of the Spirit came to him easily and smoothly."

111. Ibid., IV/3.1, 435.

112. Ibid., IV/3.1, 438.

113. Ibid., IV/3.1, 441ff.

modernity's anthropocentricism is Barth's argument that the agent who is able to salvage the human and fully immerse her in her true self is God in Jesus Christ. God is the divine wholly other who loves eternally in absolute freedom. Out of his own free will, God elects to relate to the human and reconcile her to himself and to her own self, too. In other words, Barth's alternative to anthropocentricism's falsehood is God's free election of relating to humanity in eternal love.

In his theology of God's election, Barth displays one of the main dimensions of his hermeneutics of personal nature *from* the perspective of God. The uniqueness of this hermeneutics lies not in its general tendency to interpret personhood from God's rather than the human's side, the thing that radically challenges modernity. It also lies in this very unique dimension that Barth elaborates on in his theology of election. The cornerstone of the dimension of personhood that Barth elaborates on in his theology of election is not his understanding of election as an action or a notion, but his view of God as *elector*. In Barth's mind, the person of the elector is the foundation of the act of election, and not the opposite. Election gains importance as an act by virtue of the one who elects: the divine agent comes first and then the action follows. This is why perceiving the core of Barth's theology of election requires looking at his understanding of the personal character of the infinite elector.

Who is God as elector for Barth? God the elector, Barth states, is one who loves in freedom.[114] "Electing" does not describe the nature, or form, of the actions that God makes. It defines God's essence as holy love and free lordship. How does this electorship, which lies in loving in freedom, reflect God's personhood? It reflects this personality in terms of "decision-making": God as a personal divine Being is One who makes the decision to relate gracefully to the human. This "decision-making" attribute is characteristic of God's holiness and righteousness, Barth says.[115] By looking to God's personal election, we see that the free personal self is one whose decision's nature and operation find their necessity within this self per se, and not in anything or anyone else. God is alone this personal One who loves in freedom, because his decisions are his very own creation. They are not a response to any prior demand, necessity, or decision that are made by any other. Rather, they generate the response of the other to their happening and enable this other to correspond to them with another decision. The decision, by means of which the other receives and affirms God's graceful decision, takes place, as Barth says, "in fulfillment of the prior divine

---

114. For a valuable interpretation of Barth's doctrine of election and the God who loves in freedom as an expression of God's election, see Colin Gunton, *The Barth Lectures*, chs. 6–7.

115. Ibid., II/2, 19.

decision."[116] Only God can be a real personal self since his decision-making alone is fully free, graceful, and reflective of real pleasure. God's decision of election is not only reflective of his love and relational graceful initiation (his actions). It is more fundamentally definitive of him as personal in nature. This is one of the central connotations of Barth's belief that the election of God is not only about his eternal actions, but also about God's very own mystery. Barth even affirms with this regard that since election has to do with *who* God is, we are not allowed to decide the purpose or the validity of what God personally decides to be as who he is.[117]

One of the characteristics of modernity is centralizing the notions of "self-fulfillment," "self-assertion," and "self-sufficiency" by construing these notions as expressive of the free understanding that the person makes on who he or she wants to be, or on what he or she wants to do or not to do. Selfhood is interpreted in terms of decision-making and generosity: if the human wants to relate to the world, she does this out of benevolent free will, not out of need or obligation. She makes this connection out of a generous decision that stems from self-sufficiency, not out of a need imposed on her from an external authoritative or prior other. In modernity, notions like "decision-making" and "free, benevolent willfulness" are used in the service of affirming human self-sufficiency, self-assertion, and autonomy. In Barth's theology of election, I see an implementation of the same notions, yet for the sake of proving the falsehood of human personhood that lies in self-assertion and self-enclosure. The human,

---

116. Ibid., II/2, 19. In the light of this "initiation-response" equation, Caroline Schröder's understanding of Barth's theology of providence in its relation to his theology of election makes sense. Schröder persuasively argues that if election is an item in the doctrine of God for Barth because it reflects his understanding of God's relation to his own will, Barth considers providence an item in the doctrine of creation because it reflects the dimension of God's relation to his creation as an outcome of his initial election to create them and be with them eternally. Providence, in this case, is an expression of the interaction that takes place between the human's decision to receive and respond to the graceful prior decision God made. Caroline Schröder, "'I See Something You Don't See': Karl Barth's Doctrine of Providence," in *For the Sake of the World: Karl Barth and the Future of Ecclesial Theology*, ed. George Hunsinger (Grand Rapids and Cambridge: Eerdmans, 2004), 115–35. Linking providence to election alone is what protects the earlier from wasting away by means of the human attempts to realize God's role in creation on their own or, as Schröder correctly warns, "demands it as a kind of basic right." "It is God's Spirit, in unity with the Father and the Son," Schröder affirms accurately, "who breaks into our words and our speechlessness, and who places us in our supplications at the side of a creature tormented by anticipation—and so assists our perception of faith toward an undreamed of horizon of expectation" (135).

117. Barth, *Church Dogmatics* II/2, 20–21. "[W]e resist the very being and existence of God Himself, if we raise even a question concerning the purpose and validity of this election, if we do not recognize that any such question is already answered by the fact that it is God who here decides and elects."

as Barth seems to be showing, is not the holder of the criterial image of personal selfhood. This image lies in a reality that stands over and against the human. God as such is the personal Being par excellence because God alone can make a decision by total freedom and out of grace. God is not under any obligation or need or another power's rule. God as "God" is the one who alone obliges, who is what others need, who is the powerful reference. We do not question the purposes of his decisions because he is the One who makes them. God is *the* personal, fully sufficient, fully free self because the decisions he elects are justified by *who* he is, and not by any other reason.

What modernity aspires to by attributing and detecting its inherence to the human self is now declared by Barth as definitive of, and inherent to, God's personal nature. The same notions and attributes are imported into theology to speak about different subjects; to shift the criterial prerogative from the slave to the master; from the antithesis to the thesis; from the finite to the infinite; from the ego to the Other; from the I to the Thou. This is done without necessarily questioning the validity of the prerogative per se. Paul's saying in Rom. 9:20, "But who are you, O human, to talk back to God?" is now revised and used to challenge modernist anthropocentricism: "But who are you to *replace* God, to attribute what only defines Him to the human?" Modernity's search for finding the ideal selfhood within the human is now redirected or rechanneled by Barth without deconstructing the search for ideal selfhood as such. Barth is just telling modernity: "Do not search within the human. Look at God. He is *the* personal self that is fully sufficient and truly free and autonomous." Barth is even saying, "Stop searching further. The divine self-sufficient and free one decided to show us what we are searching for by himself. He decided gracefully to make the ideal image of selfhood relatable to us." "God Himself," Barth affirms, "has communicated Himself to us and given us Himself as the answer."[118]

It is crucial here to keep Barth's shifting of the subject of personal selfhood from the realm of the human to the wholly other realm of God's being. Without it, we may misunderstand Barth's use of the notions of "decision-making" and "free election," which he imports to theology from anthropology. Barth uses the anthropological tools of his era without falling into the age's trap of anthropocentricism. This is what Barth reveals in his avoidance of absolutizing readymade concepts of freedom or electing by projecting them onto God. God is not the name of the absolute, supernatural form of human freedom and electing. If he is so, then God is a construction or an outcome of a process of human self-projection, and not another reality that encounters the human from

---

118. Ibid., II/2, 22.

without. Barth does not absolutize freedom and decision-making. Rather, he states that the characteristics of freedom and electing that the human needs to encounter in order to understand truly personal selfhood lie only and perfectly in the personal being of God, which is exposed in his eternal electing of loving in freedom.[119] Barth is not telling modernist anthropocentrists that "in the idea of God, you find the best expression or hermeneutics of human freedom and selfhood." He is saying instead, "God is the real free and personal reality *alone*. What you search for in the human exists only in the divine."

Nevertheless, the questions I may ask Barth here are: If you believe that the criterial image of personal, free selfhood lies in God alone, and if God is by default wholly other mystery beyond human comprehension, how can the image of personal selfhood that lies in God relate to us and salvage our life and understanding from the anthropocentric notion of selfhood? How can this divine image be *for us* despite God's mysteriousness and incomprehension, and despite the fact that we are not even allowed to question God about it? A possible answer Barth may offer to these questions is to say that our relating to the criterial image of personal, free selfhood becomes a possible impossibility by virtue of God's personal free decision as such. God freely and gracefully decides to relate this personal selfhood to us. And he elects to relate to us in a revelatory manner that enables us to perceive and make sense of it when he discloses himself in the human person, Jesus Christ. This is the core-content of Barth's speech on Christ as the "electing and elected" in section 33 of volume II/2, if not of his overall Christologically shaped theology.

Central to Barth's understanding of God's personal identity as free electing Deity is his hermeneutics of Jesus Christ as the mediation between God and the sinful human. This is how Barth speaks about this mediation:

> In [Christ] God reveals Himself to man. In Him man sees and knows God. In Him God stands before man and man stands before God, as is the eternal will of God, and the eternal ordination of man in accordance with this will. In Him God's plan for man is disclosed, God's judgment on man fulfilled, God's deliverance of man accomplished, God's gift to man present in fullness, God's claim and promise to man declared.[120]

---

119. Ibid., II/2, 25. This is what drives Barth to say "[God's] freedom is indeed divine and therefore absolute. It is not, however, an abstract freedom as such, but the freedom of the one who loves in freedom. It is He Himself, and not an essence of the freedom of choice, or of free choice, who is the divine subject of the electing which takes place at this point."

120. Ibid., II/2, 94.

Christ is not merely a tool that is used by God to build a relation with human beings. Jesus also is not only this ideal human person, who stands before us and relates to God on our behalf. Jesus Christ is the *relationship* that God inaugurates with the human race. He is not just the mediator of the relation; he is the relation of mediation *a se*: the relationship personified. This is what one concludes from Barth's surmising that Jesus Christ "is Himself the divine election of grace."[121] Christ, that is, reflects *ad extra* God's personal character as freely and gracefully electing Being. In this mediatorial relationship called "Christ," God stands before the human as who he is and brings the human before him. In this relationship, God shapes the human according to his will and judgment. This is not a relation where the human's will and actions are decisive of the destiny, or the direction, of the encounter of the human with God. To the contrary, once we enter the realm of this graceful election relation, which is personified as Jesus Christ, we are led, Barth says, "beyond time and beyond the nexus of the created world and its history."[122] Beyond, that is, what constitutes the realm of human self and action. The relation between the human and God occurs, *because* the human has no role in it or influence on its happening. God's eternal election and decision concerning the human identity of humans is what originates the relationship in the first place. Even the decision of making the relation is made individually by God and according to his absolute, free decree.[123]

For Barth, the relationship between God and humanity is from beginning to end God's decision and the sole story or event as/in Jesus Christ. God personified in his eternal Son, furthermore, becomes this relationship, even becomes the human other who stands before the divine and relates to him. God's relational story with humanity is actually a "one actor, many roles" narrative. The decision for this relationship is not only made regardless to the living, historical human's will or opinion, but even before this human comes into historical existence (from/in eternity). Added to this, the sinfulness of the human in his own context neither forestalls the relationship with God nor stands in the way of God's decision to bear God's own self with creation. It does

---

121. Ibid., II/2, 95.
122. Ibid., II/2, 100.
123. Ibid., II/2, 101. "In the beginning, before time and space as we know them, before creation, before there was any reality distinct from God which could be the object of the love of God or the setting for his acts of freedom, God anticipated and determined within Himself . . . that the goal and meaning of all his dealings with the as yet, non-existent universe should be the fact that in his Son He would be gracious towards man, uniting Himself with Him."

not do so because the historical, spatio-temporal creature of sin and falsehood is not, in the first place, an actor in the relationship narrative, but rather one who is acted upon by means of it. The human who stands before God and relates to him in the story is actually the human without sin, Jesus Christ.

Jesus does not only personify the relationship of election that God solely makes with the human. He is also representative of the ideal human, whom God elected to relate through eternity to every other being. Jesus, in other words, is both "the relationship of electing" and "the elected partner for the relation." Jesus makes this relationship happen not because he is fully one *of us* or because he, as an ordinary human person, has an equal influence and role to play in the relation. Jesus' contribution to the relation's occurrence stems from his divine Sonship, his "God-from-Godship" that makes him from the beginning obediently fulfill God's decision.[124] Jesus Christ is both the relationship and also the one to whom God relates, as the agent who plays the role of the fully human other that any relationship requires in order to be relational in nature. How is the relationship between God and the human possible despite human sinfulness and self-centeredness? Because it is decided and made by God. How can the human enter this relationship and become an actor in its story despite her sinfulness and self-centeredness? She cannot. As mediator, nevertheless, the divine Son becomes humanity's perfect, or even eschatological,[125] representative. As long as Jesus is both the conducted

---

124. Ibid., II/2, 101. In *CD* III/1, 54, Barth argues that the *logos asarkos*, the second person of the Trinity, is not the sole concern of the New Testament writers. To the contrary, Barth states, "the New Testament . . . does not speak expressly of the eternal Son or Word as such, but of the Mediator [i.e., *logos ensarkos*] the one who in the eternal sight of God has already taken upon Himself our human nature i.e., not of a formless Christ who might well be a Christ-principle or something of that kind, but of Jesus the Christ." Barth also repeats almost the same point in *CD* III/2, 483–84. But this is not yet, in my opinion, a Barthian way of saying that Jesus Christ is very man *like us*, or one of us in our very broken, creaturely, and sinful present nature. It is not yet a proof that, for Barth, Christ *is* the "creature which in itself is dust and ashes." He is rather the mediator in whom God's *glorification* of the creature, not the creature's condition, takes place. Barth's concern is not about the human nature's essence and the identity of the mediator, but about freeing the language of theology on the incarnation from abstractions (e.g., "the prologue [of John] is not speaking of an eternal Son or divine Logos *in abstracto*, but of a Son and Logos who is one with the man Jesus" (*CD* III/2, 483)). This resonates with Barth's Athanasian-like emphasis on the historically mediated relation between God and the human. For presentations of various aspects of Barth's "*ensarkos-asarkos*" Christology and the Christocentric extent of his theology overall, read Henri A. G. Blocher, "Karl Barth's Christocentric Method," in *Engaging with Barth, Contemporary Evangelical Critiques*, ed. David Gibson and Daniel Strange (Nottingham: Apollos/InterVarsity, 2008), 21–54.

125. Colin Gunton perceptively describes Barth's speech about God's incarnation as the human Christ "realized eschatology," language that interprets the incarnation as the threefold moment of justification. In the incarnate, we witness the wiping out of human sin and the institution of the human as covenant

relationship and the human other who relates to God in it, this God-humanity story is possible and human sinfulness does not prevent it from occurring.

In the previous chapter, I showed that the modernist understanding of selfhood circles around an emphatic prioritization of human self-fulfillment and self-assertion achieved by means of enjoying free, autonomous individualism. If this self decides to relate to any other, it should do so out of freedom to stand before another as independent and fully sufficient over against it; upon, that is, the principle that this self does not need this relation with the other in the first place. The other's condition does not influence the self's individuality or breach its self-sufficiency. It is my belief that these ideas, colored with a strong focus on notions of "decision-making" and "free electing," which underpin modernist anthropocentrism, are borrowed by Karl Barth and used in his *Church Dogmatics* to interpret God's personal nature and his relationality. God, not the human this time, is absolutely free and autonomous as a personal Being, regardless of any other. And, if God wills to relate to the finite other and opens up himself to her, he would do this in such a manner that would not allow whatsoever the other's condition and will to influence this relationship or co-generate it with him. God does this by 1) becoming personally this other, to whom he decided to relate, and 2) becoming the very relationship, which he decided to make with this other. God carries on his shoulders the weight of meeting all the prerequisites, and becoming personally all the elements, that any relationship requires to be a "relation."

---

partner. C. Gunton, *The Barth Lectures*, ed. Paul H. Brazier (London: T. & T. Clark/Continuum Imprint, 2007), 156–57. In this sense, it is accurate to call Barth's language one of realized *eschatology*, rather than one of historicality. It is also accurate, then, to conclude with Henri Blocher that founding anthropology on Christology in Barth reflects an endeavor to infer from Jesus' human nature the character of human nature in general: Blocher, "Karl Barth's Anthropology," in *Karl Barth and Evangelical Theology: Convergences and Divergences*, ed. Sang Wook Chung (Milton Keynes, UK/Tyrone, USA: Paternoster/Grand Rapids: Baker Academic, 2006), 96–135, 101–11. If for Barth, as Blocher notes, "'[the human] never at all exists in himself'; for '[the human] exists in Jesus Christ and in Him alone'" (Barth, *CD* II/1, 149) (ibid.,104), then Gunton is right in calling this Christological anthropology in Barth a language of eschatology, since the historical human does not yet exist in Jesus Christ, not even when Jesus existed in time and space. It is we who follow in our humanity the human nature of Christ by virtue of the incarnation, not the other way around. This is Barth's logic. For recent studies that link this discussion to Barth's trinitarian ontology, see, for example: Paul D. Molnar, *Divine Freedom and Doctrine of Immanent Trinity: In Dialogue with Karl Barth and Contemporary Theology* (London and New York: T. & T. Clark/Continuum, 2002); Molnar, "The Trinity, Election and God's Ontological Freedom: A Response to Kevin W. Hector," *International Journal of Systematic Theology* 3, no. 8 (2008): 294–306; and Edwin Chr. Van Driel, "Karl Barth on the Eternal Existence of Jesus Christ," *Scottish Journal of Theology* 1, no. 60 (2007): 45–61.

But does not God's becoming human to make this relationship happen mean that the human is inherent to this relationship's constitution? Not if the human we are talking about here is not the historical, ordinary finite human of sin and brokenness. God became the ideal, perfect human that such relationship premeditatively requires. He became human according to God's eternal image, and not according to the one who suffers and struggles with her sin and falsehood in history.[126] In Barth's theology, there is a general tendency (in congruence with Barth's support of Chalcedonian Christology!) to overemphasize the divine nature in Jesus Christ at the expense of the potential finiteness and brokenness of his human nature, which leads in its logic into inevitably emphasizing Jesus' perfect humanity that makes him *for us* more than really *like us*. It centralizes the substantial link between Jesus' identity and his salvific role as the eternal redeemer by stressing that the redeemer was "without sin" and how this sinlessness enabled him to elevate our humanity from its degradation. This logic invites for questioning the rate of importance that Jesus' humanity enjoys in comparison to his divinity in Barth's overall theological thinking. Christ for Barth is fully human. Yet his significance lies not primarily in the fact that he is not representative of our humanity. Barth emphasizes in his theology that Jesus represents basically the man without sin; the human, that is, whom the *Logos* took up unto himself in the incarnation. He is therefore

---

126. In his interpretation of Barth Christology, George Hunsinger argues that the former's Christological view is rooted in Chalcedonian theology: George Hunsinger, "Karl Barth's Christology: Its Basic Chalcedonian Character," in *The Cambridge Companion to Karl Barth*, ed. John Webster (Cambridge and New York: Cambridge University Press, 2007), 127–42. If this is the case, then Barth must then be following the Chalcedon and Cyril of Alexandria's understanding of the incarnation, which actually emphasizes the divinity in relation to the humanity, by also viewing the incarnation as the process of the *Logos'* embracing the flesh and taking it upon itself in almost a state of transformation. In other words, the Chalcedonian logic assumes that the broken human flesh was not actually been inhibited in its broken condition by the divine Word. It was, rather, lifted up and sort of liberated from its brokenness and sinfulness by means of being embraced by the divine *Logos*. Had this not been what Chalcedon said, there would have not been a problem with the Nestorian, non-Chalcedonian groups in the post-Chalcedonian era. If Hunsinger is right about the background of Barth's Christology, then Barth is a theologian who emphasizes, as Chalcedon, the "without sin" belief and endorses the Chalcedonian tendency to elevate Christ's flesh and humanity above the level of humanity and flesh of other human beings. On Chalcedonian Christology and post-Chalcedonian controversies, see, for example, Aloys Grillmeier, *Christ in Christian Tradition: from the Apostolic Age to Chalcedon (451)* (Louisville: Westminster John Knox, 1988), vol. 1, 414–17; 426–41; 457–63; Iain R. Torrance, *Christology after Chalcedon* (Eugene, OR: Wipf & Stock, 1998); and chapter 3, section 4 of my forthcoming book, *Orthodoxy in Arabic Terms: A Study of Theodore Abū Qurrah's Trinitarian and Christological Doctrines in an Islamic Context*, which is going to be published by De Gruyter at the beginning of 2015.

the image of the human that is intended in the mind of God; the human, that is, from whom we fell off being ourselves because of Original Sin, who we are not in our present, and who we are promised to be in his image in a yet-to-come future. If this is so, taking Barth's emphasis to its ultimate logical end would entail that Christ does not truly represent us (as our present us) in the relationship with God, but represents an image of the "human other" that the relationship requires. Only from the perspective of this conviction, one can understand what Barth means when he states, "[W]e can never say of any creature that other creatures are elect 'in it' . . . and that in its election they can and should have assurance of their own."[127] Only the ideal perfect human, who is not one like us, Jesus Christ, can stand in this relationship with God because he is not only the ideal creature, but also the Creator. What makes Jesus Christ the appropriate other in God's relationship with the human is the fact that "as elected man He is also the electing God, electing them in His own humanity."[128] Be that as it may, only when the humanity of the other, who is elected to stand before God in the relation, is unique and one of its kind, can it be ideal and universal and according to God's standards, according to Barth.[129] Otherwise, no relationship between God and any human other is a possible impossibility. It is important here to notice that Barth is not trying here to argue that the incarnation is an event that took place in God's eternal realm and will. Barth definitely avoids this trend of thought, and emphasizes that the incarnation means that the eternal will of God is temporally actualized and revealed in the life and history of Jesus Christ.[130] Barth would support this historicality of the incarnation because he is a theologian of revelation: the revealer revealed himself in human historical revelation. Yet, this does not as such entail that Barth then is supportive of viewing the incarnate as a human totally like *us*, for this would mean that the incarnate savior cannot truly save us, since he shares our sinfulness. For Barth, being "for us" (that is, with us in our

---

127. Barth, *Church Dogmatics* II/2, 116.

128. Ibid., II/2, 117.

129. Ibid., II/2, 117.

130. Edwin Chr. Van Driel is correct here in his reading of what Barth says in *Church Dogmatics* II/2, 31–31; 179: Edwin Chr. Van Driel, *Incarnation Anyway: Arguments for Supralapsarian Christology* (Oxford and New York: Oxford University Press, 2008), 86–88. Yet, there is a difference in Barth's discourse between speaking about the historicity of the event of the incarnation and about the nature of the human flesh that the incarnate *Logos* took upon himself to pursue salvation. This distinction is also Chalcedonian in nature. Defending the historicity of the incarnation event does not mean that the incarnate became exactly one of us in all the aspects of our human condition. In the Chalcedonian logic, it rather means that the incarnate replaced us, or stood on behalf of us, before God because we are not able in our sinful condition to do so by ourselves.

history) need not entail that the savior in his incarnation became *us* in our sinful humanity. It means that his humanity paves the way for us to be once again *imago Dei*. One needs to differentiate between Barth's defense of the historicity of the incarnation as an event, on one hand, and his elaboration on the nature of the human flesh that the incarnate *Logos* took upon himself and elevated to perform salvation.

Who is the other in this form of relationship through which God chooses to disclose his personal self? It seems that the other is not really "another." The other is still an item within the boundaries of God's standard relationality. The other is not "another" over and against God. He is one of God's states of otherness. Does this form of relationality exceed interiority to externality? How are this form of relationality and this notion of otherness different, really, from the modernist reduction of relationality to an activity that is made by the individual self and practiced by this self as an intrinsic experience of otherness that grants the self its self-fulfillment by means of self-estrangement? How can Jesus Christ be *our* representative if he is not really another finite over and against us, but a revelation of one of the states of otherness in God? How can Jesus be the human on behalf of *us* in the relationship with God if he is not really like us in our present historical brokenness, and our sinfulness is not part of his human condition? If Jesus' human otherness is just another face of his divine "God-from-God" nature, the relationship by way of which God reveals his personal self is something happening within God; between him and himself in the historical arena of human existence. We are outsiders and passive recipients of the outcomes of this intrinsic relation, no more, if even no less. God's election of Jesus Christ (i.e., of relating graciously to us) is just God's way of being his personal self freely and autonomously. This is not logically different from the modernist anthropocentric speech about the personal self as that which fulfills itself by means of experiencing a state of otherness that is part and parcel of its very own being. Instead of seeing this process taking place within the human, and of defining the human by this means, it seems that we have a theological attempt to see this taking place in God and in relation to his experience of otherness.

One should not stop here, but say further that Barth does not ignore human existence and does not undermine human selfhood by means of focusing on God. Barth believes that he is offering humanity an authentic hope by placing the promise of self-fulfillment and individual assertion, to which the human aspires, in the hands of God, and within the realm of God's revelation in Jesus Christ. He is not denying the human need for self-fulfillment and recognition of individuality. He rather points at where and how this fulfillment and individuality can take place: in relationship with God and by means of looking at Jesus Christ. This is what Barth argues for when he says

> [i]n this Other [i.e., Christ] that which each man is and should be for himself is presupposed and maintained, whereas without Him it could only emerge from nothing and proceed to nothing. It is exactly because of the original election of Jesus Christ that the *particular Veri* of "individualism" ... is given a lasting validity.[131]

Barth does not counter the modernist understanding of selfhood by denying its attention to individuality. He acknowledges, instead, the aspect of individuality in relation to election when he notes that God does not elect us as members in a group but as individual human beings. We relate to him in our individuality: we become the object of this relationship as individuals.[132] What Barth is avoiding, nonetheless, is a modernist-like reduction of the individual to a nonrelational, secluded being. Individuality is not God's predestination of the human; it is not the human's inescapable fate.[133] Individuality for Barth designates that from which the human is redeemed by the grace of God; therefore, it is what the human should come with, not without, in front of God. As he says himself, Barth discerns the value and depth of the negative meaning of "individuality" that makes the human look to Jesus Christ and realizes the tremendous grace and redemption God offers to the human. In this sense, Barth does not consider individuality per se a sin, but a negative reality without which the human cannot realize God's graceful forgiveness or Christ's graceful standing before God on her behalf.[134] Instead of an individuality that leads to isolation, Barth cherishes an individuality that creates relationships. God's election of loving in freedom aims at salvaging the human from isolation and redeeming her individuality by making this latter be incarnate, be itself, in relationality. Be that as it may, Barth is not anti-human or against individuality in any subordinationist, hegemonic sense of the word.

This notwithstanding, Barth still does not want to grant the human in his individuality and finitude a tangible, effective, or equally present role in the relationship that God makes with creation. Barth still prefers to speak about humanity in its perfection, in its fulfillment, which is not yet definitive of the

---

131. Ibid., II/2, 310.
132. Ibid., II/2, 313.
133. Ibid., II/2, 314.
134. Ibid., II/2, 315.

present human condition. This seems to be for him more appropriate to affirm God's sovereignty and lordship over and against anthropocentricism. This is why the other partner in the relationship between God and the human is the perfect, eschatological revelation of the *imago Dei* and not *us*. Either God is the initiator of the relation, the relation per se and the related other in the relation, or there is no possible relation between personal God and personal human at all.

Barth's understanding of personhood from God's personal decision of loving the human in freedom is undoubtedly a unique challenge to the modernist understanding of personhood in terms of individualistic self-enclosure and self-assertion. God in Barth's theology is definitely relational in this sense; definitely dynamic and open. And his understanding of human individuality on the basis of God's personal relational uniqueness is a prophetic voice against anti-otherness, anti-relationality, and anthropocentricism. This may explain why the theological anthropology of Karl Barth attracts support in contemporary theology. Being a "person," or a "personal subject," means for Barth a participation in a shared experience.[135] Barth's biblically based perspective is a blunt response to modernist individualism in a strong relational and Christological manner. It shows that "person" designates a dynamic interpersonal agent whose faculties arise only as in relation to others, and stresses that such personhood is revealed in God's revelation to the human and the world. This is why it may not be wrong to say that Barth's anthropology, as John Webster argues, is far more profound and positive than the unfair, widespread allegation that Barth sets God's sovereignty in antithesis to human freedom and individuality. Far from this, Webster states, Barth's anthropology lies in a "joyful affirmation of God's partnership with those whom he has made and remade in Jesus Christ."[136]

Having said that, even in this approach to personhood, Barth's relational theology of "personhood" slips into another danger zone when it comes close to identifying in God "personal being" and "relational existence": God is the initiator of the relation, the relation per se, and the ideal human who stands at the other end of it. I have already scrutinized Karl Barth's trinitarian terminology and showed the consequences of his replacement of "*person*" with

---

135. Ibid., III/2, 319. "If anyone has said that man is solitary let him be anathema," Barth states.

136. John Webster, "Barth and Postmodern Theology: A Fruitful Confrontation," in *Karth Barth: A Future for Postmodern Theology?* ed. Geoff Thompson and Christiaan Mostert (Hindmarsh: Australian Theological Press, 2000), 1–72, 57. Webster believes that this view is not only evident in Barth's latter writings, such as *Humanity of God*, but is also characteristic of his theology in the earlier volumes of his *Church Dogmatics*, and even "predates the start of the *Church Dogmatics* by more than a decade" (ibid., 58ff.).

"mode of being" on the doctrine of the Trinity in my book, *God Without a Face?*[137] There, I basically argued that Barth's "*Seineweise*" repeats Augustine's tendency to reduce the three in the divine Godhead into mere triadic relations and allowing the weight of emphasis, like the latter, to remain on the unity of God.[138] This attention to unity is congenial with Barth's grounding of his theology of the Trinity in his theology of revelation. For Barth, God's eternal unity as a triune Godhead is disclosed in the fact that 1) the revealer and the content of revelation are one and the same in God's revelation, yet 2) revelation is distinguished from its means, for God is distinct from the medium by, through, and in which he reveals himself.[139] Driven by his conviction that "three persons" is a linguistic expression that belongs to the dogmatic analysis, not to the ontological nature of God, Barth decided to dispense with "person" and "three persons" terminology because it threatens the revelatory structure of God's unity.[140] Be that as it may, Barth ended up proving the oneness of revelation in Christ by avoiding any concession to three *persons* in God and arguing instead for three *ways* of copying God's lordship.[141]

Even here, especially when the above logic colors Barth's understanding of the doctrine of God, the trinitarian language of "three divine persons in perichoretic relationships" is put second-rank for the sake of an emphasis on the concept of "relationship" in terms of "three modes of being." The revealedness of the "I-Thou" mode of relationality becomes more important than the infinite triune personhood of the "Thou" as such. "Being" is reduced to "communion" or "being-with," and ontology is undermined for the sake of existence. In this emphasis on making God the beginning and end of the God–humanity relationship, God's personhood becomes either mere revelatory relationality, or just "self-communion."

On the other hand, it is still valid to ask whether or not Barth's overemphasis on God's wholly otherness, in such a manner that he almost

---

137. Awad, *God Without a Face?*, ch. 3.2.2. I rely in the following lines on my analysis of Barth's trinitarian theology in that book.

138. See also Colin Gunton, "The Triune God and the Freedom of the Creature," in *Karl Barth: Centenary Essays*, 49–67, 59.

139. Awad, *God Without a Face?*, ch. 3.2.2; and Barth, *The Göttingen Dogmatics* (Grand Rapids: Eerdmans, 1991), 95–96.

140. Barth, *Church Dogmatics* I/1, 245–46.

141. Awad, *God Without a Face?*, ch. 3.2.2. Barth seems to be committed to serious thinking about the doctrine of the Trinity in its creedal and patristic versions. But, whether Barth really maintains the *patristic* concept of "*hypostasis*" is something that cannot be proved solely by showing the terminological consistency of the Barthian texts alone. Does "mode of being" truly convey the original theological use of "person" in patristic thought? I do not believe so.

denies any human active presence before God, serves his emphasis on understanding personhood from the angle of God's personal, relational character. Is it really fruitful for theology to relate to other forms of inquiry from the standpoint of God, who is totally active and dominant, and humanity, which is totally passive and receptive? If the real person in her present situation is only permitted to realize how the ideal human stands before God on her behalf, and to succumb to the outcomes of this encounter without even inquiring about it, how can this person be a genuine partner in the relationship? In Barth, the human is not even considered a partner in the relationship whose condition would make him experience rejection from God. Even the "rejected" in the relationship is not *us*, but the ideal human who represents us. Christ replaces us not only in election, but in rejection too.[142]

One cannot really be part of a relationship unless one participates personally and actively in it, as if its existence is one's responsibility and contribution, too. I cannot be part of a relationship that takes place between two others unless I take part in this relation's occurrence. Even if one of the two sides of this relation represents me, if this representative was in essence what I am *not*, he would not then be representative of me. And if the representative needs to be what I am not in order for this relationship to take place, according to the standards of the first side, then no matter how hard this representative tries to relate to the other as if he is me, he should always prove he is not me (that is, not imaging my imperfection) in order to remain in the relationship and to guarantee that the relationship remains existent. Barth's emphasis on Christ as "God from God" and Christ's perfect humanity at the expense of Christ as "one of *us*" makes his understanding of the God–human relationship almost exclusive of the human because it focuses too much on God. Overemphasizing the wholly otherness of the electing and elected, that is, the wholly otherness of Jesus Christ, over and against the human condition, serves the defense of God's wholly otherness and salvages it from the nails of anthropocentrism. But I am not sure that it salvages from anthropocentrism our understanding of the human self as such. It may rather add to the pain that is caused by anthropocentrism's nails the pain that is exerted by theocentricism's crown of thorns.

Barthian scholars (e.g., John Webster) usually defend Barth's theological anthropology by pointing to the ethical value of his attention to relationality as the core of personhood. By pointing to Barth's concern on the moral dimension of personhood, people like John Webster, for example, try to prove

---

142. Barth, *Church Dogmatics* II/2, 340ff.

that anthropology is an important part of Barth's view of the content of theology. This is the motif that produces Webster's insistence that "Barth's theology is never one in which anthropology has, as it were, to struggle to the surface from underneath the crushing weight of assertions about absolute divine subjectivity."[143] Barth combines this sensitivity to the moral aspect of human subjectivity with an evident stress on the basicality of the relation with God. He argues that apart from encountering the divine subjectivity in its actions toward us, the human cannot grasp the real core of his human subjectivity. Because God is a self-revealing divine subject, there is a possible access for the human to his own self that starts from God and ends in us.[144]

There is value in the above-mentioned attention to God's basicality for human personhood in Barth's theology. Having said that, emphasizing the moral aspect of the relation between the human and God may actually suggest that Barth goes along with his modernist age in confining personhood to moral activities. This explains, in turn, why Barth speaks about three modes of existing rather than "three persons" to define the triune personhood of God "the Father, the Son, and the Spirit." The emphasis on moral conduct in anthropology may just explain the emphasis on relation-action as expressive of self-fulfillment and self-realization instead of on "person *in* relation."

The emphatic construal of the relationship as definitive of selfhood, and the restriction of God's relationality to his relation with the ideal, and not the sinful, human, are indicative of an attempt to modify the modernist view of God as an abstract, static Being. Yet centralizing the concept of "relationship" drives Barth eventually to discard the term "person" from his doctrine of the Trinity and to end up talking instead about God's modes of relationality, or about a specific relational model in God himself; the thing that does not ultimately reflect God's relationship with *us*. Instead of defining God in terms of a Boethian individualistic personhood, Barth now defines him in terms of a relational, interactive personhood, the central core of which is God's dynamic activity as "electing and elected," as "judging and judge," and as "elected and rejected" at the same time.

It is true that Barth grounds his understanding of human personhood, and of personhood in general, in a trinitarian doctrine of God that culminates ultimately in a human modulation based on the personhood of Jesus Christ.[145]

---

143. John Webster, "The Grand Narrative of Jesus Christ: Barth's Christology," in *Karl Barth: A Future for Postmodern Theology?* Geoff Thompson and Christiaan Mostert (eds.), (Hindmarsh: Australian Theological Press, 2000), 1–72, 59.

144. Ibid., 60ff. See also John Webster, *Barth's Moral Theology: Human Action in Barth's Thought* (Edinburgh: T. & T. Clark, 1998), and Barth, *Church Dogmatics* II/2, III/1, 4.

Christ's personhood in Barth's view has clearly its own particular being, which not only lies in Jesus' relations to others, but also in his divine nature as a distinct person from the Father and the Spirit in the Trinity. However, Barth's treatment of conduct and actions as the key marks of God's revelatory presence in history (which starts with election and culminates in salvation) shapes even his trinitarian foundation. For, instead of three divine, self-distinct *persons*, Barth departs in understanding human personhood from a notion of a threefold revelatory, salvific *activity* of the divine, one Lord: God is the initiator of the relation, the relation per se, and the ideal partner who stands on the other side of it.[146] In other words, while Barth grounds personal subjectivity in God rather than in the human (i.e., in Christocentric theology rather than in anthropocentric ethics) he nevertheless maintains an action-based modernist concept of personhood that lies in self-realization. He even applies this action-based concept of personhood to the triune God: the Father, Son, and Spirit are three *modes* of God's sovereign acts in time. While Barth's anthropology correctly shows that dogmatics and ethics are inseparable,[147] his trinitarian understanding of personhood, and eventually of the three divine persons in the Godhead, fails to maintain a necessary ontological distinction between "personhood" and "relationality," which is required for evading any possible collapsing of God's infinity into his revealed-ness. Colin Gunton, accordingly, believes that because the trinitarian theology of Barth and others "is only half way out of the modalism [or 'mode of being'] that is at the root of all the problems," there is more to be said about the theological understanding of "person" than what they say.[148]

---

145. Webster, "Barth and Postmodern Theology: A Fruitful Confrontation?," 61.

146. For a critical assessment of Barth's replacement of "*persons*" with "*modes of being*" and his mistaken understanding of the patristic, mainly Cappadocian, trinitarian notion of "*hypostases*," see Awad, *God Without a Face?*, ch. 5.2.2.

147. Webster, "Barth and Postmodern Theology: A Fruitful Confrontation?," 64.

148. Colin Gunton, "The Triune God and the Freedom of the Creature," in *Karl Barth: Centenary Essays*, ed. S. W. Sykes (Cambridge: Cambridge University Press, 1989), 66. George Hunsinger disagrees strictly with those who charge Barth with modalism and states that "modalism can be charged against Barth only out of ignorance, incompetence, or (willful) misunderstanding." George Hunsinger, "*Mysterium Trinitatis*: Barth's Conception of Eternity," in *For the Sake of the World: Karl Barth and the Future of Ecclesial Theology*, ed. George Hunsinger (Grand Rapids and Cambridge: Eerdmans, 2004), 165–90, 170, fn. 5. Michael Ovey nevertheless sides with Gunton and maintains reservations about Hunsinger's opinion. He prefers to chase after some preciseness with regard to Barth's definition of "modalism" and its self-evidence before showing any readiness to share Hunsinger's trenchant dismissal of the above-mentioned charge. See M. J. Ovey, "A Private Love? Karl Barth and the Triune God," in *Engaging with Barth: Contemporary Evangelical Critiques*, 198–231, 221 (221–29). Ovey does not totally

I conclude this section by emphasizing that a personal God who elects to love in freedom, the revelationist theology of Karl Barth does not really exceed the traps of the modernist notion of the self-sufficient subject and selfhood. For, parallel to viewing God as an infinitely relational being, God is also viewed as the absolute relational *subject* whose relationship with the other is due to his very own free decision. From this combination stems, in fact, the "one divine subject, three modes of being" version of the Trinity that clearly emphasizes the relational oneness of the single divine subject at the expense of the personal distinction of the three divine persons that is not to be exhausted by or subsumed to their relations.

IV. Self, Personhood, and the Doctrine of the Trinity

The previous analysis of the relation of the notion of "person" to the notion of "relation" in modernity shows that theology needs to release itself from either drifting into a totally existentialist or a totally idealist ontology of being. In his overemphasis on the wholly otherness and beyond-ness of the incarnate God in, and not in spite of, his incarnation, Karl Barth gives the impression of supporting a reductionist hermeneutics of God's personhood that depicts the divine self as "distinguished self, purified and immunized against external influences." And, in his overemphasis of interrelationality and correlationality at the expense of otherness and beyond-ness, Paul Tillich also gives the impression of supporting another, no less reductionist, hermeneutics of God's personhood that depicts the divinized self as "individual performer of a religiously coded moral activity."[149] Neither Barth nor Tillich, or the theological approach each represents, exceeds the boundaries, challenges the foundations, or corrects the twofold reductionist philosophical understanding of the notions that happened to be commonly central in the theological and nontheological scholarships alike

---

dismiss the modalist implications from Barth's trinitarian theology, pointing instead that such a charge may be warranted by Barth's use of the term "repetition": "The idea of repetitions [in Barth] has its ostensible source in Anselm's *Letter on the Incarnation*, but represents a reading of Anselm that wrenches Anselm's argument from its original context to fatal effect, applying to the Persons what Anselm discussed in relation to nature. This commitment means God's intra-trinitarian life is reflexive, rather than being reciprocal and mutual as between three correlative subjects. Such reflexive ideas seem to fall within patristic notions of modalism, while Barth's repudiation of modalism rests on a definition that is differently drawn from the patristic sources, with no real discussion of this difference" (230).

149. I borrow these two descriptions from Michael Welker, "Is the Autonomous Person of European Modernity a Sustainable Model of Human Personhood?," in *The Human Person in Science and Theology*, ed. Niels Henrik Gregersen et al. (Grand Rapids: Eerdmans, 2000), 95–114, 102.

in modernity. They rather fall into the trap of echoing variations of this very reductionist philosophy, yet with crudely religious and theological language and content. They both wanted to achieve what Michael Welker describes as a reinforcement of "the differentiation between a self-reference given by the divine and a self-reference taken or performed in the secular world."[150] Yet they did not succeed in their endeavor because in their attempt at challenging modernity, they departed from the very same conceptual division between "personal" and "individual," "relational" and "transcendent," which modernity itself in its major trends of thought promotes and even imposes on all human sciences, including the study of religion and theology. Theology busied itself, so to speak, during the modern age with fighting over the question whether the intellectual cloth of modernity fits the body of faith or not, instead of examining whether there is a real cloth in the first place.

Paul Tillich does not claim that he is contrasting modernity or deconstructing it by his theological project. Karl Barth on the other hand clearly states that theology has nothing to do with the business of showing allegiance to modernity. Theology is self-sufficient scholarship in its own terms. It does not need to prove itself to any other fields of inquiry. Tillich believes that correlation is what should characterize theology's understanding of God's relationship to the world. However, his theological reasoning turns the subject of theology (God) and his knowability (revelation) into an *answer* to the world's needs and human existential questions—an answer, moreover, that is formed according to the modernist rules of answering questions and thinking about them. His model of correlation reflects subordination to modernity's modernization of theology. Barth, on the other hand, refuses to correlate with modernity altogether and attempts to challenge and theologize modernity from the vantage point of the revelation of God. In his endeavor to achieve this, Barth nevertheless speaks about God's self-knowledge, God's being "fully-God-by-means-of-being-his-full-wholly-otherness." He speaks, that is, theologically in a language that is actually inherent to philosophical reasoning characteristic of modernity itself. In other words, Barth's theology does not really stand opposite the riverbank of the modernist thought-form and methods of thinking. "Knowing one's self by means of one's own self per se," echoed in claims like "God is only known by God," for instance, is not a challenging, counter-principle theology with which one can confront modernity. It is rather reminiscent of the writings of people such as Hegel, Kant, and Fichte. Both of the approaches or relationships that Barth and Tillich build with modernist

150. Schrag, *The Self after Postmodernity*, 107.

trends of thought are not correlational; are not, that is, expressive of a relationship between two equally influential, self-existing, distinguished sides. They are not expressive, in trinitarian terms, of "unity-in-differentiation" forms of interaction. In its attempt to face the challenges of modernity, therefore, theology reflects failure in transcending the boundaries of modernist forms of inquiry, or in helping modernism transcend itself.

Instead, the question theology should have engaged with is whether the reductionist philosophy of "self" is appropriate for understanding divine and human personhood, or if it rather drives God, as well as the human, behind the mask.[151] Theology needs to develop a hermeneutics of divine personhood, wherein God's being is "at once that which is other or supervenient to the configurations of experience and forms of life within the immanent culture-spheres and that which exhibits a power to transfigure these configurations, forms and culture-spheres."[152] On the basis of such an ontology, we can distinguish "personhood" from "relationality" in the terminology of the doctrine of God so that the Trinity-based hermeneutics of "person" will neither allow for a reduction of being into mere movements or conduct, nor allows for obscuring relationality by turning it into an expression of subjectivist self-actualization or self-awareness.

The ontology that takes into consideration a qualified correlation of "being" and "existence" paves the way for a basic differentiation between the theological understanding of God's personhood and the understanding of human personhood. In relation to this, it is correct to recognize, as the philosopher Karl Jaspers once said, a distinction between God's being and the human's being by rendering God a transcendent Being and not a mere expression of a worldly existent unit among many others.[153] God's personhood lies in the multifariousness of his interpersonal interaction with the world. So, personhood is God's declaration of his infinite distinction, not of his inconsistency or of his indirect (i.e., mediated) relatedness. Most of all, it is an indication of God's *free* personhood, as Jaspers realizes,[154] where we encounter what is both more than personal as well as *other* than the element of finitude in personal being. "Being-with-another" is basic and constitutive of the personal identity of the human. But it is not exhaustively or preconditionally so in God's personhood, because if distinction in terms of transcendence is the *foundation* of

---

151. Welker, "Is the Autonomous Person of European Modernity a Sustainable Model of Human Personhood?," 108.

152. Schrag, *The Self after Postmodernity*, 138–39.

153. Jaspers, *Philosophical Faith and Revelation*, 138.

154. Ibid., 141ff.

personhood in God, as Jaspers notes, then God's personhood must be more than a mere ideal of communion.[155]

In his book, *The Self after Postmodernity*, Calvin Schrag follows a similar line of thought and argues that the understanding that represents a very strong sense of "transcendence" can appropriately be invested in designating the ultimate limitation of human rational comprehension.[156] In spite of the emphasis on the rationally incomprehensible nature of transcendence in such understanding, the metaphysical view of infinity as a limitation to human reason, and as a reality beyond the objective components of human life, is a positive aid to theology. It helps theology to utter metaphysically the truth of God's infinite being that exceeds all the possible subject-centered horizons that dominate the theories of understanding in modernity.[157] This is actually congenial with the theological speech on God's being as "three persons in one nature," where the nature is not less than personhood yet it is also beyond personal singularity and beyond a single personal mode of existence. The crucial issue here is whether we should define God's being *as* a specific existence or rather remember that the infinity and freedom of God prove that his being is always more than existence as one, specific personalization, although never less. Speaking, then, about three persons in God is an answer to the threat of the idea of an "inwardly lifeless God," as well as to the threat of the idea of "an outwardly functional abstract monism." It challenges these previous threats more than Jaspers and others in modernity, or postmodernity, may even imagine. Modern and postmodern theologians are quite right in believing that the Trinity is the core foundation (in modernity's words) or the core hermeneutical language (in postmodernity's words) of being in relation with "another." For, in the triune image of God each divine person recognizes the other two in their particularity and otherness. Yet a balanced theology of the Trinity should not refer to the doctrine of the Trinity in a way that overstresses the characteristic of interrelationality of God's being to an extent where we may reduce his infinite nature to an expression of a unique mode of living or of movement. The Trinity should not become a linguistic strategy for doing away with God's particular

---

155. Ibid., 144.

156. Schrag, *The Self after Postmodernity*, 116, referring to what is stated in Jaspers, *Reason and Existenz*, trans. William Earle (London: Routledge and Kegan Paul, 1956), 51–76.

157. Schrag is quite right in saying that in this regard Jaspers's existentialism is radically different from that of Jean-Paul Sartre, whose understanding of transcendence is limited to a person's exceeding of his existing self toward the human condition that is not yet his. While Sartre's transcendence is anthropomorphic, Jaspers's is not. See Schrag, *The Self after Postmodernity*, 117.

being in a manner that swallows the infiniteness of the divine as well as his existence.[158]

The infiniteness of the divine being needs to be manifest in existence so we can understand it, without denying that infiniteness means that this being is by nature beyond all contingent existence. In other words, we have to rely on a theological concept of personhood that maintains that every person of the Trinity is his-self by virtue of the relations of origin (which expresses each person's mode of existence in eternity), but every person is also his-self by virtue of his transcendence of the specific mode of his causal origin, because he is co-constitutive of the infinite and mysterious Godhead. The relations of origin do not constitute the Godhead alone, although they are substantially expressive of this Godhead. Any undermining of one of the poles of this axiom in understanding God's personhood would lead us ontologically, as Jaspers says, "either into an infinite void of inner being or into an unequivocal theistic piety that will turn [human] image and likeness into transcendence itself."[159]

It is not enough to speak about God's personal infinite nature by restricting God's infinity to his oneness. We should extend it to God's *triune* personal being. Whether they maintain the notions of "subject" and "individual self" in their understanding of personhood or not, theologians miss a very important theology of personhood if they don't take into consideration the "three *persons*" dimension, which combines God's infinity in terms of particularity with God's relational life. The best expression of "relationality in self-distinction" is "person" *because* this term cannot exhaustively define God or reduce self to a mere state of self-fulfillment. In the creedal background of the doctrine of the Trinity, "person" does not only mean communality and knowledge, but also confession and proclamation of God's sublime "*mysterium tremendum*." From the beginning, the church fathers believed that the incomplete defining capacity of "person" in the Trinity is an important prerequisite to avoid turning any theological talk about God's communion with the human into "God" per se. This was their method for avoiding tritheism, where "person" is subjected to a static definition in terms of individuality. "Person" was seen as the term that extends static definition, and, therefore, the best linguistic affirmation of God's beyond-ness.

This previous patristic tradition of "person" in the theology of the Trinity is a valid foundation for maintaining the term "person" in Christian theology for the sake of protecting God's being from the modernist emphasis on

---

158. Ibid., 165–66.
159. Ibid., 167.

individualism and self-enclosed subjectivity. Distinguishing the three divine persons from their relational movements is the hope that opens the human's personhood for new horizons of being; the modernist scopes of subjective, personal life are insufficient to open up before him. This is sufficient to show that theology needs to give up its inappropriate relation with the intellectual disciplines of the modernist conditions. In the coming chapters of this study, I will show that theology cannot run along either the philosophical alternatives of the death of the subject or of the self, and cannot apply them as they are to the subjective self of God or the human.[160] The Christian understanding of the personal subject is different from the modernist and the postmodernist ones; in that God as a personal subject is defined by means of the personhood that was revealed in and as the personhood of Christ, which is open and relational rather than abstract and self-enclosed, dynamic rather than static. It is in the light of this personhood that we know that the distinction of "person" from "relation" is not the end of personhood, but the eschatological promise that the triune personhood of God opens up before the human. It is the promise that at the end of days the human will be a real relational being with a personhood that lies in his communion with others as well as in his transcendence beyond his broken, sinful existence in the present.

The possible conflation of "person" with "relation" was not yet an issue in the writings of the theologians of modernity, who were busy developing a theology that protects God's nature from individualism and self-enclosed subjectivity. This conflation, as I will show in the following chapters, characterizes some trendy trinitarian proposals of postmodern theologians, who, instead of revising the theology of personhood from a balanced "essence-existence," or "person-relation," standpoint, take the conflation of "person-relation" and "essence-existence" into its ultimate problematic extreme. To this problematic theology I now turn.

---

160. Geoff Thompson and Christiaan Mostert, *Karl Barth: A Future for Postmodern Theology?*, 66. John Webster correctly reminds us that this is not appropriate from the point of view of theology because "what theology traces as it is taken up into the history of God is God's establishment of new humanity in Christ."

PART II

The Challenge: Trinitarian Theology and/in Postmodernity

3

The Postmodernist Conditioning

I. Setting the Scene

The second half of the last century witnessed the birth of an intellectual phenomenon called "the *post*modern condition," a condition that has deeply shaped today's intellectual scene. Opinions oscillate between belief in the possibility of a fixed definition of "postmodernity," or argue instead that it is impossible to define this multifaceted phenomenon at all,[1] let alone inquire about whether postmodernity is an expression of an intellectual breach with modernity or rather a revised extension of modernity itself.

Within this new intellectual context, theologians are faced again with the question of the nature of the relationship between Christian theology and the surrounding intellectual culture of the "postmodern *condition*."[2] They therefore relate to this condition with a caution colored by various kinds of expectations. Some theologians are fully supportive of postmodernity and believe that it is the savior of theology from the conditions of modernity.[3] Others, to the

---

1. This is what, for example, David West affirms: "'[P]ostmodern,' 'postmodernity' and 'postmodernism' are not always straightforwardly cognate terms either. They have different connotations, depending whether a historical period, a form of society, a philosophical stance or an artistic movement is in question." David West, *An Introduction to Continental Philosophy* (Cambridge: Polity, 1982), 189 (189–220).

2. Thus Jean-François Lyotard, *The Postmodern Condition: A Report on Knowledge* (Manchester: Manchester University Press, 1984). I agree with considering postmodernity "an ongoing paradigm shift in Western culture": Stanley Grenz and John R. Franke, *Beyond Foundationalism: Shaping Theology in a Postmodern Context* (Louisville: Westminster John Knox, 2001), 21. I also think that the belief that "plurality is the key to postmodernity. All known postmodern topics ... become understandable in the light of plurality" is also truly expressive of the nature of the phenomenon called "postmodernity." See West, *Introduction to Continental Philosophy*, 210. See also Jan-Olav Henriksen, "Creation and Construction: On the Theological Appropriation of Postmodern Theory," in *Modern Theology* 2, no. 18 (2002): 153–69, 155, quoting from Wolfgang Welsch's book *Unsere postmoderne Moderne* (Berlin: Akademie-Verlag, 2002), xv.

contrary, anticipate that time will reveal postmodernity to be just another anthropocentric condition that imposes on theology no less constraining criteria of verifiability than modernity.[4] If anything, this suggests that before theologians support either of these two positions they ought first to develop once more from Christian history clear answers to classical, yet principal, questions like the following: What sort of a relationship should theology have with other intellectual forms of inquiry? Should theology develop an insider view of these forms of inquiry by becoming one discourse, among many others, that speaks on behalf of these forms of knowledge and understanding? Or should theology rather maintain an outsider understanding of these new forms of inquiry, before consequently turning into a polemical opponent of a newly growing intellectual condition? In other words, should postmodernity be a condition that shapes and molds theological thinking, or should it be a new question that is asked and answered *only* from theological standpoints and on theological bases?[5]

In this part, "The Challenge," I endeavor to analyze some of the major philosophical trends of thought that shape the postmodern intellectual forms of inquiry. In the following parts, I will offer a "model"[6] that answers the question

---

3. Good examples of inviting theology for salvation from modernity *by means of* postmodernity are John D. Caputo, *What Would Jesus Deconstruct?: The Good News of Postmodernity for the Church* (Grand Rapids: Baker Academic, 2007) and Caputo and Michael J. Scanlon, *Transcendence and Beyond: A Postmodern Inquiry* (Bloomington and Indianapolis: Indiana University Press, 2007).

4. For a brief but valuable display of the various negative and positive fragmentations in theology because of the challenges of postmodernism, see Grenz and Franke, *Beyond Foundationalism*, 4–24; and John W. Riggs, *Postmodern Christianity* (Harrisburg, London, and New York: Trinity Press International/ Continuum, 2003).

5. Michel Foucault as one of the fathers of postmodern forms of thinking has once also made similar inquiries (but from the side of the postmodernist intellectual premise he supports), when he said: "What form of relation may be legitimately described between [the different divisions of mental forms of inquiries]; what vertical system they are capable of forming; what interplay of correlation and dominance exists between them; what may be the effect of shifts, and different temporalities, and various re-handlings; in what distinct totalities certain elements may figure simultaneously." M. Foucault, *The Archaeology of Knowledge and Discourse on Language*, trans. A. M. Sheridan Smith (New York: Pantheon, 1971), 10. Though Foucault's questions are challenging to the contemporary general emphasis on relativism, plurality, and relationality, they are, nevertheless, as applicable to the internal relation of the theological discourse's components per se as to the external relations between theology and other forms of discourse.

6. I do principally acknowledge with Stephen Bevans the variety of meanings "model" may hold. I follow him also in considering "models" as mere constructions that are logically formed to describe concrete relational positions. They ought to be taken seriously but not as a literal articulation of something "out there" in reality. See S. Bevans, *Models of Contextual Theology* (Maryknoll: Orbis, 2003),

of the proper relationship that theology should have with its surrounding intellectual conditions. This twofold purpose will be achieved first by displaying in this part a recent theological proposal which claims that in its central characteristics "postmodernity" represents a "theological conditioning" that essentially aims at correcting defects in theology and human secular knowledge of modernity. I will unpack the presumed logic behind this proposed theological recontextualization, before suggesting, in the last part of this study, another, more appropriate model of interaction between theology and postmodernity that attempts to restrain theology from becoming: 1) either a religious manifestation of contemporary intellectual conditions, or 2) a discourse that endeavors only to justify itself before postmodern, rational forms of understanding. Instead of making theology a "postmodern condition" and postmodernity a total "theological condition"—either of which is, in my opinion, an invocation of a modernist epistemological hierarchism that was once mistakenly followed by other, no less than referential theologians (see the second chapter of part one)—I will point to an option of relationality, wherein postmodernity can be *theologically* challenged and theology can go beyond the constraints of modernity. "*Theologically* challenged" means that postmodernity is not reduced to a mere theological phenomenon, although it is invited to acknowledge the theological dimensions of so many of its cherished notions. "*Theologically* challenged" rather than "theological condition" implies that postmodernity is questioned, and even corrected, by the theology of God the Trinity, without which an allegiance is imposed on theological assumptions or textual premises that may not, in the first place, be relevant to the concern of every contemporary inquiry.

I see such a model of theological contribution to the postmodern intellectual scene in a *correlational* form of relationality between theology and postmodern forms of inquiry. I am not offering here unconditional support for "correlation" as a notion or a model of connectedness. Rather, I argue that not every model of correlation is compatible with the nature of theological knowledge and inquiry. Thus I expose, in chapter five, two different

---

28–33. I would also follow Avery Dulles's understanding of model as "a relatively simple artificially constructed case which is found to be useful and illuminating for dealing with realities that are more complex and differentiated." Avery Dulles, *Models of Revelation* (New York: Doubleday, 1983), 30 (19–35). For other discussions on the nature of "models," see for instance Sallie McFague, *Metaphorical Theology: Models of God in Religious Language* (Philadelphia: Fortress Press, 1982), 103–44; and McFague, *Models of God: Theology for an Ecological, Nuclear Age* (Philadelphia: Fortress Press, 1987), 31–40; and Ian Barbour, *Myths, Models and Paradigms: A Comparative Study in Science and Religion* (New York: Harper & Row, 197), 29–48.

understandings of correlational relationality. On the one hand are the proposals by David Tracy, Gordon Kaufman, and Mark Taylor, and on the other hand those of Hans Frei and Francis Watson. While critiquing the first and giving support to the second, I hope to show that discussing the appropriate relation between theology and postmodernity is not only necessary,[7] but also crucial to maintaining the rational and normative integrity of both Christian theology and the surrounding intellectual paradigm(s).

Let me now move to the main purpose of this part: 1) analyzing the claim that postmodernity should be from beginning to end "theologically conditioned"; 2) pointing at the negative consequences of this claim on trinitarian theology; and 3) criticizing the understanding of "relationality" and "participation" that is invested heavily by a few trinitarian theologians, and suggesting a theological correction to it from Christian patristic tradition.

II. THE GOAL: THE AMBITION OF THEOLOGIZING POSTMODERNITY

In an anthology on postmodern theology, Kevin Vanhoozer surveys the theological schools that emerged in response to, or in support of, the postmodern campaign against any claim of "objectivity" and any belief in the existence of such thing as the "essence" of anything.[8] One gleans from Vanhoozer's survey that these theological schools emerged out of a perception of the serious threats such campaigning may generate against Christian faith

---

7. Grenz and Franke, *Beyond Foundationalism*, 4. "This checkered past confirms the vitality of Christian theology while warning of the dangers of too closely associating it with any particular form of cultural expression." My attitude toward modernity as a "past" intellectual era Christianity faced with difficulty concurs with the attitude Thomas Oden holds when he speaks about Modernity not an a corrupt enemy that needs to be totally opposed by means of appealing to the arsenal of postmodernity. I agree with Thomas Oden that any critical attitude toward modernity should not in principle be "merely censorious, embittered, negative, emotional reaction." There is something right in Oden's conviction that "there is no reason to be opposed to something that is already dead. A frustrated, anti-modern, angry, caustic, emotive reaction errs in overestimating the continuing resilience of terminal modernity and its capacity to regenerate itself intellectually." Thomas Oden, "The Death of Modernity and Postmodern Evangelical Spirituality," in *The Challenge of Postmodernism: An Evangelical Engagement*, ed. David S. Dockery (Grand Rapids: Baker Academic, 2001), 21.

8. Vanhoozer, "Theology and the Condition of Postmodernity: A Report on Knowledge (of God)," in *The Cambridge Companion to Postmodern Theology*, ed. K. J. Vanhoozer (Cambridge: Cambridge University Press, 2003), 3–25, 3. "In the first place, postmoderns reject the notion that any description or definition is 'neutral' . . . a definition of postmodernity is as likely to say more about the person offering the definition than it is of 'the postmodern.' Second, postmoderns resist . . . such things as the 'essence' of the postmodern."

and theology. For, contrary to this rejection of objectivity and "essence," and according to the tradition of doctrinal theology of revelation, the idea of the "objective truth" that encounters the human from without by means of revelation, as well as the concept of "essence" as an expression of the inner nature of God, are two principal concepts for understanding and relating to the God of Jesus Christ and the Holy Spirit. Because such concepts are foundational to Christian faith, evaluating and questioning the validity of this recent rejection of "objectivity" and of "essence" that Vanhoozer points to becomes a crucial task for contemporary theology. It may pave the way for denying theology certain particular concepts that are central to its discourse about God. In the light of this, Vanhoozer suggests, it is quite essential to ask:

> Does postmodernity present [theology] with enabling conditions and hence with new opportunities and possibilities, or does postmodernity represent a disabling condition, a condition of *impossibility* say, for discovering truth or for talking about God?[9]

In theology, there are various answers to Vanhoozer's questions. Some theologians believe that postmodernity presents enabling conditions that liberate theology from the problematic and inappropriate constraints of modernity. One of the classical claims that reflect a zeal for subjecting theology to the constraints of the changing cultural factors in the world is the one that argues against the logical and existential tenability of conceiving God as an objective reality other than the world. Such a rejection is based on the allegation that any claim of the existence of an objective, ontological, and metaphysical God is threatening to human freedom and dignity. And, eventually, any reservation of traditional theology in the light of recent developments in the surrounding cultural context is impossible and unallowable.[10] Some of the theologians who commit themselves to this

---

9. Ibid. 4.

10. Thus Don Cupitt, *Taking Leave of God* (London: SCM, 1980). Also, look at the famous response to Cupitt by Keith Ward, *Holding Fast to God* (London: SPCK, 1982). See also Colin Gunton's discussion of the debate on the doctrine of God in contemporary Western scholarship, in Gunton, *The Promise of Trinitarian Theology*, 2nd ed. (Edinburgh: T. & T. Clark, 1997), 15–29. Gunton divides Cupitt's argument into two debates. One is on the rejection of the existence of an objectively metaphysical deity. The other is on the nature of God rather than his existence. Gunton deems them to be two different debates. But Cupitt is not mainly discussing the possibility of God's existence. He is concerned, instead, about the validity or the invalidity of claiming the existence of an objective being different from humanity called God. In other words, Cupitt's concern is about the question of the acceptable identity and nature of the

perspective, as Colin Gunton shows, take their stand on the belief that the early church committed a theological mistake in looking for, and in deriving ontological and metaphysical assumptions about God, from Scripture. Because the biblical texts, Gunton explains, are just "records of experience," rather than philosophical or metaphysical texts, "we should, therefore, be free to develop a doctrine of God that conforms to our experience."[11] Such a succumbing to the surrounding intellectual conditions, as Vanhoozer and Gunton concede, takes theology into various dead-ends and imposes untenable doctrinal assumptions on the Christian understanding of God and of humanity.

Alarmed by this danger, many theologians who believe in the ability of theology to remodel the contemporary age opt for challenging *theologically* any form of external subordination directed against theology by endeavoring to subordinate the contemporary intellectual conditions to theological constraints. A number of these theologians counter the subordination of theology by calling for a theological mission (almost evangelistic in some respects) toward the contemporary (postmodernist) cultural context. Driven by strong conviction about the collapse of the project of modernity, which considered dogmatic Christianity historically irrelevant and rationally invalid, they zealously endeavor to show the substantial relevance and referential position of Christian faith for the contemporary intellectual world. We hear today, as Diogenes Allen points out, theologians who strongly affirm that

> [i]n a postmodern world, Christianity is intellectually relevant. It is relevant to the fundamental question, why does the world exist? And why does it have its present order, rather than another? It is relevant to the discussion of the foundations of morality and society, especially on the significance of human beings.[12]

---

deity that is most convenient for maintaining humanity's freedom. It is in essence one argument for nailing down ontology.

11. Gunton, *The Promise of Trinitarian Theology*, 18. "[E]ven if," Gunton continues, " it involves taking the apparently atheist path of Don Cupitt."

12. Diogenes Allen, *Christian Belief in a Postmodern World: The Full Wealth of Conviction* (Louisville: Westminster John Knox, 1989), 5–6. There are contemporary scholars who tend to argue that even from the ethical perspective, theology is the reference of proper morality that modernity missed and postmodernity ought to adopt. On the relevance of Christianity for the quest for morality in human society and even the belief that the church's discourse is the criterion for deciding what is moral and what is not, see for example Alasdair MacIntyre, *After Virtue: A Study in Moral Theory* (Notre Dame: University of Notre Dame Press, 1981); Franklin Gamwell, *The Divine Good: Moral Theory and the Necessity of God* (San Francisco: HarperCollins, 1990); and Stanley Hauerwas, *Wilderness Wanderings: Probing Twentieth-Century Theology and Philosophy* (Boulder, CO: Westview, 1997).

After exposing these trends, Vanhoozer confirms that the best approach to postmodernity is one that exceeds an "enabling-disabling," contrasting form of connectedness by means of *exclusively and narrowly* transforming postmodernity into a "theological condition." Postmodernity as a theological condition emerges into view, according to Vanhoozer, by contrasting the theologies composed in the postmodern age with their modern counterparts. From this contrast it can be discerned that the main concern of modern theologies, according to Vanhoozer, was gaining the acceptance of, and legitimization from, the modernist condition. Unfortunately, by doing this, as Vanhoozer accurately notes, modernist theologians eventually gained the respect and cultural approval of the modernist intellectual context, yet they lost their own particular Christian identity that lies in conveying the gospel message as one that is a *challenging question* to any human context, as much as an answer to such contexts' inquiries.[13] In reaction to this attitude toward the demands of the surrounding intellectual context, theology should now grab the postmodernist context to emancipate itself from the requests and expectations of the modernist context and not slavishly succumb to its preconditions.

It is crucial here to realize that while the ambition of theologians like Vanhoozer is to show that postmodernity is in fact the chance for theology to respond to modernity and to restore its autonomy and value, the real challenge for them is to prove that postmodernity would not become "the latest extra-textual framework into which theology must translate its discourse in order to be considered legitimate."[14] Valid as this concern may be, the way theologians such as Vanhoozer apply it and the goal they aim at in proving it are not fully appropriate. The practical implication of the attempt to make postmodernity theology's opportunity to gain influence is turning postmodernity into a *totally* theological condition. But this obscures an ambition to make theology the overarching framework that shapes and situates all other forms of inquiry. Theology is now proclaimed as referentially definitive of contemporary forms of inquiry. The task, as such, is to conform these forms of inquiries to the claims and components of the Christian narrative. Vanhoozer articulates this ambition of theologically conditioning postmodernity as follows:

> Theology ventures, not as a modern science, but as a theodrama that situates the human within the narrative of God's creative and redemptive activity. The suggestion, therefore, is to situate

13. Vanhoozer, "Theology and the Condition of Postmodernity," 19.
14. Ibid., 20.

modernity and postmodernity alike within the story of what relates both what God is doing in the world through Jesus Christ and the Holy Spirit to what the world is doing in response.[15]

Vanhoozer then concludes that for postmodernity to be a theological condition, theology should acknowledge that it has a mission to transform (proselytize?!) postmodernity according to a process that is from beginning to end theological and kerygmatic in essence. This mission lies, according to Vanhoozer, in promoting a "particular shape of life"; that is, in transforming postmodernity into a model "about living in accordance with the shape of the life of God displayed in the life of Jesus."[16]

Besides Vanhoozer's proposal, the endeavor to show the transformative ability of theology and its criterial role in today's intellectual scene is evident too in many other dominating, liberal and conservative, theological writings from the second half of the twentieth century onwards.

George Lindbeck, for example, sets for himself the task of recontextualizing the world on the basis, and by means of, the biblical symbols, stories, and norms. He calls this theological transformation of the world "inter-textual theology," and describes it as follows: "inter-textual theology re-describes reality within the scriptural framework rather than translating Scripture into extra-scriptural categories. It is the text, so to speak, which absorbs the world, rather than the world the text."[17] The stories and symbols of the Bible are here proposed as the tools of theology for redescribing and recontextualizing the world. For Lindbeck, theology and doctrine are the function and expression of a specific language-game and socio-anthropological life-setting in religious and God-centered terms. Doctrines are simply "forms

---

15. Ibid., 21. From a comprehensive exposition of Vanhoozer's understanding of theology as drama, read Vanhoozer, *The Drama of Doctrine: A Canonical-Linguistic Approach to Christian Theology* (Louisville: Westminster John Knox, 2005).

16. Vanhoozer, "Theology and the Condition of Postmodernity," 24.

17. George Lindbeck, *Nature of Doctrine: Religion and Theology in a Postliberal Age* (Philadelphia: Duquesne University Press, 1998), 118. Concern for conditioning the world theologically in a manner similar to Lindbeck's can be seen in William Placher's description of this recontextualization as a coherent theological explanation of how the world is to be formed according to Christian perspectives: W. C. Placher, *Unapologetic Theology: A Christian Voice in a Pluralistic Conversation* (Louisville: Westminster John Knox, 2007), 19. See also the exposition of these trends in postmodern theology by Grenz and Franke, *Beyond Foundationalism*, 3–27; and David Ray Griffin, *God and Religion in the Postmodern World: Essays in Postmodern Theology* (Albany: State University of New York Press, 1989), 1–12.

of life," and they can thus be treated as culture-shaping and context-forming instruments.[18] The theological message, that is, is a linguistic-cultural discourse that is capable of shaping human life and performance after specific webs of meaning and living that are derived from the Gospel narratives themselves.

John Milbank is another contemporary theologian who endeavors to show that many of the prominent intellectual theories and methods of interpretation (in the social sciences particularly) are in fact derived from, and shaped after, implicit theological premises. Milbank affirms that this is the case whether postmodernist scholars acknowledge their proposals' allegiance to theological rationale or not. Departing from any sense of mutuality or reciprocity, Milbank rejects the submission of theology's hermeneutic methods and claims to the conditions of any secular cultural reasoning. He argues, rather, that postmodernist fields of study should recognize the real, distinct, and influential impact of theology on *their* disciplines, which lies in "the interruptive character of Christianity and therefore its difference from *both* modernity and antiquity."[19] Before the rise of postmodernist forms of interpretation, Milbank opines, theology mistakenly borrowed non-Christian understandings of history and society and followed their interpretation of theology's relation to other sciences. This was an inappropriate decision because theology is rather the one that provides "its own account of the final causes at work in human history."[20]

Milbank believes that Western intellectual history itself reveals that theology has shown a noticeable ability to evade the suspicions and challenges other social scientific forms of inquiry posed to it. He then underscores that theology's ability to surmount such challenges stems from the following: 1) the social sciences themselves, as it appears, are "made in terms of metaphysics, and of a 'religion'"; 2) the conclusions of these sciences concerning religion and its value are as relativist and nonuniversal as any other historically shaped conclusions and theories in other social sciences. Milbank proposes that theology, as history shows, has already proven its ability to dispense with these nontheological conclusions on the nature and value of religion, treating them as unwarranted and nonabsolute.[21] Moreover, theology is not only able to

---

18. Lindbeck, *Nature of Doctrine*, 31, 69. See also, on Lindbeck's proposal and its impact on contemporary theological attempts at applying this understanding to the theology of the church and to the definition of theology as such, Najib G. Awad, "At the Dawn of 'Practice' or Re-thinking the Nature and Role of Theology and Doctrine in the Church," in *Journal of Reformed Theology* 8 (2014): 1–32.

19. John Milbank, *Theology and Social Theory: Beyond Secular Reason* (Oxford and Cambridge, MA: Blackwell, 1994), 399.

20. Ibid., 380.

21. Ibid., 260.

challenge the claims of the social sciences and critique their prerequisites, but also, and most importantly, theology develops an alternative particular, reliable understanding that penetrates beyond "any possible secular reasoning about social reality."[22] So, instead of succumbing to the intellectual challenges that dominate the intellectual scene of every historical era, theology, in Milbank's estimate, holds the natural potential of exceeding the boundaries of the rules and premises that constitute the content of these challenges. It can even assess their validity and judge their meaningfulness. This is not true only in relation to the social sciences that dominate the intellectual scene of modernity, but also, according to Milbank, it applies equally to the pervading intellectual theories of postmodernity (e.g., nihilism and the ontology of *différance*). Theology can prove itself as the generator of a needed "metaphysics of objective goodness and beauty," as Milbank says, which the postmodernist age needs in order to exceed the narrowing and limiting boundaries of modernity.[23]

Milbank goes further in arguing that theology is not only required to show its difference from other social sciences, despite the common characteristics that unify them, but also to show the other social sciences that in their discourses about the world and reality in general lie basic and constitutive elements of "a 'counterhistory,' a counternarrative of human existence, of ecclesial origination, which tells the story of *all* history from the point of view of this emergence."[24]

A reliable theological elaboration of this "counterhistory," according to Milbank, is St. Augustine's *The City of God*. Augustine's account is not only a narrative of the history of the church, but also a critical metanarrative of the history of secular society. Therein, "we discover the *original* possibility of critique that marks the Western tradition," both the religious and the secular.[25] Instead of reflecting any form of a universalized criterion of reasoning, Augustine's prioritization of peace over antagonism is shaped by a principally dogmatic and theological narrative, and is representative of a criterial ontology of peace from the angle of faith.[26] In the history wherein peace enjoys the upper

---

22. Ibid., 263.

23. Ibid., 275. "If, however, the ethical and the aesthetic are ontologically objective realities, then there is an alternative to the narrative of power, and something wider than science, which only records power, and whose truth ends with its passing . . . for only a metaphysics of objective goodness and beauty, not mere epistemology of 'human' freedom . . . can discover a realm other than that of science and technology."

24. Ibid., 389. Italic is mine.

25. Ibid., 389ff. Milbank believes that Augustine's ecclesiological philosophy of history is more practical and useful than those of Marx and Hegel. He also believes that Nietzsche's *Genealogy of Morals* is no more than "*Civitas Dei* written back to front" (389).

26. Milbank, *Theology and Social Theory*, 390ff.

hand, salvation is not restricted to the city of God (the church), but its impact extends to the world and the whole of human history. Augustine's critical metanarrative of human history, then, not only anticipates the conclusions of the social sciences about human existence. It further shapes and underpins the points of view of the sciences and their thought-forms, even if only implicitly.[27] Be that as it may, Milbank proposes that theology, or the theological metanarrative of history, should retrieve its criterial, conditioning position in today's intellectual arena, so that Christianity not only shows its difference but also reveals that it is *the* difference," the criterion of difference, for all other cultural systems.[28] The theological inquiry, which discerns truth from certain Christian religious premises and uses specific linguistic bearers different from the ones of other discourses, should maintain its difference by gaining back its referential power and conditioning ability. What is today called "the postmodern condition" is to be seen, in this case, as the inauguration of a process of making theology the new criterion that will transform every component of culture and of social sciences into an expression of the influence of theological reasoning. Consequently, theology in postmodernity has every right to claim, as Milbank says, that

> [a] gigantic claim to be able to read, criticize, say what is going on in other human societies, is absolutely integral to the Christian church, which itself claims to exhibit the exemplary form of human community. For theology to surrender this claim, to allow that other discourses—"the social sciences"—carry out yet more fundamental readings, would therefore amount to a denial of theological truth.[29]

III. THE OUTCOME: POSTMODERNIZING TRINITARIAN THEOLOGY

In the previous section, I discussed a trend in contemporary theology that ambitiously attempts to condition postmodernity by means of theological

---

27. In the following pages, Milbank takes René Girard's philosophy of history as an exemplary demonstration of the Augustinian influence (ibid., 392ff.).

28. Ibid., 381. Gavin Hyman argues that all postmodern conditions by theology characterize the radical orthodoxy of John Milbank. He claims that "Milbank thereby confronts us with a straightforward antinomy: *either* theology will 'position' other discourses *or else* other discourses will position theology." Gavin Hyman, *Predicament of Postmodern Theology: Radical Orthodoxy or Nihilist Textualism?* (Louisville and London: Westminster John Knox, 2001), 70–73 (65–94).

29. Milbank, *Theology and Social Theory*, 388.

premises. I started to argue that this approach is not a valid and productive approach, neither to theology nor to postmodernity. In this and the following sections, I will continue exposing the application of this unbalanced relation between theology and postmodernity on the specific issues of "self" and "personhood" in both trinitarian theology and postmodern philosophy. I am, in other words, moving from a macrocosmic analysis of the relationship between theology and other forms of inquiry in general into a microcosmic study of the implications and ramifications of this relationship on how trinitarian theology and postmodern philosophy interpret notions they commonly emphasize. In order to do this, I will spend the remainder of this chapter mapping major postmodernist philosophical hermeneutics of selfhood and personality, postponing the exposition of some trinitarian investments of these postmodernist hermeneutics to the following chapter. So, let us now move to study some main philosophical paradigm shifts in the understanding of "self" and "personhood."

1. The Notions of "Self" and "Personhood" in Postmodernity: Roots and Ramifications

In the nineteenth century, Friedrich Nietzsche shook the intellectual, philosophical, and religious scenes by proclaiming the "death of God." His prophet, Zarathustra, comes down from his hermetic cave on the mountain to distribute the truth that changed him while he was contemplating alone. He declares that "God is dead," and that a humanity still defined and fettered by the thought of this God needs to be overcome. Once, Zarathustra states, blaspheming against God was considered by "the religious despisers," who used to poison people by speaking about this God and forcing them to worship him, the greatest sin; the blasphemy of blasphemies. But, Zarathustra says, "God died, and thereupon these blasphemers died too."[30] Humans should now free themselves from the authority of this God by screaming "I am alone," and by becoming creators of themselves as gods.[31] Now, Nietzsche declares, "God has died: now *we* desire—that the supreme shall live."[32] "God is dead, God remains dead. And we have killed him."[33]

---

30. Friedrich Nietzsche, *Thus Spoke Zarathustra*, trans. R. J. Hollindale (London: Penguin, 1969), 42.
31. Ibid., 89–90.
32. Ibid., 297.
33. Friedrich Nietzsche, *The Gay Science, with a Prelude in Rhymes and an Appendix of Songs*, trans. Walter Kaufmann (New York: Vintage, 1974), 3:125.

Nietzsche's "God is dead" was a battle cry for reinforcing human self-assurance in relation to the "self" and to the concern about being-ness as "I-ness." Nietzsche's conviction that the Christian denial of the self-shattering, self-annihilating consequences of eagerness for power—which is exemplified in the speech about a transcendent *author* called God, whose lordship suppresses human eagerness—is what drives him to claim God's death. For Nietzsche, the human aspiration for evolution toward a stronger, progressive level of self-fulfillment that generates virtue and happiness is a destructive illusion produced by the modern Christian Western person, whether religious or merely moralist.[34] And, since this modernist delusion of progress is associated closely with Christian faith, Christianity is to be called the "religion of *pity*" that "stands in opposition to all the tonic passions that augment the energy of the feeling of aliveness."[35] Christian theologians are the worst enemies of free humanity because they offer invented imaginary causes, confuse "causal drives" with "consequential explanations," and push people, eventually, to opt for illusionary ultimate ends.[36] Every religion and morality, claims Nietzsche, the imperative of which is "do this and that, stop this and that—then you will be happy!" should be called the "great original sin of reason, *immortal unreason*."[37] And, the concept of God that underpins this religiosity and moralism is the greatest objection to existence. Redeeming the world lies in nothing other than denying this concept of "God" and any responsibility that lies in it.[38]

The intriguing claim in Nietzsche's argument is his conviction that these imaginary "driving causes" and false ends or consequences are not only forced upon human existence by means of concepts like "God," "spirit," and "free will," but notions such as "ego" and "soul" are also false and imaginary. These latter notions actually stem from the ideas of "God," "spirit," and "free will" as their products and creation. And when these false concepts of authorial deity or infiniteness and free, superior human selfhood are combined, all that we have is a hypocritical dialogue between an imaginary "God" and an imaginary anthropocentric natural history.[39]

---

34. Friedrich Nietzsche, *The Antichrist: An Essay Towards a Criticism of Christianity*, trans. Thomas Common (Mineola, NY: Dover, 2004), § 4.

35. Ibid., § 7.

36. Nietzsche points to a fourfold nature of this confusion and speaks about "the four great errors" that have deflected Western thought ever since Plato. See Nietzsche, *Twilight of the Idols, or How to Philosophize with a Hammer*, trans. Duncan Large (Oxford and New York: Oxford University Press, 1998), VI.

37. Ibid., IV.2.

38. Ibid., VI.8.

In *Twilight of the Idols*, Nietzsche points to this imaginary anthropocentric discourse of modernity by arguing that the self as it is understood in Western philosophy is in reality an expression of a dead entity. It is an empty concept, a purely mental idealism or merely moral illusion. He bluntly says that "[the human's] three 'inner facts,' the things he believed in most firmly—the will, the mind, the I—were projected out of himself: he derives the concept of Being from the concept of the I, and posits the existence of 'things' after his own image, after his concept of the I as cause."[40] The reality, to the contrary, or the factuality that *is* our life and existence, affirms Nietzsche, is "that no one *gives* [the human] his qualities, neither God, nor society, nor his parents and ancestors," nor most radically, Nietzsche continues, "[*the human*] *himself*," for "*no one* is the result of his own intention, his own will, his own purpose; *no one* is part of an experiment to achieve an 'ideal person' or an 'ideal of happiness' or an 'ideal of morality'—it is absurd to want to *discharge* one's being onto some purpose or other."[41]

Be that as it may, Nietzsche calls the human now to fight unmercifully the illusion of the possibility of a better, moral self by means of *taming* the psychology and the desires of her "I." Nietzsche describes this "taming process" as an animalization of humanity, which, instead of improving the human, makes him weak, less harmful, and ultimately "a *diseased* beast through the depressive emotion of fear, through pain, through wounding, through hunger."[42] With the end of the age of belief in God comes also the age of the realization of the legendary fictional reality of the "ego." In conclusion, not only God, but also "the single person," Nietzsche declares, "the 'individual' . . . is an error: he is nothing by himself . . ."[43]

In her perceptive reading of Nietzsche's proclamation of the death of God, Hannah Arendt helps us see the centrality in Nietzsche's thinking of the declaration that the death of the supra-natural is in essence an inauguration of the nullification of the natural too. Arendt notes that though the natural and the supra-natural are opposites, according to Nietzsche, each one of them implies the other and leads to it, since, according to the dialectically shaped mind we have lived with since the time of Plato, the two sides of the dialectic exist by virtue of the opposite's existence and the act of opposing it. Therefore,

---

39. Nietzsche, *Antichrist*, § 15.
40. Nietzsche, *Twilight of the Idols*, VI.3.
41. Ibid., VI.8.
42. Ibid., VII.2.
43. Ibid., IX.33.

the disappearance of one means also the demolition of the other. Arendt's articulation of this Nietzschean logic is worth citing at length here:

> [I]t is indeed true that once the super-sensual realm is discarded, its opposite, the world of appearance as understood for so many centuries, is also annihilated. The sensual, as still understood by the positivists, cannot survive the death of the supra-sensual. No one knew this better than Nietzsche, who with his poetic and metaphoric description of the assassination of God in Zarathustra, in a significant passage in *Twilight of the Idols*, clarifies what the word God means in Zarathustra. It was merely a symbol for the supra-sensual realm as understood by metaphysics; he now uses instead of God the word "true world" and says: "We have abolished the true world. What has remained? the apparent one perhaps? Oh no! With the true world we have also abolished the apparent one."[44]

There is no longer any "self," Nietzsche opines; the human can see in the mirror when she stares at her image simply because there is no longer an ideal, supra-natural other in opposition to, or in dialectical clash with the human, who can become anything or anyone. There is not even an ideal ego before which the human can stand, stare at, or image. Narcissus has now lost all his masks, and the world is no longer a mirror in which the human enjoys seeing his narcissistic face reflected. The belief that there is a self that is perfectly happy within itself is considered, according to Nietzsche's analysis, an illusionary fulfillment of what Mark Taylor wryly calls "comic consciousness," which has no traces in reality.[45] In his profound explanation of the target of Nietzsche's deconstruction, Taylor realizes that for Nietzsche the modern human, driven by his conviction that "God" is the absolute master, is enslaved by his narcissism and eager to murder God's otherness and shift his absoluteness to his own self. By doing this, the modern human thinks he can deny death and win absolute freedom and immortality. But, as Taylor concludes with Nietzsche, "the pursuit of self-possession actually dispossesses the searching subject. When consumption becomes all-consuming, self-affirmation is transformed into self-

---

44. Hannah Arendt, "Thinking and Moral Consideration," in *Social Research* 38 (1971): 41–425, 420 as cited in Huston Smith, "Can Modernity Accommodate Transcendence?" in *Modernity and Religion*, ed. W. Nicholls (Waterloo, ON: Wilfrid Laurier University Press, 1988), 157–66, 162.

45. Mark Taylor, *Deconstructing Theology* (New York: Crossroad/Chico, CA: Scholars, 1982), 93 (87–105).

negation... the struggle for mastery in which the self seeks to preserve itself by denying death [i.e., God] proves to be the circuitous path by which the subject pursues its own death."[46]

According to Taylor, Nietzsche's interpreters take his inaugural announcement of the death of self that inevitably follows, and even originates from, murdering God, both a structuralist and post-structuralist deconstructive step further. They assess critically the notion of the "human self," and each in his or her own way decenter the self by "shifting the locus of intentionality from the *cogito* into the conventional interpersonal systems which operate through the ego." In the light of Nietzsche's proclamation of the nihilistic disintegration of selfhood, self-fulfillment and self-enclosure are no longer constitutive of the notion of the "human self." They rather dissolve it and point to its innate, substantial deflection.[47] This outcome seems to be inescapable in the light of Nietzsche's surgical deciphering of modernity's mind.

By snatching the horizon of truth from the hands of God and assassinating God himself, as Nietzsche prophetically points out, the modernist mind nullifies completely any possible horizon of meaning or identity from which the human self can look at and infer self-understanding. Human thought finds itself sailing in an endless sea of questions, puzzles, and enigmas without a horizon that can be followed to find the right directions. We are left with Nietzsche's very challenging, but still unanswered, elementary question: "How could we drink up the sea? Who gave us the sponge to wipe away the whole horizon?"[48] Most postmodernists believe, however, that by infinitely drifting away after the passion for finding an answer to this question, humanity has now, and maybe for the first time in history, a chance to survive and acquire its real nature. The death of the modern self, as David Griffin says, "is not to be mourned. It is indeed to be hastened by promoting a postmodern vision that is more adequate to the nature of reality and that will lead to a healthier way of being human."[49]

---

46. Mark Taylor, *Erring: A Postmodern A/Theology* (Chicago and London: University of Chicago Press, 1984), 30 (19–33), quoting from Paul Ricoeur, *Freud and Philosophy: An Essay on Interpretation*, trans. D. Savage (New Haven: Yale University Press, 1970), 291.

47. Taylor, *Deconstructing Theology*, 94.

48. Nietzsche, *Gay Science*, 3:125.

49. David Ray Griffin, "Postmodern Theology and A/Theology: A Response to Mark C. Taylor," in *Varieties of Postmodern Theology*, ed. David Ray Griffin et al. (Albany: State University of New York Press, 1989), 29–62, 32.

2. IN SEARCH OF THE LOST ATLANTIS: AFTER HURRICANE "NIETZSCHE"

Today, nobody enquires about Nietzsche's question. All scholars in postmodernity build upon it and reveal a clear readiness to extract the answer from Nietzsche's very own thinking (the thing with which Nietzsche himself, in my opinion, may not be happy!). Stanley Grenz exemplifies such an attitude in his belief that by proclaiming the death of selfhood along with the death of God, Nietzsche paves the way for proclaiming the vanity of the existence of any substantial subjectified self that is happy with its self-existence alone. The self has now either been reduced to a mere collection of experiences or actions, or has "disintegrated into nothingness."[50] Grenz's comment not only demonstrates Nietzsche's central place in today's remapping of human thought and reconstructing of the rules and theories of knowing, theological knowledge included. It also summarizes a dominant philosophical position in the twentieth century that amounts to a systematic deconstruction of the history of knowledge by philosophers such as Michel Foucault.

Foucault's overall philosophical hermeneutics (what he himself describes as an "archaeological" excavation in the soil of history) aims mainly at deconstructing the unified, criterial theory of meaning in all sciences, especially the science of historical studies. He achieves this deconstruction by defending the shift in the study of history from "macro" to "micro" historiographic hermeneutics.[51] Foucault traces a similar deconstructive or fragmenting hermeneutics in the historical analysis of other disciplines' emphases on the phenomenon of discontinuity, of the "incidences of interruption."[52] What concerns me here is that Foucault reads the changes in the concept of "self" and "subjecthood" from the same angle of belief in the necessity of deconstructing all unified, criterial forms of the ego's interpretation. With regard to this issue, Foucault founds his claim about the death of the "self" or, more specifically, the "death of the subject," on Nietzsche's "death of God" and his demythologization of the "ego." He invests intensively in Nietzsche's belief that notions like "soul"

---

50. Stanley Grenz, *The Social God and the Relational Self: A Trinitarian Theology of the Imago Dei* (Louisville and London: Westminster John Knox, 2001), 123–25; referring to Robert C. Solomon, "Continental Philosophy Since 1750: The Rise and Fall of the Self," in *A History of Western Philosophy* (Oxford: Oxford University Press, 1988), 7:126.

51. Foucault, *The Archaeology of Knowledge and Discourse on Language*, 3. "Beneath the rapidly changing history of governments, wars, and famines, there emerge other, apparently unmoving histories: the history of sea routes, the history of corn or of gold mining, the history of drought and of irrigation, the history of corn or crop rotation, the history of the balance achieved by the human species between hunger and abundance."

52. Ibid., 4.

and "ego" are imaginary products of the belief in another, no less imaginary, absolute subject. Foucault does this in order to show, as Nietzsche before him, that the modernist definition of the human as an individual, self-enclosed, and fully self-conscious subject is a myth. Foucault emphasizes the claim of the death of the self in the context of his major attack against structuralism by taking Nietzsche's criticism to its ultimate nihilistic extreme, thereby paving the way for the postmodernist transformation of personhood into mere "structure" or relationality.[53]

Foucault mainly argues that the human is by nature composed of empirical, yet also transcendental, characteristics. This makes him "always open, never finally delimited, yet constantly traversed."[54] This nature frees the human from an imposed form of epistemic or ontologically defining judgments. It is no longer allowable to promote fixed possibilities for understanding who *is* the human and how the human person can *be*. There is, rather, an awareness of the prior possibility of misunderstanding who the human *is* or how the person can *be*; an awareness, that is, of "that whole realm of unaccounted-for experiences, in which [the human] does not recognize himself."[55] Foucault, in other words, is claiming that now is the time when, rather than refuting rational thinking altogether, the new *cogito* shows that the "I think" does not "lead to the evident truth of the 'I am.'"[56] The postmodern *episteme* reveals to us that the modern *episteme* that once certified the idea of the self-sufficient individual self appeared to be a mere invention of the human mind. If this *episteme* collapsed, then the image it creates vanishes too: selfhood as modernity describes it is "a face that refuses to appear in the . . . empty mirror."[57] The postmodernist *episteme*, to the contrary, calls for finding rational sense in what was not seen in modernity as thoughtful or thinkable. Anthropologically speaking, postmodernity alleges that what the subject thinks not only points to what the subject knows, but also to what the subject does not know. It points to what the self does not recognize

---

53. This term was used by Edward Said when he described humanity as "the generality of relationships among those words and ideas that we call the humanistic." Edward Said, *Beginnings: Intentions and Methods* (New York: Basic Books, 1975), 286. Said deems this view of humanity a pointer to a structuralist anthropology. However, he does not differ from Foucault in perspective, in spite of the latter's criticism of structuralism, insofar as both view the self as a collection of relations.

54. Michel Foucault, *The Order of Things: An Archaeology of the Human Sciences* (London and New York: Routledge, 2002), 351.

55. Ibid., 352.

56. Ibid., 355.

57. Taylor, *Deconstructing Theology*, 94.

as "I am." Selfhood lies in absence and not in presence, in the disappearance of individuality and its dissolving into total relationality and absolute sociality.

Within this new framework of selfhood's understanding, of the understanding of "I am," the claim that the self is or has a "being" or an "essence" is no longer affirmed, but is rather deemed questionable and even superficial.[58] The modernist anthropology that was formed after a slavish belief in a static *cogito* is as such the bondage that we need to release the human from, says Foucault. The myth of the sovereignty of the human being that lies in the act of thinking, as a single, self-sufficient "I," should now be abolished by the fact of human finitude,[59] which reveals that the self is by nature prone to nihilism and death.

Foucault constructs his conviction of the death of the self on the basis of privileging "otherness" and "specialty" over "sameness" and "generality." By doing this, he endeavors to show that the human is no longer the "oldest nor the most constant problem that has been posed for human knowledge . . . [the human] is an invention of recent date, and one perhaps nearing its end."[60] Foucault calls for the exposure of this fact by way of destroying the anthropology of modernity at its very foundations. He praises Nietzsche in particular because he regards him as the father of this destruction, who started the war alone before the troops of the postmodernist soldiers even congregated on the battlefield. Nietzsche's powerful, pioneering impact on contemporary thought lies, in Foucault's opinion, in his good news of the "superman" (*Übermensch*), because in preaching the rise of the superman and in nothing else, Nietzsche declares the "imminence of the death of [the human]."[61] Foucault concludes from this that "one now can certainly wager that [the human] would be erased like a face in sand at the edge of the sea."[62]

Foucault's view gained the support of many other contemporary continental philosophers. One of them is Jacques Derrida, who goes even further than his French compatriot in claiming that the thinking of the end of the self-fulfilled, self-enclosed image of personhood is always already prescribed even in the metaphysical discourse about the truth of the human.[63] The question

---

58. Foucault, *The Order of Things*, 354.

59. Ibid., 371–73.

60. Ibid., 386–87. See also Stanley Grenz, *The Social God and the Relational Self: A Trinitarian Theology of the Imago Dei* (Louisville and London: Westminster John Knox, 2001), 130–33ff.

61. Foucault, *The Order of Things*, 373.

62. Ibid., 422.

63. Jacques Derrida, "The Ends of Man," in *Margins of Philosophy*, trans. Alan Bass (Brighton, UK: Harvester, 2004), 121.

of meaning or truth, according to Derrida, should no longer be grounded on a thinking of being that is present metaphysically in an absolute belief in an existing being called "*the* human" or in a clearly marked humanism. In order to show that this is the case, Derrida similarly adopts Nietzsche's definition of the "superman" as that which makes up the illusion of the idealist understanding of humanism, before he (Derrida) then goes definitely beyond the speculative question of "humanhood," actively forgetting "being" and any concept of "self" or of "subject."[64]

Derrida argues for the need to break away from the enslavement to an almost demonic understanding of human "self," in which modernity caged the Western world. He claims that deconstructing this image of self is possible by means of contrasting the core of Christianity with the Platonic conception of the soul that dominates Western societies. At the center of Derrida's call is an attempt to deconstruct religion as this state of standing firm in obedience to the responsibility of a free self. Religion should rather be transformed into a responsible move beyond the relation to self into relating in ultimate alterity to the Good, to what Christianity calls the *mysterium tremendum*.[65] Derrida claims that coming to terms with this form of responsibility happens when the West breaks radically with its Greco-Roman politics and values, and restores the Christian notion of "responsibility" that is announced by Christianity's call for relationship between humans and the *mysterium tremendum*. The West, in other words, Derrida continues, should become truly Christian and exceed its Platonism, for "what has not yet arrived to or happened to Christianity is Christianity. Christianity has not yet come to Christianity."[66] By "come to Christianity," Derrida is not calling for Christianizing Western society or proselytizing the non-Christian inhabitants of the West. Such a form of religiosity is actually deemed bad sacralization and demonic irresponsibility by Derrida. "Christianity" connotes here the subject of Christian faith, the idea of God the *mysterium tremendum*—and so neither the believing followers of this faith, nor this faith's doctrinal discourse. By stretching out beyond the realm of Platonic obsession with "relation among equals" toward "relation to a transcendent Good," the human soul, Derrida claims, would emancipate itself

---

64. Ibid., 135–36. Although one can argue that both Derrida and Foucault refuse to describe themselves as postmodernist, I side with David West's belief that Foucault and Derrida "provide the most immediate point of entry in [the postmodernist] mode of thought." West, *Introduction to Continental Philosophy*, 191.

65. Jacques Derrida, "Secrets of European Responsibility," in *The Gift of Death*, trans. David Wills (Chicago and London: University of Chicago Press, 1995), 1–34.

66. Ibid., 28.

from the present and appeal to the future as a promise or a "gift" that lies in an "other." Seeking this "gift" is liberation to the human soul, because it takes the self beyond the boundaries of "at-hand," "under-control," and "in-place" into what is always "not a present," always free.

This liberation from the limits of the self by seeking after a "gift" is best reflected in Christianity, as Derrida argues, because in the idea of the *mysterium tremendum*, this gift is not another object the human can capture by means of conceptual definition. It is, rather, a personhood, a personal other, who "fixes [the soul] in his gaze while at the same time remaining beyond the reach of the gaze of that soul."[67] From the gift-hood of this personal *mysterium tremendum*, the human learns how to become a gift as such, a gift that exists in the first place when it "withdraws, hides, in fact sacrifices itself in order to give." The self reconciles with itself, becomes its soul, when it surrenders to a state of death, of living in anguish and hope, "trembling in the consciousness of sin and offering one's whole being in the sacrifice of repentance."[68] When Christianity comes to the Christianity of the *mysterium tremendum*, the human would consider, maybe for the first time in centuries, the value for human well-being of the Christian association of the value of responsibility with a readiness to be open fully to "a person such as an absolute being who transfixes [us], takes possession of [us], holds [us] in its hand and in its gaze"; as this infinite other, that is, who "first comes across [us], it falls upon [us]."[69] It throws us right into the lap of God's "gift of death," Derrida says, into the arms of which alone the self experiences a responsible "dying for the other."[70]

---

67. Ibid., 25, citing from Jan Patočka, "La Civilisation Technique," 116.

68. Derrida, "Secrets of European Responsibility," 31; and Jan Patočka, "La Civilisation Technique Est-Elle Civilisation de Déclin, et Pourquoi?," in *Essais Hérétiques sur la Philosophie de l'Histoire* (Lagrasse: Verdier, 1981); English translation: J. Patočka, "Is Technological Civilization a Civilization in Decline, and If So, Why?," in *Heretical Essays on the Philosophy of History*, trans. Erika Abrams (Prague: Peltice, 1975), 117.

69. Derrida, "Secrets of European Responsibility," 32–33. Let us keep in mind here that Derrida would not adopt the onto-theological or metaphysical implications and variations doctrinal theology adopts when using the same language as Derrida. He would rather promote a Heideggerian rejection of onto-theological meaning of the "infinite other" and would see the accurate description of this latter in Heidegger's notion of *Dasein*. For Derrida, the "infinite other" does not lie over there, outside me, as a wholly self-differentiated, self-existing reality. Rather, as Heidegger says, it "comes *from me* while falling upon me; it comes *out of me* as it comes across me" (italics are mine). Heidegger, *Being and Time*, trans. John Macquarrie and E. Robinson (New York: Harper & Row, 1962), § 57, 275 (Eng. 320). This, anyhow, is beside the point I am deriving from Derrida's attention to otherness that opens the soul up to what lies beyond its limited self.

3. OTHERNESS, IMMANENCE, AND THE IDEA OF THE INFINITE: THE PARADIGM-SHIFTING OF EMMANUEL LEVINAS

One of the most complete attempts to exceed the idea of "self-sufficient self" and attend to otherness and relationality, from which Derrida and Foucault derived their views on otherness, is offered by Emmanuel Levinas. In his book *Humanism of the Other*, Levinas calls for a paradigm shift away from understanding the self through a hermeneutics of the self that circles around egoistic needs to a different hermeneutics of the self that centralizes orientation toward the other. Levinas believes that the Western world has long followed a Platonic thought-form that mistakenly purifies thought from cultural and linguistic particularities, and views the human "other" as the mere expression of an image needed for the ego's coming to terms with itself—an absolute image, that is, that lies innately within the boundaries of the ego as such. Reducing "other" into a mere image within the self itself, according to Levinas, leads to a lethal reduction of the "self" as such into a suffocating, even deadly, hermetically sealed sphere. Elsewhere, Levinas expresses this consequence in the following words:

> The subject is in the accusative, without recourse in being, expelled from being, outside of being, like the one in the first hypothesis of *Parmenides*, without a foundation, reduced to itself, and this without condition. In its own skin. Not a rest under a form, but tight in its skin, encumbered and as it were stuffed with itself, suffocating under itself, insufficiently open, forced to detach itself from itself, to breathe more deeply all the way, forced to dispossess itself to the point of losing itself.[71]

For Levinas, the subject's imprisonment under its own skin tortures the self, throws subjectivity into self-hostage instead of allowing the self to be itself or to concede that subjectivity as such lies in "undergoing *for* the other," not "*from* the other"; lies in "otherwise than essence," "otherwise than being."[72]

---

70. Derrida, "Secrets of European Responsibility," 33. Derrida intriguingly remarks that by immersing itself in its Platonic rejection of mystery, its political disallowance of the mystical, and its Greco-Roman negligence of the "link between responsibility and the keeping of a secret," the West is too busy to realize that "it takes very little to envisage an inevitable passage from the *democratic* (in the Greek sense) to the *totalitarian*" (ibid., 34).

71. Emmanuel Levinas, *Otherwise Than Being, or Beyond Essence*, trans. Alphonso Lingins (Pittsburgh: Duquesne University Press, 1998), 110.

72. Ibid., 11.

Levinas finds the practical demonstration of Platonic thinking in the conventional understanding of philosophy as the science of thinking about the "needs" of the ego, the ego's occupation with self-anxiety, self-identification, self-happiness, and "assimilation of the world to itself."[73] It is, however, in the obsession with the journey toward the inner self, in the seeking to see *within* the eternal law of moral self (Fichte), or in the abidance in the truth within the boundaries of human reason alone (Kant), that the human discovers that "all that is human is *outside*."[74] The rigorousness of the human mind in questioning itself, distrusting its listening to itself, is not enough to free the human from the illusion called "the individual, self-sufficiently aware subject." In fighting transcendence and infinity, modernity imprisons the concept of "self" in a cage of mythically transcendentalized, oversubjectified relationality. It kills in the human any manifestation of personhood that images the ego's desire for others. The demythologization of what Martin Heidegger calls our "metaphysicalization of being" itself needs demythologization. The deconstruction of phenomenological relationality itself needs deconstruction. The actions of modernity are actually "hampered by the technique destined to make it easy and effective."[75] What is supposed to embrace the world is actually leading it to disintegration. "The 'deep inside' is no longer a world";[76] no longer *the* world, no longer what constitutes the worldliness of the world, no longer what makes meaning meaningful, personal life "personal," life a better place to be, a brand new world.

Levinas believes that the time is ripe now for the deconstruction of the metanarrative of the absolute human self. He thus argues that the Platonic form of immortal epistemology is now completely defeated, because it is not more philosophically tenable or plausible to search for a premeditated abstract human in me. Such a universalized metanarrative is now philosophically countered by a growing respect for the cultures and historical settings in which individuals stand and the linguistic means by virtue of which they express themselves.[77] The world now inescapably acknowledges that

---

73. Emmanuel Levinas, *Humanism of the Other*, trans. Nidra Poller (Urbana and Chicago: University of Illinois Press, 2006), 59, 62.

74. Ibid., 29. "Need is precisely return, the Ego's anxiety for self, egoism, the original form of identification, assimilation of the world in view of coincidence with self, in view of happiness."

75. Ibid., 59.

76. Ibid., 61.

77. Ibid., 37.

to apperceive for signification a situation that precedes culture, to apperceive language from revelation of the Other . . . in the gaze of [the human] sighting a [human] precisely as abstract [human] disengaged from all culture in the nakedness of his face, means returning in a new way to Platonism. It also allows for ethical judgments of civilization.[78]

Against this, Levinas calls for reunderstanding philosophically the notion of "desire to otherness," along with deconstructing philosophy's refusal of engagement in thinking the "Other" and its indifference about and misunderstanding of otherness, resorting instead to what Levinas describes as imaging a Ulyssesan "complacency in the same."[79] The sin of philosophy is its attempt to absorb all forms of otherness in "the same," its neutralization of all otherness.[80]

Instead of reducing the other's otherness into an element of the ego's self-fulfillment—philosophically expressed by the focus on "need"—Levinas calls for acknowledging the otherness of the other; acknowledging, that is, our desire for an otherness that is as such beyond our preconceptions and ontological boundaries. Philosophy should now be the science of understanding the *desire* of going to the other before us as a reality that is "not included in the totality of being that is expressed," but rather "arises behind all collection of being, as the one to whom I express what I express, I find myself facing the Other. He is neither a cultural signification nor a simple given."[81] Levinas calls for

---

78. Ibid., 38. On the same page, Levinas claims that "neither things nor the perceived world nor the scientific world allows us to connect with the standards of the absolute. Those are all cultural works, bathed in history. But moral standards are not embarked in history and culture." On this view I ask: Why are these moral standards not bathed in history and embarked in culture? Is not judgment as such, be it moral also, shaped to a noticeable extent, in its linguistic and cognitive shape at least, by human appraisal that is culturally colored (if not shaped)? Is Levinas forming a metanarrative, a standard concept of moral standards, after all?

79. Ibid., 26. "[P]hilosophy's itinerary still follows the path of Ulysses whose adventure in the world was but a return to his native island—complacency in the same, misunderstanding of the Other."

80. Ibid., 25.

81. Ibid., 30. For a partially similar attention to personhood as an outcome of real interaction with otherness within the context of culture and distinction, read Philip Hefner, "*Imago Dei*: The Possibility and Necessity of the Human Person," in *The Human Person in Science and Theology*, Niels Henrik Gregersen et al., Grand Rapids: Eerdmans, 2000), 73–94. Hefner, for instance, states that "personhood is achieved through our acting upon the physical, biological and cultural materials that we have inherited, so as to establish . . . an understanding of the self's relation to the world in which it lives and to the people in that world . . . the person consequentially emerges as both biological and cultural" (ibid., 73). Hefner

approaching the "Other" as a particular partner in a "face-to-face" relationship, and not in from-within processes of self-actualization. The "Other" is that reality which puts us and our knowing of "other-ness," as well as of self, into question, faces our individualistic, cognitive, existential, and emotional complacency with challenges that stem from the innate *a priori* desire in human nature for relational existence with the different.[82]

At the crossroad of separating personhood from relationality and caging it in individualism, philosophy and theology cannot escape Levinas's question: "is it really evident that 'I is another' means alteration, alienation, betrayal of self, strangeness of self, and servitude to that stranger?"[83] Opening up before the other, acknowledging relationality as the blood in the vines of personhood, is the door of the self to its essential retrieval of its inherent vulnerability; this vulnerability makes us stand naked before the other, fully and passively surrendering to his or her pain and wounds as if they are ours; as if the others are us. This is the core of subjectivity. This is personhood to the bones. Vulnerability is the address of the self's lost shore of fulfillment; it is the end of our Ulyssesan journey back home. It is this "aptitude . . . for 'being beaten'; for 'getting slapped' . . . without introducing any deliberate seeking of suffering or humiliation."[84] Intellectual sincerity and rational self-complacency lie in this form of vulnerability for and before the other. It makes the human "discover oneself totally defenseless"; makes him obsessed with others and with approaching them; makes him suffer for others, that is, "[take] care of [them], bear [them], be in [their] place, consume oneself by [them]."[85] The self, in other words, no longer finds itself in the image of Ulysses, who strives to return home where he is again what he was already. The self is now imaged in the figure of Ahasverus, the rebellious angel in Stefan Heym's novel *The Wandering Jew* who is cursed by God because he did not open his door to the crucified, tortured Messiah (the ideal other) and refused to offer him shelter and help.[86] The fallen

---

calls for a personhood grounded in triadic relationship with God, the world, and the other as thou (ibid., 83–87).

82. Michael Welker perceptively spots the postmodernist concern about being with others and the eagerness for personal, relational self-ness in Western culture in the phenomenon of the eagerness for publicity that characterizes sport and music: "It is not without reason that nowadays competitive sports and electronic popular music are the forms in which individuals can become 'public persons' with an extra large realm of resonance. The public persons in competitive sports and entertainment music mirror the way in which current societies search and long for 'the person.'" Welker, "Is the Autonomous Person of European Modernity a Sustainable Model of Human Personhood?" (ibid., 100).

83. Ibid., 62.

84. Ibid., 63.

85. Ibid., 64.

self is now destined like Ahasverus to live in eternal wandering; with no shelter, no settlement, no final destination. The only difference is that while Ahasverus's wandering is an eternal curse, the human self's wandering after its own self in the form of otherness is considered *the* only hope for the self to *be*, to acquire meaning: wandering eternally and homelessly *is* salvation; is selfhood.

Through focus on otherness, Levinas draws attentions to the mistake of transcendental subjectivity, which is not in the attempt to signify the transcendental properties of the apperception of the self that lies in "I think" or self-thinking, but rather in denying the dimension of "immanence" that makes the state of "presence with" inherent to the core of human consciousness. For Levinas, this awareness of the notion of "immanence" is emancipation to philosophy from unproductive classical metaphysics. It is what discloses clearly the fact that "philosophy is not only knowledge of immanence, it is immanence itself."[87] Transcendence, then, is nothing other than immanence subjectified, immanence present—immanence as the representation of the presence with the other, or of presence as otherness.

If transcendence is substantially characterized by immanence, and if philosophy's subject matter is no less than immanence embodied in otherness, religious discourse on "God" and its meaning can then be part of philosophical thinking. The "God" of religious experience can be part of the content of philosophical thinking insofar as it pertains to the idea of immanence; insofar, that is, as it has "a meaning that refers to a discourse, to a manifestation of presence."[88] The notion of "God" can maintain a value and relevance to human thinking and self-awareness only if it names a transcendent state of otherness that immanently comes to and abides within the human reasoning about the state of "I think." Only when "God" names an experience of an immanent state of "being with," "presence in," or "presence for" can "God" be valid to human subjective knowing. Instead of the modernist "'God' is relevant to self-awareness," the postmodern mind states that "'God' is the name of the stage of the coming to mind of the immanent state of otherness."

Levinas believes that this new understanding of "God" from the concept of "immanence" not only balances the dimension of transcendence in the philosophical understanding of subjectivity that lies in "I think." It equally balances the theological/religious discourse on the experience of the "infinite," in that it frees the idea of "God" from the limitation of the idea of "being."

---

86. Stefan Heym, *The Wandering Jew* (Evanston, IL: Northwestern University Press, 1981).

87. Emmanuel Levinas, *Of God Who Comes to Mind*, trans. Bettina Bergo (Stanford: Stanford University Press, 1998), 61.

88. Ibid., 62.

"God" is no longer under the mercy of the process of passing "from the idea of being." The idea of God, Levinas says, does not signify now "God in me, but it is already God breaking up the consciousness that aims at ideas, already differing from all content."[89] "God" is now the name of otherness, whose immanent presence in me lies in being a "wholly other" to my finite ideas; wholly other than my encompassing of "God." In other words, it names the state of transcendence in me that lies not in enclosure and self-encompassing, but in the "non-indifference of the infinite for thought: not in the placing of the infinite in thought, but wholly other than the thought."[90] "God/infinite" is for Levinas the linguistic expression of the means of emancipation for human subjectivity from the cage of "essence" and "being." The subjectivity of the self no longer draws its meaning from "essence" or "being." The "otherwise," wherein lies human kinship and the self's difference from the other, exists now in the realization within one's very own self of the immanence of a relationality that lies in otherness.[91]

Be that as it may, the journey of the self toward itself—that is, its fulfillment as a self—finds its correct final destination not in transcending relationality with the infinite state of otherness, but in this very infinite state of otherness per se. The infinite state of otherness is not a cause of self-estrangement or self-denial in the form of losing one's self because of the presence with an infinite other. It is, rather, the passage of the self toward real self-fulfillment because the infinite state of otherness names the state of immanence that the self needs to fulfill its presence as a self. The infinite is no longer against the self, because "God" names the state of "immanence-to-oneself-by-means-of-otherness" that is already in us, already within the self. This is the meaning of Levinas's saying "the difference between the infinite and the finite is a non-indifference of the infinite with regard to the finite, and is the secret of subjectivity." This is also the meaning of Levinas's emphasis that the incomprehensibility of the infinite by the finite is just "a verbal abstraction" that does not "amount to saying that the infinite is not finite." It is only a manner of speech that expresses cognitively how the idea of infinity "wakes thought up"; "affects thought by simultaneously devastating it and calling it up."[92]

Be that as it may, the infinite is not a being relating to the finite from outside. The infinite/God is the name of the state of "immanence-as-otherness" that innately lies in the finite ("in-finite") and is inherent to its subjective

---

89. Ibid., 63.
90. Ibid., 63.
91. Levinas, *Otherwise Than Being*, 176–77.
92. Ibid., 65–66.

thinking-self in its transcendence or wholeness. Apart from this notion, Levinas argues, the idea of relationship is not relational enough, because it does not allow "I think" and "be present to myself" to coexist together as equally constitutive of the transcendence of subjectivity.[93] The ideas of "God" and "infinite" matter to the human self insofar as they are expressive of a state of relationality that lies in me; that names my self-fulfillment; that relates me to my subjectivity as if this latter is an otherness that immanently abides in me. "God" here, in Levinas's words, "is pulled out of objectivity, out of presence and out of being. He is neither object nor interlocutor. His absolute remoteness, his transcendence, turns into my responsibility . . . for the other."[94] In this case, by gaining consciousness of the immanence of otherness to one's finite self, the human is not drawn into a relationship with an external other called God or the infinite, but driven into participation in, becoming part of, *an event* of relationality that, as Levinas says, "in some manner unfolds in appearing—or, in manifestation . . ."[95] For Levinas, as Sonia Sikka correctly realizes, it is the human face that makes the dimension of the infinite opened-forth; therefore, there is no knowing of the infinite or of "God" apart from the human.[96] No wonder that Levinas sees his project standing on the riverbank of Husserlian phenomenology,[97] rather than on theology, though he speaks about "wholly other," "infinite," and "God."[98]

In postmodernity, attention is paid strictly to the event of presentation or re-presentation that originates from this immanent relatedness to transcendence in terms of otherness. The event of representation, of the appearance as such,

93. Ibid., 66. "How is transcendence thinkable as a relationship, if it must exclude the ultimate—and the most formal—co-presence, which the relationship guarantees to its terms?"

94. Ibid., 69.

95. Ibid., 101.

96. Sonia Sikka, "Questioning the Sacred: Heidegger and Levinas on the Locus of Divinity," in *Modern Theology* 3, no. 14 (1998): 229–32, 311. Interestingly, Sikka accuses Levinas of imposing another violence by his very attack on the immoral violence of knowledge in philosophical reasoning. Levinas's own rhetoric, Sikka argues, "tacitly asserts that his mapping of ethical experience is the only possible one, the only truly ethical one, so that any domain of religious thought or sensibility not contained in this map must on that account be unethical, or at least non-ethical and thus indifferent to the Other and to justice" (ibid., 312).

97. On Husserlian phenomenology, read for example Rudolf Bernet, Iso Kern, and Eduard Marbach, *An Introduction to Husserlian Phenomenology* (Evanston, IL: Northwestern University Press, 1999); André de Muralt, *Idea of Phenomenology: Husserlian Exemplarism*, trans. Garry L. Breckon (Evanston, IL: Northwestern University Press, 1988); and Dan Zahavi, *Husserl's Phenomenology* (Redwood, CA: Stanford University Press, 2003).

98. Ibid., 312. Sikka strongly questions whether Levinas's project is really phenomenological or fulfills the demands implied in the term "phenomenology" (ibid., 313ff.).

is under the spotlight now, rather than those beings who appear in the event. The "I" of each side of the relation is now left behind, abandoned, and the relationship as such, its eventuality, its "experience," is what matters, what counts. "Being," Levinas says invoking Husserl, is now to be considered as "*merely* a modality of perception."[99] It is one of the forms that name the event of presentation or re-presentation in its experienceability. This is the core of Levinas's distinction between "relating to God" and "relating that can be interpreted only by means of the word 'God'" when he says

> [i]t would be advisable nevertheless to ask here whether it is a question of a transcendence toward God or a transcendence out of which a word such as "God" alone reveals its meaning. That this transcendence be produced from the (horizontal?) relationship with the other means neither that the other man is God, nor that God is a great Other.[100]

This intellectual paradigmatic shift from the ego, or the single, self-centered self, to the structure of the relational framework in which any reality, human or not, exists in orientation toward a desire of being with an-other is not only philosophical but equally theological in nature and occurrence, as Levinas's association of otherness with the ideas of "God" and "infinity" clearly show. While my concern is the theological dimensions and ramifications of this concern about the relational orientation of existence that is expressed in what Levinas calls "the desire to approach the other" in the first place, it is still necessary to locate the theological emphasis on the notion of "relationality that lies in otherness" within its wider philosophical context by talking briefly about the emphasized paradigm of "mutual participation" that seems to enjoy central place in postmodern epistemology.

4. "Let Me Be 'Otherness,'" or the Philosophical Paradigm of "Mutual Participation"

After the long-term domination of the notion of the "individual, self-related subject" in modernity, postmodernity marks the age of the philosophical and theological centrality of the notion of "relation" or "communication." This concern about relationality marks the shift in postmodern anthropology from

---

99. Levinas, *Otherwise Than Being*, 103.
100. Ibid., 108.

the modernist turn to the self or the subject into a clear critical rejection of the subject and a proclamation of its death. Individual personhood can no longer be taken for granted and can no longer be above investigation. The self is now challenged by the question: Is there really a self-sufficient, totally individual self? This underlies the postmodern rejection of any claimed standard, criterial approach to the self as an objectively and rationally defined subject. It is an assault on ideal stereotypes and metanarratives of personhood. One can say that postmodernism signifies an extreme emphasis on new connotations of "personhood," which, opposed to individuality and self-enclosure, allow the human to know who he is *only* in relation to others.[101] "Subject" or "person" now means ultimately and totally "relationality" or communicative actions. They mean that the self is a collection of relational movements in nature.

Ted Peters, the American Lutheran theologian, reflects the same postmodern passion for relationality and shows its reactionary manner to the fragmentational character of notions like "individualism" and "objectivism" by claiming that voices from many quarters around the world can be heard crying out, "enough of this! let's put the world back together again!"[102] The cardinal principle in today's world, Peters notes, is that "everything is related to everything else," and that "a philosophy of holism can overcome this tendency toward fragmentation."[103] Elsewhere, Peters describes this new anthropological understanding by saying that in postmodernity,

> [g]one is the image of the self-defined and autonomous individual; the island of personhood standing over against society. We now understand ourselves more interactively, recognizing how even our internal consciousness interacts with significant influences around us.[104]

---

101. Meic Pearse, "Problem? What Problem? Personhood, Late Modern/Postmodern Rootlessness and Contemporary Identity Crises," in *Evangelical Quarterly* 1, no. 77 (2005): 5–11, 9. This correctly reflects that "we are simply identifying some undesirable outcomes of certain historical processes, not attacking those processes root and branches."

102. Ted Peters, *God the World's Future: Systematic Theology for a New Era*, 2nd ed. (Minneapolis: Fortress Press, 2000), 17.

103. Ibid. 18.

104. Ted Peters, *God as Trinity: Relationality and Temporality in Divine Life* (Louisville: Westminster John Knox, 1993), 15.

Calvin Schrag describes succinctly the impact of the postmodern rejection of the modernist trends of totalization and unification of human experience and of the meaning of self when he says:

> Questions about self-identity, the unity of consciousness, and centralized and goal-directed activity have been displaced in the aftermath of the dissolution of the subject. If one cannot rid oneself of the vocabulary of self, subject, and mind, the most that can be asserted is that the self is multiplicity, heterogeneity, difference and ceaseless becoming, bereft of origin and purpose. Such is the manifestation of postmodernity on matters of the human subject as self and mind.[105]

The denial of the self-enclosed self by means of a heightened emphasis on the relational nature of life experiences reaches its extreme in suggestions like Derek Parfit's call for replacing speech about "self" or "I" with speech about a collection of experiences that belong to itself and point to its very own existence or nonexistence only. Instead of saying "I shall be dead," I must say, Parfit suggests, "there will be no future experiences that will be related, in certain ways, to these present experiences."[106] Such extreme empiricist reductionism articulates why the postmodern alternative understandings of "self" and "subject," and ultimately of the notion of "person," are based on a "praxis-oriented" view of selfhood, that is, according to Schrag, "defined by its communicative practices, oriented toward an understanding of itself in its discourse, its action, its being with others, and its experience of transcendence."[107] Serene Jones adds to this that the recent studies of the human self strongly and clearly show that "important dimensions of our existence that we previously considered 'natural' are, in fact, much more open to human interpretation and change than had once been believed." "The character of our embodied relationality," Jones concludes, "thus becomes even more marvelous in its complexity and its possibilities."[108]

---

105. Calvin O. Schrag, *The Self after Postmodernity* (New Haven and London, UK: Yale University Press, 1997), 8.

106. Derek Parfit, *Reasons and Persons* (Oxford: Oxford University Press, 1984), 281. See also Gunton, *The Promise of Trinitarian Theology*, 84ff. Gunton describes Parfit's analysis of personhood a "mammoth exercise in deconstruction" (ibid., 88).

107. Schrag, *The Self after Postmodernity*, 9.

108. Serene Jones and Clark Williamson, "What's Wrong with Us? Human Nature and Human Sin," in *Essentials of Christian Theology*, ed. William C. Placher (Louisville and London: Westminster John

This new replacement of "self" with "relation" is not limited to anthropology. It is also symptomatic of the methodological shift in understanding the nature of reality; an understanding that is pointed at in the writings of many philosophers from today's intellectual sphere. Jürgen Habermas's philosophical project, for example, reflects this epistemological shift.

Throughout his various writings, Habermas calls for a new hermeneutical paradigm of mutual understanding between two vocal and active subjects as an alternative to the paradigm of one-way understanding of objects by means of a referential, criterial method of rationalization.[109] The method of understanding by means of exploring the meaning and the reality of things by virtue of the rational, existential, or sensual consciousness of the knower *alone* has been exhausted, according to Habermas. It is now, therefore, the right time for developing a new paradigm of understanding based on mutual interaction between two simultaneously "knower" and "known" subjects.[110] This mutual participation transforms the subject's self-understanding relation by making the external world, to which the subject relates, a live participant and correspondent, rather than an objective static entity that is approached by neutral observation.[111] The transcendental and the empirical, the self-consciousness and that which escapes it, the procedures of reconstruction and self-critique as well as absolutism and relativism are no longer incompatible poles in such a mutual participation form of cognition. This cognition is "co-given" in such a way that evades any polar thematization.[112] Knowing any form of life requires relating to other living entities according to the actual traces of this fashion of living in history. In other words, the essence of things, the "is-ness" of something lies in its historical interaction with others. It is even the

---

Knox, 2003), 133–57, 145. Jones expresses the belief that underlies this new conviction: "The solitary individual—the wolf raised child, or a Robinson Crusoe who was born in his desert island—cannot be fully human. Just as God is God in the relations among the persons of the Trinity, so humanness involves relatedness—to other humans, to our environment, to God" (ibid., 134).

109. Jürgen Habermas, *The Philosophical Discourse of Modernity: Twelve Lectures*, trans. Frederick Lawrence (Cambridge: Polity, 1987), 295.

110. Ibid., 296. For a detailed analysis of Habermas's paradigm of mutual participation and concept of communicative action, see Habermas, "Remarks on the Concept of Communicative Action," in *Social Action*, ed. G. Seebass and R. Tuomela (Boston and Dordrecht: Kluwer, 1985), 151–78, and Habermas, *Theory of Communicative Action*, trans. Thomas McCarthy (Cambridge: Polity, 1987).

111. Habermas, *Philosophical Discourse of Modernity*, 296. "[E]go stands within an interpersonal relationship that allows him to relate to himself as participant in an interaction from the perspective of alter. And indeed this reflection undertaken from the perspective of the participant escapes the kind of objectification inevitable from the reflexively applied perspective of the observer."

112. Ibid., 299–301.

outcome of the timely, contextual, linguistic participation in mutual interaction. Relational, rather than individual, existence should now be the ground of "is-ness," not only the ground of "understanding."

Emphasizing the paradigm of communicativity, according to Habermas, pulls philosophical thought out of the modernist trap of subject-centered rationality. More importantly still, Habermas believes that doing this *completes* the project of modernity rather than displaces it. More specifically, it replaces the modernist belief in the comprehensive reason (i.e., Hegel) by means of another equally modernist belief that reason can only exist and gain necessity by virtue of the other.[113] Completion here does not mean succumbing to, and preserving, the same subject-centered paradox of exclusive-inclusive reason (i.e., something Habermas believes that Heidegger and Foucault maintain).[114] It means reinterpreting the relation between subject and reality on the basis of another modernist claim that has not yet been given proportionate attention, namely the belief that reason can only exist in communication and participation. The point here is that the cure of the modernist subject-centered disease exists already in the modernist philosophical first-aid kit. By the "mutual participation" paradigm we can show that Kant's distinction between pure reason, practical reason, and judgment is not wrong insofar as its desire about pointing to the distinction between these three forms of knowledge is concerned. Kant's distinction needs integration, however, by relating these three forms of reasoning mutually together. So, instead of dialectic and dichotomy, Habermas calls for prioritizing participation and intercommunication.

Many philosophers share Habermas's interest in a "mutual participation" paradigm. They concur with his conviction that this new paradigm helps philosophers relate theory to practice, preserving thereby, as Habermas once said, the philosophical thinking from "illusions of independence and opens its eyes to a spectrum of validity-claims extending beyond the assertoric."[115]

---

113. Ibid., 305; a belief that Habermas detects in post-Hegelian thinkers' criticism of Hegel, e.g., Marx, Nietzsche, Boehme, and others.

114. Ibid., 308–9. "Whether in form of meditative thought or of genealogy, Heidegger and Foucault want to initiate a *special discourse* that claims to operate *outside* the horizon of reason without being utterly irrational. To be sure, this merely shifts the paradox" (ibid., 308), in that it still considers that which lies outside reason as either a temporal (Heidegger) or a spatial, corporeal (Foucault) mirroring of the reason of the subject. Reason thus "remains tied to the presuppositions of the philosophy of the subject from which it wanted to free itself" (ibid., 309).

115. Jürgen Habermas, *Postmetaphysical Thinking: Philosophical Essays*, trans. William M. Hohengarten (Cambridge, MA and London: MIT Press, 1992), 9.

In his book, *Persons in Relation*, John Macmurray adopts Habermas's paradigm and argues that one of the defects of modern philosophy lies in viewing the human as an egocentric rather than a personal entity. Macmurray writes that through the course of researching the book he discovered that in modern philosophy,

> [t]he thinking self—the self as subject—is the agent of self-negation. In reflection we isolate ourselves from dynamic relations with the other; we withdraw into ourselves, adopting the attitude of spectators, not of participants. We are then out of touch with the world, and for touch we must substitute vision; for a real contact with the other an imagined contact; and for real activity an activity of imagination.[116]

Against this egocentric view of the human self, which is usually escorted in modernity with a view of the "I" as a mere thinking mind rather than an active agent, Macmurray calls for viewing the self as a "personal agent." He thus sets for himself the goal of showing that existing as a self requires being a relational and not only a spectator self. Existence itself is not possible without a personal relation to another person. And since knowing existence is only possible by participating in existence, knowing the existing self can only be tenable by being in a personal relationship with another existing person. It is philosophically essential, as Macmurray believes, to realize that the self exists only in dynamic relation with the other, "for the self is constituted by its relation to the other; that it has its being in its relationship, and that this relationship is necessarily personal."[117] By discerning the formal characteristics of personal relations we come to terms with the being of the self per se. This is not only indicative of the relational nature of being. It is also indicative of the personal nature of philosophical knowledge. Philosophy is not a science in the sense that it observes the other as an object in the world. Philosophy is the form of knowledge that offers knowledge of the self, of being, because it is a relational knowledge, in which the knower knows the other as a personal self by entering into a personal relation with him.[118]

---

116. John Macmurray, *Persons in Relation* (London: Faber & Faber, 1961), 16.

117. Ibid., 17.

118. Ibid., 28 (27ff.). Colin Gunton believes that the relational form of understanding that Macmurray supports already exists in Christian literature in the trinitarian theology of Richard of St. Victor, who, contrary to Augustine, as Gunton argues, points to the formation of personal identity in terms of the person's relations. Gunton, *The Promise of Trinitarian Theology*, 89ff., and Richard of St. Victor, *De*

For many postmodern thinkers, this relational dimension allows for the redemption of metaphysics from the fatal margin it was thrown into in modernity. Two decades after Macmurray, Harold Oliver wrote another book for the purpose of proclaiming this possibility of redemption for metaphysics. Oliver argues that understanding philosophy by acknowledging the necessity of having a relational interaction with another in order to discern one's existence contributes to the recovery of metaphysics' lost appreciation in philosophy. After it was construed an area of knowledge that is restricted to a "transexperiential" transcendent reality, there now comes the time when metaphysics can be seen, on the basis of a relational aspect of knowledge, as the relational field of truth as such. Instead of a metaphysics that drifts in its emphasis to either the pole of the subject (i.e., Idealism) or the pole of the object (i.e., Realism), philosophy as shaped by the notion of "relation" paves the way for a transpolar metaphysics founded on the relation between object *and* subject.[119]

By focusing on "relation," according to Oliver, philosophy can house a new metaphysical language about truth that is free from traditional metaphysical burdening and axiomatic tension between "subject" and "object." This traditional metaphysical trend, Oliver opines, used to look for truth in all the mistaken areas, officializing eventually a polar form of thinking: either being or existence, either subject or object, either reality or theory. The only freedom of philosophy from this archaic polarity is in prioritizing the notion of "relation," which actually makes this polarity assumable in the first place, instead of concentrating on one of the poles and not the other. This means, nevertheless, that the poles are not seen for themselves, but are completely covered up by the focus on the relation that assumes their existence. Such a relational version of metaphysics, as Oliver says, "requires that the poles be viewed as less than fundamental. The poles are subsumed under a higher category by applying to the question of their reality the strict dogma of a universal [relationality]."[120] In his elaboration on the "mutual participation" paradigm, even Habermas does not hesitate in stating a claim similar to Oliver's when he says that in such a form of understanding, the participants no longer originate or master the conditions of their interaction by means of their actions.

Trinitate, 03:3.19. Gunton sees in this a proof that theology is not a projection of other anthropological theories, as Feuerbach claims. The opposite is actually the case: anthropology stems from theology (Gunton, 90–91).

119. Harold Oliver, *A Relational Metaphysics* (The Hague, Boston, and London: Martinus Nijhoff, 1981), 101ff. Oliver states that his understanding of the relational nature of metaphysics is affected by Leibniz's and Whitehead's views without slavishly echoing them.

120. Ibid., 132 (131ff.).

The participants as such become "the *products* of the traditions in which they stand, of the socialization process within which they belong, and of the socialization process within which they grow up."[121]

Such thinking underpins the postmodern conviction that the "being" or the "is" of something is the outcome of and not the *archē* or the ground of its existence in openness to others. The identity of the person lies no longer, then, in the what-ness of the nature or the being of this person. It lies, rather, in *who* this person *becomes* in communion with others. In other words, the social, communal condition is *determinative* of personhood and of the self. This is now obviously an epistemic, conceptual paradigm in postmodernity.[122] It is the determining concept behind the hermeneutics of "self" that goes beyond the modernist view of "ego" that lies in rational and foundational self-mastering.

IV. THE THEOLOGICAL CONVERSION TO PARTICIPATION AND RELATIONALITY

In the excessive attention to "otherness" and "relationship with the other," which Levinas and other postmodernist philosophers propagate, one may find a passage toward the emancipation of "personhood" and "self" from the prison of modernity's notion of "subjectified, self-enclosed, self-sufficient ego." However, there is in this very attention to "relationality" and "otherness" a serious possibility of swallowing the self and its personal particularity by a kind of black hole—of melting into, and conflating with, the other; of being totally immersed in the other's otherness and almost part of it, so that the one's and the other's particularity and otherness (or even beyond-ness) would ultimately vanish. This, if it happens, turns "person" from an existing somebody into just a name or a "number" among many others in a society of "Borg-like" species (an extraterrestrial race in the *Star Trek* universe), whose existence is founded on an ideology of otherness that nullifies particularity by means of a new, post-communist-like fashion of neo-collectivism. This is even more dangerous in theology than in any other field of study, and it takes place when openness to, and relationship with, the other are overcentralized at the expense of self-individuation and distinction—when, that is, the Boethian definition of "person" is only selectively and partially adopted. When, for instance, human relationship with God means becoming part and parcel of God's being and personal identity, consequently turning "God" into the framework of human

---

121. Habermas, *Philosophical Discourse of Modernity*, 299.
122. Grenz, *Social God and Relational Self*, 12.

self-fulfillment, instead of maintaining God's and the human's otherness, or of affirming their individuation by virtue of the relationship between them. In some popular trends of trinitarian theology in postmodernity, this "melting into the other as the means for being one's own real personal self" is implemented in developing an understanding of the trinitarian personhood of God in a manner that turns God into an expression of a network of relationships the human is invited to claim to herself and to incarnate in her life, thus making the triunity of God the narrative (or the metanarrative) of human reconciliation with personal selfhood.

The story of this reductionist theological understanding of personhood starts from the same critical dispensation of the concept of the "self-centered, subjectified self" in the secular sphere of postmodernity. Many theologians have recently developed a robust discourse on the Christian understanding of personhood and relationality in conversation with the postmodernist attention to otherness and relationship. They do this by way of developing new hermeneutics of classical theological notions like "Trinity," "incarnation," and "church,"[123] because they believe that Christian doctrines that are constructed on these basic notions present substantial and reliable interpretations of "relationality" and "openness as otherness" that actually underpin and furnish postmodernist thought. The ambition of recontextualizing postmodernity and proving that this intellectual phenomenon is theologically conditioned has now infected trinitarian theology, too.

Driven by intellectual ambition symptomatic of this tendency, some theologians believe that their focus primarily on the doctrine of the Trinity (and secondarily on the incarnation and the church) can engender a theological correction and criticism of the modernist individualistic concept of "person" and "subjectified self." In 1989, for example, the commission on Christian doctrine in the British Council of Churches issued a report in which it stated clearly that the main purpose behind emphasizing "relationship" in today's theology is to overcome the loss of personhood because of "the pervasive individualism of the Western tradition."[124] What catches the attention in this report's ensuing statements is the emphasis on the appropriateness of the doctrine of the Trinity to defeat this loss of personhood, which does not aim to turn the doctrine of the Trinity into an anthropomorphic discourse "naively importing what we take to be important into the being of God."[125] Rather, the

123. Geoff Thompson and Christiaan Mostert, *Karl Barth: A Future for Postmodern Theology?* (Hindmarsh: Australian Theological Forum, 2000), 50.

124. *The Forgotten Trinity: The Report of the BCC Study Commission on Trinitarian Doctrine Today* (London: British Council of Churches, 1989), 19ff.

goal is to found our human personal identity on the trinitarian personhood of God in such a way that stands firm against "confusing what we are by nature with what we are as free persons"; with what, that is, we are as persons who have retrieved God's image by means and on the basis of his graceful redemptive Trinity.[126]

One should give credit to the commission's attention in this report to the dimensions of grace and otherness as also reflective of God, and not only of the human person. Unfortunately, however, the report's attention to God's grace and otherness is not symptomatic of every postmodernist theological attempt at reforming the understanding of personhood in relation to the triune God. For other theologians, focusing on the Trinity is mainly an attempt to express our human experience and conception of personhood using new, more satisfactory, and less suppressive and individualistic language. In other words, anthropology is still considered the intellectual framework for interpreting the concept of "person" even when the goal is developing a theological understanding of personhood in God. The difference now is the concern about proving that postmodernist anthropology, whether it concedes it or not, stands on theological ground and echoes theological claims. Contrary to any Trinity-based approach to personhood, this anthropocentrically theological shift is virtually shaped by the postmodern conviction that the idea of "self-enclosed subject" is an illusion invented by modernity. The subject, especially the "transcendent subject," is "simply a fictive conglomeration of fragments."[127]

Theology today adopts almost unreservedly the postmodern conviction that "'person' has more to do with relationality than with substantiality, and that the term stands closer to the idea of communion or community than to the conception of the individual in isolation or abstraction from communal embedded-ness."[128] Many recent theologians believe that this newly revived conception is the only one that can shed light on, and give meaning to, the Christian doctrine of the Trinity and can bring this doctrine center-stage as the underpinning criterion of human reasoning in today's intellectual arena. Some theologians, such as Stanley Grenz, still want to give this track a two-dimensional nature by arguing that the revival of the church's trinitarian

---

125. Ibid., 21.
126. Ibid., 24.
127. Ibid., 51.
128. Grenz, *Social God and Relational Self*, 4. Grenz is right in pointing out that this emphasis is the central characteristic of major theological trends like the evangelical, the one of process theology, and the philosophical (ibid., 5).

language would, in turn, readvocate the centrality and priority of anthropology for any theological reflection on the Trinity per se:

> Theological insights regarding the manner in which the three trinitarian persons are persons-in-relation and again their personal identity by means of their inter-relationality hold promise for understanding what it means to be human persons in the wake of the demise of the centered self and the advent of the global soul.[129]

In her book *God as Communion*, Patricia Fox concurs with Grenz's belief when she calls for placing the Trinity center-stage in today's theological, religious, spiritual, and even secular thought about human life and identity. What catches the attention in Fox's proposal, nevertheless, is her call for refocusing on the Trinity as a "*symbol*" that lies at the heart of Christian theological traditional discourse. The Trinity, Fox says, "is a symbol whose time has come" specifically to challenge the "powerful monotheistic image of God as an omnipotent, omniscient male monarch."[130] In order to achieve this goal, Fox correlates between John Zizioulas's and Elizabeth Johnson's trinitarian theologies. She sees in correlating these theologians an example of reconciliation between Eastern and Western Christian hermeneutics, one made by a male and the other by a female. And she claims that this correlation can ultimately serve the purpose of deconstructing on a fundamental level "the destructive power of sexism inherent in Christian theology and praxis."[131] The "Trinity" here is a notional symbolic tool used for the purpose of reimaging and remodeling human nature and existence. It is a means for showing that the salvation of the world from its brokenness (i.e., gender, sexual discrimination, and violence in this case) lies in the very Christian language that modernity rejects. The ultimate concern behind retrieving the symbol of the Trinity from tradition is contributing to the full humanity of all persons, to the full understanding of human existential experiences, life, and world.[132] By pointing

---

129. Ibid., 9.

130. Patricia A. Fox, *God as Communion: John Zizioulas, Elizabeth Johnson, and the Retrieval of the Symbol of the Triune God* (Collegeville, MN: Michael Glazier/Liturgical, 2001), 2. On another attempt to rethink the gender issue theologically (rather than secularly) from the doctrine of the triune God, specifically on the basis of Jürgen Moltmann and Elisabeth Moltmann-Wendel's figuring of a sexually inclusive "he" and "she" triune Godhead, see Sarah Coakley, "The Trinity and Gender Reconsidered," in *God's Life in Trinity*, 133–42. Indispensable also for a complete view of this approach is Johnson's book, *She Who Is*.

131. Fox, *God as Communion*, 18.

to the symbol of the Trinity, the contemporary world, according to Fox, can find a major tool for its pursuit of the meaning of dominant notions in today's world, like "relationality," "difference," "otherness," and "person."[133] Relying on the symbol of the Trinity, Fox concludes, "reinforces and deepens the contemporary 'discovery' that to live fully as a unique person in relation means living a life of inclusive communion with other persons and with all created entities."[134]

Fox's purpose and concern are valid and valuable. Her careful reading of Zizioulas's and Johnson's theological proposals, and her perception of major differences between each one's mindset and logic, is also praiseworthy. Whether or not, however, the attempt at offering the Trinity as the appropriate primal, foundational symbol for interpreting human life and existence represents an attention to God's trinitarian being per se and whether or not it is pursued for the sake of proclaiming God's otherness as a triune personal being are yet to be determined. One wonders what consequences may drive theology to reinforce and deepen what has already been *discovered* by the postmodernist human about the value of communality and relationality. This discovery has not happened abruptly or in a vacuum and is not presupposition-free. This discovery was made upon specific philosophical and intellectual claims that are characteristic of postmodernity, ones that are no less central, for instance, than the rejection of objectivity, selfhood, and otherness as expressions of a reality that exists in itself; in its complete distinction and wholly otherness, from outside the subjective boundaries of the human knower.

If theology's role is to show that its discourse is inherent to the reinforcement and deepening of what has already been discovered in postmodernity, theology is expected also to inhere with the reinforcement and deepening of the philosophical presuppositions that generated this discovery. The Trinity would, eventually, become a symbol in the service of "communion" and "relationality" and of the reduction of "self" and "personhood" to a collective event of relations taking place in history, on one hand, as well as in the service of the indifference to God's being as a

---

132. Ibid., 20–21. I wonder here if Zizioulas's trinitarian thinking, which departs from a strong emphasis on God's ontological otherness and freedom, serves Fox's treatment of the Trinity as symbol. Zizioulas, contrary to Johnson, would probably be hesitant to consider the Trinity as symbol of the complete humanity, though he never undermines God's concern about the human condition, to understand God. He rather moves from God to the human. Though he stresses relationality, Zizioulas is not one of those theologians who, by considering relationality exhaustively constitutive of personhood, reduce God into a model of relational existing that images the fullness of human reality.

133. Ibid., 240.

134. Ibid., 241.

self-existing, personal "Wholly Other" from without human existence, on the other. Symbols are usually used as signifiers that point to something other than themselves. They are valuable in serving certain signified things, not by virtue of themselves. Showing that the Trinity is the "symbol" that expresses what lies at the base of postmodernity's rationale is congenial with its value for serving something else that has already been discovered (i.e., communion and relationality, in this case). But this would inappropriately turn God the Holy Trinity into a mere symbol that expresses something inherent to the texture of human reality. It would be no less than a constitutive symbol, yet it would unfortunately be no more than this either: a symbol within the boundaries of human life alone.

Having in view this construal of the Trinity as the most appropriate linguistic/symbolic *means* for speaking about the human ability to interrelate, it is possible to understand why, while the belief in a personal, infinite being called God is abating alongside ontology, the sense of an awareness of a relation between us and something "outside" us is growing and taking over.[135] This very "communion-centered" notion, however, marks, as I will show in the following chapter, the unfortunate reduction in postmodern trinitarian theology of "personhood" and "subject-hood" to a mere linguistic expression of the human idea of "mutual participation," not only in relation to anthropology but also, and most problematically, in relation to the doctrine of the triune God. In this reduction appears the danger of taking hold of some dominant human concepts and forcefully projecting them onto God.[136] This is done upon the assumption that such a price is worth paying for the sake of proving that these human concepts are in substance theologically conditioned and founded.

The postmodern rejection of the subjectified self, along with the hand-in-hand stress on the inherent relation-centered definition of identity, especially in relation to the theological question of the identity and being of God, is in fact symptomatic of postmodern trinitarian theology since the first half of the last century. Many theologians, from then until now, have dedicated a large portion of their writings to criticizing the deistic transcendentalization of God and call instead for maintaining a clear attestation of God's personal and relational being.

---

135. Sven-Ake Selander, "Human Language between Christian and Secular," in *The Human Image of God*, ed. Hans-Georg Ziebertz et al. (Leiden, Boston, and Köln: Brill, 2001), 126. From this, Selander concludes that "this implies that even if the faith in a personal God is not conscious, a living relation can be maintained between man and the 'pantheistic.'" In this "pantheistic" idea, however, lies the problem of the contemporary defense of the inherent importance of God's presence for humanity's consciousness supported by Selander and others.

136. *The Forgotten Trinity*, 23.

They vehemently argue that theology as the science of God is from A-to-Z a relation-based epistemic arena, in which the knower interacts with an idea of God that expresses a wholly other *relationality*, rather than a static, abstract, and ideal object in the mind or in nature.

Ever since Karl Barth's production of *Church Dogmatics*, many theologians defended the relational nature of God's reality and his knowability by means of and on the basis of the doctrine of the Trinity.[137] They strongly defended the trinitarian nature of God as making the divine essence knowable by virtue of God's relational self-emptying, revealed historically in the Father's sending of his Son in the power of the Holy Spirit. God's triune nature is not an enclosed society of three divine realities of the same Godhead. It is rather an open personal nature in which the Father opens himself toward creatures by means of his two divine arms, the Son and the Spirit. It is this openness of the Trinity that makes God knowable to human beings and makes theology a plausibly metaphysical discipline. One can, in sum, say that almost all postmodern theologians agree with Colin Gunton's accusation that modernity displaced God and sympathize with his claim that "the displacement of God does not and has not given freedom and dignity to the many, but has subjected us to new and often unrecognized forms of slavery."[138]

Having said that, in the remainder of this part of my study I will attempt to show that the more crucial problem in contemporary theology is the trinitarian hermeneutics employed by these theologians. I am inspired by the perceptive criticism Colin Gunton offers on the displacement of God in today's intellectual condition, when he states that while today's theologians are wise to adopt philosophical criticisms against homogenous oneness, as well as the philosophical deconstruction of domination in terms of absolute unification, and to reconstruct theology in the light of these criticism's challenging claims, they are not wise to abandon any acknowledgment of God's divine transcendence because they consider it a threatening, homogenizing form of totalization imposed on the human and her freedom. While postmodern theologians are right in criticizing the Platonic concept of transcendence, they are not right in discarding the Christian concept of transcendence inherent to the doctrine of the trinitarian nature of God. As Gunton correctly reminds us, the Christian theology of transcendence is the one that acknowledges, more

---

137. For good exposition of these theologies see Claude Welch, *In This Name: The Trinity in Contemporary Theology* (New York: Charles Scribner's Sons, 1952), and Samuel M. Powell, *Trinity in German Thought* (Cambridge: Cambridge University Press, 2001).

138. Colin Gunton, *The One, the Three and the Many: God, Creation and the Culture of Modernity* (Cambridge: Cambridge University Press, 1998), 29.

than any other, human independence and freedom by leaving a space between the divine and the human, the divine and the world.[139] The postmodern rejection of transcendence and its total, one-sided emphasis on the transcendent's inherent "immanence" in the human self's subjectivist experience of itself as "otherness" undermines, and eventually misses, this important factor. A totally immanentist theology of the Trinity calls, eventually, for the human's freedom *from* God, rather than for her freedom *with* or *by* God. This last dimension is undermined because the doctrine of the Trinity, as I will argue in the following chapter, is no longer treated as a discourse on the reality of God's "being" and personal identity, but as a discourse on certain symbolic and analogical language that serves the search for a better understanding of human life.

Tossed by the strong waves of postmodern claims and conceptual inquiries, the main, if not the only, concern of a significant number of contemporary trinitarian theologians, as we will see, is to interpret the world and the nature of human life within it by means of trinitarian language.[140] When they call for human freedom by means of an interaction with God, they impose on the doctrine of God a notion of "relational participation" that sacrifices or marginalizes God's freedom and self-distinction for the sake of emphasizing relationality in terms of love and communion. This, in other words, turns God into the ideal human enjoyment of free self. Be that as it may, I hope to show in the next chapter that: 1) "it is not transcendence that is the enemy, but forms of the 'one' that fail to give due space to the many,"[141] and 2) the enemy is the forms of attention to otherness that deny God's transcendent, personal differentiation by overemphasizing relationality and defending otherness as inherent to the human at the expense of God's otherness. It is inarguably crucial to remind theology of the real subject matter of its trinitarian roots, namely to point to God's trinitarian nature in parallel to the Godhead's unity.[142] But it is at least as crucial to maintain a balanced attestation and a coherent *theo*-logical hermeneutics of the divine Trinity, so that we don't deny that the trinitarian nature of God is the ground of his self-distinction before/with the human, and not only of his relationality.

In the following chapter, I will survey trends in trinitarian theology as examples of an inappropriate relationship between theological reasoning and nontheological forms of inquiry. After this, I will point to an alternative

---

139. Ibid., 36.
140. Gunton, *The Promise of Trinitarian Theology*, 26.
141. Ibid., 37.
142. Ibid., 39.

understanding of "relationship" that is, in my view, inherent to the theological tradition of reasoning. I will not present a comprehensive exposition of all the existing trinitarian theologies in today's scholarship. In the past few decades, a vast amount of literature from all denominations and trends of thought has been produced on the Trinity in relation to God's and the human's life. I will therefore pick up a few examples that are relevant to the problem being discussed here.

4

The "Trinity" and the Evaluation of the Theological Re-Conditioning Ambition

I. "Relationship" as Reduction of the Triune Personhood of God

A careful reading of the trinitarian theologies of numerous twentieth-century theologians shows that they were clearly energized by a strong investment of the notion of "relation" in the doctrine of God, in such a manner that overrides another essential notion in the doctrine of the Trinity, the notion of "person." Aware of the foundational importance of declaring "three *hypostases*, one *ousia*" in God and as the Godhead for Christian creedal faith, those theologians avoid denying God's consistently proclaimed and confessed personhood. They clearly state that God is a divine personal reality and his trinitarian nature is of a triadic personal character. However, surrounded by a postmodernist version of subjectivism and challenged intellectually by dominant reason-centered understandings of personhood, they try to protect the concept of God from reduction to a mere theory in or about the mind, or to a pure individual, rational entity without action. They thus stress that God, according to the Bible and tradition, is a triune, dynamic, and relational reality that negates individualism and self-sufficiency, and exists relationally in itself and with the world. God is a relational Other, and knowing him requires a relation-based theology that is transpolar in nature, or that exceeds the polarity of humanity's contingency and God's infinity and focuses instead on the relation between God and the human, made possible by virtue of God's trinitarian character.

For many theologians in the twentieth century, however, the most appropriate way for developing such a theology is believed to lie in dispensing with "three persons" in and as God, and speaking instead about God's relational nature as *personal* relationality. One can easily detect in various writings on trinitarian theology during the twentieth century a tendency to avoid calling the Father, the Son, and the Spirit three divine *persons*. Karl Barth replaces "persons" with "modes of being," and Karl Rahner uses "modes of substantiation." "Father, Son, and Spirit" are deemed three modes of God's relational substantiation in, or communion with, the world that retrospectively reveals God's subsistent relations in eternity: the immanent Trinity is the economic Trinity. They are modes of relationality of one personal Lord, and not three individual Lords. "Persons" is now considered a threat to God's relationality and self-sufficiency.

Other theologians after Barth and Rahner during this "postmodern" age still follow the same track. Although many of them would not like to replace "person" with "mode of being" or "mode of subsistence" in order to avoid any possible drift into modalism, they similarly believe that what the triunity of God is all about is first and foremost a dynamic image of relationality that is seen in God and *as* God; a relationality that constitutes God not only in his relation with the human, but in his very own being. They therefore blur "person" with "relation" in the doctrine of the Trinity, instead of interpreting "person" from a relational perspective. "Person" here is defined as either "event" or "communion." Robert Jenson, for example, defines the persons of the Trinity as a "threefold identity" that expresses God's progressive interaction with the human in time.[1] John Zizioulas follows a similar track and defines "persons" in God as "communion." He then speaks about the Father, Son, and Spirit as three unique relational being-ness as communion.[2] Cardinal Ratzinger (Pope Benedict XVI) defines "person" as "total relationality" and considers the person totally and completely constituted by one's relations, possessing nothing of one's own.[3]

But is every theological concept of relationality congenial with God's relational nature, and thus to his personhood? In the following sections, I

---

1. See Robert Jenson, *The Triune Identity: God According to the Gospel* (Philadelphia: Fortress Press, 1967).

2. John D. Zizioulas, *Being as Communion: Studies in Personhood and the Church* (Crestwood, NY: St. Vladimir's Seminary Press, 1993); and Zizioulas, "On Being a Person: Toward an Ontology of Personhood," in *Persons, Divine and Human*, ed. C. Schwöbel and C. Gunton (Edinburgh: T. & T. Clark, 1999), 33–46.

3. Cardinal Joseph Ratzinger, *Dogma and Preaching* (Chicago: Franciscan Herald, 1989), 213. He even states that standing *in* relation is not expressive of real personhood (ibid., 221). For a perceptive analysis and critic of Ratzinger's and Zizioulas's understanding of personhood, see Miroslav Volf, *After Our Likeness: The Church as the Image of the Trinity* (Grand Rapids and Cambridge: Eerdmans, 1998), 29–126.

attempt to expose some exemplary trends of thought in contemporary trinitarian theology's reinterpretation of God's triune nature from this postmodernist attention to relationality. Evaluating these examples from the angle of Christian tradition will show toward the end of this chapter that there are certain notions of relationality in today's intellectual arena that are not actually appropriate for understanding God's relational being or his trinitarian relational personhood, and theology should not attempt to prove their theological origin. Instead of developing an understanding of human personhood and relationality from the relational nature of the triune God, there are recent trends of trinitarian theology that actually shape God's triune relational nature after human experiences of relational and social existence.

1. "TRINITY" AS SOCIAL PARTICIPATION IN OTHERNESS: TRANSCENDING TRANSCENDENCE

In its attempt at bringing "God" back to the arena of human thinking about the constitutive significance of the notion of "relationship" for the understanding of "self" and "personhood," trinitarian theology emphasizes God's relational nature and his historical incarnation (Christ) and progressive re-creation of the world (Spirit). Among the schools of trinitarian hermeneutics, nevertheless, there stand trends of trinitarian thinking that not only point to God's relational involvement with the world, but also, and more emphatically, God's *interdependence* on the world he is related to in terms of self-perfection. One can say that instead of departing from an interpretation of God's triune nature, these trends choose to depart from a presumption that what necessarily and naturally exists in reality is not "God," but actually "God-in-relation-to-the-universe."[4] Rather than separation or even serious ontological distinction, God and the world are in a fully interdependent, organic affinity. This affinity takes perfect shape in a specific form of sociality, wherein both the world, but also God, get enriched by each other and provide one another with something that each does not already possess. God, as David Griffin states, is now considered "essentially the soul of the universe" and that "God's relation to [the universe] belongs to the divine essence," so much so that the universe's principles exist naturally and inherently "because they exist in the very nature of God."[5]

---

4. David R. Griffin, "A Naturalistic Trinity," in *Trinity in Process: A Relational Theology of God*, ed. Joseph A. Bracken, S.J. and Marjorie Hewitt Suchocki (New York: Continuum, 1997), 23–40, 24.

5. David R. Griffin, "Panentheism: A Postmodern Revelation," in *In Whom We Live and Move and Have Our Being: Panentheistic Reflections on God's Presence in a Scientific World*, ed. Philip Clayton and Arthur Peacocke (Grand Rapids and Cambridge: Eerdmans, 2004), 36–47, 42–43.

The followers of this trend admit that if one acknowledges an eternal Trinity, one cannot possibly apply such a social form of interdependence on God. In traditional theology on the eternal Trinity, exchanging enrichment is not possible, since the relations between the three divine persons do not reflect such a dimension. Be that as it may, these trinitarian trends of thought do not primarily speak about the eternal Trinity, preferring instead to speak exclusively of the economic Trinity and God's existence in history. On the level of the relationship between God and the world, as these approaches state, interdependence is the best form, and the most coherent image, of the participatorial nature of the relationship between God and the human.[6] It is better than any other form of relationality, the argument runs, because of the real depth of mutual influence that God and the world exert on each other in their relationship.

But how can such an organic relational form of sociality take place between God and humanity when in classical theology God is considered necessary and humanity contingent? The trinitarian theology that supports a form of interdependent sociality addresses this question by arguing that God's incarnation as Jesus Christ (that is, the Christological foundations of the doctrine of the Trinity) and God's eschatological re-creation of the world (that is, its pneumatological foundations) equally state that contingency is not only characteristic of humanity but also inherent to real Deity. Interdependence is therefore the best form of relationality for shedding light on God's contingency. This is no longer questionable in the light of this realization of God's contingency. Interdependent sociality reveals contingency's inherent defining value for God's very own Being. Contingency is now one of the attributes of the Trinity that shows that God in Jesus Christ is not only fully involved in human history, but also fully influenced by human actions. It shows us ultimately, as Lewis Ford argues, that

> trinitarian concerns have no place in God apart from the way we Christians are intimately related to God, and how we conceive other salvific communities to be related to God. Trinitarian thinking concerns contingencies essential to our salvation, not to some eternal threeness of the abstract divine nature.[7]

One can eventually notice in this trinitarian approach's overemphasis on mutual enrichment between God and the human a tendency to shape divinity in the

---

6. Lewis Ford, "Contingent Trinitarianism," in *Trinity in Process*, 41–68, 48–49.
7. Ibid., 64.

image of humanity. The assumption behind this attempt is the following: apart from contingent, interdependent sociality, the triune nature of God does not only make the salvation of the Christ meaningless for us. It more drastically transforms God as such into an empty metaphysical idol. In order to defeat this danger, some trends in today's trinitarian theology contain a tendency to form a new understanding of the trinitarian being of God on the basis of the human experience of personhood and sociality that is gradually gaining the upper hand in postmodernity. What seems to be avoided, in return, is building our understanding of sociality and relationality on the relational life between the three divine persons of the Trinity, because this path is considered too metaphysical and supra-historical.

Underpinning this method of reinterpreting the Trinity on the basis of interdependent sociality is a conviction that metaphysics should be overcome in theology, and that God's transcendence should be reconsidered. This reconsideration, however, need not entail denying God's transcendence, but only *transcending* it. There are theologians today who argue strongly that in the interdependent sociality hermeneutics of the God-human relationship, "the classical idea of transcendence is transcended by allowing God to quit God's traditional transcendence and to empty God's self without remainder into the world, into the spirit of love and the affirmation of the body."[8] God is offered now a generous chance to give up his metaphysical distinction from humanity and to descend into the realm of historical existence, irretrievably giving up his eternal status. To say this more bluntly, "God's emptying Himself *without remainder* into the world" designates an offer for God to maintain existence in the world and to seek survival from extinction. The world is now offering God a redemption chance to recant his old habits of acting in human life from the vantage of an absolutist position. The court of history gives God the last chance to get a release on bail: he either gives up his lordship, power, and "wholly otherness" to love the world and melt into it completely, or he will remain a prisoner in a vicious "Azkaban," guarded by the ghosts of metaphysics' curse. God is called to either love our life's image or die suffocated with his own self.

In an attempt to show what transcending God's transcendence looks like in theological costume, Michael Scanlon, in an article titled "Trinity and Transcendence," invites theologians to trace the marks of this transcendence of transcendence in Karl Rahner's trinitarian theology. Scanlon accredits in particular Rahner's identification of the immanent and the economic Trinity.

---

8. John D. Caputo and Michael J. Scanlon, *Transcendence and Beyond: A Postmodern Inquiry* (Bloomington and Indianapolis: Indiana University Press, 2007), 3.

He believes that this identification is *the* redemptive means for God from any claim of metaphysical isolation behind his historical activities. According to Scanlon, Rahner believes that one of the major mistakes of the traditional doctrine of the Trinity lies in restricting the connotations of immanent Trinity to the inner being of God. For Rahner, this limitation is inappropriate because the Trinity is nothing else but an expression of the mystery of the salvific action that God conducts in history for the sake of human existence: the Trinity *is* the mystery of salvation.[9]

In order to fix this defect in the traditional doctrine of the Trinity, Rahner affirms, says Scanlon, that "the economic Trinity is the immanent Trinity and vice versa." By this rule, Rahner aims at showing that the mystery of the Trinity, and the theological expression of it (the doctrine of the Trinity), is not supposed to obscure the divine reality of God or place him over and against human life. The Trinity's mysteriousness does not, that is, lie in God's transcendence, but rather in God's being "a reality in the life of Christians."[10] Scanlon argues that had the story of the doctrine of the Trinity reached its happy ending with Rahner's Rule, there would have been no problem with "transcendence" in relation to God. In contemporary theology, the story, however, witnesses another chapter, which states that Rahner's Rule is qualified by successive theologians (e.g., Yves Congar[11]), who take beyond dispute all of Rahner's Rule except its last part, "vice versa." For Scanlon, the opposite actually should happen. For, "it is precisely the 'vice versa' that has proven to be the most fruitful part of Rahner's Rule for contemporary trinitarian theology."[12] Scanlon does not deny that Rahner hardly develops a clear explanation of the implications of "vice versa" in his rule. Yet Scanlon argues that Rahner provides the right track for pursuing such a development when he emphasizes that in the incarnate Christ and the divine Spirit, God strongly declares that his economic actions in history are no less than the fully free, total presence of his eternal being. Scanlon refers to what he deems one of Rahner's very few telling statements about this track:

> The unoriginated God (called "Father") has from eternity the opportunity of an historical self-expression (the divine Wisdom/

---

9. Scanlon, "Trinity and Transcendence," in *Transcendence and Beyond*, 66–81, 69.

10. Ibid., 69, and Rahner, "Remarks on '*De Trinitate*,'" in *Theological Investigations*, trans. Kevin Smith (Baltimore: Helicon, 1966), 4:78.

11. See Congar's critique of Rahner's rule in Yves Congar, *I Believe in the Holy Spirit*, trans. David Smith (London: Geoffrey Chapman, 1983), 3:13–17.

12. Scanlon, "Trinity and Transcendence," 70.

Word) and likewise the opportunity of establishing himself as himself the innermost center of the intellectual creature as the latter's dynamism and goal (the divine Spirit). These two eternal possibilities (which are pure actuality) are God, are to be distinguished from each other, and are to be distinguished by this distinction also from the unoriginated God.[13]

Scanlon concludes from the above quotation that Rahner proposes the key meaning of the Trinity to be the freedom that makes God become, as such, "radical nearness as self-gift to the world."[14] Through the paradigm of interdependent sociality, Scanlon fashions God's freedom after the human experience of freedom. Accordingly, he argues that as human freedom lies in "the ability to determine oneself, to construct oneself over the course of a lifetime of self-enactment,"[15] the Trinity basically reveals that God's freedom is also reflective of the same ability of progressively (or historically) constructing his divine self's eternality. Time, in other words, is the fuel of freedom not only for the human but also for God. History is not only the arena of the process of "becoming-ness" of the community of God, but for the "becoming-ness" of the God of the community as well. The "vice versa" is the key tool for unearthing the mutual interdependence sociality that links "God with us" to "God *in se*"; the Trinity to humanity. As the divine Trinity is a "co-doer" with the human self, the "vice versa" criterion makes the human self equally a "co-doer" in the divine Trinity itself.

This logic naturally furnishes for Scanlon's allegation that "God, too, has a history: God becomes the kind of Deity God wills to become by using all of time with eternity as its fruition. God *becomes* actually triune in a divine history."[16] How can we transcend, then, the boundaries of God's transcendence

---

13. Ibid., 71, and Rahner, "Oneness and Threefold-ness of God," in *Theological Investigations*, trans. Edward Quinn (New York: Crossroad, 1983), 18:118.

14. Scanlon, "Trinity and Transcendence," 71.

15. Ibid., 71.

16. Ibid., 72. Italics are mine. Scanlon, in almost a proof-text manner, cites Rahner's saying "only when . . . within a concept of God that makes a radical distinction between God and the world, God Himself is still the very core of the world's reality and the world is truly the fate of God Himself, only then is the concept of God attained that is truly Christian" (ibid., 72, citing from Rahner, "Christian Concept of God," in *Theological Investigations*, trans. Hugh M. Riley [New York: Crossroad, 1988], 21:191). Snatched from its wider, exact context of argument, this sentence turns Rahner inappropriately into a panentheist or process theologian. Rahner is as emphatic as Barth on the centrality of revelation and God's relational nature. Yet he does not part from Barth's attention to the Christian patristic maintenance of God's

by means of the Trinity? This can be done, according to Scanlon, by treating the Trinity as an expression of the process of God's free decision to become, or to acquire, his eternal self by means of living in the Son and the Spirit as a participant in the human temporal process of self-fulfillment. It can be done, in other words, by *historicizing* the reality of God the Trinity.[17] The historicization of the Trinity entails viewing "eternity" as "the everlasting fruition of time."[18] Eternity is time at the end of its process of evolution; time in its maturity; time in ages' fall. God is now the Spirit that temporalizes the world by placing its progress within history as it should be, that is, within a true historical nature of history that essentially lies in God's personal process of becoming the eternal kingdom of salvation for the world. God becomes the name of a triune unfolding of time, which ultimately eternalizes God by making the Trinity the eternal realm of salvation (i.e., self-fulfillment) for humanity.

2. "TRINITY" AS TRANSCENDING HISTORICAL DISCONNECTION: ROBERT JENSON AND THE TEMPORALIZATION OF ETERNITY

In this section and the following two, I will present three examples of contemporary trinitarian theologies that reinterpret the Trinity from the angle of an exclusive emphasis on relationality and stand in the line of the endeavor to transcend God's transcendence. I will start this section and the following with two Lutheran theologians from the United States, Robert Jenson and Ted Peters. I will start with the proposal of the senior of the two, Robert Jenson, leaving the proposal of Ted Peters to follow. It is not my attempt here to develop a comprehensive analysis of Jenson's, or of Peters's, theological thinking. Far from this, I will confine my study to Jenson's understanding of the triune being of God in *The Triune Identity*, which he wrote during the 1980s.

Right from the first pages of the preface of his book, Jenson places before his readers what he considers the most daunting question before religion in today's world: the question of God's identity. Jenson argues that a general definition such as "God is the object of ultimate concern" is not useful religiously. For any ultimate concern as such is empty if those who are identified with it are not sure primarily that what they are concerned about is right and reasonable. One needs religiously to base first the concern about any

---

otherness, even if Rahner's understanding of the rate of the "wholeness" of this otherness differs from Barth's.

17. Scanlon, "Trinity and Transcendence," 77. Scanlon refers here to Joachim of Fiore's belief that the progress of history unfolds nothing other than the history of progress in God's self.

18. Ibid., 76.

ultimate on an authentic answer to the question, "Which possible God is real?"[19] Furthermore, if those who are answering the question "Which possible God is real?" are Christians, they inevitably refer in their answer to the God whom Jesus Christ in Scripture calls "Father," and who, in turn, empowers his Son with the Spirit and enables us also to call him "Father" by virtue of the same Spirit. According to Jenson, this has always been the answer Christianity offered ever since its genesis. It is therefore common sense for Christians today, too, to identify God by relearning and reproclaiming the triunity of God.[20] Referring to and relying on the history of the doctrine of the Trinity does not mean, however, Jenson adds, just echoing literally or mechanically the statements of tradition without any further ado. To the contrary, it means reversing this tradition's elements critically to "develop proposals for its reform and further development."[21]

Setting before his eyes this development goal, Jenson starts his reidentification of the triune God by running an inquiry about the general, primal use of the word "God" in people's life. It is of crucial importance to perceive here that Jenson's attention to the use of the word "God" in the context of people's life-setting is in fact an approach to religiosity from the perspective of the relationship of the human life with time, or even *as* temporal, historical events. Jenson's reliance on the notions of temporality and historicity recur in his later elaborations on the identity of God, the relationship of God with humanity, and the relationship of time and eternity. Jenson will present himself as a theologian of revelation who believes in the possibility of using God's revelation in Jesus Christ as tenable, and as a valid foundation for temporalizing God's eternity and historicizing the divine's transcendence. He will identify his trinitarian thinking by identifying God himself as an expression of an event-based temporality in which humanity is eschatologically promised to participate and identify.

Jenson claims that the reality of time in human existence makes itself apparent in a twofold manner: time stands as a past, which we remember and attribute our origin to, and as a future, which we anticipate and look toward as our end. Between these two poles of time, Jenson notes, the human lives in a kind of a struggle, standing astride two ends that are often estranged and far from attached to each other. One cannot maintain one of these poles and

---

19. Jenson, *The Triune Identity*, xi.

20. Ibid., xii. "Those who suppose Christianity to be true, and therefore wish to answer so, must in our time relearn the answer's depths and subtleties, that is, they must learn—and carry further—trinitarian piety and thought."

21. Ibid., xii.

give up the other, nor can one keep them together without real unity between them. Both—the past as the element of human memory, and the future as the element of human expectation—are equally constitutive of present human life. So, instead of falling into an "either/or" dead-end, Jenson suggests that we ought actually to reconcile these two poles and bring them slightly closer to each other by the help of a third element. This element is what Jenson calls "eternity." Reading through Jenson's elaboration enables the reader to realize that Jenson is suggesting his own notion of "eternity." Eternity is not here a designation of the nonhistorical; it is not the opposite of time; it is not the a-temporal or a-historical. Jenson's "eternity" is this element that enables the happening of the transcendence of the disconnection between the past and the future.[22]

Being an element inherent to time's self-fulfillment and integrity makes eternity the element that enables time to turn into "life" or to become a narrative of living; a story of *becoming* a living; an event of living that can be given a "name." And, if this "time as life" is to be identified in religious terms, the union between the past and the future that makes time "life" should be given no other name than "God." In this shift from "life" and "time" to "God," and later "eternity," lies the crux of Jenson's theology of the Trinity. The core of this crux, moreover, is Jenson's belief that "God" is the *name* of that union between the past and the future of human temporality. The need for knowing who God "is" is necessitated by the demand of knowing "how our lives hang together" as one temporal story, one historical body, wherein the future and the past unite together without disconnection. Jenson sees the Christian version of his thinking in nothing else but the doctrine of the Trinity and in no other than the Christian liturgical naming of God as "Father, Son, and Spirit."[23] These three are not three persons, or forms or realities combined together as one God. They are together one name; and insofar as they name "God," they are also three identities for the same reality that holds the one name God. More crucially, and intriguingly still, "Father, Son, Spirit" is the proper name of our temporal life as creatures whose past and future are given the chance to be united in a way that transcends any disconnection. It is the name of human history in its full, complete, and perfect historic identity.

Does the playing of the role of the name of the union between human history's past and future have any implication on how one should understand the nature of "God" as a name? In Jenson's answer to this question appear signs of an adoption of an "interdependence sociality" model of relationality between

22. Ibid., 1–5.
23. Ibid., 5.

God and humanity. The interdependence aspect appears in Jenson's projecting of human experience of timely existence and change onto God's being and life. Jenson repeats a description of time by means of movements and actions. Taking this description into consideration, one can argue that if Jenson would apply the same definition to what names time, he would end up saying that what names the union of the past and the future should also be defined by means of action and movement. If the name, in other words, defines the nature of what it names and not only its mode of presence, "God," as the name of life in its two temporal sides' total attachment, should name what defines this life and identify with it. And, if time is defined by actions, "God" as the name of the union of the two components of time (past and future) should also be defined as activity.

It is my belief that a logic similar to this one lies behind Jenson's principal treatment of the "Father, Son, and Spirit" as three identifying activities or events, rather than three *hypostases* or three distinct centers of action. And it also underlies his claim that "in the Bible, the name of God and the narration of His works . . . belong together."[24] Linking God to his works is not meant here, for example, as a defense of the authenticity of the salvific actions of Christ from the perspective of the patristic logic that "what is not assumed by the *logos* in His incarnation is not redeemed." This is not essentially an attempt to define God's personal character by means of his actions, or proving the divinity of the Son or the Spirit by means of the ontological designations of their actions. This is rather Jenson's special way of reading the scriptural attestations of God's activity as if they define God's being *as* mere action. This appears in his claim that the biblical authors always resort to a description of certain actions God does whenever the question of "Who is God?" is raised. In the Old Testament, Jenson proceeds, the question of "Who is God?" is answered by God's talk about his actions in Israel's life (e.g., "I will punish you for your ways . . . then you will know that I am [yhwh]" (Ezek. 7:4); "I will establish my covenant with you, and you will know that I am [yhwh]" (Ezek. 61:62) And in the New Testament, the same question is answered by referring to God's acts in Jesus Christ: he is the one who raised Jesus from the dead.[25]

Both the exodus and the resurrection, Jenson concludes, are the answer of the Bible to the question "Who is God?" Moreover, they *are* what "Father, Son, Spirit" names. The "triune name," as Jenson calls the Trinity, is the name of these eternal activities that unite the past and the future of human time and turn history into "life." Jenson believes that it is not unusual that the triune

---

24. Ibid., 7.
25. Ibid., 6–8.

name has been habitually used by the church in its life and throughout its long history, even "when there is no special reason to do so."[26] Actually, if we concurred with Jenson's suggestion that the Trinity is the name of life components' (memory and expectation) transcendence of disconnection, we would not find it necessary to look for a tenable reason to use the name "Father, Son, Spirit." For, like "God," "Trinity" is just a proper name, a signifier that inclusively signifies the very act of finding reason for using this triune name as well. If "finding a reason" for anything is part of the activities that the triune name names (as the name of life), finding a reason for using the triune name is itself named by what we are trying to find a reason for its use as a name. This would be like finding a reason for reasoning in a certain way by means of using the same reason, the reliability of which we are trying to justify in the first place. More important, nevertheless, than the reason for using this name would be this name's temporal origin, according to Jenson's logic. What matters more would be showing that this name is not forced on our life. It is a name that generates *from* life as such to name it. This is also why, rather than considering it a given knowledge, we will find it crucial to declare with Jenson that "the triune name did not, of course, fall from heaven; it was made by believers for the God with whom we have found ourselves involved."[27] Looking from Jenson's angle, this makes sense, of course, since the names of things are usually made by naming agents. It is, of course, another no less valid question to ask if turning the Trinity into a mere name is theologically appropriate. But, from Robert Jenson's perspective, this latter is not a question. It is rather itself questioned and replaced.

In the light of the above understanding, "God" and "Trinity" are to be considered proper names that define activities. Proper names for which activities? Proper names for the eternal that unites the activities of the past with the events of the future, turning human history into one life narrative. How does this understanding affect theology? According to Jenson, it makes theology quit defining God by time-neutral characters (e.g., "God is whoever is omnipotent") and starts, instead, identifying him temporally as "whoever raised Israel's Jesus from the dead."[28] If "God" names certain actions that make the past and the future transcend their disconnectedness, "God" should be identified by, or even *as*, a historical narrative. There is no historical narrative that can identify God according to the Bible except for the event of Jesus. Jesus is the work of the event that identifies this God who names the union of the past and the future.

---

26. Ibid., 10.
27. Ibid., 12.
28. Ibid., 21.

"God," says Jenson, "'is' Jesus." Therefore, "God" defines "what happens with Jesus"; more specifically "what particularly happens with Jesus that compels us to use the word 'God' of this 'Father' in the first place."[29] And, since "God" names the union of the past *and* the future in our temporal life, "God" is not only what *happened* to Jesus, but also "what *will come* of Jesus and us, together."[30] Jesus' narrative, or even Jesus *as* a historical narration of salvation as event, is the possibility of "God's identifiability," in Jenson's words,[31] because Jesus himself is an action that "God" *does*, or even the action that "God" *is* as a name. And if "God" names the temporality in its transcendence of disconnectedness, identifying "God" should, as Jenson states, be done by pointing "with all three of time's arrows in order to point out this God." Why threefold pointing? "Time does have three arrows that are inescapable."[32]

In relation to these three arrows of time, Jenson interprets the Trinity. The triune name's particularity for Jenson lies ultimately in this particularity's reflection of these arrows of time and in naming them. It is in this organic subsistence in time, or even subsistence *as* time in its fullness and perfection, that the Trinity makes sense and truly attests to the God of the gospel, according to Jenson. The gospel's Trinity is grounded in God's revelation and has no meaning when it is bound with a timeless sense. The Trinity acquires meaning when it is seen as an *event* that takes place within the three-dimensional history of Jesus' redemption. "The temporal structure of [Jesus'] event," says Jenson, "must be left as ultimate in God."[33] In other words, Martin Luther's theology of the "hidden God" is a drastic proposal, Jenson affirms. "God" is far from any hidden-ness. "God," to the contrary, "defines Himself in these events of our own time and history."[34]

In the light of the foregoing thinking, the natural following move in Jenson's thinking is to substantially reconsider the value of what he calls "the traditional Hellenistic interpretation of God." Jenson believes that because of the Hellenistic influence on Christian theology, the Greek metaphysical a-temporalization of deity and speech about "the distance of God" infiltrated the gospel's attestation of the God who is fully involved in history and ontologically bound to the temporal incarnation and life of its *Logos*. Coming from a

---

29. Ibid., 22.
30. Ibid., 23, where Jenson carries on saying "the event by which God is identified—Jesus' resurrection—is the event in which Jesus is future to himself and to us."
31. Ibid., 24.
32. Ibid., 24.
33. Ibid., 26.
34. Ibid., 28.

Hellenistic culture into Christianity, the first followers of Christ, argues Jenson, found themselves confronted with the necessity of finding out how they could be Christians notwithstanding their Hellenistic culture; how they could, that is, Christianize their Hellenism.[35] One of the unfortunate ways for making this happen was setting the biblical notion of God alongside the Hellenistic notion of "real deity," which, according to Jenson, led eventually to "abstracting ['God'] from time with negative analogies."[36] The result of opting for this solution, according to Jenson, was speaking about "God" as an abstract, hidden, and certainly a-temporal reality. For Hellenistically framed minds, upon hearing about the "God" of the gospel as "the God the Beginning, God who is our fellow man Jesus and God the fulfillment," says Jenson, the first question to ask is: "but what is the timelessly self-identical Something that *is* all these three? What is the time-immune Continuity which must be the Being of the real God?"[37]

In Jenson's opinion, what is more pivotal than answering this question is asking whether the question per se should be adopted and considered as appropriate, sensible theological inquiry or not in the first place. And he believes that the question as such should be displaced, for any answer to it would be heretical and contrary to the content of the gospel.[38] In the place of this inquiry, Jenson calls for paying attention to the patristic doctrinal tradition's concern about deciphering the trinitarian network of relations between God, his incarnate *Logos*, Jesus Christ, and God and his Christ with their spiritual presence in the community of faith.[39] In the history of doctrine, Jenson pinpoints the Cappadocian fathers' theology of the Trinity and conducts his very special reading of their literature, chasing therein after evidences that might support his own proposal. In their speech about a relational dynamic nature that lies in the personal interrelationships between the Father, the Son, and the Spirit in the Godhead, the three Cappadocians, according to Jenson, rescued, before any other church father, "God" from any abstract identification that lies in changelessness and timelessness. "God's identity" in the writings of the Cappadocians, as Jenson reads them, means "God *seeking* His identity."

---

35. Ibid., 61ff.
36. Ibid., 62.
37. Ibid., 64.
38. Ibid., 65. In Christian history, the two major heresies that originated from the attempt to answer this question, instead of discarding it altogether, according to Jenson, are modalism and subordinationism.
39. Ibid., 68–92.

In his paraphrasing of what he believes was claimed by the Cappadocians, Jenson concludes: "God" is what he is only in remembering what he was and hoping for what he will be.[40] The notions of "remembering" and "hoping" are already considered by Jenson to be constitutive of the meaning of time, history, and human personhood. In this definition that he now develops out of his special reading of the patristic literature, he points out that these two notions are not only definitive of human personhood. They are also definitive of God. This appears further clearly in Jenson's speaking about God's trinitarian identity in the following way:

> [T]hat there is even one identity of God means that God is personal, that He *is* God in that He *does* Godhead, in that He chooses Himself as God. That there are three identities in God means that this God's deed of being the one God is three times repeated . . . and so that only in this precise self-repetition is God the particular God that He in fact is. God does God, and over again, and yet over again—and only so does the event and decision that is this God occurs.[41]

Using "does" and terms that designate activity is Jenson's way of following the lesson he believes we should learn from Gregory of Nyssa and other fathers: "God's" "is" is to be identified *as* God's doing. "God" is predicated of "divine activities toward us."[42] "Father, Son, Spirit" names what happens to us in our timely narrative that seeks perfection. "Father, Son, Spirit" are not three actors, among which the name of an action (God) is divided. The action itself is a process that begins from "Father," gains presence through "Son," and reaches its final perfect form as "Spirit." "Father, Son, Spirit" names the process that is finally one activity called "God": "there is one event, God, of three identities."[43]

What does the foregoing understanding of the triune God's identity tell us today? For Jenson, it tells us that we have to free trinitarian theology from the notion of divine timelessness. This ought to be pursued by way of considering the relationship between the "immanent" and the "economic" Trinities.[44] As with those theologians to whom I referred in the previous section, Jenson also supports the centralization of the "vice versa" phrase in Rahner's Rule (i.e.,

---

40. Ibid., 110. "As a person . . . I am what I am only in that I remember what I have been and hope for what I will be."
41. Ibid., 111.
42. Ibid., 113.
43. Ibid., 114.
44. Ibid., 139ff.

the economic Trinity is the immanent Trinity and vice versa): the economic Trinity *is* the immanent Trinity fully and indistinguishably. Instead of differentiating the immanent from the economic ontologically, Jenson proposes distinguishing them *chronologically*. The immanent Trinity is the final perfection, or, as Jenson says, "the eschatological reality of the economic Trinity."[45] By deleting timelessness from the theology of God, Jenson argues, theology no longer needs to speak about the eternal relation between the begetting Father and the begotten Son as necessarily different from the relation between Christ and the God he calls "Father." Instead of this, theology should speak about the eternal relation of begetting between the Son and his Father as the *final outcome* of their temporal interaction as the history of Jesus Christ.[46] It follows from this that every speech about the relational dynamic between the three persons in eternity has not happened yet in God's history, because God is still an event in a temporal process of happening. This dynamic identity called "God" will happen fully, however, because it is already in a state of happening eschatologically. This perfect identity is "God's" "final self-expression, by which He establishes His identity for us and for Himself."[47]

This brings us back to the beginning of Jenson's discussion when he started by talking about temporality. It is from temporality that eternity is now defined. What is eternity? It is the Trinity per se, since this latter is the perfect image of God's temporality. The Trinity is no other than the name of the future complete identity of the transcendent disconnection between the past and the future, which we can ultimately call "God." This is the meaning of Jenson's concluding claim, that "what happens between the human Jesus and his Father and the believing community *is* eternity."[48] This is also the meaning of his belief that God is the name of the event that transcends the disconnection between the beginning of time and what it will become (eternity). "To be," Jenson ends up saying, is to be "interpretive relatedness across time." And "to be God is to anticipate a future self by an inexhaustible interpretive relation to another that God Himself is."[49]

---

45. Ibid., 140.
46. Ibid., 140.
47. Ibid., 140.
48. Ibid., 141.
49. Ibid., 182.

3. "Trinity" as the Eschatological Solution of Time-Eternity Paradox: Ted Peters and the Wholeness of Temporality

Along with Robert Jenson, another Lutheran theologian, Ted Peters, pursues the same attempt at transcending God's transcendence by turning eternity into the perfection of time. In his book, *God as Trinity*, Peters endeavors to show that the Trinity is the key answer to the question of the proper understanding of God-human communication on the basis of the renewed emphasis on relationality in today's intellectual arena. The Trinity designates no other truth than "the eternal one enters time, and time thereby enters the divine life. And it stays there, even unto eternity."[50] Peters states clearly in his preface what he wants to argue, thereby showing his standing within the stream of imaging God's triune personhood after a human image of relationality:

> [T]he incorporation of time into eternity takes place through the eschatological incorporation of the temporal creation into the eternal *perichoresis* of the three persons that characterizes the trinitarian life. The eternity-time paradox is resolved eschatologically. This is what this volume attempts to underscore and develop in today's Trinity talk.[51]

In order to pursue this goal, Peters departs from pointing out that the primal question the doctrine of the Trinity is responsible for attending to is "How can our eternal God relate to our temporal world?,"[52] with all the secondary inquiries this question leads to, such as: Is it appropriate to understand eternity as timelessness? And should absoluteness mean opposition to relationality?

The development of appropriate answers for these questions, and ultimately to the question of God-world relationality, should begin, says Peters, with conceding that such answers can only be found in the doctrine of the Trinity. Does this mean any and every doctrinal discourse on the Trinity? Far from this, the doctrine of the Trinity that Peters puts center-stage is one that is grounded in the temporal experience of God's incarnation as attested to in the Bible.[53] The Trinity shows that God stands at the two sides of the borderline between eternity and time, and that eschatologically he breaks this

---

50. Ted Peters, *God as Trinity: Relationality and Temporality in Divine Life* (Louisville: Westminster John Knox, 1993), 8.
51. Ibid., 8–9.
52. Ibid., 14.

line down and incorporates into his own life the history of his relation with the world. This organic link between God and the world makes the notion of "relationship" not only the salvaging means for the understanding of human self from individualistic, absolute ideas of modernity, but also for God from the abstract, metaphysical trends of thought as well. The notion of "relationality," Peters argues, offers a warrant interpretation of the nature of triune identity, in that it reveals that "the fullness of God as Trinity is a reality yet to be achieved in the eschatological consummation" of creation.[54] God is waiting for the fulfillment of the human self to become fully his triune self, too.

But why did Christian theology not answer the question of the Trinity's meaning from the angle of the organic relation of eternity and time in centuries past? Peters believes that theology holds the responsibility of delaying the switching into the path that he and other theologians suggest today. Theology holds back its progress by adopting the presumption that the triune God is by default a mystery that exceeds our apprehension. The overemphasis on the mysteriousness of God leads theology ultimately, as Peters believes, to the trap of the "mysteriorization" of the doctrines of God and the Trinity: God, as well as the human interpretation of God's identity (theology), are both placed beyond analysis or conceptualization by being deemed incomprehensible. Contrary to mystery and incomprehensibility, however, the Gospels' attestations of God in Jesus Christ, and of the scriptural God in general, both invite us to consider the possibility of God's giving up mysteriousness; breaking away from it when he created the world, raised Jesus from the dead, and related in the Spirit to us. The Trinity is this answer that invites us to discern these biblical declarations when it reveals that God's relation to humanity is his transcendence of mysteriousness; his transcendence of every transcendence. God's mysteriousness lies no longer in absoluteness and beyond-ness. Rather, it lies in the paradoxical, surprising power and nature of God's ability to transcend absoluteness and transcendence primarily because he is absolute, and not in spite of it. The mysterious is God's disclosure that "eternity is affected by temporal contingency," as Peters says, and the drama of Golgotha is the story of the trinitarian life of God in eternity.[55]

If the God of Scripture is this substantially relational and temporal reality, should not we reconsider the appropriateness of distinguishing the immanent

---

53. Ibid., 15. "If one moves to the Trinity proper," Peters claims, "we find that God incarnate in Jesus Christ and present in to us as the Holy Spirit places God within the spatial and temporal horizon of our experience."

54. Ibid., 16.

55. Ibid., 20.

Trinity from the economic Trinity in theology? This is Peters's next question, which he answers by affirming that the immanent and the economic Trinity are but one, single reality, and not at all "a double Trinity of six figures, three authentically eternal and three accidentally temporal."[56] As with Robert Jenson, Peters refers to Rahner's Rule and claims it is the foundation of the doctrine of the Trinity. And when he faces the claim that Rahner's Rule paves the way for a possible jeopardizing of God's freedom by collapsing the two dimensions of the Trinity together, Peters resorts to a chronological understanding of the relation between the immanent and the economic Trinity: the immanent Trinity is the eschatological perfection of the economic Trinity.[57] He praises the soundness of making eternity and immanence the outcome of God's economic, temporal intercourse with the world. This chronological, eschatological understanding shows, in his opinion, that eternity and temporality are not mutually exclusive and that relationality is constitutive of God *a se*, and not only of God's presence with the world.[58] Relationality marks in God's eternal being the divine infinite openness to live the state of beyond-ness as an act of transcending his very own transcendence and opting for the future of his own self-perfection.[59]

If the previous account describes Peters's thesis, how does he verify this thesis in the ensuing chapters of his book? Peters begins his argument by noticing that within the time span that separates the beginning of the second half of the twentieth century from today, theological stances toward the Trinity have noticeably changed. Around the 1950s, the challenge for theology was to bring back the doctrine of the Trinity to the center of theological reasoning and bring it back from the margin of secondary speculation toward which it had been thrown. However, Peters claims, the challenge for theology is now to develop a discourse on the Trinity that will correct the doctrine of God's metaphysical obscurantism and exceed the marginalization of relationality and temporality vis-à-vis God's being. Viewing himself as a theologian standing within the stream of addressing this challenge, Peters suggests that the right trinitarian approach that can make this correction is "to conceive of God as in the process of self-constitution, a process that includes saving relationship to the world right in the definition of who God is."[60]

---

56. Ibid., 21.
57. Ibid., 22ff.
58. Ibid., 24.
59. Ibid., 25. "The trinitarian being of God is still open. God has a future in history as well as in an eschatological future. The *perichoresis* of Father, Son and Spirit is being carried out in time and through a history that is not done yet."
60. Ibid., 82.

In order to develop the needed trinitarian correction to the traditional doctrine of God, Peters refers again to Rahner's Rule. Rahner argues, according to Peters, that the divine reality that Jesus' salvific actions uncover before our eyes is *a se* the divine Godhead. We do not experience God in general first and then encounter his economy of salvation as *his* economy. Rather, we first experience God in the economy of salvation and build afterwards on this experience a general knowledge of divinity. Peters acknowledges that the belief that the immanent Trinity finds its very identity in the temporal events of the economy of salvation is not Rahner's personal conviction, but the interpretative variation that his rule was made to say by successive theologians (e.g., R. Jenson, J. Moltmann, E. Jüngel). This notwithstanding, Peters believes that these theologians' stretching of Rahner's Rule to such an end is justified by the fact that "Rahner [himself] is on the brink of saying that God relates to God's self through relating to us in the economy of salvation."[61] What Rahner is ready to say is that the roles the Son and the Spirit play in human history are not just roles they play before humanity for its sake. These roles are definitive of what the Son and the Spirit do in the triune Godhead, as well as definitive of what the Trinity as such "is." Rahner believes, as Peters argues, that denying this organic link between economy and immanence would imply that the activities of Jesus and the Spirit do not introduce God's identity. If particularity in terms of role in history does not identify a particularity in the Godhead itself, "then what we learn from the economic Trinity has no warrant for applying to the immanent Trinity—that is, a genuine revelation of God has not taken place."[62]

Peters, however, notes what he deems a limitation that keeps Rahner's thinking trapped behind the same boundaries of the classical, metaphysical theology, which departs from God's eternity and absolute aseity, and he tries to work out the relation of this aseity to God's activities *ad extra*. Emphasizing the belief that "*because* God in His immanence is relational and complex, so His activities and relations should reflect this complexity" does not, in Peters's opinion, take Rahner's logic beyond the boundaries of metaphysical theology. It rather keeps God eventually unrelated and shrouds the dilemma of God's perfection and relatedness in neologisms. It does not offer an explanation about how "a God who does not change internally [can] actually change externally."[63]

---

61. Ibid., 97 (96–103). Peters cites Rahner's saying "the Trinity is not for us a reality which can only be expressed as a doctrine. The Trinity itself is with us." Rahner, *The Trinity*, trans. Joseph Donceel (New York: Crossroad, 1997), 39.

62. Peters, *God as Trinity*, 99.

63. Ibid., 101 (100ff.).

Peters believes that the immutability of God, and Greek metaphysical speculation's influence on theology, should be seriously questioned. Taking Rahner's Rule beyond the limits of the notion of immutability and Greek metaphysics happens by means of reviewing the time-eternity relationship in such a way that "what happens in the history of salvation becomes constitutive of the content of eternal life."[64] Instead of speaking about God's "is," we speak now about God's "becomes" or even about God as an "outcome." Peters acknowledges other theologians, like J. Moltmann, W. Pannenberg, L. Boff, process theologians, R. Jenson, and C. M. LaCugna, who put Rahner's Rule, in his opinion, on the right track of development, crystallizing and sharpening, thereby, the core of Rahner's proposal.[65] Upon the contributions of these theologians, Peters builds his own interpretation of the Trinity. He believes, nevertheless, that the main thesis these theologians are yet to claim is the following: "the divine process of self-constitution through intercourse with the world's history"[66] is definitive of God's being as such. While these theologians pave the way for exploring this thesis, they do not trade into this way themselves. Peters believes that unless we trade into this path and walk to its end, Rahner's Rule would not fully serve the purpose of restructuring the doctrine of God.[67]

64. Ibid., 102.
65. Ibid., 81–145.
66. Ibid., 145.
67. Missing Peters's understanding of Rahner's Rule and the elaboration on it in other theologians' writings, which he develops in his book, would lead to a misunderstanding of his speech about God's alterity in his last two chapters. Miroslav Volf, for example, stops at Peters's speech about God's alterity, citing from *God as Trinity*, 186, his saying "God alone is God," and places Peters on the side of those who defend a disjunctive rather than conjunctive understating of *imago Dei* theology. Contrary to those who say that humans copy God in all respects, Peters, according to Volf, states that humans do not copy God *at all*. Volf, "'Trinity Is Our Social Program': The Doctrine of the Trinity and the Shape of Social Engagement," in *Modern Theology*, 3, no. 14 (1998): 403–23, 404–5. Contrary to Volf, and from Peters's discussion of Rahner's Rule and what he thinks this Rule's interpretation is yet to consider, Peters would not be a total disjunction theologian who would refuse any copying of God by the human altogether. On page 186, from which Volf cites in his paper, Peters states clearly that the human cannot just copy God because God alone is God. This notwithstanding, Peters states that this is the case *especially* and *certainly* in relation to political and social justice and ruling issues. He wants to say that our participation in God's triune life and self-fulfillment, which Peters argues to prove throughout his book, does not exceptionally make us copies of God the ruler or king in our leadership and kingship. When it comes *specifically* to kingship, we certainly cannot copy God. One can certainly ask Peters here why, when it comes to kingship, we cannot copy God, but can do so elsewhere. But one should, in my view, keep in mind that Peters himself, when it comes to other aspects of the God-human relationship, is as much a

Aiming at going where other theologians have not yet journeyed, Peters argues that in order to see how God's being can substantially link to history, we should reconsider our understanding of time and eternity in theological scholarship. In a method similar to the one of Robert Jenson, Peters pursues an interpretation of eternity that ultimately aims at temporalizing it in such a manner that divine absoluteness and relationality are brought into intensive convergence. The classical definition of eternity construes it "contra-time" or against temporality. This is why eternity defines the divine in traditional theology, since in this theology God is by default totally simultaneous and in perfect possession of limitless life.[68] On the other hand, "time" names the thing that determines and defines succession and distinction between past, present, and future possibilities. One of the main connotations of time is history in the sense of our reality's triadic identity as "passage, decay and death."[69] Now, Peters explains, if we depart like Augustine and Gregory of Nyssa from the assumption that eternity is supra-temporal, and restrict eternity to life and time to death, God, as eternal, would no longer be capable of causing temporal effects. And temporal causes, in turn, would not produce any effect on eternity. But, if this is the case, there cannot be any possible link between God and creation: God is fully dissociated from the affairs of the world.[70]

In contrast to this classical dichotomization of time and eternity, Peters refers to the understanding of "time" in quantum physics as an "edgeless" and "open-ended" reality to find therein a new way for bringing time and eternity together in theology. He suggests seeing eternity as the name of "the wholeness of the edgeless time." Peters notes the notion of "wholeness" popular in today's physical and biological theories, and he reveals his conviction that this notion deserves theology's attention and accreditation. "Can we," he asks, "conceive of a temporal whole to the cosmos precipitated by an eschatological event that brings fulfillment to all inertial frames of references?"[71] And then he answers that such a temporal whole is theologically tenable if what is meant by it is the whole of history, since "eschatological wholeness has to do with fulfillment, with consummation of the entire history of creation that preceded it."[72] The fulfillment of history's wholeness requires incorporating the notion of eternity

---

theologian of conjunctive, and not disjunctive, *imago Dei* as any theologian of social trinitarianism. He differs in details, not in method and content.

68. Peters, *God as Trinity*, 147–49.
69. Ibid., 150–51.
70. Ibid., 152.
71. Ibid., 169.
72. Ibid., 170.

into the understanding of the nature of history. Yet the notion of eternity that is appropriate for this is the one that both affirms the spatio-temporal origin of this history and redemptively brings it to its whole goodness. History needs God to reach its completeness in time. Otherwise, history would be a prisoner of an endless fragmentation of its parts. To add a trinitarian dimension to the wholeness of history on the basis of time's need of eternity (God) to fulfill itself, Peters states that the Trinity is the signifier of the reciprocal, dialectical relation that integrates the parts with the whole and makes them mutually inclusive and interdependent. The Trinity is the proper signifier of the time-eternity dialectic because it states that "the eternal has become temporal. The infinite has become finite. And the work of the Holy Spirit anticipatorily binds the parts to the whole, the present to the future, the expectation to its fulfillment."[73]

How can the notion of "whole temporality" shaped by eternity and trinitarian significations contribute to the theological understanding of the triune God per se? Peters answers this question as follows:

> As trinity, God is both eternal and temporal. God is the transcendent and hence eternal source of the created world. God is also immanent to the world as one finite being among other beings, as incarnate in Jesus of Nazareth, as a single objectifiable person in a single temporal-spatial frame of reference. God is also paradoxically immanent and transcendent as the Spirit, which ties times together and which promises the consummate unity of the whole of time in the eschatological kingdom of God.[74]

What are the implications of this understanding of the triunity of God? The first implication Peters extracts is that in order to speak about the triune God as a God who is actively and influentially related to creation, temporality and not only eternity should be constitutively inherent to who God is in himself.[75] The subjection of the divine Son to all the vicissitudes of ordinary existence in the incarnation is more ontologically constitutive for God's being than we think, according to Peters. It says that the incarnation reflects one dimension of God's becoming his self-perfection. The second implication, on the other hand, is as God in the Son communicates his divine attributes with

---

73. Ibid., 170.
74. Ibid., 171.
75. Ibid., 173. "To understand God as Trinity in the economy of salvation requires that God be both temporal and eternal."

us, his involvement in our existence communicates our attributes with him and takes our temporality, decay, and death up into his very eternal life. The incarnation tells us that God's eternal reality is no longer outside time, not only practically (in terms of salvation) or epistemologically (in terms of self-disclosure), but ontologically, too. The *perichoresis* of the Father, Son, and Spirit includes as part of its wholeness the history of the world and nature. And "eternity embraces the alpha and the omega plus whatever happens in between."[76] It is now possible to claim, Peters continues, that "if we say that God is infinite, it follows that the divine infinity includes the finite world."[77]

God as absolute and God as relational are no longer two separate identities that God holds in two different settings, one eternal and the other temporal. God's absoluteness is one of the characteristics of his relational identity: God as absolute relationality. "Absolute" just designates the total mutuality, the whole *perichoresis* that characterizes God as triune relationality. Speaking about the absoluteness of relationality, however, would be incomplete apart from discerning the fact that God's salvific relation to humanity in all its temporality is constitutive of the absolute relationality of God's whole nature. The absolute relationality of God is eschatologically seeking its total perfection by virtue of God's relationship with world history. God is seeking his becoming "God-in-relationship" when the work of salvation, or, as Peters says, "the economic Trinity [itself] is complete."[78] How can a God proceeding toward the fulfillment of the wholeness of his absolute relationality be a salvific promise for us? In this dynamically and fully economic triune God, we have love and grace coming to claim our lives from within our history, not from without; from an intimate mutual interdependence standpoint, not from a standpoint of opposition. The Trinity, Peters concludes, makes sense to us because "it offers us an opportunity to remind ourselves that the God of the beyond has become intimate, that the God of the creation has entered our world as its redeemer and sanctifier, and that we have good reason to hope for resurrection into the new creation."[79] Unless God the Trinity is this wholeness of our historicity, God's existence is futile and empty of meaning for the world, no matter how strongly verifiable and irreducibly evident his existence may be.

---

76. Ibid., 175.

77. Ibid., 176, which means, according to Peters, "the coming into existence of eternity—at least salvific eternity—is contingent . . . [and] the arrival of consummate eternity creates the wholeness of time."

78. Ibid., 181.

79. Ibid., 187.

4. IMAGING THE "TRINITY" AFTER HUMAN COMMUNAL SOCIALITY: PAUL FIDDES AND PARTICIPATION IN GOD'S BEING

Paul Fiddes, of the University of Oxford, took the same trend of trinitarian theology to a similar logical extreme in his *Participating in God*. In this book, Fiddes sets before himself the task of presenting acceptable language to speak about a *triune* God by starting methodologically from the historical, doxological experience of the Trinity in the church and ending up eventually with the doctrinal conception of the Trinity, rather than the other way around. Fiddes chooses this epistemological method because, according to him, it successfully solves the Christian dilemma of speaking about a "personal God" as meaning "three persons." As such, Fiddes argues, the "personal God" language is not meaningful from a purely logical standpoint because: 1) "three persons" can never mean "one personhood" for the modern mind, and 2) the idea of God, who is believed to be different in nature and other in existence from the human, cannot logically include the claim that God is "person." The logical paradox of the Trinity can be challenged by questions such as "How can God be truly personal, and yet also three persons? How much can a human word like 'person' apply to all the infinite and unique reality of God?"[80]

Can the previous conflict be sorted out by rejecting the personal connotations in the language of God? Fiddes does not think so because Scripture speaks about God in personal terms. The solution, in his opinion, lies instead in distinguishing the personal terms about God from the doctrinal notions of "personhood" that were developed in the doctrine of the Trinity throughout history. The history of doctrine shows Fiddes that the negative impact of the dilemma of speaking about "personal" and "persons" at the same time can easily enhance theological reasoning. This dilemma becomes seriously problematic whenever, instead of perceiving the dimensions of distinction and experience as the primal concern of the doctrine of the Trinity, theology turns the Trinity into a puzzle that baffles the believer's mind. To the contrary, what the fathers of the church originally wanted to articulate by the doctrine of the Trinity, according to Fiddes, is "the richness of the personality of God that they had found in the story of salvation and in their own experience."[81] Although they consciously think of one God, their experience of this God's salvation story points to a God who acts in a fatherly manner by means of a relation to a human figure, Jesus Christ, who responds to this fatherly action by a son-like obedience, dedication, and love. The father's focus is on this father-son relation

---

80. Paul Fiddes, *Participating in God: A Pastoral Doctrine of the Trinity* (London: Darton, Longman & Todd, 2000), 3.

81. Ibid., 5.

of salvation because they experience this relation and its implications in their communion together. By virtue of the joy of this communion, they acquire hope in the future of renewal in terms of a "Holy Spirit," whom they associate with the God who relates in a fatherly manner to Jesus as his Son.

By means of this experience, Fiddes concludes, "the early Christians moved back in thought from the activity of God in ordering the household (*oikonomia*) of the world to the being of God within God's own self." This process entails, according to Fiddes, that "the God who *makes* communion in the world must already *be* communion."[82] The church fathers express this communion in their description of God's being by the idea of procession within God's eternal substance. "The two missions in the world, of the Word and the Spirit, were based on two 'processions' in the inner being of God."[83] What follows from this is the belief that the theological understanding of the ministerial task of the church (i.e., pastoral/practical theology) should be based on an understanding of Christian human and communal experience from the trinitarian processions that constitute God's being. The purpose is primarily to see "how *participation* in this triune God affects both our images of God and our acts."[84] In the following chapters of his book, Fiddes meets this goal by arguing that the real image of community lies in God's being, for God in himself is an interrelational network. His argument, as it will be clear from the following analysis, amounts to a conclusion that the Word and the Spirit are not the agents of procession in God, who are reflected in their two divine missions in history. The Word and the Spirit are two processions in God; therefore they are God *as* two missionary *movements* in which the human participates and realizes by her worship and prayer.

Fiddes believes that the new experience-based orientation to the Trinity is expected to avoid two mistaken versions of trinitarian thinking: 1) pluralism that stresses the existence of three *persons* in God at the expense of his oneness, and 2) modalism that stresses God's single nature at the expense of the reality expressed by virtue of the persons. The core problem of these two mistaken views is that they undermine the central place of the notion of "relation" in the doctrine of God. Moreover, epistemologically, these views approach the Trinity from outside as observable, objective entities that can neutrally be described by means of any limited finite mind and senses.[85] Against these two observational approaches to the Trinity, Fiddes offers a *participatorial* approach that negates

---

82. Ibid., 6. Italics are mine.
83. Ibid., 7.
84. Ibid., 8.
85. Ibid., 12.

the object-subject dilemma and concentrates on the notion of "relation" per se. Knowledge here is acquired by participation in God's trinitarian relational being, which reveals that the Trinity is of an experiential and not a speculative nature.

The belief in the experiential nature of the Trinity is the only reason Fiddes can find for the use of "person" for God.[86] The orthodox fathers undermine this dimension, according to Fiddes, by investing heavily in the Greek terminologies of "*ousia*" and "*hypostasis*." Though their concern about reconciling unity and particularity in God is crucial, this investment in Greek metaphysical terminology, as Fiddes believes, does not really produce a satisfactory solution because it lacks a clear explanation of what "*hypostasis*" (i.e., person) would in this case really mean. The vagueness of "*hypostasis*," nevertheless, is gradually cast away, according to Fiddes, when some fathers focus on this term's relational connotation. They shift the focus from the philosophical difference between "person" and "essence" into a more fruitful definition of "person" as "relation." And, "Father, Son, and Spirit" become a network of relations of paternity, filiation, and spiration. If "*hypostasis*" is in this case "personhood," and if personhood is "relation," then "*hypostasis*" is no more, and no less, than "relation." Moreover, if "*hypostasis*" also means "substance" as it means "relation," then the divine substance or the divine essence *is* "relation." Consequentially, Fiddes states, personal relations are not to be added to the being as an extra. Being itself is a relation, so that "to be and to be in relations become identical."[87]

One of the major modern misconceptions of this original patristic trinitarian thinking for Fiddes lies, nonetheless, in denying that "person" in God basically means "otherness in relationships." An equal misconception also lies in turning this otherness into a form of individuality and alone-ness. Fiddes believes that this drives theology toward the inappropriate construal of Father, Son, and Spirit as three *objects*, each with his own particular consciousness.[88] What theology needs in order to overcome this misconception is a specific notion of "relation" that integrates "person" with "personage," "self" with "openness to other," "individual" with "communal," and "unity" with "diversity."[89] Theology needs to develop a notion of "relation" derived from a certain personal language about God that propagates a relation constituted by

---

86. Fiddes elsewhere states that in the doctrine of God "the single word 'person' is only a stopgap, as it were" and nothing else. Fiddes, *The Creative Suffering of God* (Oxford: Clarendon, 1988), 204.
87. Ibid., 15.
88. Ibid., 16–17.
89. Ibid., 19–28.

participation. This mode of relationality is most appropriately derivable from the triune God, where the three in God are a *perichoresis* of relationships that are mutually constitutive of what each relation in itself is. Rather than merely imitating an imaginary Godly life in our life after the model of the Trinity, Fiddes calls for a trinitarian understanding that enables Christians to participate in God's life and being in an experiential manner. Such participation requires a reassessment of the church's traditional language of "person" to see whether it reflects an existential, human language that humanity imposes on God because it suits its own varied life expectations, or whether it is a language that we address to God because he himself reveals to us that his essence, his "is," is "personal relations."[90]

Fiddes's conviction is that the relational language exemplifies a way forward into God, despite the limitation inherent in its human origin. This language is more appropriate than the language of "being" because it "has the capacity to be a language of participation, pointing to engagement in God and drawing us into such involvement."[91] Talking about God as three personal relations, then, is the best demonstration of the relation of participation. It is a language in which one speaks about something one participates in. One here is part of the subject of one's experience and of the media that express it, rather than a distinct, separate observer. Be that as it may, such a language of participation requires, in Fiddes's conviction, a serious redefinition of the notion of "person" in the Trinity. "Person" should not mean something particularly subsisting in a relational mode of existence. It should rather mean "subsisted relation." This means that "there are no persons 'at each end of a relation,' but the 'persons' are simply the relations."[92]

Fiddes credits here Thomas Aquinas, who, before anyone else, offered the most complete definition of person as a subsistent relation. Aquinas reveals to us that it is subsistent relations that we call "Father, Son, and Spirit," and nothing else. Fiddes, nevertheless, still takes the notion of subsistent relations a step further than Aquinas's insistence that the three subsisting relations are only *the same as* the one *ousia* of God, by stating that the subsisting relations *are* the *ousia* itself. By this distinction, as Fiddes believes, Aquinas misses the focal conviction of the Eastern fathers that God's being is communion or fellowship, rather than three persons in communion. It is therefore necessary, as Fiddes believes, to equate "subsistent relations" with "being in communion," and to speak about God as an "event of relationships" or as "three movements of

---

90. Ibid., 29–30.
91. Ibid., 33.
92. Ibid., 34.

relationships subsisting in one event." The triune God must not be "visualized as three individual subjects who *have* relationships," for this does not allow any knowledge of God by virtue of participation. Participation demands a God who is by nature "an event of relationships" that happens as God per se, that makes God *happen*, so that the human can participate in God.[93]

By viewing God's triune nature as a network of relations rather than as persons, Fiddes believes that he reconciles ontology with epistemology. He states that "the being of God is understood as event and relationship, but only through an epistemology of participation; each only makes sense in the context of the other."[94] "Father, Son, and Spirit" within this context are convenient to express epistemologically the movement of relationships in its ontological dimension, for these names express modes of relations we are familiar with and in which we are capable of personally imitating and sharing.[95] This entails that "using names for God, then, must always lead us into *movements* of divine love, which cannot be reduced to a relationship between a subject and an object."[96] Instead, therefore, of relating to God as someone to whom we address our desires as another, God *is* now the desire in which we pray: God is a state of participating in which we share and by which we experientially perceive the meaning of sharing. We cannot name or think of "Father, Son, and Spirit" apart from this form of participation, because when we talk about the Trinity we do not encounter personal agents on the ends of our relationships with the divine. We rather participate in a specific transcendent flow of relationships.[97] The analogy between the human and God is thus reduced to an analogy in terms of relation, not of person. Instead of "three living realizations of [distinct] centers of actions," theology, according to Fiddes, should speak of "three living realizations of movements or directions of action."[98]

---

93. Ibid., 36–37. Elsewhere, Fiddes states that "'Trinity' expresses the idea that God is a complex being, happening as a communion of relationships or movements of being which are characterized by their relationships to each other." Fiddes, *The Creative Suffering of God*, 201.

94. Ibid., 38.

95. Ibid., 41–42. "To say, for instance, that the Father eternally generates that Son is a way of saying that there is a movement like a father sending a son in which we share" (ibid., 41).

96. Ibid., 44.

97. Ibid., 50, 73.

98. Ibid., 85. Fiddes offers here an alternative to Wolfhart Pannenberg's trinitarian understanding of God's personhood. However, his phrase "three living realizations of *separate* centers of action" proves his misunderstanding of Pannenberg's view. Pannenberg does not speak about separate but rather *distinct* centers of action. Thus I maintain Pannenberg's terminology by replacing "separate" in Fiddes's quotation with "distinct" in my text.

Fiddes's concern about presenting a practical/pastoral doctrine of God for the sake of the church's ministry is valid and useful. Also, his interest in showing God's dynamic, relational, and open nature, which negates any observation of God as a dead object, is necessary as it reflects a foundational Christian belief about the identity of God. Having admitted that, it is not quite theologically appropriate, in my conviction, to achieve this goal by conflating the notion of person with the notion of relation, especially when this conflation is done on the basis of an ontological conviction that God per se is a "movement of relationships," and that this event of relationships does not happen outside the human's experiential, epistemic participation. Fiddes may be right in thinking that "it makes perfectly good *grammatical* [my italics] sense to speak of a *perichoresis* of *movements*,"[99] especially from a postmodernist belief in the foundational place of language in the realm of knowledge and meaning. But does it make good and accurate doctrinal sense even for Thomas Aquinas, who, according to Fiddes, is the pioneer contributor of the definition of "persons" as "subsistent relations"? It is my belief that one can raise the same question before the trinitarian proposals Robert Jenson and Ted Peters present, for they also rely heavily on the notion of "relationality." They opt almost in the same way for reducing God's substance and personal agency to an expression of an ideal form of relationality, claiming like Fiddes that the relationalization of God's being is definitive of the patristic thinking about God and the Trinity.

In the following sections, I will discuss the accuracy of Jenson, Peters, and Fiddes's one-sided reliance on the notion of "relationality" by putting it face-to-face with a theological understanding of "relationship" and "personhood" from the doctrinal tradition of the church. I will refer specifically to the notion of "relationship" in the theology of Thomas Aquinas, whose theology offers probably the most complete elaboration on the notion of "relationship" (if Boethius and the Cappadocians offer the most complete theologies of "personhood"). The questions I will tackle are: Does the theological tradition from which contemporary trinitarian theology derives its notions of "relation," "participation," and the "Trinity" allow for the allegation that movements of relationships can distinguish themselves from each other without agents to distinguish them?[100] Can relationships really exist by and in themselves? And can we speak theologically of participation as sharing *in* God's being that makes God *happen*, or *become*, or even gain *self-perfection*? Should not we rather follow

---

99. Ibid., 73.

100. Ibid., 85, where Fiddes states that the three living relations of movements "can equally be conceived as distinguishing themselves from each other."

Thomas Aquinas in speaking about a graciously given participation *with* God in his trinitarian existence in a threefold dynamic and relational action in history?

In order to shed stronger light on the inaccuracy of the reduction of the three persons to "movement of relationships," we need to go back to the trinitarian tradition that can most probably be the source of the contemporary popular notion of "subsistent relation" and "participation." This will take us back to the Scholastic period, where the doctrine of the Trinity was rigorously understood in the light of a strong association with a renewed (revisionist, I would say) interest in the Aristotelian notion of "relation." This will, more specifically, take us, as I mentioned above, to Thomas Aquinas, who is considered by the majority of theologians and philosophers as one of the most prominent Western thinkers of "relation" and "participation." I will show that the theological overemphasis on relationality represents in fact an echoing of Aquinas's trinitarian theology of "subsistent relations." Yet, as I will show, by its indifference to the full scope of Aquinas's understanding of "participation," this attention to relationality originates an inappropriate theology of "personhood" and of "relationship" in the doctrine of God, as well as in anthropology.

II. An Alternative Notion of "Relation" to Balance the Reductionism of Trinitarian Theology[101]

1. "Relatio" in Medieval Philosophy and Theology

Medieval philosophy scholars believe that Scholasticism pioneered a coherent and fully structured philosophical inquiry on the notion of "relation" in the history of thought, although the idea of "relation" itself was first philosophically analyzed so much earlier by Aristotle. The long delay of philosophizing on the notion of "relation" till the age of Aristotle may be due to the fact that at this point there was no single term in Greek language for "relation," but rather a phrase that expresses the prepositions "to" and "toward" and designates the state of being "toward something" (τά πρός τι). This may explain why in later centuries the notion of "relation" was given in Latin the specific term

---

101. I have published parts of my discussion in this section and my elaboration in the ensuing sections on Aquinas's notion of participation and relationality as Najib G. Awad, "Thomas Aquinas' Metaphysics of 'Relation' and 'Participation' and Contemporary Trinitarian Theology," in *New Blackfriars Review* 93, no. 1048 (2012): 652–70.

"*relatio*" that designates "reference, bearing, or toward-ness," and was construed "a relative that signifies the substantive meaning of something so ordered or referred."[102] In the Scholastic period, and by the help of Aristotle's philosophy, "*relatio*" was studied and thematized as a specific categorical accident that only exists in the subject in respect to another subject. There, for the first time, we see a serious inquiry about the distinction between relations and their causal foundations. We find, that is, detailed answers to the question: Is relation caused by a foundation, or is it just this foundation named in connection to something else?[103] This is what turned "relation" into a primal philosophical notion for the first time in the history of thought and generated the diverse theories of the notion during the Scholastic period.[104]

Of great importance to my study is the fact that the origin of the interest in the concept of "relation" is not purely Aristotelian or exclusively philosophical, but also theological in nature. For the theologians of that period, the driving force for studying the notion of "relation" was the attempt at forming a solid rational interpretation of the doctrine of the Trinity and establishing a lucid understanding of the idea of God's relation to his creation.[105] This goal, one must say, was achieved by a strong, almost one-sided, reliance on Aristotle's philosophy. In the light of this latter's understanding of the idea of relation, the fathers of this period understood the three divine persons of the Trinity as constituted by a network of relations.[106] This conceptual framework demonstrates a crucial view of the ontological status of relation as such, which is characterized by a plurality of meaning that in the following centuries became the fountain of many succeeding theories of relation in Western thought.

Postmodern theology noticeably inherited from the ontological thinking of people such as Thomas Aquinas, Dun Scotus, William of Ockham, and others different answers to the question of whether the relation is identical with the things that are related to each other by its means or not.[107] This heritage shapes, as it seems, the way by which many theologians today speak about "person" and "relation" within the realm of the theology of the Trinity. A trace of this impact, as I showed in the previous sections, is detectable in Robert Jenson and

---

102. "Relation," *New Catholic Encyclopedia*, 2nd ed. (Washington, DC: Catholic University of America Press/Gale & Thomson Learning, 2003), 12:40–44.

103. Ibid., 12:41–42.

104. See Rodolph Gasché, *Of Minimal Things: Studies on the Notion of Relation* (Stanford: Stanford University Press, 1999), 1–13.

105. Ibid., 2.

106. Mark G. Hanninger, S.J., *Relations: Medieval Theories 1250-1325* (Oxford: Clarendon, 1989), 1ff.

107. Ibid., 2. "Is a real categorical relation distinct from its foundation?"

Ted Peters's reliance on the model of "interdependent sociality," and in Paul Fiddes's reliance on the notion of "subsistent relation." I will now show that such a notion of relationality is borrowed from Thomas Aquinas's trinitarian theology, yet it is today interpreted and used for understanding God's trinitarian nature in a manner different in substance and content from that of Aquinas.

The key category for understanding both the Trinity and creation in Thomas Aquinas's theology is the category of "relation." Since Aquinas relies heavily on Aristotle's philosophy of substance in his writings, we need to look briefly at some of the central ideas Aristotle offers with regard to the notions of substance and relation, before, that is, we look at Aquinas's implementation of these ideas in his own theology. The patristic scholar Lucian Turcescu helps us in this task as he offers in one of his books a brief yet valuable explanation of Aristotle's use of the Greek phrase τά πρός τι, which principally means in Aristotle's writings "things [said] in relation to [something else]."[108] In order to grasp coherently Aristotle's interpretation of this phrase, especially his view of its conceptual relevance to his notion of "substance," Turcescu sets before himself the task of looking first at Aristotle's twofold definition of "relation" in *The Categories*, before viewing this definition afterwards in the light of Aristotle's understanding of "substance" and its relationality in *The Metaphysics*.

In *The Categories*, Turcescu states, Aristotle defines τά πρός τι as the name of "all such things as are said to be just what they are, of or *than* other things, or in some other way in relation to something else."[109] What things are is primarily said by means of comparison to something else, or to a different other. Aristotle's definition of relation, however, does not stop there. He rather follows this first interpretation with a qualification, which he deems necessary lest substances should also be construed as relatives. It is not accurate, Aristotle thinks, to consider the aforementioned understanding of relation inclusively definitive of substances. The substances cannot be spoken of as if in essence relations because they are by default these entities that are what they are by virtue of themselves, and not by virtue of any causal relation to another. Be that

---

108. Lucian Turcescu, *Gregory of Nyssa and Concept of Persons* (Oxford: Oxford University Press, 2005), 30–35.

109. Ibid., 3. "What is larger is called what it is *than* something else (it is called larger than something); and what is double is called what it is *of* something else (it is called double of something); similarly with all other such cases." Turcescu quotes from *Aristotle's "Categories" and "De Interpretatione,"* trans. J. L. Ackrill (Oxford: Clarendon, 1963), 6a36–40. He also relies on the discussion of the same issue in Fabio Morales's "Relational Attributes in Aristotle," *Phronesis* 3, no. 39 (1994): 55–274, and to a lesser extent on Charles H. Khan's "Questions and Categories: Aristotle's Doctrine of Categories in the Light of Modern Research," in *Questions*, trans. Henry Hiz (Dordrecht: Reidel, 1978), 227–78.

as it may, Aristotle, as Turcescu notes, qualifies his initial definition of relation in the following words:

> Now if the definition of relatives which was given above was adequate, it is either exceedingly difficult or impossible to reach the solution that no substance is spoken of as relative. But if it was not adequate, and if those things are relatives for which being is the same as being somehow related to something . . . then perhaps some answer may be found. The previous definition does, indeed, apply to all relatives, yet this—their being called what they are, of other things—is not what their being relatives is. It is clear from this that of someone knows any relative definitely he will also know definitely that in relation to which it is spoken of.[110]

Turcescu concludes from the above Aristotle's conviction about the inappropriateness of calling substances relations. Substances are "endowed with a comparatively complete sense." For instance, "a head or any such substance can be known definitely without necessarily knowing definitely that in relation to which it is spoken of."[111]

Turcescu believes that Aristotle's threefold categorization of relatives in his *The Metaphysics* sheds stronger light on the core implications of Aristotle's view in the *Categories*. There, in *The Metaphysics*, book Delta (5), section 8, Aristotle defines substances as those things that "far from being predicated of some subject, the other things are predicated of them."[112] Afterwards on section 15 of the same book Delta, Aristotle echoes the same idea of "predicating things without being predicated of them" as he divides relations into the three following categories: 1) relations said according to number, 2) relations said according to capacity, and 3) relations said according to the link between the measure and the measurable.[113] On the two categories of relations, Aristotle says "the account of something else is involved in what [these relations] are, not that what they are is involved in the account of something else."[114] In other words, these two categories of relation are inapplicable as definitions to

---

110. Turcescu, *Gregory of Nyssa and Concept of Persons*, 32; quoting from Aristotle, *Categories*, 8a28–35.
111. Turcescu, *Gregory of Nyssa and Concept of Persons*, 32–33.
112. Aristotle, *Metaphysics*, 5.8.i.
113. As articulated in Turcescu, *Gregory of Nyssa and Concept of Persons*, 33–34 echoing Aristotle, *Metaphysics*, 5.15.
114. Aristotle, *Metaphysics*, 5.15.

substances. Since what they are is not involved in the account of something else, they cannot be constitutive of the substances, of which other things are usually predicated; they are not, that is, themselves predicated of some other subjects.[115]

Only when it comes to the third category of relation (i.e., said according to the link between the measure and the measurable), Aristotle picks up a possible intersection between the notion of "relation" and the definition of substance he earlier suggests in the same book Delta. As the substance is that which other things are predicated of, this third category of relations is said to be that which the account of something else is related to, or as those measures by means of relating to which other things are measurable, as Turcescu implies in his reflection on the same Aristotelian text.[116] This is, according to Aristotle, the one and only case when the substance can be seen as relative: when the relation is necessary to substantiate what is predicated of it, not for the substance's *is* per se.

2. "RELATIO" IN THOMAS AQUINAS'S THEOLOGY

Like Aristotle, Aquinas views relation as a mode of being distinguished from the substance, yet also characteristic of the external things' connectedness to the substance. According to Hans Meyer, this Aristotelian understanding lies at the background of Aquinas's belief that "relation depends for its being not only on the existence of its subject but also on the existence of something besides this subject."[117] Thus "relation" represents for Aquinas (and Aristotle) the least and the weakest form of being-ness because its existence is not by virtue of itself, but by virtue of its subject and of the existence of something else besides its subject.

This is not to mean, however, that "relation" is a meaningless, fictitious idea of the mind. "Relation" is an accident, is a category, because it inheres in the being of its subject. Because it is real, "relation" is expressive of the substance of a real, existing subject. It is fair to say, as Meyer does, that Aquinas does not deny the existence of relations as *real* accidents, nor does he reduce all realities to mere relations. He believes that "a real relation presupposes the existence of two real *supposita*, really distinct." In other words, "a subject is required from which the relation proceeds, and another subject really distinct from the first to which the relations extends."[118] "Relation" is never inherent in another, nor is it in reference to other subjects. The subject of relation, on the other hand, can have

---

115. See again *Metaphysics*, 5.8.i.

116. Turcescu, *Gregory of Nyssa and Concept of Persons*, 34.

117. Hans Meyer, *The Philosophy of St. Thomas Aquinas*, trans. Fredric Echoff (St. Louis and London: Herder, 1954), 114.

118. Ibid., 115.

more than one form of relation with another subject or with other subjects. It can have these multiple forms of relationality simultaneously without any one of them being referred from another. All relations are rather in reference to a certain substance or subject as their foundation. This is theologically reflected in Aquinas's view of the relation between God and creation. God is related to creation by various forms of connectedness. These forms are founded on God because they are modes of relations between members who belong to two different levels of being. Because he is infinite, God is prior to creatures in nature. Therefore, the relation between him and creatures is founded on God, whose knowability by virtue of this relation is prior in importance to the relation by which God is known to creatures.[119]

The same understanding of relation characterizes Aquinas's proofs of God's existence. He proceeds from proving the existence of a first cause by means of tracing a certain relation of causation and moves into an understanding of God's being and of the Trinity. This epistemic movement from the relation between the cause and the effects up to the first cause is the main form of relation that provides the human with knowledge about God. This causal form of relationality provides, in Aquinas's opinion, knowledge of God's existence in relation to the world, despite the deficiency this knowledge holds due to human limitation and finiteness.[120]

Having said that, when it comes to God's being in himself, regardless, that is, to God's relation with creation, Aquinas is keen on departing from his previous differentiation between the relation and its subjects, and from identifying substance and existence in God. God for Aquinas is an infinite, simple, and necessary being who, contrary to creatures, does not receive his existence from another. God is being itself, and his existence is his very own being-ness, which is not in reference to any relation with another.[121] This underpins Aquinas's trinitarian thinking in his *Summa Theologica*. There, he starts his ontology of God by showing that, contrary to the human being whose being a human and his humanity are not wholly the same, God's being divine and his divine being are identical. The distinction between being a human and humanity is an expression of the fact that the human is composed of matter and form. To the contrary, since God is not composed of matter and form, "He

---

119. Ibid., 118.

120. See William W. Young III, "From Describing to Naming God: Correlating the Five Ways with Aquinas' Doctrine of the Trinity," *New Blackfriars Review* 999, no. 85 (2004): 527–41, 529. Young shows that because of its deficiency, Aquinas restricts the knowledge boundaries by means of this effect-cause form of relation to God's existence in relation to the world, not to God's triune essence.

121. Meyer, *The Philosophy of St. Thomas Aquinas*, 90ff.

must be His own Godhead, His own life, and whatever else is thus predicated of Him."[122] Because God's being-ness is not caused by an external agent, and because God is a self-efficient cause of his being (since he is the first efficient cause), God's being-ness (i.e., that he exists) and God's essence (i.e., what he is) are one and the same thing.[123] It is expected, in the light of this stress on the identity of substance and existence, that Aquinas proceeds from there to a discussion on God's unity before studying his triunity. For Aquinas, "one" means simplicity and indivisibility. Since there is no division between being-ness and substance, "being" corresponds with "one."[124] And, because "one" designates indivisibility, it is opposed to the "many" as the divisible is opposed to the indivisible.[125] As "simple Being," God, then, is one, and his being one opposes any possible plurality in his Godhead because God is undivided and not a composite in substance. "God is God, and He is this God. It is impossible therefore that many gods should exist."[126]

But, what about the Trinity—Father, Son, and Spirit? How can their existence as the Godhead concur with the previous emphasis on unity and oneness by means of identifying substance and existence? Here, Aquinas resorts to the concept of "relation" in order to show that for which the Father, the Son, and the Spirit stand. Aquinas believes that the Trinity designates in essence a possibility of procession in God. However, he insists that this procession is not an outward act done by God, as if God is causing something less than him in nature (i.e., Arius's understanding of the Son's being as less than the Father's), or as if he assumes an imagery figure before creatures (i.e., Sabellius's modalism). Contrary to both extremes, Aquinas states that "procession" expresses something inherent in God himself in a manner similar to the intelligible word that proceeds from the speaker yet remains in him.[127] This inward relation of procession means that what proceeds in God is God as well, is of the same substance. This literally applies to God's generation of his Word, or the Father's begetting of the Son. Because in God the relation's subject is identical with its relation, and because "in God the act of understanding and His being are the

---

122. Aquinas, *The Summa Theologica*, trans. Laurence Shapcote, in *Great Books of the Western World*, ed. Mortimer J. Adler (Chicago: Encyclopedia Britannica, 1990), 1:1.3.3. All my following quotations of Aquinas are taken from this version.
123. Ibid., 1.3.4.
124. Ibid., 1.11.1.
125. Ibid., 1.11.2.
126. Ibid., 1.11.3–4.
127. Ibid., 1.27.1.

same,"[128] the Word that proceeds from God is called the Son, and the generation of the Son and the Son's nature are identical.

This inward procession and its identity with God's being indicate that relations exist *really* in God. These relations' reality lies in that they all proceed from and move toward the same principal substance.[129] Moreover, God's relations *are* his essence. Their being-ness is of the being-ness of the divine essence, for "in God relation and essence do not differ from each other, but are one and the same."[130] But does Aquinas mean that these relations are totally identical in God? He does not, because Aquinas believes that the notion of "relation" he relies on presupposes an other toward whom the subject moves to relate. This means that there is a distinction between the two ends of the relation. A similar distinction appears as well in God's relations without threatening God's one and simple nature. This distinction in God is not in his nature but in his modes of relationality.[131]

What would the previous entail with respect to the three divine persons, Father, Son, and Spirit? For Aquinas, "person" signifies an existing single substance with a clear individual being. It does not mean the substance's existence that connotes its nature. It rather means the substance per se in its individual singularity as an existing reality.[132] Aquinas believes that "person" suitably names God's essence, because despite his difference from creatures in nature, God is the perfect being in whose being we have the real and absolute individual subsistence in a relational nature. God is a "person" in that he is a self-subsisting, communicable individual. "Communicability" is central to Aquinas's following interpretation of the three divine *persons* in God. He believes that "person" in the human designates individuation and particularity of *this* or *that* person. In God, however, the case is different, for "person" does not signify particularity as an accident in a nature. It rather signifies the nature itself, which is its own relations. In trinitarian terms, the Father's personhood is his fatherhood because his fatherhood lies in his relation to, or his origination of, the Son. The fatherly nature of the Father is not a sign of a particular individuality but of a relation. So, the Father's person is his fatherly relation.[133] It follows from this that the Father per se is a relation of fatherhood since "that which subsists in the divine nature is the divine nature itself."[134] In other

---

128. Ibid., 1.27.2.
129. Ibid., 1.28.1.
130. Ibid., 1.28.2.
131. Ibid., 1.28.3.
132. Ibid., 1.29.1.
133. Ibid., 1.29.3–4.

words, the Father is a fatherly relation that subsists in its own nature. The Father cannot be a personal subsistence of a divine nature because the nature is its own subsistence. And this nature cannot be a nature that has relation, because the relation is not an accident of a substance in God but rather the divine substance itself subsisted. This is the inevitable conclusion of saying that "a relation is a *hypostasis* subsisting in the divine nature."[135]

The previous exposition of Aquinas's trinitarian logic shows that Aquinas partially identifies substance and accident, existence and essence in his interpretation of "person" in the doctrine of God. Some scholars believe that Aquinas deliberately implements this Aristotelian metaphysical trend in his speech on the Trinity, rather than in his understanding of "person" and "relation" in general, for considerable apologetic reasons.[136] Such an apologetic language has led many modern theologians to believe that Aquinas is the pioneer of the total equation of "person" and "relation." They attribute to him, in other words, the collapsing of the particular personhood of God's Trinity in the relations this Trinity makes.

Nevertheless, a careful reading of Aquinas's trinitarian logic within the wider context of his thought supports William Young's recent claim that in *Summa Theologica* Aquinas reminds us that he is basically trying to explain the "*notions of persons*" in God rather than developing "personal notions."[137] These notions are constitutive of the knowledge of the persons, without which we are unable to know God because of our human limited reason. It is true that Aquinas does not, for instance, say that God's persons do not separately exist in God's substance but they are God in essence for they are three subsisted persons who are truly one essence in their relations. However, I believe that one can explain why Aquinas does not do this. He seems to believe that it is basic to maintain the ontological difference between the human and God in being. The best way to do this is to show that other than the human, "relation" and "person" in God are identical. This, in other words, means that the purpose of Aquinas's argument here is *epistemological* and not ontological in concern. His argument, as Timothy Smith says, in questions 2–26 of his *Summa Theologica* spurs a

---

134. Ibid., 1.29.4.

135. Ibid., 1.29.4.

136. Thus believes Robert L. Richards, S.J., *The Problem of Apologetical Perspective in Trinitarian Theology of St. Thomas Aquinas*, in *Analecta Gregoriana*, 131.B.43, 110–12. According to Richards, the apologetic purpose appears in that "Aquinas has relied on the metaphysics of relation to give systematic structure to the plurality of persons subsisting in the unity of the divine essence" (ibid., 111).

137. Young, "From Describing to Naming God: Correlating the Five Ways with Aquinas' Doctrine of the Trinity," 539, and Aquinas, *The Summa Theologica*, 1.40.1.

discourse on the persons of the Trinity that aims at showing the foundational necessity of the three divine persons for understanding the human degrees of knowing God, if not of knowing in principle, in this life and the life after.[138]

Aquinas's logic is followed clearly in Jenson, Peters, and Fiddes, especially in their emphasis on the priority of relations over substance by means of reducing "person" to mere "relation." However, their adoption strips Aquinas's claims of their wider and main logical framework and epistemological concern. It undermines the fact that Aquinas is not actually making the notion of "relation" the foundation of the reality of God. He is not trying to fit God's being into a criterial, preconceived notion of "relation." He is not subjecting the reality of God to a notion that is satisfactory to human reason. Aquinas is rather sorting out a logical confusion in the human mind about God's "oneness-in-Trinity" or "Trinity-in-unity" by the help of a notion that is supposed to be perceivable for the human. In order, therefore, to perceive and redeem the real dimensions of Aquinas's ontology of "relation" and "person," we need to look at Aquinas's understanding of the notion of "participation." By studying this third key notion, I endeavor to show that, by emphasizing the relational aspect in God's nature, Aquinas was not imposing on the doctrine of God a concept of "relation" that denies the subjects on the ends of the relationship, and was not, therefore, making God an expression of a movement of relations in which the human substantially participates. In other words, Aquinas's ontology of participation is a challenging criticism to the postmodern theology of participation in God.

III. A Trinitarian Metaphysic of the Notion of "Participation"

As I argue above, scholars believe that Aquinas derives his notion of "relation" from Aristotle. Aristotle distinguishes "relatives" from "relations" as such and speaks about relatives that have their relatedness by virtue of themselves and those that have their relations by virtue of relatedness to the other. In either case, "relation" is a category or a predicate *of* a relative, and not a relative per se. By this, as B. Mattingly says, Aristotle confines all the commentators who confuse "relation" with "relative."[139]

---

138. Timothy L. Smith, *Thomas Aquinas' Trinitarian Theology: A Study in Theological Method* (Washington, DC: Catholic University of America Press, 2003), 48–60.

139. *New Catholic Encyclopedia*, 12:43. Mattingly refers to Aquinas's *Commentary on the Metaphysics*, and *De Potentia*, 7–8, to show that Aquinas derives from the above mentioned Aristotelian distinction his conviction that the study of relatives is prior to that of their relations: the "what" is prior to the "how."

C. Phan believes that Aquinas applies this distinction of "relation" and "relative" to his understanding of the relationship of the Father and the Son in the Trinity. Aquinas believes that this trinitarian relationship consists of: 1) at least two existing terms related to each other; 2) an existing ground for the relationship, and in the Father and the Son's case this ground is begetting; and 3) an existing relationship as such. For Aquinas, as for Aristotle, the first characteristic of relation is that it does not exist in and by itself, for it is not a substance but an accident. "It does not subsist in itself but exists in another."[140] The second characterization of "relation" in Aristotle construes this latter as an accident, which, as Gasché says, "amounts to the property, inhering in a thing, of being-toward-another."[141] His belief that relation as "*prose ti*" should not only be perceived from its subject, but also with respect to another thing, has generated the Scholastics and Aquinas's inquiry: "Is being-toward-another possible without a movement away from and ahead of the subject of the relation?"[142] One has to say that this metaphysical inquiry is not essential only because it points to the basicality of the "openness-toward-another" characteristic of every relation. It is primarily essential because it acknowledges an existence of a subject for the relation. This importance is forcefully stressed when it is juxtaposed with another question: "What is the status of the subject, wherefrom the relation seems to originate, if relation is essentially a being-toward-other? And how does the nature of such an outgoing subject affect, in turn, the relation's nature?"[143] From presuming that "there is no relation . . . without a prior opining of the possibility of being-toward-another, by which the subject is allowed to arrive 'in' the place of the other,"[144] it clearly ensues that the idea of relation is meaningless without the relation's *subject*, and without constructing the relation with *another*. It is meaningless to speak about a relation without discerning its two ends, for no relation would ever happen without originating from a subject and destining toward *another*. Even if the relation is as such constitutive of its subject's identity, the relation per se is neither the identity of this subject as such, nor is it its own subject.

It is within the framework of this understanding of relation as the orientation of a subject toward another that Aquinas understands the notion

---

140. Ibid., 12:45.

141. Gasché, *Of Minimal Things: Studies on the Notion of Relation*, 2.

142. Ibid., 7. A similar inquiry may also underlie the shift in modernity from the attention to "what is a relation" to an attention to its knowability, which is associated with an emphasis on the knowledge of relation by means of participation *in* and *as part* of it.

143. Ibid., 8.

144. Ibid., 9.

of "participation." Aquinas uses the notion of "participation" in his ontology of God's being. Yet Aquinas departs ontologically from an acknowledgment of the necessity of the doctrine of the real distinction (not separation) between "essence" and "existence"; so that in his investment of the notion of "participation," Thomas maintains the difference between the contingent and finite, and the noncontingent and infinite, realities. For Aquinas, this difference is a basic constituent of the Christian belief in the world's origination from an infinite Creator. Aquinas concludes from this that "being related to God is a reality in creatures, but being related to creatures is not a reality in God."[145] One should again say here that the distinction between nature/essence and existence/actualization does not mean for Aquinas that essence can be without existence. It just means that the essence can sometimes be perceived without having a specific subsistence in the created universe.

Aquinas's acknowledgment of the distinction between the "essence" of the thing and the "being" through which this thing "*is*" is noticeably combined with an understanding of "participation" as "taking part in something." He invests herein the Aristotelian conviction that what belongs to something by participation can be predicated of it substantially.[146] This is how he understands the equal divinity of the Father, Son, and Spirit. Because the Son and the Spirit participate with the Father in the divine substance by virtue of proceeding from the Father, divinity is predicative of their own nature. Having said that, Aquinas differs radically from Boethius, who speaks about a single form of participation, in that Aquinas distinguishes between various forms of participation that are developed according to each subject's condition. One of these forms of participation is that of the caused effects that participate in what is attributed of their cause. This form applies, for instance, to the human's participation in God's goodness, according to Aquinas. Here, "good" is an additional predicate, in which the human participates by virtue of being caused by God as God's creature. This form of participation is different from the form of participation of the Son in the Father's essence in the Trinity. The Son's divinity is not an additional predicate opposed to the Son's substantiality. It is a substantial predicate of his nature, which lies in the Son's and the Father's equal constitution of one divine essence along with the Spirit. There is, then, an

---

145. Aquinas, *The Summa Theologica*, 1.50.2, as quoted by Peter Hick, "One or Two? A Historical Survey of an Aspect of Personhood," *Evangelical Quarterly* 1, no. 77 (2005): 41. Hick correctly realizes that Aquinas's focus on humanity's relation with God is not identical in conception with the contemporary stress on the constitutive significance of relationship for human identity.

146. See Rudi A. Te Velde, *Participation and Substantiality in Thomas Aquinas* (Leiden, New York, Köln: Brill, 1995), 11–13.

ontological distinction in the concept of "participation" with regard to God-human relations and with regard to Father-Son-Spirit relations.

Within the framework of "cause-effect" relationship, Aquinas uses the notion of "participation" to speak about the existence of created beings as *derived* from the being of God. According to Julius Weinberg, this derivation does not mean for Aquinas that the being of creatures is a "particle of the being of God." As a spiritual reality, essence in God is distinguished from the action reflexive of God's subsistence. And "participation" here means that creatures can *imitate* the way by which God exists.[147] The possibility of tracing similarity and perceiving a possible imitation by creatures of God's existence is based on the logic of causality, which as such implies a distinction between the cause/causer, the causal process and what is caused. In this imitation, there is a clear concern about emphasizing the degree of similarity that renders the creatures' participation in God's existence demonstrative of his substance. However, there is no denial here, as Norbert Metga notes, of the imperfectness and inadequacy of the caused effects, which prevent their full identification with the cause.[148] This is also why despite his appreciation of theological language and his rejection of limiting it to negation (emphasizing instead that human language does reflect a true knowledge of God), Aquinas stresses the language of causality when he speaks about participation with regard to God (*via causalitatis*) in order to maintain a clear distinction between God and our understanding of, and language about, him.[149]

It is in the light of his qualification of language, and in the context of his qualified notion of "participation," that we have to read Aquinas's conviction that analogy is the most appropriate method for conceiving theological language.[150] In his use of analogy, Aquinas is mainly interested in the relation

---

147. Julius R. Weinberg, *A Short History of Medieval Philosophy* (Princeton: Princeton University Press, 1966), 2:50–54.

148. Norbert W. Metga, *Analogy and Theological Language in the Summa Contra Gentiles: A Textual Survey of the Concept of Analogy and Its Theological Application by St. Thomas Aquinas* (Frankfurt am Main: Peter Lang, 1984), 62. Metga calls this understanding of participation in terms of imitation or likeness the "analogy of proportionality" and sets a double sense of "proportion" in Aquinas's thought (64–66). For another analysis of Aquinas's notions of proportion and proportionality, see Laurence Paul Hemming, "*Analogia non Entis Sed Entitatis*: The Ontological Consequences of the Doctrine of Analogy," *International Journal of Systematic Theology* 2, no. 6 (2004): 118–29.

149. See Battista Mondin, S.X., *St Thomas Aquinas' Philosophy: In the Commentary on the Sentences* (The Hague: Martinus Nijhoff, 1975), 87–102.

150. Ibid., 103–19. Miroslav Volf sides with the analogically shaped relation between God's being and humanity in relation to the link between the doctrine of the Trinity and ecclesiology, arguing that "'person' and 'communion' in ecclesiology cannot be identical with 'person' and 'communion' in the

between the "analogates." Analogy in essence is a linguistic relation that is not its own end. It is a relation that essentially pertains to analogates, to distinguished sides. This relational essence of analogy means that understanding Aquinas's view of analogy is possible restrictively in relation to his notion of "relation," especially when he speaks about the relation between God and the human. As this relation implies, besides unity, a diversity that lies in the difference between God and creatures that cannot be narrowed down; "analogical relations," which imply participation, also include besides the dimension of unity an aspect of diversity. This diversity appears through the fact that the relational analogy is grounded in an existence of distinct analogates, which differently appertain of similar properties because their particularities as subjects are real.[151]

This essential understanding of analogical language, and of analogy as such, on the basis of a notion of "relation" that acknowledges analogates—rather than on the basis of denying the agents at the two opposite ends of the relation—clearly shows an avoidance of reducing the subjects in the analogical language about the relation between God and humanity into mere forms of speech that originate from the human's mind, when this latter takes part in a conversation with the former. It strongly criticizes the trinitarian understanding that states that "the closest analogy between the triune God and human existence created in the image of this God is not in persons [i.e., not in analogates] but in the personal relationships themselves."[152] Karen Kilby also makes this point when she accurately points out that what Aquinas wants from speaking in his doctrine of the Trinity about three subsisting relations (Fatherhood, Sonship, and Spirithood) in the divine essence is not using the idea of "relation" to clarify, or even determine, the manner according to which the human ought to think about God. Aquinas, as Kilby states, "begins with the category of relation as he takes it to be normally understood, and then introduces as many modifications as necessary to make use of it in speaking of something internal to God."[153]

---

doctrine of the Trinity; they can only be understood as *analogous* to them." Volf, *After Our Likeness*, 199. Volf correctly states that the absence of this analogical mediation of the relation between God and his community either deifies the church or denies God his divine being.

151. Mondin, *St Thomas Aquinas' Philosophy: In the Commentary on the Sentences*, 111. "Therefore, it seems proper to conclude that for St. Thomas the essential constitutive of analogy in general are two: 1) it is a principle of unification, 2) this unifying principle is a perfection (quality, property, etc.) that is realized in several beings (or is predicated of several subjects according to different degrees)."

152. Fiddes, *Participating in God*, 49.

153. Karen Kilby, "Aquinas, the Trinity and the Limits of Understanding," *International Journal of Systematic Theology* 4, no. 7 (2005): 414–27, 421–23.

This Thomist principal belief is specifically pertinent to the postmodernist theology that tends to turn God's relational personhood into an image that ideally exemplifies the human relationality and personhood. If God's triune relational nature is beyond our comprehension, we cannot, then, turn the triune nature into a notional foundation for human relationality; a foundation, that is, that is epistemologically measurable, rationally capturable, and conceptually fixed. We cannot do this because the divine nature is beyond our rational boundaries, and because, by default, the idea of "criterion" presupposes that something must be bounded, determined, and measurable in order to work as an assessment means. Our language about the relational nature of God cannot fully capture God's relational nature per se. We can make the doctrine of the Trinity's language a criterion for measuring the accuracy of a general conception of "relation" and "personhood." Yet this does not make us naturally part and parcel of the triune life and being of God just because we image in our human life what the doctrinal language of relationship and personhood states. The overconcern about grasping the trinitarian nature of God may be the reason behind the excessive eagerness to turn God's trinitarian relational being into an absolute exemplifier of our own ideal relational, communal human nature. In the face of this enthusiasm, Thomas Aquinas offers a relational understanding of the triune God that does not turn him into a criterial model, the imaging of which we are called to in our life. It is an understanding that reminds us, rather, that "there are at least some aspects of what we must say about the Trinity, of which we can have no grasp whatsoever."[154] By remembering this, we avoid reducing God's being to a mere notional modifier of human reality.

From allocating the notion of "participation" within an analogical framework that acknowledges analogates, Aquinas sets various levels of participation in relation to his theory of the hierarchy of being and of metaphysical analogy. He concentrates therein on the form of the finite entities' participation in existence (*esse*), and he distinguishes participation in universal existence (*esse commune*) from self-subsisting existence (*esse subsistens*), which signifies God himself. For Aquinas, these two forms of existence are different from each other.[155] And God and the human are different from each other with regard to these two forms of existence. God is not the name of a universal concept, a state of existence, or an act of being. God is a self-subsisting being with his very own existence. The human, to the contrary, belongs to the entities

---

154. Ibid., 427.
155. John F. Wippel, "Metaphysics," in *The Cambridge Companion to Aquinas*, ed. Norman Kretzmann and Eleonore Stump (Cambridge: Cambridge University Press, 1993), 85–127, 95 (93–99).

of the universal form of existence. Consequently, participation in general existence does not, in Aquinas's opinion, allow created beings to share in the divine self-existence of God (*esse subsistens*). The only possible form of participation between God and created beings is by means of sharing in God's likeness, in his divine image; as the effect holds the image of its cause.[156] By this, Aquinas maintains God's self-existence as *someone*, rather than as something, in which the human participates. "Participation" means here that all existing beings are caused by one, primary *being*. It is a form of participation that is realified by virtue of sharing in the state of existence that is caused by, or comes from, God (e.g., participating in the human image of Jesus Christ).[157] God is an extrinsic, and not an intrinsic, cause of creatures' existence. Thus his essence is also laid open by means of God's very own existence, not by means of the human's intrinsic understanding of existence.

This qualified, proper theological understanding of participation is obscurely twisted when participation becomes the key notion for reducing the three divine persons in God into a mere threefold relational movement. If God's Trinity is merely relations, and if the human's person-like language is an expression of the human participation in the triune movement (which is God in essence), participation, then, implies that the human is a phase in God. This becomes an inevitable conclusion in light of the fact that human language is, after all, the creation of humans themselves, and also in the light of the allegation that participation connotes "being-part-of-something," and not "being-in-the-likeness-of-someone." On the basis of this alleged understanding of participation, existing in a relation is already inherent to the participant per se. It is not caused by another subject that is self-subsisting. This twisted view of participation is correctly played down by a theology of participation like Aquinas's, where God is the self-subsisting origin of the general existence in which humans participate.

IV. Relating to the Other as "An-Other"

The exemplary proposals on the Trinity I exposed in the previous sections give a sufficient idea about the main problem in one of today's most popular approaches to the doctrine of the Trinity. In their attempt at correcting the

---

156. Ibid., 96–97.

157. Ibid., 97, where Wippel correctly realizes that "Aquinas uses the language of participating 'by likeness' in the first and pure act, or subsisting *esse*, in order to avoid any possible suggestion that participation in the divine *esse* might mean that in some way a creature is a part of God."

classical metaphysical speech about God's transcendence, infinity, and otherness that reduces God into an *a se* divinity, theologians such as Robert Jenson, Ted Peters, Paul Fiddes, and others believe that maintaining an abstract distinction between divine nature or substance and other natures does not serve the purpose of protecting God's freedom and omnipotence. According to them, what maintains God's divine freedom, instead, is defending God's total, organic interdependence on the world and relationship with the process of history. God decided upon his free will to become incarnate as Jesus Christ and made the world an agent in his self-constitution. In making the relationship to the world constitutive of his self-becoming, God practices his divine freedom fully and omnipotently as the divine exalted deity of biblical attestation.

What these theologians do not, however, realize in their narrow attention to God's freedom is that by showing that freedom lies completely in relationality, they undermine the fact that freedom is a freedom of *someone*, and not an expression of a "free something." If "God" is just the name of a certain ideal form of relationality, it does not matter any more; it does not even make sense, if this relationality is free or not. Freedom is an attribute of active *agents*, not an attribute of things or actions. Even when we say, for example, "free mind," "free speech," or "free thinking," freedom here is not designative of the speech as such, but rather of the *speaker's* manner of communication, the *thinker's* mindset, and the cognitive rational capacities of the agent who makes the thinking and gives the speech.

To defend the free nature of a form of relational process of self-constitution we tend to name "God" is to defend a notion of freedom that is completely different from the Christian theological speech about divine freedom as one designative of a divine triune *agent* with personal identity. Defending the free nature of the triune model of relationality that the aforementioned scholars propose may be proven by them as a self-validating conception in its own terms. Yet, this as such does not mean that what they are defending is really the freedom of the God of Scripture, who is a particular infinite Creator *different from* creation. In the Bible, God is a free divine *agent* or *actor*. He is not the title of "free relationality" or "free process of self-constitution." So, defending God's freedom by reducing God's subjective identity into his divine relationality does not defend *God's* freedom, because it deletes "personhood" from the understanding of God's identity for the sake of centralizing "relationality." Freedom is useless when it no longer indicates anything about God's personhood, or when it is used as a means to reduce this personhood into mere process of communality. By reducing God's eternity into another form of historical temporality, God turns into a state of communion conditioned by the human understanding of relationality, presenting in the long run a deity that needs the world's experience of communion and relationality in order to be actual and a real, existing divine entity. George Hunsinger is quite right when he says that

> [a] Creator whose being is conditioned and restricted by the creation is not Israel's Lord. An eternity dependent upon and limited by its interaction with time is not compatible with the God of free and sovereign grace. The processional view of eternity evacuates God of His deity . . . and makes eternity dwindle into some sort of finite infinity. For God's eternal being is . . . inextricable from the temporal being of the world.[158]

Against such a reduction, Christian theological tradition, even that of the Cappadocians, consistently maintains that God is "three divine persons *in* relationships," not a "threefold process of relationality"; is "divine essence with particular, triune existence," not "triune existentiality." Against this reduction, also, Thomas Aquinas maintains that 1) by default "relationship" is something that takes place between two related entities: it is what happens between two distinguished sides and what actually points at their self-differentiation, and 2) without these two sides the relationship itself is naught; it does not exist at all.

In a paper titled "Problems of a Trinitarian Doctrine of God," Wolfhart Pannenberg detects the roots of this reduction of God's trinitarian personhood to a mere threefold network of relationality. He detects such reduction in the contemporary obsession with critiquing the traditional doctrines of God and the Trinity. And, he contextualizes this obsession in the recent trendy criticism of metaphysics and the conviction that theology can develop today an anti-metaphysical appropriation of the doctrine of God on the basis of the doctrine of revelation.[159] Pannenberg notes that the attempt at basing the doctrine of God on the doctrine of the Trinity, which became the ruling method in modern theology since Karl Barth, stands behind the conclusion of many theologians—who tried to link the being of God to the triune work in the cross

---

158. Hunsinger, "*Mysterium Trinitatis*," 167.

159. Wolfhart Pannenberg, "Problems of a Trinitarian Doctrine of God," in *Dialog* 4, no. 26 (1987): 250–57, 250. "A considerable number of contemporary theologians, while hardly in agreement over other issues, converge in looking at the doctrine of the Trinity as an inexhaustible resource which allows Christian theology to make constructive use of anti-metaphysical and atheistic criticisms of the concept of God, and, indeed, in such a way as to make possible a deeper appropriation of the specifically Christian concept of God contained in the revelation of Christ."

and the incarnation—that if the Trinity is the foundation of God's identity, the incarnation and the cross have an *ontological* relevance for the being of God.[160]

Notwithstanding the value of understanding the nature of God from the doctrine of the Trinity and not from the divine essence's oneness and simplicity, contemporary trinitarian theology, argues Pannenberg, is still stuck in the circle of treating the triune God "as a single subject, thinking of the Trinity in terms of its self unfolding."[161] The difference lies only in restructuring the notion of essence in the doctrine of God strictly upon the idea of "relationality." One of the unfortunate outcomes of this restriction lies in constituting the trinitarian persons of the Godhead as purely forms of divine relationality. By reducing personhood to relationality, Pannenberg perceptively notes, modern trinitarian theology let the two substances that stand at the end of every relation be sucked into the relation itself. Modern thought, in Pannenberg's words, "unloosed the idea of relation from this link to the concept of substance [that we inherit from Aristotle], and indeed, reversed the situation by subordinating the concept of substance to the idea of relation."[162] By putting the notion of "relation" above that of "substance," nature was reduced to a "totality of pure relations." In consequence, the personal distinction of the three divine persons is reducible into "movements in history" and the distinction between God and creation (which is, as Pannenberg states, *the* foundation of the possibility of God's being truly *all in all*[163]) is now dissolved. By denying "substance" by means of "relation," we can no longer find an appropriate foundation upon which we can prove that these relations that represent a divine process of self-constitution *are* ultimately one God. This oneness can, nevertheless, be preserved when the

---

160. Ibid., 251. Pannenberg concedes that this conclusion is reflected in his own argument in a paper titled "The God of History: The Trinitarian God and the Truth of History," where he maintains that "the reciprocity in the relationship of the divine persons makes room for the constitutive significance of the central time and change for the divine eternity . . . for the Father, the actuality of his own Godhead depends upon the working of the Son and the Spirit toward the realization of the kingdom of God in the world" ("Problems of a Trinitarian Doctrine of God," 252), referring to Pannenberg, "God of History," 76–92.

161. Pannenberg, "Problems of a Trinitarian Doctrine of God," 252. Pannenberg sees this in Robert Jenson's and Eberhard Jüngel's proposals among others, admitting that he himself has not yet developed a full elaboration that shows his distinction from these theologians with regard to this point. For an attempt at showing Pannenberg's difference here, read N. G. Awad, "Futural Ousia or Eschatological Disclosure? A Systematic Analysis of Pannenberg's Trinitarian Theology," *Kerygma und Dogma* 1, no. 54 (2008): 37–52, 39–43; as well as Pannenberg's own elaboration in the remainder of the paper I refer to in these paragraphs ("God of History," 253ff.).

162. Pannenberg, "Problems of a Trinitarian Doctrine of God," 253.

163. Ibid., 257.

doctrine of the Trinity grounds the discourses on the essence and the attributes in the doctrine of God, instead of reducing this doctrine into a mere discourse on relationality. The doctrine of God should not be exhaustively identified an interpretation of relationality in trinitarian terms, even if such interpretation is appropriate for understanding the Trinity.

In dissolving the substances into the relationships that stand at their two ends, the doctrine of the Trinity itself needs to be questioned before one can use it as a question to correct the doctrine of God. By the help of Aquinas's understanding of relationship, I tried to pursue this questioning. I endeavored in this chapter to draw the attention of postmodern trinitarian theology to a substantial difference between the traditional, Christian investment of the notions of "participation" and "relation" in the doctrine of the Trinity, on one hand, and the attempts of many of them at showing the central place of relationality in the Christian discourse on the Trinity, on the other. In these attempts, the notions of "participation" and "interdependence" are key tools for interpreting the idea of "relationship" and the criteria that decide what is the right language and hermeneutics for the concept/symbol of the "Trinity." Contrary to this approach, in Aquinas's theology, the notion of "relation," understood and interpreted on the basis of the triune being of God, constitutes the meaning of "participation." In other words, while in many of today's trinitarian theologies the language of "participation" and "interdependence" decides God's triune being, God's triune being decides which language of participation is appropriate in Christian tradition. Some contemporary theologians merely pay lip service to the idea that God defines everything but instead develop theological proposals expressing how *they* want God to accommodate their convictions. The fathers of the church, whom these theologians tend to make echo their own ideas, leave their silence and speak as if they are standing right in front of the divine other, whose trinitarian personhood reveals the Lord's face they should mirror, not the mirror that should reflect their condition.

On the other hand, the patristic use of the notion of "relation" for explaining the triune Godhead aims to explain "personhood" in God in a way that intends to avoid division, individuality, or plurality in the divine nature. On the contrary, the previous examples I displayed indicate that there is today a dominant tendency to adopt the traditional Christian notion of "relation" in order to justify the dispensation while acknowledging an existence of three "persons" in and as God. The three divine persons are reduced to three "subsistent relations" in order to validate the centrality of the notion of "participation" in the doctrine of God, and to project the notion of "participation," which is appropriate to human selfhood, over God. It is not easy to explain in a logical way how the human can participate in a self-existing *Other* of three-personal nature called God, for it is impossible to speak about one human participating in another. It is easier and more conforming to human logic to speak about human participation in a relational event or movement; that is, a human person's participation in *something* that is rather innate to her self's process of self-reconciliation. It is now a central attempt in many contemporary interpretations of the Trinity to show that the human self's Ulysses-like journey toward its Edyssa; toward, that is, its home—that is, where Ulysses' mere retrieval of his kingdom and turning back into his old identity indicate that "otherness" is just a stage of getting lost away from home—images almost literally in God's being and God's life. The question "Which is the truth, is [the human] in the image of God, or God in the image of [the human]?" is countered in postmodernity by asking "What would God be without us?," and then responding: "a call without echo, a force without effect, a principle without practice."[164] It is perceivable from this perspective why the goal of writing a trinitarian doctrine of God may easily become interpreting a notion of "participation" that strongly negates a real distinction between God and the human, and stresses otherness as just an intrinsic moment of self-actualization that lies in relationality and return to one's own self by means of objectifying this self in a state of otherness. This is why "participation" and "relationality" in such proposals are snatched from the traditional theological, and actually more appropriate, context such as the one we see in Aquinas's writings.

Thomas Aquinas's theology of relation and participation teaches contemporary theology the following. First, it teaches us that sharing the postmodern intellectual obsession with notions of "relation" and "participation" should not be executed without maintaining the criterial place of the theology of God in understanding these notions. Aquinas adopts the notions of "relation" and "participation" from Aristotle and thus shares tangibly in the intellectual interest of his era. Yet, his understanding of these notions is grounded in the doctrine of God: God's relational nature is the foundation of our understanding of participation and relation. Ulysses' journey may be the story of a human's life of self-seeking and being-ness, but it is not the story of God.

Aquinas's theology teaches us today that emphasizing God's relatedness to creation can be achieved without reducing God to an ideal image of a human existential relationality by means of rejecting his transcendent, personal

---

164. Questions posed by the cursed, eternally wandering Ahasverus in Stefan Heym's novel, *The Wandering Jew* (Evanston, IL: Northwestern University Press, 1981), 122, 266.

otherness and reducing him, eventually, to a mere symbol of intersubjective otherness that is innate to human existence. Stating that God is intrinsically relational is fundamental to a Christian theology of God. It has substantial importance for the doctrine of salvation, because only a relational nature can show the value and the real impact of God's salvific action on human's life. A God who is not relational in nature is useless and meaningless to any other, even if this God holds the most sublime feelings and intentions conceivable. Having said that, the relationality of God should not be an excuse for ignoring the question of God's being and his particular self-existing self for the sake of his actions and connectivity. Such a dissipation of being, as Mark Heim correctly notes, will eventually rule out the reality of "relation" itself. It would indicate a full regard to a pure relation with no distinctive persons or "ones" to have a relation.[165] Emphasizing God's personal otherness as self-existing being (and not as a name for relationality) does not imply that rejection of the reduction of God to mere movement of relations (in which the human's participation is required for the sake of movement of itself) is a strategy for defending an abstract, immutable, and isolated form of deity one more time in the history of human thought. Emphasizing God's otherness and trinitarian personhood points, rather, to the necessity of structuring hermeneutics for a notion of "relation" that is more conceptually convenient for theological ontology than the one dominant today.

We need to retrieve a theology capable basically of showing that while there is an ontological gulf that does not allow finite creatures to experience a form of participation in the infinite so as to have knowledge of what it is like to be God, such an ontological gulf is overcome by virtue of God's trinitarian life in time as an infinite being who can know what it is like to be a finite creature, without, however, turning his otherness into a state within the human story of self-fulfillment. We need to retrieve such a theological understanding in a qualified way so that we don't dissolve the fact that such an overcoming of the ontological gulf is possible for the infinite because it is transcendent and distinct from the finite in its very own being. We need to maintain the transcendence characteristic of God's personal being in order not to turn the participation of God in the finite's realm of existence into a panentheistic or one-sidedly, human-centered, immanentist relationality. Even God cannot execute such panentheistic participation because all knowledge that God has of the finite is always embedded in his infinite divine mind. Otherwise, God's interaction with

---

165. Mark S. Heim, *The Depth of the Riches: A Trinitarian Theology of Religious Ends* (Grand Rapids: Eerdmans, 2001), 24.

the human makes him lose some of his attributes;[166] makes him, that is, lose his personhood.

The panentheistic concept of "personhood" is no less problematic with regard to the human's being and life, especially if the interpretation of these latter is claimed to be derivable from the being and life of the triune God of Scripture. I side completely with Kallistos Ware's affirmation that the anti-panentheistic view of personhood, which reflects a distinction between personhood and relationality, is characteristic of the Bible's attestation of personal relationships. This is evident in the biblical speech about the relationships between the three persons in the Trinity, especially the relationship between the Father and the Son. "In the Gospel," Ware correctly states, "when Jesus prays to His Father and the Father replies, surely more is involved than an overlapping between 'two manners of subsisting.'" "And," he continues, "when the fourth gospel interprets the relationship between Father and Son in terms of mutual love, let us keep in view the truth that only persons are capable of such love; 'movements' or 'ways of being' do not and cannot love one another."[167] If humans are "transcripts of the Trinity,"[168] everything the Trinity is, including the distinction between the divine persons and their relationships, should be imaged (undoubtedly with appropriate qualifications) in the human nature. So, if in the triune God personhood and relationality are not reduced to each other, human personhood also should not be reduced to mere movements of subsisting or relating, though this personhood should be relational in nature in order to really image God's triune personhood. Only when this distinction between personhood and relationality is maintained, the image of the triune God, as Ware says, truly "comes to full realization in the 'between' that unites 'me' with 'neighbor' and 'I' with 'thou' in a bond of love."[169] Without this distinction between the person and her relations, the "between" concept is meaningless.

In addition, I also side completely with a similar critique that Miroslav Volf launches against the total identification of personhood and relationality in relation to human reality. I believe, with him, in the accuracy of the problematic anthropological implication of such identification and its threat to human

---

166. See Gordon Knight, "The Theological Significance of Subjectivity," *The Heythrop Journal* 1, no. 46 (2005): 1–10, 4.

167. Kallistos Ware, "The Holy Trinity: Paradigm of the Human Person," in *The Trinity, East/West Dialogue*, ed. Melville Y. Stewart (Dordrecht, Boston, and London: Kluwer, 2003), 227–43, 234.

168. Ibid., 235.

169. Ibid., 235–36.

freedom. Volf is right in saying that the freedom God bestows on the human by means of the relations he enjoys with him

> presupposes that the person constituted and determined by these relations is in fact not identical with those relations, but rather is able to stand over-against and relate to its social and natural environment, and that it is able to make something both of its relationships and of itself as a being that stands in such relationships.[170]

The person, as Volf affirms elsewhere, "is always already outside of the relations in which he or she is immersed." Therefore, "non-assertiveness of the self in the presence of the other," Volf concludes, "puts the self in danger either of dissolving into the other or being smothered by the other"; especially if the other is dominantly powerful, and this self is weaker and can easily be at the mercy of the stronger side's manipulation or violation.[171] Only when one's personhood is not totally constituted by its relationships, but gains recognition of its otherness in and through them, the personhood of the other is also recognized in its otherness; in its particular self as that which is "not-mine" and cannot be one day abbreviated into what is "mine." The otherness of the related sides can be maintained in its particular alterity strictly when the relationship enables the related sides to define themselves *through* the relation, and not *as* it.

I side anthropologically as much as theologically with the ontological premise Volf is defending above because I believe that the postmodernist total identification of "person" and "relation" replaces the modernist constraining emphasis on self-enclosed individualism by another no less constraining relation-based collectivism. Such collectivism is mistakenly thought to be demonstrative of God's image in the communal life-setting of the church. It in

---

170. Volf, *After Our Likeness*, 186. Volf correctly argues, in addition, that even if our notions of "personhood" and "relationality" were formed after personhood and relationality in the Trinity, there are basic limits to this modeling. Trinitarian personhood and relationality can be applied to human communality, Volf argues, in analogues and creaturely and not univocal sense. Volf, *After Our Likeness*, 198–200; and Volf, "'The Trinity Is Our Social Program,'" 405.

171. Volf, "'The Trinity Is Our Social Program,'" 410. Siding with Volf's view here does not mean that I fully support social trinitarianism in all its claims. I do agree with Karen Kilby's warning of the serious amount of "projection" the social interpretation of the doctrine of the Trinity exerts on the understanding of God's eternal nature and like her, I do believe that the speculation on the social or any other kind of analogy for the Trinity should not be considered a first-, but rather a second-order set of rules to deploy the Christian vocabulary on God in a proper manner. Kilby, "Perichoresis and Projection: Problems with Social Doctrines of the Trinity," *New Blackfriars Review* 81, no. 956 (2000): 432–45.

fact turns the church into a form of a communal cocoon that dissolves personal particularity and distinctive freedom in a collectivist network of premeditated forms of communality; the cocoon that is not in principle different from the collectivist social cocoon of the communist, or even Islamic/Arabic, societies (such my homeland Syria, or Lebanon, where I worked and studied), where the "I am" that designates personal particularity dissolves in an obligatory form of relations and becomes the "not-I."[172] I concur, eventually, with David Brown's retention of the understanding of personhood in terms of "center of self-consciousness" in relation to personal relationality. This earlier dimension of personhood does not oppose the latter dimension of relationality. It rather affirms its happening and makes its distinction real. For, as Brown says, "only if an individual is aware of himself as an agent, and the distinct cause of a particular action, does it make sense to speak of him as a person [i.e., as a relational being] at all."[173]

To take this argument to the wider framework of the theology-postmodernity relationship, if modern panentheism links God ontologically to the world in a way that turns the world into a function of God's being, therefore disabling creation to become itself, as Gunton charges,[174] the postmodern theological panentheism, as I endeavored to show in the second part of this study, develops an existentially organic link between the human and the idea of deity in a way that turns God into a mere function of the human's self-becoming identity, thus disabling God from being a self-existing, Wholly Other infinite Being.[175] Postmodernity and postmodern theology strongly attend to the concept of the "other," and they argue that there is no existing self and no existing reality without the other. However, they forget that the other, especially when this other is meant to be God, must, as Rowan Williams says, "precisely *be* other—not the fulfillment of what I think I want; the answer to my lack."[176] Jürgen Moltmann once very pointedly asked: "Is the Godhead just a screen for all possible projections, with the slogan 'what's your fancy?'

---

172. Ibid., 187. Against this, Volf states that "one can derive the unity of the church already from the plurality of its members instead of grounding it in the claim that the church is a single subject, a unity which does not respect the independence of communally determined persons" (ibid., 189).

173. David Brown, "Trinitarian Personhood and Individuality," in *Trinity, Incarnation and Atonement: Philosophical and Theological Essays*, ed. Ronald J. Feenstra and Cornelius Plantinga Jr. (Notre Dame: University of Notre Dame Press, 1989), 48–78, 69. By "self-consciousness," Brown means "awareness of oneself as a distinct entity" (ibid., 70).

174. Colin E. Gunton, *The Promise of Trinitarian Theology*, 2nd ed. (Edinburgh: T. & T. Clark, 1997), 209.

175. On the various trends of panentheism in contemporary theology, see the collection of papers in Clayton and Peacocke, *In Whom We Live and Move and Have Our Being*.

Is Christian faith a religious supermarket?"[177] My answer, as I argued here, is that God is definitely not the fulfillment of the human search for the meaning and image of her being. God is the *Other* who makes the human in his image specifically by refusing to be a screen for all possible human projections.

By discerning the personal nature of God that lies in the distinction between his triune personhood and his trinitarian, relational activities, I am going to look in the following chapters for a trinitarian hermeneutics of personhood in which we maintain a logical distinction, to which Thomas Nagel once pointed, between "knowing something about the personal identity of someone from her behavior and relations" and "knowing how it is like to be a person with this kind of personality and what it is for this person to behave with and relate to others in the way she does."[178] Beside the question "What is it like to be a person?" there stands another equally important one: "What is it like to be *this* or *that* person you are?"[179] Later on, I will point to a theological reflection on such an inquiry on personhood in other trends of trinitarian theology. But, before I do this, let me turn back to the main frameworking issue within which I started mapping the theology-postmodernity relationship. At the beginning of the previous chapter, I argued that there is a theological trend in today's scholarship that attempts to show that postmodernity is from beginning to end theologically conditioned discourse(s) and that the narrative, which postmodernity offers as a deconstruction to modernity, is actually inherent to the narrative that Christianity wrote about faith and God throughout the centuries. In the succeeding parts of that chapter and this one, I argued that the outcome of this zealous throwing of Christian theology into the arms of postmodernity has produced an unfortunate reconstruction of theological reasoning after the intellectual and conceptual conditions that are definitive of postmodernity, e.g., notions of "relationality," "otherness," "participation," and "transcending transcendence." Before I bring this part to an end, I would like to make some final, concluding remarks on this attempt to theologically condition and recontextualize postmodernity and its negative, ultimately nonrelational, consequences, and on what I believe should be characteristic of a proper relationship between theology and postmodernism's forms of intellectual inquiry.

176. Rowan D. Williams, *Lost Icons: Reflections on Cultural Bereavement* (Edinburgh: T. & T. Clark, 2000), 153.

177. Elisabeth Moltmann-Wendel and Jürgen Moltmann, *God—His and Hers* (New York: Crossroad, 1991), 35.

178. Thomas Nagel, "What Is It Like to Be a Bat?" *The Philosophical Review* 83 (1974): 435–50.

179. Knight, "The Theological Significance of Subjectivity," 2.

V. Concluding Remarks: The Validity of the Re-Conditioning Ambition

One should not, in my opinion, deny the principal validity of challenging the allegation that theology needs to rely on a sociological "reading" of itself *from outside* its own disciplinary boundaries in order to understand itself and to be acceptable to other forms of knowledge. It is also the duty of theologians, in my view, to show the difference of Christianity from both modernity and antiquity, if this task is meant to disclose the particularity of the theological discourse and the uniqueness and otherness of the subject matter of faith, that is, God. Such a task becomes a problem and an obstacle before theology itself, however, when it invests in reactionary affirmations such as: all "scientific" theories are themselves "theologies or anti-theologies in disguise." They are, that is, theologically conditioned, if not even "theological conditions" in nature.[180] It is my belief that such a theologization approach attempts at nothing other than resisting the conversion of Christianity into a ghetto by turning Christianity into another no-less-ghettoizing framework; by, that is, showing that the Christian narrative is *the* criterion, the one and only criterion, for understanding the postmodern condition. This is what makes many recent theological projects derive ideas and concepts for theological inquiry from the postmodern writers and their precursors, hoping, rather inappropriately, to show thereby that theology and postmodernity are just two sides of the same coin.

One can initially consider the previous "conformity-leadership" debate a positive warning to theology about the challenges that face it, and the responsibilities that may be required from it, in the contemporary intellectual context. It is undoubtedly crucial to realize that postmodern conditions may turn out to be an exodus from the constraints of modernity into another conditional phenomenon intolerant of the theological proclamation of a self-existing, infinite divine Creator/*archē*, because this last belief is considered one of the prevailing ideologies of modern thought. However, I believe that one should remain equally mindful of the manner by which theology tends to deal with this threat. Theologians need to be fully aware of the side-effects of the recontextualization strategy into which they heavily invest. This awareness becomes more crucial in light of the fact that there are theologians who already

---

180. Ibid., 3. "Contemporary theologies which forge alliance with such theories are often unwittingly rediscovering concealed affinities between positions that partake of the same historical origins."

either "call themselves postmodern" or "have been described as such,"[181] without discerning the possibility of such a challenging outcome.

One of the important theological tasks today, in my opinion, is examining in specific the validity and the intentions of the theologies that *call themselves* postmodern. Those who *have been considered* postmodernist, or *whose language may make them seem so*, may not actually be postmodern in intention, or may not even concede themselves to be so, even when their advocates, similarly to the postmodern theologians par excellence, say that "theology cannot simply react to culture, but must approach it from a particular context of worship and life."[182] We need to scrutinize the validity of theologies that bluntly purport to recontextualize postmodernity. The proposed transformation of the postmodern condition into a theological condition presents theology per se as an absolute, single referential criterion for an intellectual condition that emphasizes relativism in a way that does not tolerate any kind of authority. This theological conditioning would equally impoverish theological thinking as such from its own particular content, which stems from a belief in a triune God who interacts with creatures in a manner that acknowledges the human's particular nature, as well as maintains God's trinitarian, personal self-distinction. In other words, while it is legitimate to show that there is a substantial place for theology in the postmodernist arena of intellectual inquiry, it is necessary to abstain from turning the contemporary forms of cognitive inquiry into a theological condition *only* and *totally*. We need, first, to see if the mere concern about proving a legitimate pretension to the postmodern throne is itself theologically a necessary, valid, or appropriate ambition or not. It may end up being just another way of acquiring autonomy in a new phase of human history, so that what was confiscated from theology in modernity is now paid back with interest by the postmodernist conditions of cognitive inquiry.

It is more appropriate to go beyond both "postmodernity as a condition of theology" and "postmodernity as a theological condition" toward another option in which theology and postmodernity reciprocate enrichment and challenge between each other, in a way that revises and balances postmodernity rather than proclaims it a new form of theologization as such. This qualification of the relationship is important for theology as much as for contemporary intellectual conditions. As it maintains the postmodern necessary principle of

---

181. See the preface to *The Cambridge Companion to Postmodern Theology*, ed. K. J. Vanhoozer (Cambridge: Cambridge University Press, 2003), xiv.

182. Gunton, *The Promise of Trinitarian Theology*, 17. There are recently postmodern theologians who made similar claims to Gunton, but without maintaining his theological sensitivity to God's transcendence and his particular objective being.

plurality and diversity, it also releases theology from the demand of proving its qualifications before the postmodern condition. Theology does not need to earn such recognition because: 1) postmodernity does not acknowledge any universal criterion of legitimating; 2) there is no *one* postmodern trend of thought to which theology must show allegiance and for which it should be a constitutive condition; 3) the postmodern condition itself should prove its proper contribution to theology on the basis of the theological doctrine of a God who is neither an expression of a textual infinite meaning nor a linguistic signification of favored ideas, like "charity," "hospitality," "justice," and "gift."

This last point should be constitutive of any model of interaction we concede between theology and postmodernity. Postmodernity may prove that it is not a new bondage to theology. However, this does not make postmodernity the savior of theology from subordination to certain intellectual presumptions, or at least it does not make it directly so. What is not "bondage" is not by default necessarily "savior" or "means of salvation." It is crucial to maintain an awareness of the dangerous implications of a fundamental postmodern rejection of the existence of an objective reality, of the subject as a particular self, and of the idea of "essence." The contemporary forms of cognition (as with any other forms of rationality that dominated history at one era or another) should not be the conditioners of God's ontological reality, even if they happen to help theology overcome certain problematic conceptual constraints, or even if they revealed readiness to become in the long run an expression of theological condition. Viewing any secular intellectual form of inquiry as a theological condition in substance may become a new form of conditioning to theology itself, when, for example, it entails an undermining of God's transcendental reality and the ontological characteristics of his divine nature. It is a challenge for postmodern theologies that attempt a total theological recontextualization of postmodernity to show if this project can be tenable *theologically* without any serious attention to the ontological nature of God's transcendental reality that we encounter in Jesus Christ.

I agree with Stanley Grenz's description of the threatening dimension of the theological conditioning and contextualization of postmodernity when he says that the eagerness to gain a hearing from the postmodern world by showing theologians' gravitation to certain recently popular and appealing issues in order to reveal the plausibility and intelligibility of theology may not work, because such a gravitation may not attract the interest of a "culture whose attention is fixed in other directions."[183] I also believe that such gravitation may even have an opposite effect on the role of theology in the church itself. It may just lead the church to ignore all kinds of theological discourses, good or bad, in recent times, and listen instead to other voices that may be problematic, as, for instance, the claims of recontextualization. Eventually, this would echo the earlier theologians' endeavor to show theology's competence vis-à-vis the modernist condition, which has also led the church to listen to voices other than the voices of theology.

---

183. Stanley J. Grenz and John R. Franke, *Beyond Foundationalism: Shaping Theology in a Postmodern Context* (Louisville: Westminster John Knox, 2001), 11.

PART III

The Proposal: Trinitarian Theology and Postmodernity: In Correlation?

5

Correlation and/as Hierarchism, or What We Do Not Need

I. Correlation as a Method of Subordination

According to George Hunsinger, one of the trends that offer a promising theological relationship with postmodernity is that which calls for a dialogue between theology and secular inquiry *from* the standpoint of the doctrinal and confessional claims of the Christian faith.[1] The relevance of this dialogical approach, Hunsinger opines, stems from its representation of an overlap and, ultimately, a reconciliation between confessional and doctrinal theology (i.e., "evangelicalism," as Hunsinger puts it), on one hand, and contemporary hermeneutics of "method" and "meaning" on the other.[2] In this dialogical approach, one reaches a stage where one can finally dispense with the obligation of choosing between either maintaining a liberal/evangelical split (usually seen

---

1. George Hunsinger, "Postliberal Theology," in *The Cambridge Companion to Postmodern Theology*, ed. K. J. Vanhoozer (Cambridge: Cambridge University Press, 2003), 42–57, 42–42ff. According to Hunsinger, this trend of thought starts with the postliberal approach of Yale theologian Hans Frei. Frei's postliberal approach is reminiscent of Karl Barth's methodological movement from the traditional to the modern, from the confessional theology of the tradition and its ecclesial commitment to a theological method shaped in dialogue, and in dialectic, with secular methods and disciplines: "The logic of Frei's theology tended to move from the particular to the general, from the ecclesial to the secular, and from the confessional to the methodological." According to Hunsinger, this method distinguishes Frei's approach from the one of his Yale colleague, George Lindbeck, who follows the opposite approach. Thus Hunsinger calls Frei's project "postliberal" and Lindbeck's "neoliberal." Contrary to this, Stanley Grenz still considers Lindbeck one of the pioneers of *postliberal* theology (Grenz and Franke, *Beyond Foundationalism*, 5–6). I personally side with Hunsinger's "postliberal-neoliberal" distinction, and, therefore, place Lindbeck with those who try to turn postmodernity into a theological condition, while I see Frei's approach as a promising relation between theology and any secular condition.

2. Hunsinger, "Postliberal Theology," 4. Frei's approach is, in the first place, an answer to modernism, not to postmodernism. However, this approach applies, in my opinion, to the discussion of the relation between theology and postmodernity. It works as a relevant modeling of a balanced correlation.

as characteristic of modernity), or one-sidedly promoting a purely liberal conversion of theology by means of premeditated secular methods.[3] In Hunsinger's analysis, there is a call for theology to develop a correlational identity in which theological hermeneutics is done within a postmodern context in a manner that maintains a logical and principal distinction between meaning and truth, between God's reality and the linguistic, textual attestation to it.[4]

Graham Ward seems also to support a similar call for a correlational form of interaction that supposes theology to be one of the constitutive elements of the postmodern condition. Ward follows an approach similar to Hunsinger's in speaking about, first, the useful role that the postmodernist, popular method of deconstruction can play in theology, and, second, the impact that theology can have on the project of deconstruction within postmodernity. In his proposal, however, Ward warns of a possible slip into an emphasis on one side of the correlation at the expense of the other side; turning correlation into an arena of hierarchy or domination, which the present world fought so hard to get rid of when it criticized absolutism and authoritarianism in modernity. Ward alludes to this danger:

> Deconstruction might be employed by a theological project to draw attention to the operations of the linguistic sign, but it cannot be "theologized" per se because then the *nihil* would be the condition for naming God.[5]

In other words, Ward invites theologians to keep in mind, as they implement nontheological methods of interpretation in their reconstruction of theology, that if they take for granted every postmodern project that leads naturally to a theological meaning, and if they insist on interpreting postmodernity as a theological discourse, they may find themselves not only obliged to consider as theological everything postmodernity claims, but also to consider as theological everything *it does not* concede. If, for example, the deconstructionist emphasis on the centrality of language and of "*différance*"

---

3. Ibid., 45. This may suggest that Frei's view is more like "reinterpretation" than "redefinition" of the propositional content of theology.

4. Ibid., 48. Texts, accordingly, mediate realities that both precede and transcend their textual embodiment.

5. Graham Ward, "Deconstructive Theology," in *The Cambridge Companion to Postmodern Theology*, 76–91, 84.

is deemed a theological discourse, the theological recontextualization of postmodern deconstruction requires that the postmodern denial of the existence of a transcendent, self-existing Being or origin (*archē*) should also be considered as a theologically proper claim. Contrary to such a pure theologization of postmodernity, Ward cautions against treating "deconstruction" as essentially a theological concept, and advises viewing "deconstruction" and assessing its validity for theology from the angle of the doctrinal propositions and norms of the Christian faith.

There is a need, then, for qualifying the eagerness of many contemporary theologians to prove that postmodernity is a purely theological condition. For the sake of achieving such a qualification, a correlational understanding of the relation between theology and postmodernity is needed in today's scholarship. The question to be tackled in this chapter in the light of Keith Ward's valid warning, nevertheless, is the following: What form of correlation is valid between theology and postmodern forms of intellectual inquiry, and what is not? In this chapter and the following, I will expose two models of correlation presented by two groups of theologians who take seriously consideration of the intellectual changes that secular human thinking and scholarship bring to human religious history. The first model, and the subject of this chapter, is that which is present in the work of David Tracy, Gordon Kaufman, and Mark Taylor. The second is in the work of Hans Frei and Francis Watson, and will be presented in the following chapter.

In this chapter, I will show that the models of correlation found in Tracy, Kaufman, and Taylor fail to exceed the conditioning rules of postmodernity. They actually subordinate theology to these rules, and its content is controlled by them. On the other hand, Frei's and Watson's models of correlation represent, in my opinion, a balanced form of correlation that maintains theology's and postmodernity's self-integrity and particularity. They call for a relationship between theology and other forms of intellectual inquiry that maintains the distinction and integrity of each side of the relation, without undermining the unity that appears in their reciprocal interaction.

II. David Tracy's Revisionist, Correlational "Theology"

In his book, *Blessed Rage for Order*, David Tracy presents a theology founded on a correlational relationship with postmodern forms of inquiry. Tracy starts his book by pinpointing the core difference between the "modern" and the "postmodern" forms of human inquiry or models of humanity. According to Tracy, the modern understanding of the human self imposes on human existence the image of an autonomous, lonely, rational critic who claims total freedom from religious (here, Christian) traditional norms, as well as calling for the development of an absolute understanding of human capacities and reason that are capable of enhancing the reality of human autonomy.

On the contrary, the "postmodern" condition represents a blunt disenchantment with, and total opposition to, the previous sanguine view of human rational and individual abilities. Like modernity, postmodernity departs principally, as Tracy argues, from a strong belief in the necessity of self-criticism and liberation from any absolutization of the present. Yet, in the case of the postmodern understanding of human self, this self-criticism is solely interpreted, says Tracy, "as a demand for 'self-transcendence': a radical commitment to the struggle to transcend our present individual and societal states [i.e., no matter how autonomous they may be] in favor of a continuous examination of those illusions which cloud our real and more limited possibilities for knowledge and action."[6] Although modernity and postmodernity join each other to a certain extent in the concern for a full-scale critical self-understanding, Tracy indicates here that postmodernity relies on this very paradigm of self-criticism in deconstructing modernity's view of the human self. It waters it down from within primarily by showing that the modernist understanding of the rational, autonomous individual self is nothing but an "illusion" or a myth. "Self-transcendence" is used in postmodernity as an expression of disenchantment with these illusions about human self-sufficiency, for the human is neither "as autonomous nor as critical as his pronouncements would suggest." The human is rather in a radical need for "self-transcending personal and societal liberation."[7]

Rather than giving up the critical assessment, and far from reacting to liberal modernity by retreating into one form of intellectual conservatism or another, postmodernity, Tracy argues, holds to the ethical demands of the liberal spirit born in modernity. This time, though, postmodernity applies the critical exigencies of the previous phase both on modernity and on itself. In other words, it sets before itself a commitment to a constant self-transcendence that enables the human to be free from an illusion like "the free person is free from all illusions." It enables her to be disenchanted with any mythical belief in the possibility of complete disenchantment. In sum, the postmodern paradigm of "self-transcendence" states that in order to fly free from the cage of the

---

6. David Tracy, *Blessed Rage for Order: The New Pluralism of Theology* (Chicago and London: University of Chicago Press, 1996), 11.

7. Ibid., 12.

modernist view of the rational human being we need the "emancipatory power of human rationality itself."[8]

What would theology do in the light of this postmodernist shift? Tracy believes that theology should take the postmodernist call for self-transcendence seriously and change itself into an epistemological discourse reflective of this new paradigm. After deconstructing the modernist claim of absolutism by means of the same criteria of absoluteness that modernity recognizes as fundamental, Tracy proposes a new form of theology he calls "revisionist theology." He presents this theology as one that is, in his opinion, compatible with the newly dominating forms of human inquiry in the postmodern intellectual atmosphere. Rather than either isolating itself from the postmodern context of cognition or succumbing to it completely, Tracy invites theologians to acknowledge the need for maintaining the theological ideal by looking for new methods of cognition and new sources for fulfilling this ideal. He believes that the theologian (i.e., postliberal, in specific) must realize that "both secularity and traditional Christianity should be challenged in accordance with publicly available criteria for meaning, meaningfulness and truth."[9]

The main characteristic constitutive of this revised version of theology for Tracy is *correlation*. But why correlation and nothing else? Tracy believes that it is correlation in particular that seals for theology the following two sources as central to its methodology: traditional Christian texts, and common human experience and language.[10] The roots of Tracy's understanding of "correlation" are elucidated further in a subsequent work, *Plurality and Ambiguity*. There, Tracy gives the correlation between Christian tradition and general human experience and language, which he calls for in *Blessed Rage for Order*, a more general character that exceeds the realm of religious thinking and calls it "conversation." For him, the notion of "conversation" is the best expression of such a correlation between theology and other secular forms of inquiry because it is a key designation of the correlational communication between religious discourse and a general scientific theory of hermeneutics. In this conversational model of relationship "postmodern hermeneutics," as Tracy argues, "is the test of any interpretation of any religion; at the same time, religion . . . is . . . the best test of any theory of interpretation."[11] According to Tracy, the theologian applies a conversational model of interaction to her theology when she 1)

---

8. Ibid., 13.
9. Ibid., 33–34.
10. Ibid., 43ff.
11. David Tracy, *Plurality and Ambiguity: Hermeneutics, Religion, Hope* (New York: Harper & Row, 1987), ix–x.

continually searches for "adequate expressions of the religious dimensions of our common experience and language," and 2) finds a method of interpretation capable of "discarding *at least* the central meanings of the principal textual expressions of Christianity (viz. the scriptural)."[12] By correlating the results of these two tasks, the theologian then determines the two components' "significant similarities and differences and their truth-value."[13]

The correlational method is what grants theology acceptance in postmodernity, according to Tracy, because "contemporary Christian theology is best understood as *philosophical reflection* upon the meanings present in common human experience and the meanings present in the Christian tradition."[14] This philosophical reflection is oriented toward a metaphysical dimension inherent in the theistic meanings sown in the soil of both the common human experience and language, and the Christian tradition.[15] By nature, religious discourse consists of inquiries about human condition in general: theology is from beginning to end a human-made production. Therefore, any human person can offer answers to religious inquiries without necessarily being a confessed religious believer or a professionally designated theologian.[16] The secular interpreters, moreover, can even correct and revise any theological claim when they realize any irrelevance, inadequacy, or obscurity in its conventional language.[17] Theology is not, in sum, just a discourse open before, and tolerant of, the requirements and demands of other forms of inquiry in today's scholarly arena. Theology is further conditioned and shaped by these demands and is appraised according to these requirements and expectations.

Tracy's description of theology as a philosophical reflection is worth attention and analysis. By "philosophical reflection," Tracy means an invocation of the epistemological methods that are usually used in philosophy to explicate and investigate every phenomenon that appears to human consciousness by means of "self-transcending," of "rising above," or of "going beneath" this phenomenon to "discover the most basic presuppositions or (more critically

---

12. Tracy, *Blessed Rage for Order*, 48–49.

13. Ibid., 53.

14. Ibid., 34.

15. Ibid., 52–56, 172–203, where Tracy speaks about the "transcendental or metaphysical mode of reflection" as a method of hermeneutic constitutive of the revisionist theology for which he calls.

16. Tracy, *Plurality and Ambiguity*, 86. "Any human being can interpret the religious classics because any human being can ask the fundamental questions that are part of the very attempt to become human at all, those questions that the religious classics address."

17. Ibid., 88.

formulated) 'conditions of possibility' of that phenomenon."[18] According to Tracy, this form of theology cannot be constructed upon the classical Christian theism of the church.[19] Only by speaking about God as an objective ground *in* reality rather than speaking about the objective reality of God per se, can the concept of "God" 1) have a cognitive relevance to human religious language and experience, or 2) become useful for a correlational theology that reflects philosophically on religion from both common human experience and Christian tradition. Be that as it may, the constitutive contents of Christian faith, say the objective reality of God, becomes one of the basic "*cognitive, human-made claims*" for the Christian common religious experience and language.[20] It becomes the correlational cognitive form of speech that theology needs to unveil its rational intelligibility and compatibility for the common human experience in general. Only by deeming the religious reality of God one of the *cognitive* postulates, "God" can be considered an appropriate concept for a correlational theology and for hermeneutics of traditional Christian texts.

Rather than the question of the objective reality of God, the fundamental inquiry is now whether or not, in the theological thought that departs from a correlational relation with other forms of rational inquiry, it is by any means valid to include metaphysical language (i.e., to speak about the objective reality of God, for example) in hermeneutical and philosophical investigations. For Tracy, "a primary task of metaphysical reflection should be the investigation of the cognitive claims of religious language,"[21] so that the possibility of a cognitive use of language in Christian religion becomes evident to the postmodern context and the process of correlation achieves its purpose. In other words, the only acceptable metaphysics is one that offers an interpretation affirmative of, rather than confrontational with or distinguished from, the acceptable meaning of the metaphors and symbols of this language as they are used in the general postmodernist arena of thinking. If, for example, "God is love" is a constitutive metaphor in Christian traditional language, the metaphysical hermeneutics we apply to this language should seek this metaphor's meaning in a philosophically and cognitively tenable manner that accords with the scientific trends of research in today's intellectual arena. We

---

18. Tracy, *Blessed Rage for Order*, 67. In Tracy's view, this understanding of philosophy is what makes it doubly characterized as phenomenological and transcendental.

19. Tracy, *Plurality and Ambiguity*, 147. As an example of such theism, Tracy alludes to Aquinas and Calvin (fn. 9), who state that God and humanity are ontologically distinguished, and that God is a wholly self-existing, objectively infinite other.

20. Ibid., 146ff.

21. Ibid., 160.

cannot say God is love and then speak metaphysically about this God as impossible and unchangeable in nature,[22] because this metaphysical language is no longer deemed scientifically and epistemologically reliable. We have to revise our understanding of God according to the present understanding of charity or love, rather than understand love *from* the nature of God. God should image, should symbolize, love, and not the other way round.

The central concern of Tracy's previous proposal is to show that the claims of any given religious language can be transformed into truly *cognitive* and tenable allegations by reconstructing them according to a general criterion of intellectual inquiry, interpretation, and validation. Theologians need to verify that the recently prevalent rules of cognition and intelligibility are inherent within theological discourse and claims. Developing correlational or conversational theology, therefore, does not aim to show that the religious discourse represents a particular form of cognitive inquiry. It does not try to show that what theology alone can uniquely represent as a form of understanding, other forms of cognition ought to take seriously and accept objectively. It aims instead at showing that theology is a transformable discourse; a discourse in a constant state of flux. It can be changed in such a manner that makes it demonstrative of an external criterion of interpretation that is gaining prevalence in today's postmodernist era. Discourse on God's trinitarian being, for instance, becomes in this case just a hermeneutical form of explication used to show that religious language on the divine can offer philosophically meaningful speech on the general intellectual understanding of human existence and being.

Metaphysics concerned about "the objective reality of God" is now within the boundaries of the postmodern criterion of intelligibility alone. What we have is a correlational theology that states "both what metaphysics *is not* and [what is] the general character of a contemporary metaphysical analysis."[23] Every metaphysical language that is neither internally coherent nor adequate for humanity's common religious experience and religious tradition is not "metaphysics." And theology that takes this metaphysics on board is not a proper theism. More crucially still, any conception of "God" that evades showing the necessity of "the transcendent" for properly understanding the

---

22. Ibid., 161. Tracy suggests that the proper metaphysical language for solving the cognitive meaning of "God is love" is the process thinking of people like Charles Hartshorne and John Cobb, rather than classical Greek thinking. He says on Hartshorne's position: "to my knowledge, no other single thinker in modernity has proposed as carefully formulated and evidential a series of alternatives to the classical dilemmas of theists and non-theists alike" (ibid., 174).

23. Ibid., 172.

common experience of every human being, religious or not, and the validity of the religious tradition for human life in general, and beyond any narrow cognitive boundaries at the same time, is inconvenient for a revisionist correlational reconstruction of theology.[24]

Tracy's perception of the core concern of postmodern intellectual conditions usefully demonstrates that thinkers are required now to 1) point to inappropriate forms of cognition, and 2) to offer alternative key notions expressive of a critical self-transcendence. The question of "how we know what we know" is not, in other words, discarded, but rather tackled by means of showing that the nature of knowing is better grasped via notions other than the ones offered in modernity. Knowing in the light of "transcendence" means constantly exceeding the present, thus postponing meaning to the future (*différance*) and mastering a specific language game.

Having said that, what decides whether the adjudicated form of religious language based on metaphysical expressions is cognitively intelligible or not? Is the criterion of judgment Tracy suggests the outcome of the correlation process (i.e., both theology and other forms of inquiry produce the criterion of meaningfulness by virtue of their correlation), or is there rather a prior rule that decides the form, the content, and the ultimate conclusion of the correlation before the process takes place? If the second option is the case, is the correlation based on this prior criterion truly expressive of a mutually active encounter of two equal forms of inquiry?

The correlational model Tracy proposes does not seem really *correlational* because it shapes the assumed correlation itself by a presupposed understanding of "cognitive intelligibility," without first allowing theology to ponder whether this criterion is compatible for understanding the objective reality of God or not.

In his elaboration on "transcendence" in relation to his construal of theology as a "philosophical reflection," Tracy seems to be investing in a horizontal version of transcendence that lies in going beyond the present phenomenon of human existence into its originating *a priori* postulates, regardless of whether these postulates are specific existential experiences or "experience" as a concept. "Transcendence" here is the "basic *a priori* condition of all human living and thinking,"[25] which lies within the boundaries of human experience and awareness alone. Now where would God fit into this form of transcendence? Is God a "Wholly Other" from outside these boundaries of

---

24. Ibid., 175ff. Classical theism, according to Tracy, is not pertinent to the revisionist correlational theology because it "fails to meet the legitimate criteria for logical meaning" (ibid., 180).

25. Tracy, *Blessed Rage for Order*, 68.

awareness? It does not seem so. "God" is rather one of the *a priori* experiences, whose role is to originate in the human person a specific religious behavior. Such a theological hermeneutic can easily surface in a correlational theology defined, like Tracy's, as merely a "philosophical reflection."

Tracy believes that the philosophical criterion of reflection is suitable for theology because both theology and philosophy acquire their self-understanding within the same hermeneutic circle. Both, Tracy concludes, "*must* be involved in philosophical reflection upon our common human experience and language."[26] But is the common involvement of philosophy and theology in the same hermeneutic circle inherent to what they are, or is it rather circumstantially due to certain contemporary rules determinative of the game of intellectual inquiry from outside both of them? Why *must* theology be involved in a philosophical reflection of the sort Tracy is calling for to gain acceptance in postmodernity? What makes such involvement an obligation? Is it the nature of theology itself? Is it theology's duty toward other disciplines? Or is it theology's recent fate of hardly seeking the acceptance of other intellectual disciplines? If the transcendental moment in philosophical reflection merely means disclosing "the true conditions of the possibility of [the human] experience,"[27] the theological reflection on the transcendent would turn into an endeavor for comprehending the *a priori* postulates and presuppositions, which originated the experience and the language and are inherently human-centered. In this case, theology is just another form of philosophical inquiry about the human and her religious consciousness, no matter how correlational it appears to be. It is an invocation of a Kantian-like "religion within the boundaries of reason alone" set out in the following form: theology within the cognitive boundaries of postmodernity alone.[28]

In such an understanding of theology, correlation is the tool for giving up a theological claim, rather than the means by which this claim positively and integrally contributes to the intellectual context. The theological claim this form of correlation is ready to give up is the belief in the objective reality of God. This is evident in Tracy's saying that the adequate criterion of analysis in revisionist theology is the one that *only* clarifies "the exact philosophical meaning of the symbol, concept, image, metaphor, or myth and experience

---

26. Ibid., 69.

27. Ibid., 69.

28. Even if we said that "experience" should not be confined to sense experience and should rather include a human person's consciousness of herself as a "self," this does not take theology beyond the boundaries of the belief that, as a "philosophical reflection," theology is just an investigation into the linguistic and experiential components of humanity's orientations.

each discloses."[29] In other words, the experiences and linguistic bearers are *meaningful* only if they disclose as genuinely as possible the authentic lived experiences of the community that uses this language. There is no indication of any meaningfulness for these experiences that stem from their relation to the objective reality of God. "Meaningfulness" here designates the authenticity of certain experiences as "religious" rather than as *theological* (i.e., reflective of a divine, self-existing truth in an encounter with the human) phenomenon.[30] "God" is here a particular *concept*, and theology, as one of many other postmodern philosophical discourses on common human experience and language, is responsible for showing how this concept functions as a fundamental "belief" or "condition" of possibility of all our experiences.[31] Theology is not in a correlation with other forms of inquiry as a distinguished "other," but one among many other forms of expression of the correlational character of postmodern forms of inquiry.

III. Gordon Kaufman's Liberal Theology of Correlation

The liberal theologian Gordon Kaufman is another major theological voice who departs from a clear adoption of the preconditioning values of postmodern pluralism. Kaufman considers the contemporary pluralistic worldview to be the cornerstone in any attempt at developing a correlational relationship between theology and other intellectual forms of inquiry.

In an article titled "Doing Theology from a Liberal Christian Point of View," Kaufman defends associating theology with liberation. He claims that liberating the theological and religious discourses from traditional absolutism and authoritarianism by exposing their claims on God, the human, and the world to critical revision is what makes liberal theology the most appropriate demonstration of theology's openness to correlation with other forms of understanding and knowledge. Such a correlation, according to Kaufman, is in fact necessitated by the fact that "liberation" as a principle lies at the very heart of the Christian gospel and its intellectual discourse, "theology." The good news of the Christian gospel calls in essence for a liberation from all sorts of domination and absolutism by virtue of the graceful role of the divine other. Be that as it may, the objective "liberal" in "liberal theology" is not characteristic

---

29. Tracy, *Blessed Rage for Order*, 69.

30. Ibid., 70. "Philosophical reflection would aid . . . by determining whether these texts and events bear a limit-character which would *logically* allow the analyst to apply the meaning 'religious' to them."

31. Ibid., 71.

of a narrowly bounded, specific branch of theological thinking. "Liberal" is definitive of what theology is all about. Liberal theology is *the* theological discourse proper because the core of the Christian ethos is a primary concern about "human liberty, human liberation, human freedom." "Liberal theology" is from beginning to end "the good news about how the various kinds of human bondage are overcome." It is Christian faith in a state of calling for a specific form of truth reconstruction that demands fundamental criticism, careful examination, and assessment of all the given propositions on truth and value.[32]

If this principle of liberation is inherent to the being of theological knowledge, theologians should concede the need for all the available scholarly and scientific methods of examination and assessment to make theology relevant and meaningful to the liberating demands of the human condition. It is time for them to realize, in Kaufman's words, "that the central Christian claims about human freedom demand a willingness to use modern methods of radical criticism within theology itself," incorporating, therefore, into the theological hermeneutical arena "whatever could be learned about humanity and the world from scientific and historical research and from philosophical reflection."[33]

What is the outcome of such a liberation-oriented, critical understanding of the nature and task of theology? The outcome is a necessary conditioning correlation between our knowledge of God and our knowledge of the world, between theology and other fields of study. Why necessary? Because it alone makes theology a tool for liberation. Why conditioning? Because it assumes that the venues and aspects that liberal theology should deal and converse with are to be detected according to the expansive scope of modern knowledge about the world, humanity, and history. Whenever these secular fields of understanding and research take a new turn, theology should be ready to correlate with these new changes by getting along with and conforming to the newly decided expectations. It is a correlation in which theology reacts in total response and in full hospitality to the changes surrounding it. Theology would be considered "an ongoing *process* of thinking and rethinking" when it gets involved in a correlation that demonstrates its readiness to "'absorb' every change in scientific insight and allow such a change to shape its understanding of the message of Christian faith."[34]

---

32. Gordon Kaufman, "Doing Theology from a Liberal Christian Point of View," in *Doing Theology in Today's World*, ed. John D. Woodbridge and Thomas E. McComiskey (Grand Rapids: Zondervan, 1991), 397–415, 397–98.

33. Ibid., 401.

34. Ibid., 402.

The more that theology correlates with other fields of knowledge and absorbs their claims, the more historically conscious it proves itself to be. As a liberating "science" of God and creation, theology correlates with the "bio-historical" conditions and changes of the world when it becomes an "essentially 'imaginative construction' of a picture or conception of humanity, the world, and God."[35] Theology, Kaufman's claim indicates, should be a mirror. Whenever the world poses before it, it should image this *world's* profound mysteriousness, its infinite truth that exceeds all religious symbolism and rituals. Rather than imaging the mysteriousness of a "Wholly Other" divine Being, theology mirrors the profoundness and mysteriousness of the world. "God" is the name, the "image/concept," in Kaufman's words, that names this state of infiniteness. Admitting the contingency of human nature in comparison to an infinite God is taken on board here not necessarily because of a concern about God's otherness and infinity, but basically because: 1) admitting the limitation of our knowing, or our profound unknowing, according to Kaufman, can alone liberate us from ignorance and lack of understanding.[36] And 2) because "theology, if it truly speaks of God, always simultaneously becomes social criticism and ethics," that is, a contextualized religious discourse that aims at humanizing every culture.[37]

Why should theology not be primarily a discourse on God's infinite otherness in his relation with the human? Ought it to focus instead on the human's encounter with the fact of human contingency and the way for exceeding it? Because theology, as a discourse on God's otherness in relation to the human, has through the past centuries treated the other forms of intellectual inquiry in an authoritative manner. In his article "Critical Theology as a University Discipline," Kaufman accuses classical theology of authoritarianism and elaborates on what this authoritarianism stands on. He argues that the authoritarianism of theological reflection stems from the belief that "God had been decisively revealed to humanity in the history of Israel and especially in and through the ministry, death, and resurrection of Jesus Christ."[38] Kaufman

---

35. Ibid., 405.
36. Ibid., 406. "Only and with the acknowledgment of our profound un-knowing can the *symbol* 'God' turn us—by a kind of indirection—toward its intended referent: the ultimate source and content of our humanity, the ultimate mystery of life." Italics are mine.
37. See Gordon Kaufman, *God, Mystery, Diversity: Christian Theology in a Pluralistic World* (Minneapolis: Fortress Press, 1996), 52.
38. Gordon Kaufman, "Critical Theology as a University Discipline," in *Theology and the University*, ed. David R. Griffin and Joseph C. Hugh Jr. (Albany: State University of New York Press, 1991), 35–50, 35.

thinks that this belief implies that truth is determined before the theological, critical investigation and seeking after it even begins. Truth is not, then, discovered by way of human intellectual work. Its authenticity and truthfulness are rather given and assumed on its own sole authority. Such a form of authoritarian theological thinking, according to Kaufman, is incapable of persuading us of its validity. It is no longer even tolerated after the rise of critical and intellectual methods of knowing. Any authoritarian approach to religious claims is precarious and stands on strongly shocking ground.[39] Today's intellectual forms of inquiry do not tolerate any other form of inquiry except one that is evidently critical. Theology that is sensitive to contemporary thought should, rather, be critical in nature. Theology should become that field of study "that is done with full attention to, and is thus an expression of, critical consciousness . . . that opens itself willingly to severe criticism from outside perspectives."[40]

Rather than enjoying a criterial position among other forms of intellectual inquiry, theology is supposed to prove to these other forms its readiness to dispense with authoritarianism and play a critical, especially self-critical, task. The critical task that truly correlates theology with the historical process of changing human conditions, according to Kaufman, is one that seeks to understand religious belief as an existential phenomenon that is reflective of "fundamental features of human existence." One of the theologians' major tasks today, as Kaufman elsewhere states, is "to ascertain just which beliefs and concepts inherited from tradition are still viable, and to determine in what ways they should be reconstructed so they will continue to serve human intellectual and religious needs . . . theology can no longer look simply to authoritative or normative decisions or situations in the past for its principal guidance. It must orient itself toward that future into which we are (quite rapidly) moving, a future which is open and indeterminate in many respects."[41]

In light of the above, "faith" becomes a purely rational mode of cognition, and "theology" becomes that field of study which offers the proper language

---

39. Ibid., 36. This is especially the situation of theology in the context of the university, affirms Kaufman.

40. Ibid., 38. Elsewhere, Kaufman states the same idea in the following manner: "It is often held, for instance that Christian theology is primarily the exposition of Christian doctrines or dogmas, as though these doctrines and dogmas were given that the theologian must simply accept, and that he or she is then called upon to explain or interpret. But according to our thesis this is once again the wrong way around . . . doctrines and dogmas then, are not simply to be accepted. They are to be examined, criticized, and often rejected, in the light of the image/concept of God that finally commends itself to us." Kaufman, *God, Mystery, Diversity*, 44.

41. Kaufman, *God, Mystery, Diversity*, 22.

for showing that this concept means, as Kaufman states, "men and women live out of and on the basis of their trust in and loyalty to what they take to be most meaningful, previous, and important in life; that human lives are always oriented by some (perhaps implicit) center [or centers] of value; and that it is out of underlying faith-commitments such as these that humans act and live in face of the unknown future into which they must inexorably move."[42] Theology has a mission in today's world as a public intellectual and critical discourse that would be "preparing intellectual tools and methods for helping to address humanity's major worldwide problem of finding ways to encourage the great diversity of human groups around the globe to live together more peacefully on our rapidly shrinking planet."[43] The public-ness of this peace-fostering theology lies, according to Kaufman, in the fact that its claims and content are not readymade presumptions and are not convictions that are restrictively shared by persons with closely similar faith-commitment. Instead, it is a discourse that is pluralistic and dialogical in nature. It is a theology that emerges "in the conversation among persons of different faith-commitments, as they work together seriously in their collective attempt to understand and assess their diverse forms of orientation."[44]

Does Kaufman call for transforming theology altogether into a discourse on the religious human alone, with no role for God to play in it whatsoever? As I showed earlier, Kaufman believes that theology is a discourse on "God" as much as it is on human reality. The core of the matter for him is the role of the idea of God and its implications in relation to human knowledge and understanding. The importance of the term "God" (i.e., as it is spoken about by Christian tradition) lies in its expressiveness of Christianity's concern about universalism in a way compatible with today's emphasis on religious pluralism.[45] "God," Kaufman thinks, is a *symbol* pertinent to today's concern about pluralism because it is one of these human expressions that connotes a center of devotion outside any limited individual or self-enclosed concept of "self." It symbolizes a "from outside" center of concern that draws the self out of narcissism. In the same line of thought, Kaufman construes "salvation" and "humanization" as mutually connotative of the same meaning.[46] The notion of "salvation" that the

---

42. Kaufman, "Critical Theology as a University Discipline," 40.
43. Ibid., 41.
44. Ibid., 45.
45. Kaufman, *God, Mystery, Diversity*, 26.
46. Ibid., 28. "We must be prepared radically to criticize and reconstruct traditional ideas of God, if God is to continue to serve as an appropriate object of devotion for our time, one who truly mediates to us salvation (humanization)."

world may allow theology to promote is the one that turns the dehumanized modernity into a fully and factually humanized reality. Theology is asked to participate in developing a global life-setting that is "directed toward the fulfillment of all human beings and all societies, no matter what their cultural or religious traditions and commitments are."[47]

In his book *An Essay on Theological Method*, Kaufman tackles the subject of the value of the concept of God for theological knowledge in extensive details. He explains that even in its highest forms of criticism, theology is not to dispense with the foundational role that the concept of "God's revelation" plays in Christian faith. Theology should just disallow such a divine revelation to tell the scholar "how to begin [the] theological work . . . [to tell] us where we as theologians, as human thinkers, can or should turn to do theology."[48] Elsewhere, Kaufman offers an alternative to revelation when, to the contrary, he states that "what is necessary or required to build a humane order *in this world* should be made the central criterion both for assessing our theological beliefs and for determining the character of the theological task."[49]

Kaufman's words here not only speak about the place of the idea of God within the process of theological inquiry. They also offer an alternative understanding of theological inquiry itself. It means that theology is just a "grammar" of a specific form of interpretation and reconstruction of the meaning of a collection of vocabularies from a rather common, publicly used language—language that "everyone knows, understands and uses." So much so, that every one can belong to the theological circle of inquiry and thinking "simply by virtue of speaking and understanding English."[50]

In his book *God the Problem*, Kaufman shows the implications of this understanding of theology on the notion of God. He argues that the term "God" as such does not in fact name the transcendent Being that religious people worship and believe in, but rather our mental, imaginative construct of the idea of the divine.[51] "God," whose self-existence is religiously taken as

---

47. Ibid., 35. "The Christian concern for the salvation of all women and men is primarily a concern for their full humanization" (ibid. 39). "It is the task of theology," Kaufman adds, a couple of pages later, "to define and clarify and interpret the criterion of humanization, to engage in reflection and discussion leading to deeper and fuller understanding of its significance and import, and to attempt to measure and assess in its terms the great claims and emphases about human life and destiny made by the various religious and cultural traditions of humankind" (ibid., 40–41).

48. Gordon Kaufman, *Essay on Theological Method* (Missoula, MT: Scholars, 1979), 3.

49. Kaufman, *God, Mystery, Diversity*, 24.

50. Kaufman, *Essay on Theological Method*, 8–9.

51. Gordon Kaufman, *God the Problem* (Cambridge, MA: Harvard University Press, 1972), 82–115. Kaufman distinguishes between "the *real* referent of the name" of the real entity and "the available

factual, "is not available for our direct inspection or querying," according to Kaufman. It is rather God's idea that is "largely verbally or intra-linguistically" grasped (even generated).[52] Although Kaufman concedes that God per se can be a real, existing, even transcendent Being, he holds Kant's conviction that such a Being is beyond the limits of human reason. Therefore, it is beyond knowledge.

Be that as it may, what matters for Kaufman is what theology speaks about by means of the term "God." He does not see "God" in theology as designative of a transcendent Being who exceeds the realm of reason. He rather reads this term as an expression of a purely "mental or imaginative construct,"[53] made by the human mind, in accordance with the human, historically shaped condition. Instead of negating God's existence altogether, Kaufman segregates God in his transcendence from the realm of the correlation between theology and other forms of intellectual inquiry, leaving religious discourse on God, at the same time, at the disposal of the conditioning language game of postmodernity. He maintains that unless theology plays the game of speaking about and interpreting reality according to the rules of the predominating human intellectual forms of inquiry, the theological talk about God will be perennially unconvincing to the world. Unless theology adopts fully and unreservedly the linguistic-cultural constituents of human knowledge, the symbol "God" would no longer be the designation of "the Creator of heaven and earth" or "the Lord." It would not, that is, be expressive of what the human means and understands by means of this symbol. Theologians should use the term "God" in such a manner that convincingly helps people grasp the intimate relation of the religious imaginative notion of the divine to "every aspect and feature of the world and every dimension and quality of experience."[54] Theology should redefine and reconstruct the symbol of "God" so that its meaning becomes accessible in the same way other forms and structures of meaning are accessible in certain cultural contexts. Theology is not a valid and valuable discourse of knowledge if only those who believe in God are its makers. Rather, "it should be possible for believers *and* unbelievers alike to reach considerable agreement in descriptions of the available God."[55]

referent" of it. The real George Washington, for example, is not exactly the available Washington, the reality of whom is reconstructed in our mind because the particular George Washington, the historical person who lived in a specific time and place, is no longer at hand (ibid., 84).

52. Ibid., 84.
53. Ibid., 86.
54. Ibid., 92. "Anyone who takes the notion of God seriously will apprehend the whole structure of meaning within which he lives as oriented toward and grounded upon this most profound resource of meaning and being, and the available God will thus be grasped, phenomenologically speaking, as himself 'objective' and 'real.'"

If this is the only role the notion of "God" (i.e., the subject of theology and the content of faith) can, or even must, play in the called-for critical and liberating form of theology, the correlational character of theology does not lie in inherent particularities that are specifically and uniquely accorded to its core subject. Theology, rather, finds itself in correlation with other fields of intellectual or grammatical forms of inquiry just because it is one among many other similar, sometimes even more reliable, public discourses. What other discourses leave intact and under-studied in the vocabulary of human public language—ones like "sacred," "holy," "divine," and "God"—theology is given the duty of reflecting on, criticizing, and refining, so as when once we needed to use these terms, we may do so in better ways. Only such a religious cognitive discourse could make the belief in the reality called God relevant to today's world. It is the job of this discourse to show that human language on the divine is in essence "talk about life and the world, about our deepest problems, about catastrophe and triumph, about human misery and human glory. It is about what is really important in life, how we are to live, how to comport ourselves, which styles of life are genuinely human and which dehumanizing."[56] "God" is, as Kaufman believes following Kant, one of the conceptual means by which theologians develop an understanding of the world.[57] At base, as Kaufman states,

> [t]he criteria for assessing theological claims turn out in the last analysis, thus, to be pragmatic and humanistic. This is not because theologians are necessarily committed to pragmatic or utilitarian conceptions of truth in general, but rather because such considerations—when understood in the broadest possible sense—are the only ones by which a way of life, a world view, a perspective on the totality of things, a concept of God, may ultimately be assessed.[58]

---

55. Ibid., 95. Italic is mine. What makes God's life and active existence conceivable in reality is interpreting God as "implying a conception of the universe as through and through moral, a world within which personal and purposive action is continuously effective and determinative" (ibid., 113).

56. Kaufman, *Essay on Theological Method*, 13–14. Because it all falls down into a matter of linguistic expression, Kaufman believes that one can speak about the human condition and the world by using terms other than "God." The priority of "God" as that which means human condition is simply due to historico-cultural factors related to the context of Western culture (ibid., 14–15).

57. Ibid., 32. "The theologian's task is to construct a conception or picture of the world—the whole that contains all that is and all that can be conceived—as pervaded by and purveying a particular kind of (humane) meaning *and* significance because its grounding lies in an ultimately human reality."

58. Ibid., 76.

It is my conviction that Kaufman's approach calls, like that of Tracy, for a correlation between theology and other intellectual forms of inquiry that eventually serves the purpose of proving theology's readiness to succumb to the conditions of other fields of study and to do whatever it takes to gain accreditation and recognition today. The question I raise before Kaufman's proposal is whether such a model of correlation represents a real mutual and reciprocal conversation. "It takes *two* to make a conversation." Kaufman is right in affirming this when he speaks about theology as a particular conversation partner. However, to hold a mutual conversation we need more than acknowledging two conversers. We should allow each one of them equal space of expression and influence in the process of interaction. Theology should not just react openly and charitably to the claims of the conversation's counterpart. Theology should also be encountered as an active and contributive partner in its own terms and according to its own premises.

To take this to Kaufman's discussion, let me try to show how mutuality and equality challenge Kaufman's accusation of theology of authoritarianism. In principle, Kaufman's criticism of the authoritative attitude that makes theologians take for granted the accuracy and referentiality of certain claims and convictions and refuse to expose them to scrutiny is valid and worth pondering.[59] Yet should theology question and scrutinize itself because today's intellectual scene is intolerant of any authoritative form of knowing, especially the religious one, as it has never been before? Is this the reason why theology should be self-critical and raise questions: to meet the demands of the historical changes and renewed conditions of a new human context? Is there not something inherent to the conversation partner called "theology" in itself that indicates a particular critical and critiquing character uniquely attributable to theology alone? Why should having certain definite answers to theological questions be designated as "authoritarian"[60] rather than a *particular* understanding of "definite" in terms of "founded" instead of "final"? Why should this be considered "authoritarian," unless such an assessment of theology is itself made in an authoritarian manner?

Kaufman believes that in today's pluralistic world, theology should be that discourse which emerges from the conversation between the members of different faith commitments. It should be the religious discourse that is made by believers and unbelievers alike. This is another understanding of theology that

---

59. Kaufman, "Doing Theology from a Liberal Christian Point of View," 408–9ff.

60. Ibid., 409. "To take the authoritarian approach to theology is to presume certain answers to [theological questions]."

turns it into just a form of inquiry subjected to a dominant, preconditioning context. In today's interreligious dialogue between Christians and Muslims, for example, the concern about allowing the conversation to generate the religious truth that guarantees peace between these two communities obliges Christians sometimes to speak with a very low voice, or even maintain silence, about the divinity of Jesus Christ, the trinitarian nature of God, the crucifixion, and so on. In such a public theology that yearns for peace and co-formation of religious truth like the one Kaufman calls for, Christian theologians are expected to not threaten the potential of peace by critical assessment of the other's convictions. They are only expected to be as critical as possible about the "traditional" claims of Christian faith alone. In other words, theology is not really an equal partner in a dialogue, but an intellectual servant. It is not addressed as already a discourse with a complete, unique identity of its own before the dialogue begins. The form and the identity of theological discourse are here the *function* of the correlation. They do not substantially or uniquely contribute to the conversation by virtue of their particularities. Theology awaits, instead, the conversation to reward it with something it can hold as an acceptable and satisfactory identity and role in the contemporary context. This is precisely the backdrop of the conviction that within the process of theological inquiry the "claim about God's guidance and revelation will be a conclusion not an opening premise, it rests upon prior foundations in experience, reflection and reasoning, and these must be uncovered and made clear if we are to come to genuine understanding of what we are doing when we are theologizing."[61]

IV. Mark Taylor's Dialectical Correlational "A/theology"

In Mark Taylor's theological project we have an attempt at correlating theology with other theoretical grounds that are inherent to the Western contemporary era. The core purpose of this correlation, as Thomas Altizer notices in his forward to Taylor's *Deconstructing Theology*, is the renewal or rebirth of theology that, according to Taylor, lies only in salvaging theology from its premodern, pretheoretical ecclesiastical tomb, into which theology was buried by people like Karl Barth and Paul Tillich alike.[62] Mark Taylor, Altizer states, is this theologian who has the mission of saving theology from the fangs of the dragon called "the church." Altizer believes that Taylor is the most qualified for this mission because the latter is "the first American post-ecclesiastical systematic

---
61. Kaufman, *Essay on Theological Method*, 3–4.
62. Mark C. Taylor, *Deconstructing Theology* (New York: Crossroad/Chico, CA: Scholars, 1982), xi.

or philosophic theologian, the first theologian free of the scars or perhaps even the memory of church theology, and the first theologian to address himself solely to the purely theoretical or cognitive problems of theology."[63]

Altizer claims that one of the major afflictions in ecclesiastical theology lies in turning theological language into "a solitary and isolated language, referring to nothing whatsoever outside of itself."[64] And Mark Taylor is one of the genuine leaders who promises in his theological proposal to take theology out of its linguistic dead-end; out of its dark and closed narrow circle into the light of an eschatological ultimatum. Why is Taylor's proposal qualified for this task? Because, says Altizer, Taylor is one who, among others, discovered that the salvation of theology from its meaninglessness lies only in breaking it down; in deconstructing theology's very own thinking of God. It is in "deconstruction," as Mark Taylor himself states, that the resurrection of theology finds a chance to happen. This new philosophy of deconstruction "harbors a radically new theology, a *secular*, post-ecclesiastical theology, which can both draw on and respond to distinctively postmodern experience."[65] It is in the postmodern atheism that is rooted in religious language and rationale, according to Altizer and Taylor, that theology has a promising chance to postmodernize and re-create itself; can become truly a "postmodern theology."[66]

In order to achieve this goal, Taylor endeavors to re-create theology by applying to theological thinking a process of self-negation. He does this by applying to theology a Hegelian dialectic method of interpretation. He departs in his total reliance on Hegel's dialectical thinking from a twofold conviction that 1) Hegel's dialectic of "differentiation-alienation-reconciliation" is nothing less than the true road of the self toward real, full selfhood.[67] So, any proper theological hermeneutics of selfhood should also walk on the same road. And, 2) Hegel's insistence that "every concrete actuality includes *in its own self* its other as definitive and constitutive of itself"[68] should become the foundation of any understanding of relationality or co-relationality, including the correlation of theology and philosophy. The appropriate form of correlationality between any two forms of thinking, as almost all Taylor's writings show, is one that relies on a dialectical reason that lays bare "the thoroughly relational character of concrete self-identity."[69]

63. Ibid., xii.
64. Ibid., xiv.
65. Ibid., xix.
66. Ibid., xx.
67. Ibid., 1–22.
68. Ibid., 25.

But how does dialectical correlation save and resurrect theology from its dead-end meaninglessness? Taylor answers this question by deconstructing the relationship theology made with modernity since the time of Karl Barth onwards. According to Taylor, the rise of the modern age's awareness of the reality and influence of relativism in matters of knowledge and hermeneutics has put all disciplines, including theology, into very serious disarray. Theological language, consequently, almost lost its validity and fell into a state of paralysis.[70] Theologians found themselves faced with a very serious challenge to prove the validity of theological language in the face of this condition. This was Karl Barth's main concern, Taylor continues, when he claimed that "theological reflections perpetually focus on the absolute and transcendent Word of God."[71] Barth, Taylor concedes, acknowledged the value of relativism in relation to all religions and religious studies. Yet he resiliently insisted that Christianity defeated relativism because *it* is founded upon revelation, which, in turn, does not succumb to the rules of interpretation and scrutiny to which other forms of inquiry are subjected.

Taylor thinks that in this Barthian anti-relativist attitude lies the core of the failure of Christian theology. Theology should launch a serious correlation with relativism, instead of retreating to a "precritical naïveté" (in Taylor's words) that makes theology intolerable to the modern age. Theology's course, Taylor argues, "must pass through instead of around relativism."[72] If Hegel's belief that apart from the other, from the moment of otherness, there is no self-fulfillment is correct, theology is not itself unless it passes through the moment of relativism and correlates with it. Relativism should be a moment in theology's self-fulfillment; in becoming its theological self. Theology cannot be a discourse about truth unless it takes seriously the fact that "truth is relative because meaning is contextual and being is relational." The relativity of truth, however, lies not in asserting a multiplicity and polytheism that borders on nihilism and perpetual conflict. It rather lies, Taylor affirms, in its dialectical relational nature, wherein "co-implicates mutually constitute each other."[73] Theologically, this means that God and the world are mutually constitutive of each other, not only epistemologically, but primarily ontologically. "God and the world cannot exist apart from one another. God forever becomes incarnate, and the finite is always in the process of becoming reconciled with the infinite."[74] Meaning, affirms

69. Ibid., 29.
70. Ibid., 45.
71. Ibid., 46.
72. Ibid., 47.
73. Ibid., 48.

Taylor, "is thoroughly dialectical or completely relational."[75] So, any meaning the reality of God holds is not self-generated; it does not lie in God per se, but in God's constituting relation with the human. Without this correlation with the human, God is not only denied his infinite self. God is not *at all*. Apart from relational ontology, theology is meaningless and has no existence at all, since its subject matter (God) as such is also destined to be subjected to the same relational, dialectical ontology too. The axiom "identity-within-difference and difference-within unity"[76] is not only expressive of a method of knowing that helps theology understand itself in connection to history and other forms of inquiry. It is more radically an ontological process that defines theology's nature as much as its subject matter. One can even go as far as saying that this ontology suggests a new subject matter to theology: dialectical relationality, which is expressive of the fact that "there is no thing-in-itself, for self-relation is always mediated by relation-to-other."[77] Theology, then, is "theological" when it expresses this ontology. On the other hand, the subject matter of theology demonstrates this ontology when the self-relating God dies, and the God who cannot *be* unless in relation with the human lives. This essentially relational ontology makes theology an epistemic moment in the process of human self-knowing and acknowledges God as a moment that serves the purpose of negating finiteness in order for this finiteness to reach self-fulfillment.

Of crucial significance here is to realize Taylor's belief that although theology and relativism, God and the human, are called to correlate, this correlation does not depict coalescence or the relational image of an interaction between two independent opposites. Taylor is actually calling theology to be involved in a correlation that makes it and its subject matter a moment in the human epistemic "self-conscious explication of [one's] radical unity."[78] The correlation Taylor calls for is not between "theology *and* relativism," "God *and* the human," "finite *and* infinite." It is in fact correlation of "theology *within* relativism," "God *within* the human," "infinite *within* finite."[79] Missing this "within" and Taylor's Hegelian interpretation of the nature of this "within"

---

74. Ibid., 49.
75. Ibid., 50.
76. Ibid., 53.
77. Ibid., 55.
78. Ibid., 57.
79. Ibid., 59, as it can be gleaned from Taylor's speech about "being *within* becoming; unity *within* plurality; identity *within* difference; truth *within* truths; constancy *within* change; peace *within* flux."

will prevent perceiving the essential meaning of Taylor's understanding of hermeneutics in his saying that

> hermeneutics, in other words, presupposes an interplay of the familiar and the strange, a reciprocity of identity and difference in which each becomes itself through dialectical relation to the other.[80]

At face value, this claim seemingly reflects an understanding of correlationality reminiscent of the patristic theological notion of *perichoresis*: unity-in-distinction. But, in fact, Taylor's understanding is not an invocation of such a theologically orthodox notion. His principal point of departure, in the first place, is Thomas Altizer's declaration of the death of this very God of Christian orthodoxy along with the discourse expressive of it (orthodox theology): not only God (*theos*), but also his Word/Son (theo-*logos*) are equally dead. In addition, Taylor grounds his revival of theology in a Hegelian dialectical logic that entails that the terms of "strange" and "difference," which he uses in the above quotation, are not meant to stand over and against the terms "familiar" and "identity," as if each is expressive of distinguished, independent, and self-existing realities. Taylor rather refers by these terms to "the *state* of estrangement" and "the *state* of differentiation" into which the familiar and the identified need to convert in order to acquire self-actualization and achieve self-reconciliation.

Only when we keep the "within" preposition in sight, do we grasp accurately Taylor's model of correlation. He himself alludes to this hermeneutic key when he speaks, for instance, about "identity-*within*-difference," and when he states that the journey of the self that takes place through becoming an "other"; through becoming "otherwise," should become an "Odyssey"; a return home, a return of the self to its selfhood, in a closed-circled journey from-*within*. Ultimately, the journey should not stop at the shore of the strange other in her otherness and strangeness. The journey should terminate at the homeland shores. Only there, the self overcomes estrangement, according to Taylor.[81] Correlation as a dialectical relation of mutual constitution lies in this "within-ness" that is intrinsic to the process of self-actualization and never extrinsically linked to the self as fully self-existing, different other.

---

80. Ibid., 67.
81. Ibid., 67–68.

Again, here, the primary inspiration for Taylor's view of otherness as "self-objectification," rather than "self-existing object," is Hegel's dialectic. Hegel states, according to Taylor, that

> consciousness of objects reveals itself to be the self-consciousness of the subject. Self-consciousness, on the other hand, necessarily involves realizing the self as an object. Put differently, self-consciousness is impossible apart from self-objectification . . . the desiring subject seeks to assert its own substantiality and independence, . . . it destroys the independent object and thereby gives itself the certainty of itself as a true certainty, a certainty that has become explicit for self-consciousness itself in an objective manner.[82]

The following main station in Taylor's correlational dialectic for the sake of reforming and reconstructing a theology beyond the boundaries of orthodoxy is his correlation of the modernist claim of the "death of God" with the postmodernist claim of "the death of selfhood." "If theology is to have a future," according to Taylor, "we must learn to speak of God godlessly and of self selflessly."[83] How do we do this? By converting theological epistemology from concentrating on an assumed absolute author, whose truth is *represented* in human, linguistic, and nonlinguistic signifiers, into decentralizing the author. This decentralization can be pursued by concentrating on the signifying means and their interpretation: from the author (God), into what images him, and from representation (revelation) into interpretation (hermeneutics). "Creative interpretation" now replaces "mimetic representation," and "as the death of God implies the birth of the Word, so the death of selfhood implies the birth of the text."[84]

To take this to theology, we should no longer speak about one, single subject matter as the central concern of theology, be it God or the human self. In the light of relativism, no one can claim one monolithically standard interpretation or understanding of such a subject matter. Even if the point of departure for theology is an assumed single subject, the final outcomes are shaped by various, relative hermeneutics of this subject, and singularity is destined to end with plurality. The subject matter of theology, therefore, is

---

82. Ibid., 72–73. See also Taylor's *Journey to Selfhood: Hegel and Kierkegaard* (Berkeley: University of California Press, 1980), 181–262.

83. Taylor, *Deconstructing Theology*, 89.

84. Ibid., 96.

no longer "God," but the plurality of textual meanings that signify the human relation with the infinite. These meanings are now constructed via cheerily temporalized interpretations. Theology's subject matter is now the "text" that speaks or signifies the plurality of the infinite's interpretations. The infinite as such, in turn, is no longer encountered in himself because the transcendent's presence lies now in its *absence*. God's arrival, Taylor says in a clear Derridean fashion, "is delayed, His presence infinitely deferred."[85] Theology is a discourse on God's absence, on the deferral of God's truth in the unknown, infinite future. Theology is not "*theo*-logy." It is "*a*-theo-logy," and what guarantees a future for theology is proclaiming the *death* of God in the sense of his "*différance*" and absence, not of his proclamation or affirmation. Theology is demanded here to join the human sciences in proclaiming the disappearance of "author-ity" by declaring the disappearance of God, which alone correlates theology with the postmodernist discovery of the death of selfhood. Taylor quotes a long paragraph from Thomas Altizer, whereby the latter offers a clear explanation of the passage through which Taylor drives theology:

> [O]nce the ground of an autonomous consciousness has been emptied or dissolved, then there can be no individual center of consciousness, or no center which is autonomous and unique. With the disappearance of the ground of individual selfhood, the unique "I" or personal ego progressively becomes a mere reflection or echo of its former self. Now the "I" takes into itself everything from which it had withdrawn itself, and therefore it ceases to stand apart. In losing its autonomy, it loses its own unique center or ground, and thereby, it loses everything which had once appeared as an individual identity or "face." Facelessness and loss of identity now become the mark of everyone, as everyone becomes no one, and the "I" is inseparable from the "other." Individual selfhood does not imply or literally come to an end or disappear; it appears in the other. Only in the other does the individual appear or become real, for it is only in the eyes or the glance or the touch of the other that the individual becomes himself.[86]

---

85. Ibid., 97.
86. Ibid., 98, citing from Thomas Altizer, *The Descent into Hell: A Study of Radical Reversal of the Christian Consciousness* (New York: Seabury, 1979), 155.

Let me try to apply the claims of this paragraph on theology. If theology adopted the belief that there is "no center which is autonomous and unique," God's otherness and lordship could be denied because uniqueness and autonomy are descriptive of God's otherness and lordship. Furthermore, if theology accepted as constitutive of its subject matter the belief that "the 'I' takes into itself everything from which it had withdrawn itself, and therefore, it ceases to stand apart," God would earn his being and identity from his opposite, the finite human. God would not exist apart from what he derives from his opposite. God, then, certainly "loses everything which had once appeared as an individual identity or 'face.'" For God to be God in this case, God should be stripped of his identity as a particular personal Being. And theology would stand one last chance for survival by becoming a discourse on God's death or God's lack of identity. If everything the "I" *is* is derived from its opposite, the death of selfhood would become the ground of every theological discourse on God. And if theology's identity lies in that which is not theological (its opposite), theology should only be an interpretation of "the death," "the absence," the "lack-of-self" condition, since theology's opposite lies in "the death of selfhood."

But why does theology's subordination to such a process of reshaping and re-creating grant its survival? Because, to cite Altizer again, "only in the other does the individual appear or become real, for it is only in the eyes or the glance or the touch of the other that the individual becomes 'himself.'" "The death of God" here becomes the *content* of theology, and the question of God's identity becomes the *function* of the organic relation of "the divine's absence or death" ideas to the "the death of selfhood" one. The more we evade speaking about God, the more theological language and speech become. The more we focus on the human self-formation that lies in the dialectical relation with otherness, the more our speech is meaningful as "a/theology," since God's face appears in its hidden-ness behind the face of the finite. The more God is absent, the more he makes sense. And the more theology is nontheological, the more theology gains meaning. The core subject of theology is not affirming God, but rather negating him. It is a Hegelian-like theology that is based on the principle that "essence is pure negative activity that relates itself to itself in otherness."[87] What kind of otherness? An otherness, the substance of which is death, that is, an absence in *différance* and dissolution. In the dialectical relationality between "death of God" and "death of selfhood," as Taylor says, "the divine is reborn in self, even as self is reborn in the divine."[88] Unless theology *kills* God, unless God

---

87. Taylor, *Deconstructing Theology*, 101.
88. Ibid., 102.

is banished and erased, theology cannot rise up as a reliable, really theological, discourse, and God cannot actually become his self.

The philosophical soil of Taylor's theological thinking does not really help him offer any guarantee that sowing this seed of dialectic would eventually produce an attestation of God that is congenial with Christian Scriptures and the notion of "revelation." Taylor's hope and promise is godly—the idea of God has a place in it. Yet his tools and logic are bereft of God and make his goal self-defeating.

Taylor's subsequent writings actually point to this self-defeat. In his book, *Erring: A Postmodern A/theology*, Taylor resumes calling for theology to deconstruct or de-theologize itself. Instead of reunderstanding God by means of interacting *within* "death of God," for example, Taylor takes to its ultimate extreme his earlier invitation of self-deconstruction, for theology to become "a/theological" discourse on deconstruction as such. This time, Taylor adds to his early Hegelian logic a Derridean-like conviction that deconstruction *as such* is "the hermeneutics of the death of God."[89] If theology is "the death of God" discourse, and if the core hermeneutics of this discourse is deconstruction, then the subject matter of theology is nothing other than deconstruction per se. Now, this deconstruction discourse is given the name of "a/theology." Taylor considers this "a/theology" the means for reconciling what theology and philosophy have always considered exclusively and evidently opposed and nonequivalent notions.[90] Against this opposition, Taylor proposes "a dialectical inversion that does not have contrasting opposites unmarked, but dissolves their original identities."[91] Taylor uses deconstruction as a tool to enable theology to achieve this dialectical inversion. He argues that by means of deconstruction, theology can question all its traditional systematic forms and create new openings for the religious imagination.[92]

To this project of "a/theology," Taylor also incorporates the notion of "erring." By this term, Taylor expresses his view of theology as a discourse in a state of constant movement, of perpetual wandering around, of nomadic roaming after the mistaken notions of "deity" and "infinitude." He calls the theologian an "a/theologian" and describes her as someone "driven to consider and reconsider errant notions."[93] In the process of doing this, the "a/theologian"

---

89. Mark Taylor, *Erring: A Postmodern A/theology* (Chicago and London: University of Chicago Press, 1984), 6.
90. Ibid., 8–9.
91. Ibid., 10.
92. Ibid., 11.
93. Ibid., 12.

becomes neither "theological" nor "nontheological," Taylor explains, but always roaming "in-between" this "neither-nor" in a constant nomadic state of transgression of all the notions at hand. "Erring" is not the *name* of this "in-between-ness." It defines it totally. "The a/theologian," Taylor states, "asks errant questions and suggests responses that often seem erratic or even erroneous. Since his reflection wanders, roams, and strays from the 'proper' course, it tends to deviate from well-established ways."[94] This nomadic journey called "a/theology" has no final destination and no starting point of departure. Its fate is to be always unfinished and its words to fall always in-between. Therefore, it is appropriate, according to Taylor, if not even mandatory, to realize the *heretical* nature of "a/theology." This nature is not something against "a/theology." On the contrary, delving into heresy, affirms Taylor, is an unavoidable transitional phase for the happening of a/theology. It is the nature of a/theology to wander along completely erratic boundaries.

What kind of a theology, or "a/theology," is produced by the deconstruction of theology through the dialectical correlation between "death of God" and "death of selfhood"? What is the core of this production and its subject matter? The second half of Taylor's *Erring: A Postmodern A/theology*, especially chapter five on God, offers his answer to these questions. Taylor argues there that the process of deconstructing theology generates eventually deconstructive a/theology. In this deconstruction of theology, theology really begins; in "murdering God" God truly lives and in the disappearance of the self the self truly appears. Negation is now the criterion; is now the beginning; even the beginning of rebeginning. Here, Taylor again proposes Hegel's philosophy as the foundation of his proposed "a/theology," this time with a primal focus on Hegel's axiom "difference constitutes identity."[95] The so-called "a/theology" does not image theology as a field of inquiry that represents a different form of writing, and it speaks about endlessness of difference in writing. Theology is a new form of writing (though it may be inscribed in the words of the old writing[96]), the canon of which are the texts of Hegel, Kierkegaard, Nietzsche, and Derrida; these apostle-philosophers of the life that lies in death; of the presence that lies in absence, of the presence that lies in constant, endless openness.

94. Ibid., 13.
95. Ibid., 98. Taylor, nevertheless, alludes to the fact that he is taking Hegel's thinking into new frontiers when he claims that Hegel himself "is not always sufficiently aware of the radical implications of his analysis of the philosophy of identity"—as if Taylor is here "murdering" Hegel, deconstructing his philosophy, in order to open before it a new valid venue of existence.
96. Ibid., 99.

What kind of "God" does this "a/theology" consider as its subject, if ever? What kind of *theos* can this *logia* write? It is a *Theos*, Taylor says, that is shaped after the image of Jesus on the road to Emmaus, walking with the two disciples and conversing with them without them recognizing him. Taylor's comment on this event deserves quoting at length:

> Here presence is absence, and absence presence. Jesus' followers see but do not see; they listen but hear only the silence of an empty tomb. "When he was at the table with them, he took bread and blessed and broke it, and gave it to them. And their eyes were opened and they recognized him; and he vanished out of their sight." . . . And what did they "see"? They recognized presence in absence and absence in presence. This unending (*inter*)play is the eternal (re)inscription of (the) words(s).[97]

What are the theological implications of this reinscription of the content of "a/theology"? According to Taylor, the basic role of "a/theology" is expressing the incarnational nature of the death (not the presence) of God. It aims at articulating the reality of God's death, as well as this death's real presence in the world. It proclaims the fact that in his appearance as other than himself, God makes known that "the God who alone is God disappears." God as Lord or Creator is no longer there. God is now the name of the wording on the creation of "the infinite play of interpretation."[98] Theology is now "the word"—the *logos* that emerges out of the writing we produce in an attempt at interpreting and inscribing the fact of the death of deity. "A/theology" is nothing other than "a critique of the notion of transcendent God." And the "a/theologian" is one who welcomes this death and builds upon it. In "a/theology," "God is what word means, and word is what 'God' means [notice the quotation marks!]. To interpret God as word is to understand the divine as scripture or writing."[99]

One may glean here that Taylor rejects traditional theological understanding (usually common in Western thinking) of the role of words. Taylor, as one may think, strictly unifies "word" and "God" without necessarily totally identifying them. One may think so on the assumption that Taylor adopts the traditional differentiation in the notion of "word" between the signifier and the signified, and that he concurs with the belief that since the meaning of a word lies in what it refers to, words remain always subservient

---

97. Ibid., 103.
98. Ibid., 103.
99. Ibid., 104.

to what they signify (i.e., to what lies *behind* them as primary and they secondary).[100] But, far from adopting this understanding, Taylor aims at deconstructing it and banning its use from theological reasoning. For Taylor, no transcendentalism is to be allowed so as to make God a signified that enjoys priority over certain signifying words. The opposition between "signified" and "signifier" has, rather, to be called into serious questioning. This distinction between "signifier" and "signified" is not real. It is rather the creation of a self cognizing itself. The signified for Taylor is an imaginary creation of the conscious self. The self creates this imaginary postulate for and in itself and uses it as a criterion for judging itself.[101]

Taylor concedes that when we become aware of this fact we no longer distinguish the word from what it signifies, neither in terms of independence, nor in terms of superiority. Be that as it may, "God" is a "word." "God" is a sign, a linguistic expression. And the written scriptural attestations are not writings *about* God any longer. They *are* God inscribed. This is what Taylor himself suggests when he says

> the word "God" refers to the word "word" and . . . the word "word" refers to the word "God": although the word is a sign, the signified is not independent of and qualitatively different from, the signifier. In as much as the signified is a signifier, the sign is a sign of a sign.[102]

Scriptures are the linguistic enactment of the death of God. They are God's death "word-ed"; they "mark the death of God."[103] The word, insofar as *logos* is here meant, is no longer God's revelation, but rather the disclosure of God's death; if not even a disclosure of death in the sense of absence and disappearance. And, if the signified is the signifier, "in the beginning was the word" means "in the beginning was death," and "the word was God" means "the word was death," or "the word was absence." The age of God has ended. The age of the word, of death, has begun. The era of the transcendent's revelation ended. Begun, instead, is the era of writing that allows for no form of hierarchy. "God" no longer governs "world"; "eternity" no longer governs "time"; "presence" no longer opposes "absence"; "spirit" no longer overrides

---

100. Ibid., 104–5.
101. Ibid., 105.
102. Ibid., 105.
103. Ibid., 118.

"body." In the era of writing, difference and identity mutually constitute each other. "Expressed more concretely," Taylor says,

> difference resists the totalitarianism of identity, just as identity resists the anarchy of difference. This relation of opposites is not exclusive or hierarchical. In writing, neither identity nor difference is prior, proper or pure.[104]

In the "a/theology" that names and expresses this form of writing, finitude and infinitude are one and the same thing. The "infinite" names that which is *in* the finite; that which is inherent to the finite. The in-finite is that *within* which the finite realizes itself. And, by virtue of this self-realization, the infinite is its "self" by means of being *in* the finite.[105]

V. WHEN IS CORRELATION CORRELATIONAL?

In the previous pages, I examined three proposals that aim to correlate theology with other forms of inquiry. Each of these proposals demonstrates good intentions toward theology, in that each endeavors to salvage theology from all that may be preventing a serious appreciation of its value as a field of knowledge in the eyes of the people of today, or in denying theology the chance to contribute to the goodwill and advancement of human life in the contemporary academic and scholarly world. Each theologian discussed wants to reclaim theology's valuable role in human life by means of reconstructing theology itself in a manner that will show the ability of Christian religious discourse to adapt flexibly to the intellectual and existential changes of human history. Theology, they argue, is not a closed-circle form of knowledge. It is not a hegemonic, totalizing discourse that places God and religiosity over and against the human and the world. Theology is an open, dialogical discourse because the God it speaks about is a totally relational and interactive thing. It makes perfect sense in the light of such an intention to show that theology is correlational in nature, and even to reconstruct theology in a manner that makes it in form and content a pure correlation.

---

104. Ibid., 109.
105. Ibid., 113–14. "The finite is not merely other than and opposed to the infinite but is actually an 'interior' dimension of infinitude, . . . finitude and infinitude are neither simply opposed nor mutually exclusive. To the contrary, they enact a ceaseless play in which each becomes itself in and through the other" (ibid., 114).

Notwithstanding the validity and value of this intention, Tracy's, Kaufman's, and Taylor's understandings of "correlation" and their expectations of theological discourse that stems from the reconstruction they make are questionable and problematic. They impoverish theological discourse and turn the subject matter of theology into a speech about "God" that is not in fact expressive of the God of Christian faith, the God of Scripture, and Jesus Christ's revelation. They actually produce a theology that is hardly *theo*-logical in content, let alone the form. They speak about "God" *beyond* God, even "God" *against* God. Their theology's "God" is considered the redemptive means to an assumed problem the Christian God of Scripture and revelation causes. On this belief, they tend, as Thomas Guarino correctly notes, to defend and adjudicate theology's truth-claims by making them revisable and acceptable according to "publicly warrantable criteria," and they justify this move not by theological but rather philosophical reason and assertions.[106]

In following this path, these theologians, however, no longer correlate theology with other forms of intellectual inquiry. They rather transform theology into another form of inquiry that fits the public domain but does not necessarily speak on behalf of the historical Christian faith. But how tenable is it as a *Christian* approach to justify Christian truth-claims publicly, apart from faith? And, as Guarino asks persuasively, "if we cannot stipulate that the faith that seeks understanding extends a certain priority to revealed truth and its linguistic formulation as doctrine, can we ever make any final determinations about Christianity's ultimate content and message?"[107] More importantly still, can we really claim that the correlation method that does not take into consideration the continuity of "the material identity of Christian faith and doctrine in and through history,"[108] but denies any ontological basis for such continuity, is truly correlational in nature?

In their correlational model of relationship between theology and contemporary forms of inquiry, Tracy, Kaufman, and Taylor do not actually co-relate theology with postmodernity. They rather re-create theology according to the rules and preconditions of the postmodern other. Is this an appropriate correlation? I tried in the previous pages' critical analysis to show that it is not. Such a model of correlation does not demonstrate a real reciprocity and correspondence between two equally influential, fully distinct, and proportionately active sides; the characteristics, that is, that are constitutive

---

106. Thomas G. Guarino, *Foundations of Systematic Theology* (London and New York: T. & T. Clark/Continuum, 2005), 316 (311–37).
107. Ibid., 318.
108. Ibid., 319.

of any proper correlation. Tracy, Kaufman, and Taylor offer an important and serious deconstruction of theology. Yet they do not deconstruct the method of deconstruction itself. The proper correlation requires a proportionate deconstruction of the correlation's two sides, not of one for the sake of, or according to, the standards of the other.

Mark Taylor, for example, deconstructs everything ecclesiastical theology says about God. Yet he does not deconstruct the postmodernist "death of God" and "death of selfhood." He rather builds upon them as he calls theology to reconstruct itself into a discourse *about* God's and self's death. David Tracy, on the other hand, calls for deconstructing theology by means of reimplementing the notion of "transcendence" or "infinity." Yet Tracy also adopts a postmodernist notion of "self-transcendence" and makes it the criterion for theology's deconstruction of itself, without deconstructing this very criterion in itself and examining its validity as a criterion for theology in the first place. Kaufman, nevertheless, calls theology to correlate with postmodern conditions by means of living in a constant readiness for *absorbing* all the intellectual and philosophical changes that take place in today's scientific arena, achieving thereby a total liberation of Christian religious discourse from any accusation of irrelevance. Yet Kaufman, like his other two colleagues, borrows the logic of absorption and liberation from the postmodernist sphere and applies it as theology's conduct and thinking criterion, without deconstructing and reevaluating the plausibility and relevance of such logic from the standpoint of theology's particular identity and epistemological tools. In these three scholars' proposals, we have a "one-way-track" correlation model, suggested as the means for granting theology a valuable role and validity in today's scientific arena. But, "one-way-track" correlation is not a "correlation" at all.

In order for theology to be in an appropriate correlation with other forms of inquiry, theology should be granted the right and the space to say to postmodernity: "I do not agree. What you offer does not speak to me; it does not speak about me as *I am*; it does not speak about *my* God, but about the God of either your wishful thinking or your nightmares. It speaks about a 'God' and 'theology' about which you and I cannot agree." Theology, as a partner in a co-relation, must be able to deconstruct postmodernity as much as it allows postmodernity to deconstruct it. Otherwise, any new criterion of reconstruction offered to salvage theology would turn into a form of slavery or hegemony exerted over theology. Against this, theology must interact with other forms of inquiry in a correlation that takes place between two equal sides, each with its own particular identity, and each with openness for change and transformation by means of the other.

Is such a fully correlational correlation possible? In the following chapters, I will argue that, yes, it is perfectly and fully possible. The last three chapters of this book will be my proposal for the appropriate correlation in which theology and other forms of inquiry should get involved. In the first chapter, I will suggest Hans Frei's and Francis Watson's proposals on the relationship between theology and other fields of study as an appropriate model of correlation that contemporary theology can rely on in today's intellectual context. In the following chapter, I will trace the existence of this correlational model in trinitarian theology. I will argue that the model of correlation Frei and Watson offer is actually derived from the theological arena itself because its logic is inherent to the trinitarian understanding of the notion of "*perichoresis*," which implies "unity-in-self-differentiation." In the last chapter, I will point to the theological approach of Jürgen Moltmann and Wolfhart Pannenberg (with particular stress on the latter) as *the* best available model of relationality we have so far in theological reasoning about correlation as *perichoresis*. In Moltmann's, and more specifically, Pannenberg's social trinitarianism, I find the most appropriate answer for both the question of the proper relationship between theology and secular intellectual forms of inquiry, and the question of the proper understanding of the notions of "personhood," "selfhood," and "relationality."

6

Correlation beyond Hierarchism

I. Introduction

In contrast to the intent of postmodern theologians such as David Tracy, Gordon Kaufman, and Mark Taylor to prove that "correlation" is key to theology within a postmodern context, I will show in this chapter that there is another understanding of correlation that is more suitable for construing the integral relationship within theological scholarship. I argue that the analyses of Hans Frei and Francis Watson on the relation between theology and secular forms of inquiry offers a more proper model of the correlational relationship.

II. "Correlation" as a Conceptual Notion

Introducing the method of correlation he pioneered developing in his systematic theology, Paul Tillich establishes a threefold meaning to the term "correlation." "Correlation" first designates the correspondence between the elements inherent to one and the same thing. Secondly, "correlation" names the logical interdependence between two things standing in polarity to each other. "Correlation," nevertheless, means thirdly the interdependence of two things that undergirds the possibility of their existence in reality, not only their tenability within the boundaries of theoretical cognition.[1] Tillich believes that theology is by default correlational in nature such that it combines its components and claims under one inclusive, coherent rubric and orients its practical implications, whether theologians acknowledge this nature as definitive of theology or proceed without explicit recognition.

According to Tillich, the core value of the notion of "correlation" lies in the fact that it negates in principle any domination or overshadowing of one of the correlated sides by means of making it dependent by any means on the other

---

1. Paul Tillich, *Systematic Theology* (Chicago: University of Chicago Press, 1967), 1:60 (60–66).

side. The interdependence characteristic of any form of correlation implies that the correlates co-respond and co-question each other. This "co-operating" or "co-acting" that forms an interactive relationality between two correlates takes, according to Tillich, the shape of "a circle which drives [the human] to a point where questions and answers are not separated."[2] Moreover, this circle is not just an event that happens and ends in time and space, Tillich points out. This interaction, interdependence, or correspondence is, rather, inherent to the identity, to the reality of what the two correlates *are*. Tillich sees this ontological dimension expressed in theological thinking in the God-human relationship. With this relationship, theology 1) correlates by formulating questions about this relationship that are demonstrative of human existence and answers that are derivative from divine disclosure, and 2) it conducts interpretation by correlating between finitude and the infinitude that grounds this finite and separates itself from it. Correlation appears in theological thinking when this latter "makes an analysis of the human situation out of which the existential questions arise, and it demonstrates that the symbols used in the Christian message are the answers to these questions."[3]

Discussing correlation as a question-answer circle definitive of theology as such, Tillich seems to pay disproportionate attention to mutuality of influence for the sake of highlighting the dimension of particularity in terms of the role between the two correlates in theological reasoning: God and God-talk play the particular role of answering; they represent the "answer" pole. Whereas the human and the human condition itself play the particular role of questioning, they represent the "question" pole. Langdon Gilkey may be right in saying that Tillich acknowledges the equal roles of philosophy and theology in answering the questions of ultimate concern, so that both, and not theology alone, express answers to ultimate questions that our finitude and existence pose.[4] However, contrary to Gilkey, this does not yet prove that Tillich's question-answer correlation is proportionately reflective of equal mutuality when it comes to questioning. For, while philosophy is given the space to participate in making the answers for ultimate human questions, theology does not seem to be given, in Tillich's model, a space for participating in raising the questions, or in even

---

2. Ibid., 1:61.
3. Ibid., 1:62.
4. Langdon Gilkey, *Gilkey on Tillich* (New York: Crossroad, 1990), 73 (56–78). "*Philosophical/theological analysis* uncovers reflectively the ultimate questions that our finitude and existence pose—as, in turn, theology, will reflectively express the answers received through participation in the revelation present within a given religious tradition. Theological analysis of meaning in union with philosophical analysis of structure therefore, asks the question."

questioning the raised questions and assessing their validity from the standpoint of God and revelation.

In Tillich, as Gilkey also realizes, the question should always be reflective and expressive of an *existential* dilemma, not of a theological challenge or critique to this very considered existence.[5] Theology for Tillich, as Gilkey admits, "is the theoretical task of interpreting the symbols of its tradition in the light of the questions of human existence to which these symbols 'have been found' existentially to be an answer, or *the* answer . . ."[6] Theology is not, in other words, a discourse that also challenges the questions of human existence by means of its religious symbols. How can theology be so if its symbols were in the first place developed *from* the conditions of human existence and *for the sake* of reflecting this existence, and not from any standpoint related to a reality that is counterpart to this existence and in distinction from it? God is interpreted in Tillich's correlation solely as "the answer to the questions and dilemmas of our finitude . . . namely as the ground and power of being,"[7] which prevents God from being a counterpart to this ground of being and a question to it from without—notwithstanding Tillich's statement that the questions do not only receive answers that are pertinent to their existential character. The questions are also asked "under the impacts of the answers."[8] His application of correlation as a method of theological reasoning that circles around particularity in terms of role indicates that he views particularity as exclusivity and specification: the divine's role is restrictively answering, and the human's role is restrictively asking. By equating particularity with exclusivity, Tillich's detailed interpretation betrays his principal definition of correlation per se.

One has to admit, nevertheless, that Tillich speaks about particularity in terms of "unique influence" and "acknowledging of self's and other's differentiation." He says, for example, that though the theologian asks philosophical questions and the philosopher asks theological questions, the earlier should not decide what is true philosophically and the latter should not state what is true theologically,[9] if they want to conduct a correlational form of thinking and interaction. Correlation as interdependence means that each of the correlates maintains its uniqueness and particular role by acknowledging and opening up before the particularity of the other's questions and answers.

5. Ibid., 73–74.
6. Ibid., 74, referring to Tillich's *Systematic Theology*, 1:9, 23–24, 117, and 129.
7. Gilkey, *Gilkey on Tillich*, 74.
8. Tillich, *Systematic Theology*, 1:62.
9. Ibid., 1:63.

If Tillich had wanted to be loyal to his understanding of correlation, he would have centralized this dimension of particularity (i.e., in terms of uniqueness and acknowledging the self's and the other's differentiation). What he did, instead, was to reduce particularity to role-exclusiveness by limiting questioning to one fixed pole and answering to the other fixed pole in the correlation. This is also what seems to be derivatively applied in theological hermeneutics in the twentieth century, such as those of D. Tracy, G. Kaufman, and M. Taylor (see my discussion in the previous chapter).

In this chapter, I will call for discerning more carefully the overshadowed elements in the notion of correlation that Paul Tillich suggests as a key method for theologization and for "theology-postmodernity" relationship. I find implicit within Tillich's perception of mutuality and particularity as constitutive components of the notion of "correlation" an invitation to discover that genuine correlationality does not actually point to, or lie in, the particularity of the roles restrictively and exclusively conducted in the correlation. It primarily lies in, and points to, the particularity of the content, of the object, of the foundational truth, that the answers and the questions convey, express, or represent, each in its own terms and difference. This particularity of Christianity does not primarily or correlatively lie in its role as the one that is supposed to provide answers. This particularity lies, instead, in the fact that the answers Christianity gives and the answering method it follows, as Tillich correctly affirms, "are dependent on the revelatory events in which [these answers basically] appear."[10] Avoiding Tillich's understanding of the dimension of particularity in terms of content and subject matter can be achieved only if, contrary to him, one does not overemphasize Tillich's claim that the answers "are *dependent* on the structure of the questions which they answer" and places center-stage, instead, Tillich's other belief that the answers cannot be *derived* from analyzing the context and the constituents of the question and the questioning side. It should, on the contrary, be presented as answers *to* or *for* these constituents and content; as answers from outside.[11]

The bottom line of calling for particularity that lies in the subject matter and the method of answering and questioning, instead of in the practices of questioning and answering and their confinement to one of the correlates and not the other, is to take Paul Tillich's valuable proposal of the method of "correlation" beyond the reductionist, inappropriate implementation of it. The

---

10. Ibid., 1:64.

11. Ibid., 1:64. Though unfortunately underdeveloped in his *Systematic Theology*, this logic underlies Tillich's saying "God is the answer to the question implied in human finitude. [Yet] this answer cannot be derived from the analysis of existence."

trick here is to search for a model of correlation that is more correlationally balanced to apply to the relationship between theology and other intellectual forms of inquiry. Such a model of correlation should depart from an acknowledgment of the particularity of each of the correlates, not by limiting their influence and reducing their identity to a specific role each plays, but by acknowledging each other's particular content, method, object, and form. Such a model should also invite the correlates to step beyond their closed circles and change on the basis of their particularities, and not in spite of them. It should show, the difference and distinction between the correlates notwithstanding, that it is possible for a positive relationship of mutual influence to happen between them. And it should be based on unity-in-differentiation that neither transforms one side into a mimesis of the other, nor submits to the other hierarchically. It rather should make a cross-fertilization between theology and other disciplines possible, without making the assertion of the truth-claims of each side of the correlation, as well as the recognition of such assertion, an indication of a lapse into any ideological or criterial authoritarianism. As a matter of fact, Christian tradition itself, Thomas Guarino reminds us, already carries evidences of such a correlation, or "intertextual mutuality," as it reveals that "a certain critical correlation between Christian faith and 'secular' wisdom . . . has been classically sanctioned in the Christian tradition."[12] Guarino's description of this correlationality between theology and other fields of inquiry is worth citing here at length.

> In this . . . understanding of correlation, theology is not captive to Enlightenment modernity, neither in its traditional form nor in its contemporary metamorphosis as communicative rationality. Nor is theology bound to assert the truth-claims of Christian faith and doctrine absent the benefit of further philosophical, even metaphysical (taken in broad sense) support . . . the normativity of the gospel message is proclaimed. However, this evangelical primacy does not need to result in a dichotomous either/or, so that a proper correlation between theology and the disciplines . . . is repudiated.[13]

12. Thomas G. Guarino, *Foundations of Systematic Theology* (London and New York: T. & T. Clark/Continuum, 2005), 321.

13. Ibid., 322. Guarino personally still wants to acknowledge a higher, more ascendant position for the truth-claims of Christian theology on the basis of bestowing upon revelation a criterial position. I do think that going along the track of recognizing an ascendancy to the revelatory narrative may actually lapse correlation into another, no less hierarchically twisted end, unless one keeps in mind that the revelatory narrative itself is not a criterion about truth in general but about God's truth, which is beyond any form of truth related to human understanding that other disciplines are supposed to deal with and

In the remainder of this chapter, I will outline Hans Frei's and Francis Watson's views on the relation between theology and other forms of inquiry. In their proposals, I find two balanced and appropriate understandings of "correlation," according to which theology should relate to or with other fields of study. In their hermeneutics of correlation, I find a more promising model of relationality that can salvage theology today from the extremes of turning theology into a postmodern condition, and from turning postmodernity into a theological condition. In the two ensuing chapters of this last part, I will show how the same understanding of correlation Frei and Watson call on is supported and implemented in J. Moltmann's and W. Pannenberg's trinitarian thinking, as well as their understanding of the relation between theology and other disciplines or between theology and secular thinking.

III. HANS FREI: THE BOUNDARIES OF CORRELATION

In a collection of posthumously published papers, Hans Frei draws the boundaries for a proper interaction between theology and philosophical theories of knowledge. He basically argues that one of the most necessary tasks of theology is to scrutinize the modernist construal of theology, both in its internal dimension as a specific religious description, and in its external dimension as an instance of a general class of academic, scientific disciplines based on a more or less philosophical system of inquiry (*Wissenchaftslehre*) that reflects a more general and critical system of human cognition.[14] Frei exposes five types of attitudes to theology that are expressive of this modernist view. According to these types, the degree of theology's involvement with general disciplines of inquiry varies. It ranges from an involvement that stresses the prioritization of the philosophical conditioning of theology over the theology's role of reflecting on the religious practice of a certain community (type one), up to a form of involvement that stresses the exclusion of theology from any

---

converse with theology about. Revelation has a criterial position only *ad intra* theology and not in theology's conversation with other disciplines on reality in general. Even Pannenberg, who supports considering God the foundation of reality in its totality, would consider *God* and not revelation as this foundation. In addition, Guarino's belief that theology's need for a kind of *prima philosophia* "appears to be demanded for the sake of the intelligibility of revelation itself" (ibid., 323) is reminiscent of the no-less-problematic passion of theologically recontextualizing nontheological forms of inquiry into the biblical metanarrative and using them in the service of retrieving a central position for theology, which I pointed to earlier in part two, chapter three.

14. Hans W. Frei, *Types of Christian Theology*, ed. G. Hunsinger and W. C. Placher (New Haven and London: Yale University Press, 1992), 1–7.

participation in general inquiry by restricting its role to the self-description of Christianity (type five).[15] Frei believes that the major common problem in these five types lies "not in what it affirms about Christianity but in what it appears to *deny* about the character of theology as part of Christianity."[16]

In his other writings, Frei consistently expresses support for Barth's theological methodology. This is probably the reason behind calling his approach "postliberal" theology.[17] Here as well, Frei's support of Barth's view of the relation of theology to philosophy is noticeable. If Frei were to adopt one of the five types, he would choose the fourth type, which, in his opinion, is the most expressive of Karl Barth's theology. This Barthian type accepts a degree of combination of theological norms with methods founded on general disciplines of inquiry. However, it refuses to view this combination as a "correlation between heterogeneous equals." It rather states that "the practical discipline of Christian self-description governs and limits the applicability of general criteria of meaning in theology, rather than vice versa."[18] Relevant to this is Frei's criticism in an earlier essay of two mistaken characterizations of Christian theology as either a philosophical discourse on religion or a sociological discourse on religious life and practice. There, Frei argues that instead of pointing to specific theological and philosophical dimensions in Christian faith for the sake of gaining a deeper understanding of this faith, these two characterizing forms endeavor to show that philosophy and sociology are constitutive of theology: they make theology what it *is*.[19] Instead of maintaining the self-descriptive character of theology, these two forms reduce theology to a mere descriptive means for another predominant criterial condition. Theology, in this case, becomes an expression of a religious eagerness to acquire intelligibility according to the rules of a certain theory of knowledge. It is a

---

15. Dan Stiver thinks that Frei's fifth type falls eventually into "fideism," "where Christian theology only attends to itself without reference to anything outside." He also states that postmodernity drives theology to this fideistic corner, "removing it from the larger playing field altogether." Dan R. Stiver, "Theological Method," in *The Cambridge Companion to Postmodern Theology*, ed. K. J. Vanhoozer (Cambridge: Cambridge University Press, 2003), 170–85, 176.

16. Frei, *Types of Christian Theology*, 5 (italics are mine). Frei focuses here on the first and the fifth types. However, his perceptive note applies to all the types exposed.

17. According to Placher's introduction to Frei's essays, "postliberal theology" is the name that was originally given to Frei's Barthian-like theology by George Lindbeck. See Hans Frei, *Theology and Narrative: Selected Papers*, ed. G. Hunsinger and W. C. Placher (Oxford and New York: Oxford University Press, 1993), 3.

18. Frei, *Types of Christian Theology*, 4. For an earlier version, see Frei, *Theology and Narrative*, 94–116.

19. Frei, *Theology and Narrative*, 96–97.

correlation in which theology is seen as "a supertheory to *mediate* [philosophy and sociology] and explain both as autonomous contents undergirded by a single structure."[20]

At face value, Frei's previous critique may show that the response to any secular, historical characterization of theology should be in converting this secular content into a theological condition, where the theological criterion of inquiry becomes prior to the philosophical ones in shaping all human concepts. But, far from being the case, a careful reading of Frei's statement about the problem that lies in what is *denied* rather than in what is affirmed about theology reveals that Frei is not here concerned about developing a theological transformation of the general theory of inquiry, but about disallowing any imposition of external criteria over theology for all sorts of nontheological reasons. This pinpoints what certain extra-theological conditions *deny* to and about theology. It neither imposes a theological norm over a general condition of inquiry, nor rejects the theology's correlation with external conditions in the absolute. Frei, rather, endeavors to ground the relation of theology to the surrounding intellectual condition in the *undeniable* inner coherency of Christian faith, which *is*, for Frei, what makes theology a valid and a valuable form of inquiry among many others. Denying this inner coherency is a problematic twist to the correlation between theology and any general theory of inquiry. And displaying the negative outcomes of such a denial summarizes Frei's theological criticism of modern epistemological methodology.

The point of departure of Frei's criticism of the theological adherence to modern epistemology is a rejection of the Bultmann-like dictum: all theological assertions are anthropological assertions. This dictum stands as a "survey of the largest part of the theological household's convictions," not only in the eighteenth and nineteenth but also in the twentieth century. This is why, according to Frei, the central content of Christian doctrine, Christology, has been primarily shaped by a preoccupation with the historical Jesus and his *work* rather than the divine person of the Christ of the *kerygma*. In conclusion, theology, like philosophy, "has been agitated by epistemological and ontological rather than metaphysical questions."[21] Such a methodology, where actions are constitutive of nature (in the light of the Kantian praxis-ethics framework of religion), has turned theology into a secularly conditioned and

---

20. Frei, *Theology and Narrative*, 101.

21. Frei, *Theology and Narrative*, 28. Frei explains that for him "ontology" designates an inquiry in the concept of being that is considered as an anthropologically based inquiry, that is, as an inquiry that considers human beings "the indispensable focus for the apprehension of being." In other words, Frei is not really against theological ontology, but against onto-anthropology.

constrained discourse. "Systematic theology," as Frei says, "has largely been an endeavor to unite the doctrines of Christ and the Spirit at the level of immanence rather than transcendence."[22] For Frei, theology found itself obliged to "validate the *possibility* and, hence, the meaning of Christian claims concerning the shape of human existence and the divine relation to it, even though the *actual occurrence*—and thus the *verification* of the claim—is a matter of divine, self-authenticating action and revelation."[23]

It is important that Frei's alternative to the previous subordination of theology to a general condition of inquiry is not a claim of a theological counterattack, by which theology re-conditions and recontextualizes the general intellectual context whenever it has the chance. Rather, Frei calls for a third approach in which theology is first understood and Scripture is first interpreted on its own terms and from its own truth-claims. He suggests that the systematic inquiry about the meaning of Christian narrative (written or proclaimed) should be: "What does this narrative say or mean, never mind whether it can become a meaningful possibility of life perspective for us or not?"[24]

Is Frei calling for an authoritative theologization that shapes all kinds of interpretation and draws boundaries to all levels of meaning? Frei may be doing this with regard to the intra-development of theological inquiry itself. In this regard, Frei's warning against the absence of textual authority makes sense. As he correctly shows, without the authority factor, reading and interpreting theological texts would reflect whatever the interpreter personally wants the material to say, and it may also be an interpretation based on unlikely extra-theological presumptions.[25] This by no means implies that Frei is imposing a theological method of interpretation over *all* forms of human knowledge, or over *all* historical and intellectual conditions. His view is just a baseline for a possible theological re-understanding of certain epistemic criteria by means of discerning theology's distinction first.[26]

22. Frei, *Theology and Narrative*, 29. Such a conditioning of theology proves for Frei that "Kant's *Religion Within the Limits [of Reason Alone]* contains *in nuce* almost all the problems systematic theologians have worried to and fro since his day."

23. Frei, *Theology and Narrative*, 30.

24. Frei, *Theology and Narrative*, 40.

25. Ibid., 40.

26. It is worth noting that Frei's view of authority does not represent even a moderate version of the doctrine of infallibility or of the doctrine of literal inspiration. It is rather a reflection of the following understanding of the Bible: if there is no hermeneutical approach that is completely unbiased and nonsubjectivist (not even the historical-critical approach, since its supporters bring into their hermeneutical inquiry an anthropological and Kantian subjectivist premise), let the authoritative criterion

It is understandable, in the light of the previous, why Frei sides with Barth's claim that what makes theology an authentic and valuable procedure of inquiry is not its commensurability with a general dominating discipline of inquiry in a certain historical situation, but the fact that theology is a discourse about God.[27] Frei's support of this view stems from his concern about maintaining a degree of theological dependence on philosophical secular aspects that are available and appealing to theology in certain conditions, provided these aspects are controlled by the premises of proper theological inquiry.[28] Frei supports this approach because it does not turn the relation between theology and any general philosophical condition into a systematic super-theory that imposes theological connotations over all levels of meaning, in such a way, that is, that makes any discourse unnecessarily crypto-theological. This in turn prepares for a free and balanced interaction between theology and other intellectual discourses. It 1) maintains properly the social, communal structure of the Christian language of faith that expresses a theology done in interaction and relationship;[29] and 2) it shows that rational inquiry is not alienated from the theological realm of understanding, although it exists within this realm fragmentarily. This fragmentary presence does not prevent interpreting the theological discourse in recourse to philosophical inquiry, since Christian theology, according to Frei, does not bring its own technical conceptual tools with it.[30] These two points indicate that the relation between theology and any general condition of inquiry is necessary and inevitable, provided that theology would neither describe this general condition affirmatively (or conformingly), nor seek to prove its competence and legitimacy according to this condition. Theology should not succumb to a process of inquiry that denies it one of its substantial norms or expects it to pursue the denial of such norms.

---

of our interpretation of Scripture be *theological* rather than anything else. The issue here is claiming the sole validity of theology for interpreting Scripture. See Frei, *Theology and Narrative*, 42.

27. Frei, *Types of Christian Theology*, 38–46.

28. Ibid., 41.

29. Ibid., 74. We should be careful lest we identify Frei's point with George Lindbeck's reduction of theological discourse to a mere linguistico-grammatical practice that is generative of truth. Frei, on the contrary, acknowledges the existence of a norm or norms for theological language that are distinct from the language and its practice per se. See George Hunsinger, "Postliberal Theology," in *The Cambridge Companion to Postmodern Theology*, 42–53.

30. Frei, *Types of Christian Theology*, 81. Frei is here discussing the relation of theology to philosophy in the light of an interpretation of Barth's definite rejection of the characterization of theology as *Wissenschaft*. Frei thinks that Barth's strict rejection of this categorization does not yet prove Barth's total rejection of all kinds of interaction between theology and secular knowledge (78–91).

IV. Francis Watson: The Validity of Disciplinary Boundaries

An attractive alternative for the understanding of correlation is found in Francis Watson's view of the relation between hermeneutics and systematic theology, which he develops with the challenges of the postmodern condition clearly in mind. In an essay titled "The Scope of Hermeneutics," Watson states the following:

> Origen's question about the relationship between literal and theological senses is still with us in various forms; but it must be answered by a way of criteria internal to theological discourse and not only by appealing to general hermeneutics which, if it is interested in this issue at all, will see it only as an instance of a more universal problem. Theological hermeneutics will have much to learn from general hermeneutics, but it will have much more to learn from theology itself.[31]

It can be easily noticed that Watson is not speaking here, or in the following pages, about the relation and the impact of the theological and the general (modern or postmodern) inquiries over each other. He is actually talking about the relationship and the disciplinary boundaries between two areas from the theological field itself. However, the *"crossing-boundaries"* model of interaction he calls for here applies to the issue of the required relation between theology and postmodern forms of inquiry.

According to Watson's claim, theological inquiry should not be practiced on the basis of, and should not be constrained by, extra-theological conditioning predicaments that undermine the substantial foundations of theology itself. Theological inquiry should be done by means of its own theological rules and doctrinal norms. Such interiority not only preserves the integrity of Christian religious thinking. It also disallows any demoting of theology into merely one contextual expression of the postmodern (or modern) condition among other equally relative ones. Rather than allowing an external conditioning to theological inquiry, we ought to: 1) pinpoint the positive contribution of theology to Christian religious practice and communal life itself, as Watson correctly states; moreover, we ought to 2) point to the positive impact of theology over the world surrounding the church, which is just as valuable and transforming for this world as it is claimed to be for theology.

---

31. Francis Watson, "Scope of Hermeneutics," in *The Cambridge Companion to Christian Doctrine*, ed. C. E. Gunton (Cambridge: Cambridge University Press, 1997), 65–80, 71.

Such a possible correspondence and mutual enrichment between theological and general inquiries (or general and theological hermeneutics, in Watson's words) is stressed by Watson's opinion on the validity and value of the existence of disciplinary boundaries.[32] Watson discloses a clear, critical view of the existence of disciplinary boundaries between different fields within theological inquiry, together with a parallel admittance of its partial convenience. From his opposition, as well as from his admittance of its partial necessity, one can infer points that are relevant to the issue of the relation of theology to postmodernity.

In the first place, Watson acknowledges a degree of convenience and necessity in the existence of disciplinary boundaries. He states that "faced with the difficulty of mastering extensive fields, it is a reality to know that this field has its limits and that one has no responsibility for that which lies outside those limits."[33] One elaboration on this is that a similar relief can stem from the fact that any internal limitation should not be a proof of the weakness or the disqualification of this field of inquiry, and it should not entail, therefore, that this field must contradict itself in order to succumb to certain external measures and gain general acceptance. In other words, the disciplinary boundaries are necessary, for example, for supporting the tenability of the theological discourse about the existence of a transcendent divine Origin before other postmodern discourses, since these boundaries indicate that it is not the responsibility of these postmodern discourses to judge the validity of such a claim in theology.

On the other hand, Watson is equally critical of disciplinary boundaries. He believes that these boundaries should not necessitate a total seclusion and relativism that would eventually distort any positive, and even necessary, mutuality between different forms of knowledge. Once such boundaries are overdrawn, as Watson says, they "are not only restrictive, they also grossly distort precisely the objects that they are intended to demarcate and protect."[34] To take this within the context of the theology-postmodernity relationship, the following can be suggested: If, on the basis of the disciplinary boundaries criterion, theology surrenders the task of studying the impact and the role of language in understanding truth and meaning to the postmodern philosophers, theology will inevitably miss the influence of the linguistic and contextual nature of Christian worship on the formation of so many doctrinal claims and on the interpretation of the history of doctrine.[35] If, on the other hand, postmodernity discards the doctrinal claims about the being of God, the God-

---

32. Ibid., 72ff.
33. Ibid., 73.
34. Ibid., 74.

human relationship, God's transcendence, and so on, on the basis of a conviction that such dogmatic views are irrelevant and unacceptable according to certain anti-ontological premises, postmodernity will eventually miss a form of inquiry that is capable of reforming both its oversubjectivist and relativist reaction against modernity, and its anti-ontological, overimmanentist interpretation of truth and meaning, of the idea of the "Wholly Other" and even of the concept of "love/charity." By denying that theology can turn the deconstruction of modern metaphysics back to what has been deliberately forgotten or undermined by the postmodern reaction, namely "the particular being of God,"[36] postmodernity misses the profound dimension of a valid criticism. In other words, it misses the fact that in its overemphasis on the absoluteness of the idea of presence that always lies in absence (i.e., *différance*), postmodern deconstructionism becomes itself another form of the transcendentalism it claims to deconstruct in modernity.[37]

What is, nonetheless, more important after denying the segregation of theology from postmodernity is the question of the mode of the appropriate interaction that begins when each one crosses its own boundaries toward the other: Should theology cross its boundaries to condition postmodernity, to be conditioned by it, or to dialogue with it in a way that grants theology its particular nature and its influential impact on an external condition that ought always to be distinct?

Watson's understanding of the relation of biblical studies and theology in his book *Text, Church and World*[38] presents a coherent answer to this question in a manner reminiscent of Frei's view. Watson starts his argument by acknowledging the necessity of tackling the components of Christian theology in their own particularity, without, that is, imposing on them a general criterion of interpretation. He emphasizes the particular nature of the biblical texts, stating that this particularity deems any subjection of Scripture to the control of a "single reading-perspective" unlikely. Such an indiscriminate subjection of

---

35. Ibid., 78–79 (67–71). Watson alludes to the importance of this contextual factor and reveals an acceptance of its influence on theological hermeneutics when he calls for understanding the theoretical reflection on the practice of interpretation (i.e., hermeneutics) in "local" terms, that is, "in relation to the practice of a specific interpretative community."

36. Stephen D. Long, "Radical Orthodoxy," in *The Cambridge Companion to Postmodern Theology*, 126–45, 134 (133–36).

37. Long, "Radical Orthodoxy," 130 (127–30). "[The postmodern] ontological violence is as metaphysical as the modern standpoint postmodernity deconstructed." Once this is realized, Long continues, "it allows theology to outnarrate postmodernity's efforts to overcome metaphysics."

38. Which Hunsinger describes as "an excellent example of recent postliberal hermeneutics." Hunsinger, "Postliberal Theology," 28, fn. 17.

the biblical texts to an overarching, extra-theological reading criterion is not, according to Watson, congenial with the fact that in Christian faith "the written artefact is valuable only in so far as it permits access to that which is other than itself."[39] The postmodern deconstructionist belief that "there is nothing outside the text" does not, therefore, apply to the theological text, and should be qualifiedly applied to theology. This qualification neither means subjecting the theological understanding to a general rule of interpretation that denies a conviction about the distinction between the religious text and the reality it mediates, nor does it deny that the postmodern belief in the close link between the text's linguistic character and its meaning is also applicable to the biblical texts. Rather, it reminds theologians that despite the principle of distinction, the link between the reality and its mediating text is strong and substantial.

Similarly to Frei, Watson acknowledges that biblical interpretation and doctrinal theology should correlate with the surrounding encompassing social and intellectual sphere, despite all the possible conflicting results this correlation may cause.[40] Moreover, Watson alludes to a correlation that allows for a theological modeling of certain secular conditions of inquiry. He sets for himself the task of understanding the world *theologically* by pointing to the full participation of theology in the world—for theology itself, according to Watson, is an open sphere of inquiry. In this mode of correlation, the world's condition of inquiry is considered as both necessary for mediating theological truth-claims, and as openly exposed to theological questioning about dimensions that only theology is capable of addressing in a sufficient way. Watson nevertheless stresses that such a theological qualification to the idea of "world" does not reduce the world to a theological idea. It also does not subject theology to the constraints of a certain worldly concept that misrepresents and misconceives the truth of the theological discourse. One of the dangerous consequences of the correlation of theology with postmodernity is the relativization of either theology or postmodernity to such an extent that it jeopardizes their self-integrity. In the postmodern context, theology's unqualified and subordinating openness may lead to the total denial of the concept of universality, which is basic for theology's understanding of God and his relation to creation. Such subordination to relativism is not a sign of a balanced relation, because renouncing the theological claim of the universality

---

39. Francis Watson, *Text, Church and World: Biblical Interpretation in Theological Perspective* (Edinburgh: T. & T. Clark, 1994), 2.

40. Ibid., 7ff. Watson elaborates on this by speaking about the place of theology in the realm of the university.

of God's truth is a distortion of a substantial component of the Christian message. Watson affirms this:

> If one wished to strip [Christian truth] of its universal pretensions, reading it and the biblical narratives from which it is derived as simply one story among others, then it would be hard to differentiate this program from the world's assumption that the Christian story is simply false.[41]

The interdisciplinary approach is, therefore, necessary for studying, as well as developing, the relationship in which theology and postmodernity relate to one another as two concentric circles. The challenge, though, lies in the extent of correlation that each would execute with, and each would allow to, the other in such a relationship. According to postmodernity, every text has an infinite range of meanings that is always differed by and deferred to the future. The meaning of the text exceeds mere literal reading. However, postmodernity does not show readiness to concede that this "*différance*" may point to a linguistic transpiring of something that lies *beyond* language itself and even generates it. Instead of this, postmodernity states, according to Watson, that "we have at our disposal nothing but sign, and the idea that we cognate outside language in order to attain to 'reality' as self-contradictory."[42]

On the contrary, theology seems to be too charitable in its attitude toward postmodernity. It overgenerously embraces the deconstructive claims in their anti-theological terms, and it is sometimes too ready to dispense with any dogmatic concept that may conflict with these claims. This was recently done, for instance, in the manner of overemphasizing a claimed similarity between the postmodern rejection of any ontological description of God's reality and the mystical apophatic language of Negative Theology.[43] It is quite interesting here that the main postmodern promoters of such a rejection of ontology refuse personally this charitable assimilation and deny such allegiance to negative theology, maintaining in response a strict rejection of theological discourse about God in its mystical version.[44] Theologians show readiness to review

---

41. Ibid., 10.
42. Ibid., 80.
43. Ibid., 80–81ff.
44. See Derrida's rejection of any claimed similarity between his philosophy and Negative Theology in: Derrida, "How to Avoid Speaking: Denials," trans. Ken Frieden, in *Derrida and Negative Theology*, ed. Harold Coward and Toby Foshay (Albany: State University of New York Press, 1992), 73–143. And see also the difference between Derrida's and Marion's interpretation of Pseudo-Dionysius, in Thomas A.

and reconsider Christian beliefs in light of the questions that are put by postmodernity,[45] whereas postmodernist philosophers are not judging their assumptions and positions in the light of an objective, open consideration of the questions of theology. Like modernity, postmodernity seems to be trapped in a judgmental, hierarchical attitude toward the theology of God. And, like modern theologians, the majority of postmodern theologians are trapped in an eagerness to gain a place within the newly dominating philosophical condition. Both postmodernist philosophers and theologians, like their modernist predecessors, are trapped in the same mistaken correlation.[46]

The balanced theological approach to postmodernity should rather go beyond the category-mistake trap of modern and postmodern philosophy and theology and develop instead a theology that grows out of an *"encounter with and resistance to"* the surrounding conditions. So far, contemporary theology has generally admitted the necessity of the encounter, but, to a noticeable extent, it has succumbed to the postmodern rules. What is yet to be done by theology is to maintain a perceptive and a reasonable degree of *resistance*. Denying the importance of this resisting standpoint threatens, in the first place, the Christian concept of "God,"[47] as much as the modernist condition that threatened it in the past. By reducing the idea of God to a mere expression of a transcendental textual meaning, postmodernism does not address theology on its own terms. Therefore, postmodernity should not only be taken seriously, but should also be responsibly encountered by theology.

For such an "encounter-in-resistance" correlation to take place in a fruitful and not a polemical way, nevertheless, it needs to be executed by two sides that consider the other an "important dialogue partner which will assist in the shaping of its form and substance even as it is resisted."[48]

Carlson, "Postmetaphysical Theology," in *The Cambridge Companion of Postmodern Theology*, 58–75, 69ff.

45. Like, for example, when theology speaks about its truth-claims merely as "intra-systematic" forms of speech that has, like any other form, its own language, rather than as a "meta-discourse" or a truth-claim that is legitimized upon a metanarrative related to God. Watson, *Text, Church and World*, 83ff.

46. Watson, *Text, Church and World*, 84. "The unbelieving philosopher who demonstrates the irrationality of belief in the existence of God participates, along with the anxious apologist who hastens to the defense of this belief, in a category-mistake."

47. Ibid., 85. According to Watson, the Derridean view of textuality would reinscribe God as merely immanent within textuality, so that "the so-called metaphysical attributes of God are covertly transferred to textuality itself."

48. Ibid., 86.

V. Concluding Remarks

In his two-volume *Systematic Theology*, Robert Jenson makes the following perceptive statement: "If theological prolegomena lay down conceptual conditions of Christian teaching . . . that are more than a formal demand for coherence and argumentative responsibility . . . the prolegomena sooner or later turn against the *legomena*."[49] In searching for a correlation model such as the one presented by Hans Frei and Francis Watson, I have tried to show that there are in theological scholarship good examples for developing a relationship between theology and other forms of intellectual inquiry that take seriously Jenson's warning of the prolegomena's turning against its "*legomena*." Ultimately, Guarino is right in his belief that "Athens and Jerusalem are not in entirely different spheres; both reason and faith are gifts from God."[50] The challenge, nevertheless, is to find a proper, balanced form of relationship between faith and reason that maintains each one's particularity and truth-claims in a mutual circle of "asking-answering" or "transformation-preservation." The challenge, that is, is to find a correlation that makes Christian theology "always open to new ideas and new points of view that will further illuminate the deposit of faith, even while maintaining the material continuity and abiding nature of Christian truth."[51]

Miroslav Volf once accurately reminded us that "method is message," since method and content mutually shape each other in theological reasoning.[52] By choosing the right method of correlation to develop a valuable and appropriate relationship with other intellectual forms of inquiry, theology not only plays the role it is expected to play as the discourse on the truth of God in the world. More crucially, it sends to the world the right message about its identity, its truth-claims, and God's relation to creation. Theology, in other words, becomes God's message to the world on the possibility of building a relationship that combines identity and unity in a mutually balanced way. Theology becomes God's message about the possibility of imaging his relational life in human life. By carefully thinking about its methodology, it gives a message about a correlation shaped after a *perichoretic* form of relationality, wherein the correlates are not only interdependent and co-influential to each other from outside, but

---

49. Robert Jenson, *Systematic Theology* (Oxford and New York: Oxford University Press, 1997), 1:9.

50. Guarino, *Foundations of Systematic Theology*, 329.

51. Ibid., 329.

52. Miroslav Volf, "Theology, Meaning & Power: A Conversation with George Lindbeck on Theology & the Nature of Christian Difference," in *The Nature of Confession: Evangelicals and Postliberals in Conversation*, ed. Timothy R. Phillips and Dennis L. Okholm (Downers Grove, IL: InterVarsity, 1996), 46.

also interact in a personal manner that makes them interior to one another. This profound interiority does not, as Volf elsewhere states, deny each side's particular identity and truth-claims. It rather shows that the mutual interiority between the two sides is the strongest evidence that their identities are not self-enclosed or hierarchically related.[53]

It is this form of correlation that we should shape after the triune nature of God. Any correlational model that does not maintain the distinction between its two correlates, and does constructs the mutual interaction and correspondence between them on their distinctions, fails to serve the purpose of understanding the relation between God and the human, or how God's triune identity models our human social living. Miroslav Volf is perceptively correct in warning us that overemphasizing the claim "God is our social program" may lead to an inappropriate theology of the Trinity and of the God-human relationship. Reducing God's trinitarian nature to the mere image of our own sociality entails, Volf warns, that every characteristic of this nature should also be inherent to our own personal and social being. So, the perichoretic interiority of the three divine persons should mirror a similar interiority on the human level. But such a correspondence, Volf persuasively argues, is impossible, for human persons cannot be internal to one another as the three divine persons of the Trinity are.[54] Be that as it may, the correlation of the Trinity with human sociality should be reflective of God's agency in making human life social and relational *after his likeness*. God as the agent of sociality, who correlates with us in a relation of union-in-self-differentiation, is the divine Spirit who enables personhood (self-particularity) and sociality (other-concerning relationality) as equally constitutive correlates. God as the Spirit is the agent who makes sociality and personhood in human existence equiprimal. He is not the name of this equiprimality. Volf concludes from this that "the question is not whether the

---

53. Thus Miroslav Volf, "'The Trinity Is Our Social Program': The Doctrine of the Trinity and the Shape of Social Engagement," *Modern Theology* 3, no. 14 (1998): 409. Volf derives this from a direct look at *perichoresis* in the life of the Trinity itself: ". . . the sources of *perichoresis* for thinking about identity are as rich as for thinking about unity. For it suggests that divine persons are not simply interdependent and influence one another from outside, but are *personally interior* to one another. . . . Every divine person is indwelled by other divine persons; all the persons interpenetrate each other. They do not cease however to be distinct. Rather, their interpenetration presupposes their distinctions' persons who have been dissolved in some third thing cannot be said to be interior to each other. The distinctions of the persons notwithstanding, their identities partly overlap. Every divine person is and acts as itself and yet the two other persons are present and act in that person."

54. Miroslav Volf, *After Our Likeness: The Church as the Image of the Trinity* (Grand Rapids and Cambridge: Eerdmans, 1998), 191ff. See also a brief yet perceptive analysis of Volf's point in Anne Hunt, *Trinity: Nexus of the Mysteries of Christian Faith* (Maryknoll, NY: Orbis, 2005), 126–30.

Trinity should serve as a model for human community; the question is rather in which respects and to what extent it should do so."[55]

To take the same point to the realm of the proper correlation between theology and other forms of intellectual inquiry, I conclude that the question today is not whether or not theology should correlate with other forms of intellectual inquiry. The question is, rather, *in which respect and to what extent* this correlation should take place. What people such as Francis Watson and Hans Frei tell us by their models of correlation, and what Miroslav Volf tells us by his critique of "the Trinity is our social program," is almost one and the same principle: God is God; we are not God; and, as we cannot simply imitate God,[56] theology is theo-logy, and other forms of inquiry are not theology just because, or even when, they speak about "the Wholly Other" or the "Infinite Transcendent." Theology does not become one of these forms of inquiry by simply repeating their claims and using their linguistic dictionary; nor can nontheological forms of inquiry be deemed inherently theological simply by using terms familiar to the theologian's ear. As God's substantial distinction from humanity does not prevent a correlation of unity-in-self-differentiation between them, the distinction between theology and other forms of inquiry is not an obstacle against their correlation, but the foundation and the generator of such a correlation.

---

55. Volf, "'The Trinity Is Our Social Program': The Doctrine of the Trinity and the Shape of Social Engagement," 405, and Hunt, *Trinity: Nexus of the Mysteries of Christian Faith*, 127.

56. Volf, *After Our Likeness*, 192–95.

7

Perichoresis of "Person" and "Relation" and Trinitarian Theology

I. The Immanent and Economic Trinity Reconsidered

One of the main characteristics of modern trinitarian theology lies in the important emphasis it places on the ontological and epistemological unity between the immanent and the economic Trinities. Both Karl Barth and Karl Rahner, as two major theological voices in the modern age, emphasize that the immanent and the economic Trinities are identical: God is his revelation, or the salvific actions of the three divine persons in history reflect the intra-trinitarian relations of the three *hypostases* in the eternal Godhead. In order to maintain the substantial identity of the immanent and the economic Trinities, Barth and Rahner stress that the salvific actions of the Father, Son, and Spirit and their distinctions do not point to multiple centers of origin: the Father, the Son, and the Spirit are not three separate divine sources, and the trinitarian actions do not define three individuals. The economic triune salvific actions are revelatory of God's transcendent, one, and single immanent divine being. They are, in other words, three modes of subsistence of the one divine essence of God.

Among the two, Karl Rahner's understanding of the Trinity has occupied the center of the theology of God's triune nature since the second half of the twentieth century. What is known as "Rahner's Rule" (*Grundaxiom*) undergirds almost every theological proposal on the triune life of God ever since the publication of Rahner's *The Trinity*.[1] In this text, Rahner argues for the need

---

1. The German text where Rahner sets his rule "Die 'ökonomische' Trinität ist die 'immanente' Trinität und umgekehrt" is: "Der dreifaltige Gott als transzendenter Urgrund der Heilsgeschichte," in *Mysterium Salutis, Grundriss heilsgeschichtlicher Dogmatik*, 2, hrsg. J. Feiner u. M. Löhrer (Einsiedeln: Benziger, 1974).

to develop the doctrine of the Trinity beyond the boundaries of contextual or biblicist interpretations, advocating instead for the construction of serious, theologically developed hermeneutics. This theological development of the church's understanding of the Trinity is achieved for Rahner by reinterpreting every doctrine of faith, especially the incarnation and salvation, *from*, and as a variation on, the doctrine of the Trinity.[2]

Rahner is, of course, fully aware that one of the central claims of Christian faith is the divine mysteriousness and incomprehensibility. Rahner himself affirms that the mysteriousness of God is fundamental and indispensable for theological reasoning. "Even in the vision [i.e., where the divine gives himself to us]," Rahner states, "God remains forever incomprehensible."[3] Therefore, Rahner adds, "the dogma of the Trinity is an *absolute mystery* which we do not understand even after it has been revealed."[4] "Trinity" and "mystery" are not contradictory terms. They actually belong together in essence, and the Trinity, in fact, is the depth of the concept of mystery.[5]

But, if the Trinity is a mystery beyond human comprehension, and if it is absolutely so, how can we understand any other theological doctrine from it? The core of Rahner's answer to this question lies in his notion of God's "self-communication." In *Foundations of Christian Faith*, Rahner states what he understands by God's self-communication. When God communicates with us, Rahner says, he does not just convey to us some truths *about* who he is by means of one vision or another. When God addresses us, he communicates his very own self, his own most proper reality. God's self-communication is an ontological event that makes God in Godself known, and not only things about him.[6] God's self-communication is the eternal, incomprehensible divine reality relating to humanity, as Rahner says, for the sake of making God known and

---

2. Karl Rahner, *The Trinity*, trans. Joseph Donceel (New York: Crossroad, 1997), 9ff. With regard to the incarnation, for instance, Rahner suggests a trinitarian reading of the divine's becoming human as a reflection of the grace of the eternal *Logos*, the second person in the Trinity, instead of the grace of "God-man" or the divine *monos* who became human.

3. Ibid., 46. "The Trinity," Rahner continues, "is a mystery whose paradoxical character is preluded in the paradoxical character of [the human] existence. That is why it is meaningless to deny this mysteriousness, trying to hide it by an accumulation of subtle concepts and distinctions which only seem to shed more light upon the mystery, while in fact they feed [the human] with verbalisms which operate as tranquilizers for *naïvely* shrewd minds, and dull the pain they feel when they have to worship the mystery without understanding it" (ibid., 47).

4. Ibid., 50.

5. Ibid., 51.

6. Rahner, *Foundations of Christian Faith: An Introduction of the Idea of Christianity*, trans. William V. Dych (New York: Crossroad, 1989), 116–17.

possessed in immediate vision and love.[7] The ontological nature of this divine self-communication, moreover, is apprehensible to the human because it points to an ontological link between God and humanity: God's self-communication corresponds ontologically to the human's essential being, which in turn lies in self-communication too.[8] God's self-communication is a revelation of God's very own being because the three divine persons of the Godhead, Rahner states, are ontologically related to us; are intrinsically and absolutely linked with us.[9] For Rahner's theology of divine self-communication, as Nancy Dallavalle rightly notes, "the triune God of salvation history is the self-communication of the triune God of eternity; the human experience of God in the events of the history of salvation *is* the human experience of the very mystery of God."[10]

On the basis of this ontological correspondence between the human and God's triune self-communication, Rahner argues that the Trinity should not be isolated from human reality because it is a mystery. "There must be a connection between Trinity and [the human]," Rahner affirms.[11] The Trinity, in other words, must be the mystery that redeems the human and saves her from the state of self-presence, which the human self was deprived of due to sin. The Trinity is the mystery of salvation because only in realizing that her humanity lies in corresponding ontologically to the triune self-communication does the human become who she is by nature.

Be that as it may, Rahner concludes, God's self-communication should be a revelation of God's very own self. Otherwise, it is not salvific to the human self and does not make it what it is in essence. This self-communication will only be, in this case, a discourse on some facts *about* the human self, without

---

7. Ibid., 117–18.

8. Ibid., 117.

9. Rahner, *The Trinity*, 14–15.

10. Nancy A. Dallavalle, "Revisiting Rahner: On the Theological Status of Trinitarian Theology," *Irish Theological Quarterly* 2, no. 36 (1998): 133–50, 135. Dallavalle offers a valuable interpretation of "Rahner's Rule" in relation to his linking of it to Christology, incarnation, and the doctrine of Grace. Dallavalle may not be far from truth in stating that the rather incommensurable interpretations and resources Rahner offers on his axiom makes this latter contradictory in implications: "On the one hand, the theology of the expressive symbol that grounds Rahner's treatment of the incarnation is seen to maintain in tension the ontological distinction between God's life and God's life with us. On the other hand, while the innovations that underlay his understanding of the doctrine of grace . . . support well his assertion that Grace is the *self*-communication of God, they also collaborate systematically to threaten his claim of an ontologically distinct 'immanent' Trinity" (ibid., 135). I do not agree with Dallavalle's conclusion that Rahner's trinitarian thinking has impoverished modern trinitarian thinking (ibid., 150). This impoverishment is due to the misuse of Rahner's Rule by modern trinitarian theology.

11. Rahner, *The Trinity*, 21.

really enabling it to become itself. God's self-communication is ontologically bound to the salvation of the human self. Thus God in his revelation is God in his very own essence. We cannot, Rahner affirms, "neglect the experience of the Trinity in the economy of salvation in favor of a seemingly almost gnostic speculation about what goes on in the inner life of God." We cannot forget, he continues, "that the countenance of God which turns towards us in this self-communication is, in the trinitarian nature of this encounter, the very being of God as He is in Himself, and must be if indeed the divine self-communication in grace and in glory really is the communication of God in His own self to us."[12] In other words, "the 'economic' Trinity is the 'immanent' Trinity, and the 'immanent' Trinity is the 'economic' Trinity."[13] If the immanent and the economic Trinities are not mutually co-reflective of each other, God's revelation is not only unsalvific, but, more crucially, not revelatory or communicative. God's self-communication, on the contrary, is salvific because it unpacks the very self of the human before her, in that it makes the human realize that God is "the incomprehensible ground of [the human] transcendent existence."[14] If this is what the Trinity is supposed to declare, the mutual identity of the immanent and the economic Trinity should be the criterion of the real meaning of the doctrine of the Trinity.

The impact of Rahner's trinitarian thinking on the following theology of the Trinity is unsurpassed. Christoph Schwöbel attributes to Rahner the reelevation of the doctrine of the Trinity to the center of attention in the systematic construction of the components of Christian faith based upon his emphasis on the identity of the immanent and economic Trinity. According to Schwöbel, Rahner correctly identified that the subordination of the treatise "*De Deo Trino*" to the "*De Deo Uno*" in much of theology undermines the claim of the doctrine of the Trinity, both metaphysically and historically, in such a way that prevents this doctrine from playing its biblically and dogmatically constitutive role in reflecting the essence and identity of the God of Jesus Christ. Rahner's emphatic criticism of this subordination paved the way, Schwöbel

12. Rahner, *Foundations of Christian Faith*, 135.

13. Rahner, *The Trinity*, 22. Rahner explains this conclusion in the *Foundations* in the following words: ". . . with regard to that aspect of the Trinity in the economy of salvation which is given in the history of God's self-revelation in the Old and New Testaments we can say: in both the collective and individual history of salvation, there appears in immediacy to us not some numinous powers or other which represent God, but there appears and is truly present the one God Himself. In His absolute uniqueness, which ultimately nothing can take the place of or represent, he comes where we ourselves are, and where we receive Him, this very God Himself and as Himself in the strict sense." Rahner, *Foundations of Christian Faith*, 136.

14. Rahner, *Foundations of Christian Faith*, 137.

states, for subsequent theological attempts that argue that the doctrine of the Trinity, rather than being a mere appendix of the doctrine of God, is "the gateway through which the theological exposition of all that can be said about God in Christian theology must pass."[15]

In a relatively recent book on Rahner's theology, Svein Rise goes further in arguing that it is from Rahner's theology of the identity of the immanent and the economic Trinity that contemporary theology receives its willingness to clear the concept of "person" in the doctrine of the Trinity from all subjectivity, and to deny consequentially any notion of personhood that contains "self-consciousness" as one of its components.[16] Instead of departing from an understanding of the concept of "being," Rahner, according to Rise, starts his theology of the Trinity, in Athanasian fashion, from discerning the actions of salvation; the starting point that inevitably alludes to the philosophical rejection of the subject and the emphasis alternatively on praxis and communicative activity. Here, God's threefold action of salvation corresponds to a parallel threefold form of subsistence in eternity, rather than to three persons. Rahner stresses that "*hypostasis*" means a relational form of appearance to the divine essence, rather than expressing three related and distinct persons.

Rahner insists on this interpretation for two reasons. First, he wants to protect trinitarian terminology from individualism by rejecting the contemporary understanding of "person" as a being with its own free center of conscious and free activity.[17] Against this understanding, Rahner affirms that what personhood refers to in relation to the divine essence is a unicity in

---

15. Christoph Schwöbel, "The Renaissance of Trinitarian Theology: Reasons, Problems and Tasks," in *Trinitarian Theology Today: Essays on Divine Being and Act*, ed. C. Schwöbel (Edinburgh: T. & T. Clark, 1995), 1–30, 5–6. One has to say here that rather than adopting a traditional affirmative criticism to Rahner's identification of the immanent and the economic Trinities, Schwöbel prefers to point to a possible qualification to Rahner's axiom in the form of an inquiry: "Is the 'is' of his phrase [i.e., the immanent Trinity *is* the economic Trinity] to be interpreted in the sense of strict identity implying the indiscernibility of identicals, or is some other interpretation of the relationship of immanent and economic Trinity to be preferred?" (7). As it will appear from the following pages, I exhibit here the clear critical approach against Rahner's axiom because it is in the idea of total identification that many trinitarian theologies derived from Rahner's axiom lies the problematic ontological identification of "person" and "relation."

16. Svein Rise, *The Academic and Spiritual in Karl Rahner's Theology* (Frankfurt am Main: Peter Lang, 2000), 110 (107–14). Others would go further in arguing that Rahner's *Grundaxiom* is responsible for the blurring of the distinction between person and nature in modern trinitarian theology. See Neil Ormerod, "Wrestling with Rahner on the Trinity," *Irish Theological Quarterly* 3, no. 68 (2003): 213–27, 214–20. I personally think that this blurring is the fruit of a certain reading of Rahner's logic that attempted to stress historicity over eternity, and epistemology over ontology, by means of his Rule.

17. Rahner, *Foundations of Christian Faith*, 134.

essence that "implies and includes the unicity of one single consciousness and one single freedom, although the unicity of one self-presence in consciousness and freedom in the divine Trinity remains determined by that mysterious threeness which we profess about God when we speak haltingly of the Trinity of persons in God."[18] Secondly, he wants to avoid any extreme ontological segregation between God and the human that can be based on God's infinity and human finitude. And thirdly, and most importantly, he wants to deny any divisive opposition between God's modes of subsistence. Rahner believes that the relational understanding of personhood he suggests is the only appropriate means of preventing any suggestion of an "I-thou" link between the persons of the Trinity—a relation of over-against-ness, that is, that implies an ontological difference, an unbridgeable rift, between the "I" and the "thou."[19] Because of these three reasons, Rahner refuses to acknowledge in the Trinity three self-conscious, freely distinct persons. He rather supports an emphasis on an existence of three salvific moves of substantiation that are expressive of one, autonomous consciousness.[20] In sum, the main conviction that originated from Rahner's identification of the immanent and economic Trinity is articulated later by the Lutheran theologian Ted Peters. Peters writes: "The trinitarian life is itself the history of salvation. . . . To put it more forcefully: the fullness of God as Trinity is a reality yet to be achieved in the eschatological consummation."[21]

This brief exposition of Rahner's reduction of the immanent and the economic Trinity to identical modes of subsistence of one divine being provides the backdrop for the discussion to be pursued in the following pages, locating it within the framework of the ontology of personhood in the doctrine of God of modern and postmodern theology. My argument so far is: 1) modern trinitarian theology pursues a modalist trinitarian theology through the derivation of the three divine persons' identity, as well as the deduction of their being, from the one, single divine God; there is a subsuming of the threeness of the persons into the concept of a single personal God. 2) Nevertheless, in postmodern trinitarian, *anhypostatic* theology (the theology that evades speaking about three "persons"

---

18. Ibid., 135.

19. Svein Rise, *The Academic and the Spiritual in Karl Rahner's Theology* (Frankfurt am Main: Peter Lang, 2000), 111.

20. On Rahner's refusal of "person" and the modalist or nonmodalist implications of his "modes of subsistence," see Marc A. Pugliese, "Is Rahner a Modalist?" *Irish Theological Quarterly* 2, no. 28 (2003): 229–49, and the earlier argument in William Hill, *The Three-Personed God: The Trinity as a Mystery of Salvation* (Washington, DC: Catholic University of America Press, 1982), 144–45, 179, 215, 254–55.

21. Ted Peters, *God as Trinity: Relationality and Temporality in Divine Life* (Louisville: Westminster John Knox, 1993), 16. See also my analysis of Peters's trinitarian logic in part two, chapter four.

in the Trinity), which derives its view of the "three divine movements" from the single absolute idea of love, there is another form of reducing the three persons in the Trinity into the concept of a single relationality characterized by mutual participation. One can say that the doctrine of the Trinity proceeds in modernity and postmodernity as follows: from singularity to modality, and from modality to movement. The modalist version of the Trinity, in which "the moments in the self-consciousness [of the Trinity] have no subjectivity of their own"[22]—have no, that is, self-distinct personhood—is now taken to its ultimate extreme in postmodernity, in that God per se is not even conceived to be a single personal subject any more, but an expression of a relational action whose existence lies in the relational existence of the human self. Postmodernity does not only continue the eradication of the plurality of persons in God by reducing them to modes of being in one, divine subjectivity. More problematically, it eradicates the divine subjectivity per se by making God the name of the ground of our self-consciousness, self-existence as persons.

The previous modalist dead-end in the ontology of "person" in relation to the doctrine of God brings back the tracing of its origin, as many theologians of the twentieth century argue, to the tendency of totally identifying the immanent and the economic Trinity, and leads us eventually to conclude that theologians should criticize the rejection of subjectivity in the context of the hermeneutics of the Trinity. Some theologians have, in fact, already met this challenge by defending the necessity of acknowledging three equally self-conscious and autonomous centers of action in the Trinity. Other theologians, whose trend of thought is my concern in earlier chapters, take a different approach and blame Rahner for not taking his relation-action paradigm to its natural ultimate conclusion.[23] They argue that instead of just talking about "three modes of subsistence" as the meaning of "persons" in the Trinity, there should be a further emphasis on the relations of love in (and as) God in such a way that makes God per se a *history* of movement and of change characterized by charity and participation. Such emphasis on making God per se a history of love movement marks not only the theological figuration of the rejection of the notion of the subject. It also marks the beginning of the postmodern rejection

---

22. As Pannenberg describes this trend of thought in his *Systematic Theology*, trans. Geoffrey W. Bromiley (Edinburgh: T. & T. Clark, 1991), 1:295.

23. Recently, others, who are not my concern in this study, go even further in calling into question the value of Rahner's rule altogether, if not deny it any theological validity and tenability as well. See for instance Bruce Marshall, *The Trinity and Truth* (Cambridge: Cambridge University Press, 2002); and Randal Rauser, "Rahner's Rule: An Emperor without Clothes?," *International Journal of Systematic Theology* 1, no. 7.1 (2005): 81–94.

of a necessary distinction between God's personal being and "God's personal attitude vis-à-vis the human person,"[24] which is necessary to show that God becomes mutable as one who is in essence an immutable being, not as an ideal expression of a real state of mutability.

The only exit for the trinitarian ontology of personhood from the misuse of Rahner's total equation of the immanent and the economic Trinities does not primarily lie in reducing "person" in the Trinity to "action" or to "relation." It lies, rather, in reckoning deeply with a claim put forward by one of the twentieth century's most prominent theologians, Wolfhart Pannenberg:

> If the trinitarian relations among Father, Son and Spirit have the form of mutual self-distinction, they must be understood not as merely different modes of being of the one divine subject but as living realizations of separate centers of action.[25]

This means that the metaphysical ontology of personhood that avoids subsuming or collapsing "person" and "relation" into each other should once again have a central place in trinitarian theology and in the theology of personhood.

In this chapter, I would like to go back to the first group of critics of the total identification of the immanent and the economic Trinity according to Rahner. I will pinpoint in their theology an acknowledgment of a divine Trinity of three self-conscious, free, and autonomous persons. I refer to this acknowledgment because I believe that this approach to "person" and "relation" in the doctrine of God exemplifies a balanced adoption of, and allows for an appropriate impact on, the secular, philosophical notions of "person" and "relation," wherein theology is neither considered an antagonist nor deemed a follower, but rather viewed as a discipline that discerns its distinction as much as it respects its relational openness. I will refer first to Jürgen Moltmann's trinitarian ontology of person, before I focus more closely on Wolfhart Pannenberg. Both theologians reveal deep awareness of their surrounding intellectual sphere, and both seek a considerate dialogue with modern and

---

24. Rise, *The Academic and the Spiritual in Karl Rahner's Theology*, 113.

25. Pannenberg, *Systematic Theology*, 1:319. Colin Gunton also concurs with this approach by saying that "the person is neither an individual, defined in terms of separateness from others, nor one who is swallowed up into the collective." Gunton, *The Promise of Trinitarian Theology*, 2nd ed. (Edinburgh: T. & T. Clark, 1997), 13. Gunton strongly follows Pannenberg in laying the relationality and the unity of the Godhead in the otherness and particularity of the three divine persons and considers this ontological trinitarian nature of God the foundation of human personhood.

postmodern conditions. This, in my opinion, appears most noticeably in their understanding of the notions of "personhood" and "relationality" in the Trinity. Both want to interpret aspects of God's nature in conversation with the secular, anthropological interpretation of the same notions. Yet both seriously acknowledge a substantial distinction between the meaning of personhood and relationality in relation to the Trinity and in relation to human nature. I further claim that this applies even more evidently to Pannenberg than to Moltmann, for while the latter tends almost to turn the persons in the transcendent Trinity into an idealized copy of the salvific characteristic of the historical Trinity when he discusses the impact of God's revelation on his divine attributes, the former maintains the difference between the persons and their relationality even when he discusses God's attributes on the basis of a central consideration of the three persons' self-differentiation.

II. Expanding Karl Rahner's Trinitarian Paradigm

In his book *History and the Triune God*, Jürgen Moltmann reveals that he is one of those who would consider themselves principally in favor of taking Rahner's rejection of "three subjects" in the Trinity to its ultimate end,[26] although he also launches a trenchant critique against Rahner's theology of religion—the wider framework that Moltmann believes characterizes Rahner's thinking—in such a way that indicates that Moltmann's intention exceeds Rahner's "anonymous Christian" theory. Moltmann believes that Rahner's concern about the relation between universality and relativity alludes to a deeper question related to the doctrine of God: "How can an absolute, the infinite, eternal God, be depicted by a relative, the finite, limited human people of God?"[27] In other words, how can we speak of God's divine, eternal being by means of human concepts? What makes a form of speech that uses terms like "person" and "relation" possible for God? Rahner, according to Moltmann, believes that this is possible because everything God reveals of himself is already inherent in the human person. In other words, Christian faith is just "the awakening of the inner divine grace in human beings, and being a Christian is then an actualized form of being human."[28] Moltmann disagrees with this, believing that it is a

---

26. Jürgen Moltmann, *History and the Triune God: Contributions to Trinitarian Theology* (New York: Crossroad, 1991), 110. "Honoring a theological teacher means taking up the conviction about the work of God he has stimulated and carrying it *further*." Italic is mine.

27. Ibid., 111.

28. Ibid., 116.

purely existentialist form of exclusivism that in essence negates inclusive and free universality.[29]

In contrast to Rahner, Moltmann believes that the possibility of speaking about God's being in human and temporal terms is more ontologically basic than Rahner thinks: God's communication with humanity (i.e., exemplified ultimately in the acts of creation and re-creation) is itself an expression of the *history* of God, or the history of God's relational existence as such. The Old Testament's idea of "Sabbath" or "divine rest" is, for Moltmann, an expression of the completion of the historical process of God's experience of his relational reality. Having, so to speak, gone out of himself in bringing forth creation into existence, "God turns round," Moltmann says, "on the Sabbath and returns to Himself in the Sabbath rest. God is completely present as Himself."[30] In other words, God's being is eschatologically oriented and is shaped after the image of a process. It is an invitation to existence that he extends to humans and experiences with the human. This eschatological, processive movement is fully revealed in and as the human person, Jesus Christ. This state of being-ness, in addition, discloses that God himself is a fully active and progressive movement of salvation that aims at its final rest and self-fulfillment. But, more importantly, this form of being-ness, which is revealed in the incarnate Jesus Christ, also shows that humanity is in essence shaped after becoming itself by virtue of a perfect participation in the divine nature, which becomes possible to this humanity by way of becoming in the image of Christ's humanity.[31]

Moltmann applies this eschatological, processive understanding of God's life as an expression of divine historicity to the doctrine of the Trinity. In contrast to idealist concepts of "being" that are derived from the metaphysics of the concept of "absolute subject,"[32] Moltmann starts his understanding of the divine trinitarian reality from God's dynamic, historical act of salvation. He believes that this act generates another definition of being-ness, in which salvation history is ontologically identical with the process of self-fulfillment that takes place within the Trinity in its own eternity.[33] Moltmann affirms that this history is not a Hegelian-like arena of God's coming-to-himself by

---

29. Ibid., 114–18. Moltmann believes that this weakness appears in Rahner's theology of the relation of nature and grace, where he identifies "being really human" with "being Christian," which reflects, in Rahner's view, the Christian classical and problematic identification of the church with the kingdom of God.

30. Ibid., 118.

31. Ibid., 119.

32. Ibid., 80ff.

33. Ibid., 82.

means of self-alienation and then self-reconciliation. It is, rather, a process of interaction between God and human beings, as if this latter is an "other" different from God. In this sense, the history of the Trinity becomes none other than the history of the saved human person. For, "'salvation' means being taken up by the trinitarian history into the eternal life of the Trinity."[34]

In order for the reality of salvation to be expressive of such a participatorial nature like the one pointed at above, God's triune being and its relational, dynamic, and progressive nature, according to Moltmann, should not only be stressed in opposition to the conventional (basically medieval) abstract metaphysical concept of "supreme substance." It should be also emphasized in opposition to the modalist, monistic notion of "absolute subject." By "absolute subject," Moltmann means the cognitively preconceived and postulated, ideal absolute ground that underpins the human soul, and lies not in an external reality that stands over against the human, but rather within the human's own self per se.[35] In this case, speaking about God is restricted to and preconditioned by the conditions of the human self: God exists insofar as he represents or images the state of the human's awareness of her subjective existence as a self. It is in this form of anthropomorphic subjectivity that God becomes the image of an ideal, absolute personality that is reflected by means of subjective relationships.

In contrast to the classical paradigm that underlines the unity of the divine essence as the starting point for reflection on the triune God, Moltmann calls for a new methodological approach that avoids the disintegration of the Trinity into abstract monotheism.[36] Instead of one, self-enclosed, self-related absolute subject, Moltmann invites speaking about the dynamic, open divine identity by means of pointing to a process of a trinitarian, eternal self-differentiation in God himself. Because God is a triune self-differentiating personal subject, we can speak about God's self-disclosure. This is not, however, to mean taking the notion of "self-differentiation" into a Hegelian monistic conclusion, where the Trinity would become just an expression of an abstract idea of an absolute single subject that reflects itself in three *modes* of being. The triune self-differentiation is rather to be seen as an expression of a historical revelation of God in relation to the human in the person of Jesus Christ.[37]

---

34. Ibid., 83.
35. Jürgen Moltmann, *The Trinity and Kingdom of God: The Doctrine of God* (London: SCM, 1998), 15.
36. Ibid., 17.
37. Ibid., 19. "The present book is an attempt to start with the special Christian tradition of the history of Jesus the Son, and from that to develop a historical doctrine of the Trinity."

By pointing to the historical relation of the Son, Jesus, to God as the foundation of the trinitarian self-differentiation of God in himself, and of God with the human, Moltmann supports the strong link between the *opera ad intra* and the *opera ad extra trinitatis*. However, he is critical about the ontological conclusion Barth and Rahner glean from this identification in relation to the personhood of the Father, the Son, and the Spirit. He accuses Rahner of Sabellian or idealist modalism. He then responds to Rahner's rejection of anything that could mean three "subjectivities" in relation to divine personhood by saying that subjectivism does not always represent a threatening notion of individualistic, secluded, and self-centered subjectivity. Within the modern notion of personhood is also included an understanding of a subjective openness to the other; an aspect that theology should not ignore or undermine.[38] By rehabilitating the terms "*hypostasis*" or "person" in the doctrine of the Trinity by means of "modes of subsistence," Rahner, according to Moltmann, not only narrows the scope of the dynamicity of the relation between the human and God; he also prevents any mutual self-differentiation between the three divine persons as such.[39] Eventually, identifying God's oneness in essence with his self-communion would, according to Moltmann, also endanger the distinction between God and the world. God's action would not then be an action of self-communication with an other, but rather an action of self-expression within his own self. Here, as Moltmann says, "the absolute subjectivity of God becomes the archetypal image of the mystic subjectivity of the [human] person who withdraws into himself and transcends himself."[40] This is against the real nature of the triune God of Jesus Christ, who is related to the human as an "other" because he is an open, inviting Trinity in nature.[41]

By emphasizing the organic relation of self-differentiation in God's life, Moltmann wants to show that God's nature is the basis for understanding human personhood. God's triune being should illumine the concepts of "person" and "relation" in regard to human selfhood. From God's triune identity as Father, Son, and Spirit, we realize that person and relation are complementary concepts. No concept may subsume the other and be made a generic term including the other. Personality and relationality exist alongside each other as

---

38. Ibid., 145 (144ff.).
39. Ibid., 146. "Because the modes of subsistence within the Trinity do not represent distinct centers of consciousness and action, there cannot be any mutual 'thou' between them either. . . . But if there is no 'thou' within the Trinity, then there is not really any *mutual* love between the Father and the Son within the Trinity either, since 'mutual' presupposes two acts."
40. Ibid., 148.
41. Ibid., 149.

equally original. This is why "Father" and "fatherhood" exist simultaneously in God; neither precedes the other in existence. However, their distinction is also evident in that one can address a father (*pater*) but not fatherhood (*paternitas*). Both "relation" and "person" stand alongside each other as equal yet distinct identifying items of being. Therefore, Moltmann concludes, "neither reduction nor subsuming is allowed" between them.[42] In this sense, the *perichoresis* of the three persons is neither exhaustive of their personhood, nor is it the originator of the persons. *Perichoresis* is an expression of both the divine persons *and* the divine relations. It is *perichoresis* that expresses the complementarity as well as the distinction of "person" and "relation." The divine persons, therefore, do not only exist for the relations with one another. They also exist to express each other's distinction and freedom. They do this in such a way that the distinction of person and relation becomes the foundation that discloses that "the perichoretic integration of the persons in relation is complementary to their manifested distinction."[43] Subsuming of "person" into "relation" results, as it does in much modern and contemporary theology, in turning God into one absolute subject of three modes of subsistence. There is also a parallel subsuming of the three divine persons into three modes of lordship of the one absolute deity. Hence, Moltmann is right to point to the dangerous consequences of overemphasizing God's lordship at the expense of his Trinity, which characterizes Barth's and Rahner's threefold conceptual construction of God's self-communication.[44]

There is an equal danger in defining the persons of the Trinity by a single, limited form of relationality: reducing their relationship to their common nature.[45] In the history of doctrine, it was primarily Augustine, according to Moltmann, who tried to expand the range of the relationships between the three persons by speaking about the mutual relationality between the Father, Son, and Spirit in terms of origination and love. However, Augustine went so far in emphasizing relationality that he almost reduced the persons to mere relations.[46] Contrary to this Augustinian approach, Moltmann sides, albeit critically, with the Eastern concept of "*hypostasis*" that evades identifying

---

42. Moltmann, *History and the Triune God*, 85.
43. Ibid., 86.
44. See Elisabeth Moltmann-Wendel and Jürgen Moltmann, *Humanity in God* (London: SCM, 1984), 94ff.
45. Moltmann, *The Trinity and the Kingdom of God*, 171.
46. Colin Gunton shows that Augustine's approach inflicted the worst damage in this regard on the personhood of the Holy Spirit by turning the Spirit so clearly to a mere relation between the Father and the Son. Gunton, *The Promise of Trinitarian Theology*, 30–55.

"person" and "relation." In the Eastern patristic mind, as Moltmann notes, personhood is constituted by "relation" without exhaustion, because relation, in turn, is not without persons. The Eastern fathers, as Moltmann argues, knew that modalism can also be expressed by means of conflating "person" and "relation," thus denying the reciprocal relationship between them.[47] If the persons are mere relations, then God is nothing other than a triple self-repeating reality. This, as Eastern theology correctly shows, "not only dissolves the trinitarian concept of person; it does away with the interpersonal concept of relation as well."[48] The balanced way of looking at "person" and "relation," as Moltmann gathers from Eastern theology, is obtained by maintaining the genetic connection[49] between them, rather than total identification. The belief that the person actualizes himself only by seeing and encountering another is not possible unless the person and the opposite other are distinct from the relation between them.

In the Trinity, Moltmann concedes, we need to rethink "person" and "relation" *together* as two distinct concepts in order to show God's dynamic and active nature.[50] Personhood cannot then be reduced to an expression of roles or social functions (i.e., *persona*). "Person," rather, designates a unique personal being-ness that is really revealed in, rather than hidden behind, its very own relations. "Revealed in its relationships" does not mean that person is to be conflated with relationship. Such a possibility is a slip into modalism.[51] If "person" and "relation" are both fundamental, then the three in God are "persons-in-relations," not "personal relations." Any contemporary version of theology that varies on the second option simply invokes a modernist trinitarian modalism in a postmodern fashion.

---

47. Ibid., 172. "It is true that the Father is defined by His fatherhood to the Son, but this does not constitute His existence; it presupposes it. . . . Here there are no persons without relations; but there are no relations without persons either."

48. Ibid., 173. This is also the conviction of Thomas Aquinas as I discussed earlier in part two, chapter four.

49. One should here add reference to the ontological distinction to complete and qualify Moltmann's proposal. As I will show, Pannenberg's trinitarian theology also offers an attestation of this qualification of the ontology of personhood.

50. Moltmann, *The Trinity and the Kingdom of God*, 174.

51. Moltmann-Wendel and Moltmann, *Humanity in God*, 97.

III. Trinitarian Theology and the "Self-Differentiation" Ontological Paradigm

In this section, I will focus on the theology of Wolfhart Pannenberg, which, in my opinion, has not yet been fairly, comprehensively, or deeply studied or appreciated in the Anglophone world.[52]

Where Moltmann departs from Rahner's version of the identification of the immanent and the economic Trinity, Pannenberg aims at interpreting Rahner's rule in a way that exceeds both total identification and segregating prioritization. He searches for a certain dynamism that maintains God's self-differentiated, self-sufficient nature, which is from eternity to eternity itself, side by side with God's free interaction with time in a way that makes him experience a personal eschatological disclosure at the end of time. Roger Olson is correct in realizing that Pannenberg achieves this by showing that the Trinity is "the key to understanding the unity-in-difference of immanent and economic relationship between future and present."[53] The triune dynamic of self-disclosure, as Pannenberg believes, explains this relation between the past and the future by means of showing that the existence of God's self in the fullness of its historical activity *retroactively* reveals that God is already from eternity to eternity the triune Lord, is eternally and temporally who he is in essence. Understanding Pannenberg's version of Rahner's Rule requires a perception and serious appraisal of the previous concern. Christoph Schwöbel is right in saying that

---

52. This is my belief after the past ten years or so of my academic life, research, and involvement in theological scholarship in the West. On both sides of the Atlantic, English translations of Pannenberg's literature are displayed in almost every theological bookstore, university, college, or seminary library, alongside scores of volumes of secondary literature and doctoral dissertations written on his theology. Yet grasping the real extent of the versatility, comprehensiveness, and coherence of Pannenberg's systematic thinking is, in my opinion, so far beyond reach. On the British side, Pannenberg's contribution is generally considered Hegelian and foundationalist. Against Hegelianizing Pannenberg's thinking, I wrote a master's dissertation that was later published as "Revelation, History and Idealism: Re-examining the Conceptual Roots of Wolfhart Pannenberg's Theology," *Theological Review* 1, no. 26 (2005): 91–110. On the other hand, on the North American scene, he is deemed a spokesperson for "process ontology" and "ontological eschatology *ad intra trinitatis*" in the "Old Continent." Against deeming Pannenberg an advocate of process ontology I also wrote "Futural Ousia or Eschatological Disclosure? A Systematic Analysis of Pannenberg's Trinitarian Theology," 37–52. Neither form of categorization is fair to the width, or the depth, of Pannenberg's thinking.

53. Roger E. Olson, "Wolfhart Pannenberg's Doctrine of Trinity," *Scottish Journal of Theology* 43 (1990): 175–206, 201. However, I disagree with Olson's overaffirmative conviction that "without question Pannenberg's doctrine of the Trinity emphasizes the economic Trinity" (ibid., 196). I think that the degree of certainty in this claim needs to be carefully scrutinized, lest Pannenberg's trinitarian ontology be misunderstood.

Pannenberg's exposition must be read in two ways: as an application of the doctrine of the immanent Trinity to the divine economy, and as an application of the divine economy to the trinitarian doctrine of God. Only if it is read from these two perspectives does the point of the relationship of immanent and economic Trinity which Pannenberg intends to make become clear.[54]

Pannenberg's critical extension of Rahner's Rule is also leveraged in engagement with Karl Barth's qualified identification of the immanent and the economic Trinity. Pannenberg takes a critical approach to the Barthian modalist version of trinitarian ontology. One of Pannenberg's main criticisms of Barth's doctrine of the Trinity is his conviction that Barth grounds his doctrine of the Trinity in a conceptual, rather than a historical, notion of revelation.[55] If it is true that the important developments of trinitarian theology in the twentieth century are blossoms from Barthian roots,[56] Pannenberg is one of those who believe that the prevalence of modalism in much of modern theology is also from the same source.

Pannenberg, however, concurs with the move by Barth to align closely the doctrine of the Trinity with revelation, and in making the notion of "relation with God," which lies in God alone (*sub ratione Dei*), the basic key of theology.[57] This underlies Pannenberg's belief that we can speak of God only in relation to reality in its wholeness.[58] Conversely, all reality cannot be spoken of in its totality away from its relation to God. It is necessary, therefore, to show that the all-determining reality of God is implicit in all finite realities.[59] It is nevertheless equally important, for Pannenberg, to realize that God's implicitness in finite reality does not undermine God's infinity. The organic relation between God and the finite reality of creation is itself based on God's infinity, which is expressed by his personal self-differentiation. This is what entails, according

---

54. Christoph Schwöbel, "Rational Theology in Trinitarian Perspective: Wolfhart Pannenberg's *Systematic Theology*," *Journal of Theological Studies* 2, no. 47 (1996): 498–527, 508. Thus Pannenberg's "approaches 'from below' and 'from above' are seen as strictly complementary" (ibid., 511).

55. Christiaan Mostert, "Barth and Pannenberg on Method, Revelation and Trinity," in *Karl Barth: A Future for Postmodern Theology?*, ed. Geoff Thompson and Christiaan Mostert (Hindmarsh: Australian Theological Press, 2000), 89–95; also, Pannenberg, *Systematic Theology*, 1:296ff.

56. Peters, *God as Trinity*, 82.

57. F. LeRon Shults, *The Postfoundationalist Task of Theology: Wolfhart Pannenberg and the New Theological Rationality* (Grand Rapids: Eerdmans, 1999), 92ff.

58. Pannenberg, "Kerygma and History," 1:94.

59. Pannenberg, *Theology and Philosophy of Science*, trans. Francis McDonagh (Philadelphia: Westminster, 1976), 330.

to Pannenberg, that the basic discourse on the relations between the infinite God and the finite world is not the doctrine of creation or anthropology, but rather Christology.[60] Pannenberg regards anthropology a fruitful field from which one can build up a speech about God. However, Pannenberg does not imagine that there is any obvious, direct way from anthropology to theology, from human experience to true speech about God. Nor does he overlook the fact that the decision about the truth of human attempts to speak truly about God "rests with God Himself."[61] Christology, therefore, is to be pursued "from below" as the venue of knowledge of the trinitarian personhood of God that is revealed in both the incarnate Son's self-differentiation from the Father and the Spirit as the second person in the Trinity, and in Jesus of Nazareth's self-differentiation (characterized by obedience) from his God as a fully human person. The difference between God the infinite and the finite human makes their relationship epistemological in nature and personal in manner, without this implying that they are mutually co-constitutive of each other's reality.

The previous argument is related by Pannenberg to the understanding of personhood as a self in relation to another self. His understanding of the "self-other" relation departs primarily from the question: "Do we know that we are not 'other' because we are self, or do we know that we are self because we are not 'other'?"[62] According to Jacqui Stewart, "I know that I am a self by knowing that the 'other' is not 'me'" is Pannenberg's option.[63] This is most probably true because it is congenial with Pannenberg's understanding of personhood in relation to the Trinity and self-distinction; on the basis of the person's awareness of the other's difference from him, the Son acquires self-consciousness of his sonship in obeying the Father who is distinct from him.

This explains why Pannenberg follows Martin Buber's dialogical personalism in his understanding of the relation between the "self" and the "other," the individual and the social, within his anthropology. Dialogical personalism is Pannenberg's route of escape from the traps of either drifting toward abstract individualism or falling into a prioritization of the social or of society over the individual.[64] This is why being and existence, personhood and

---

60. Wolfhart Pannenberg, *Jesus—God and Man*, trans. Lewis L. Wilkins and Duane A. Priebe (London: SCM, 1968), 406. "Thinking about christology in connection with God's relation to the world in general and especially in connection with his relationship to humanity in the course of its history . . ."

61. Mostert, "Barth and Pannenberg on Method, Revelation and Trinity," 77, pointing to Pannenberg, *Systematic Theology*, 1:56.

62. Jacqui A. Stewart, *Reconstructing Science and Theology in Postmodernity: Pannenberg, Ethics and the Human Sciences* (Aldershot, UK and Burlington, VT: Ashgate, 2000), 73ff.

63. Ibid., 74.

roles, need to be equated with, and related to, each other without confusion or domination.[65] The person is a "person" only in the wholeness that is not at the disposal of any form of "another," but rather "characterized by a hidden 'inside' and by freedom."[66] Freedom is a substantial characteristic of personhood, for freedom is what shows that, though relationally conditioned, personhood is capable of distancing itself from objectification and impersonalism, as well as dwelling in and attending to personal relationships at the same time.[67] The real capacities and dimensions of freedom appear most profoundly in relation to God. By basing personal freedom on God's transcendence, we come to terms with the personhood that always exceeds its social situation and relational existence, so that even if personhood lies in the relational appeal to another, personhood should be, as Pannenberg says, "critically independent in reference to the concrete form that social relations may take at any given time."[68]

This anthropological distinction of "self" from "other" in relation to personhood brings us systematically back to the three theo-logical foundations of Pannenberg's notion of personhood: ontology, Christology, and the Trinity.

1. PERSONHOOD AND ESSENCE

For Pannenberg, the understanding of "person" as a self-distinct, active subject rather than a mere expression of relationality lies in the relational nature of God's essence. Pannenberg principally believes that the existence of things is strongly related to and is expressive of their essence. It is in its functional, active existence that the essence of the thing manifests its distinct nature from all other essences. The same applies to God, who for Pannenberg "finds manifestation in the working of his power, and we know the distinctiveness of his essence, and differentiate it from others, by the characteristics of his working."[69] The works of God, while not directly capturing the essence in its totality, reveal the essence's attributes. This is not to say that the essence of God is hidden *behind* the attributes that are ascribed to it. Rather than this, the attributes *are* those of

---

64. Pannenberg, *Anthropology in Theological Perspective*, trans. Matthew J. O'Connell (Edinburgh: T. & T. Clark, 1985), 180ff.; after, that is, the manner of Rousseau and Marxism or nationalist notions, according to Pannenberg.

65. Ibid., 225ff.

66. Ibid., 235.

67. Ibid., 240ff.

68. Ibid., 241. Pannenberg continues saying: "It follows that the self-assertion of the individual against others and society need not be simply an egoistic rebellion of the part against the whole. It can also be the expression of a call to a more perfect fulfillment of the human destination of community."

69. Pannenberg, *Systematic Theology*, 1:359.

the essence itself; they belong to it.[70] This organic link between the attributes and the essence, manifested in the attributes' appearance in the essence's actions, shows why the attributes are more revelatory of the person, of the personal essence, than the names. While names are universally distributable and common among many things, the attributes that are designative of the essence's self-differentiation by means of its actions are not. They, rather, tell us specific things about the person. The person's uniqueness is primarily known by way of the attributes, not the names.

Having said that, Pannenberg does not jump from the previous discussion to the conclusion that the person's essence *is* his relational actions, since these actions reveal the essence's characteristics. Pannenberg maintains a distinction between the essence and the relational actions of the person, in that he acknowledges that the person is "more than the attributes,"[71] and in that his emphasis on the ontological link between the essence and its actions as revelatory of its attributes is not a total identification of the essence and the actions of the person, but rather a pointing to the actions as revelatory of the essence's *uniqueness and distinction*. The attributes manifested in the actions do not exhaustively capture the essence that is thereby personified. They rather disclose the distinction of the person from other persons. By this logic, Pannenberg believes that he can exceed two problematic ontologies in theology. The first is the one that conceals the essence behind the attributes and stresses its utter unknowability. And the second is that which totally equates the essence with the attributes, making them constitutive of the essence.[72] Because the history of theology, in his appraisal, has led the debate on the relation between the essence and the attributes into one of these dead ends, Pannenberg decides to deconstruct the philosophical and theological claims behind this debate and to offer instead a balanced understanding of the notion of "essence."[73]

In the first place, Pannenberg points to the philosophical trend of thought that started in modernity as a response to the Aristotelian understanding of the relation between "essence" and "attributes." He argues that against the construal of relationality as a category or an accident external to the substance, modern philosophers, pioneered by Kant and Hegel, subordinate substance

---

70. Ibid., 360.

71. Ibid., 361.

72. Ibid., 361–62ff. Pannenberg points to Gregory Palamas as the earlier exponent and champion of the first approach in the East, and the council of Florence (1330) and Thomas Aquinas as the first exponents of the second approach in the West.

73. Ibid., 364ff.

to the category of relation, claiming that the only possibly conceived truth about anything is its relations. The essence per se becomes an expression of a relational phenomenon, and relationality specifies the concept of "essence" as such.[74] The theological outcome of this reduction of essence to relationality in theology, according to Pannenberg, is the affirmation that God's essence lies in his relationship with the world. "Transcendence," as Pannenberg shows, is this time inappropriately deemed an expression of a form of supra-natural relationality. The challenge before theology, however, is to find a way by which it views God's essence from a relational perspective without slipping into one of the problematic dead-ends of the implementation of the notion of relationality in the doctrine of God.[75]

Away from either placing the essence of God agnostically behind its relations or making the relations totally constitutive of God's essence, Pannenberg views the relation between "essence" and "relation" by the help of the notion of "action." He develops a notion of "action" wherein the action and the actor are distinguished. The action for him is "a mode of being of the one who acts."[76] It displays essential qualities of the one who makes the decision of the action, although the act that is done in exchange with another may mean that the action not only characterizes the one who acts but also the one who is exchanging the action. If the one who acts is acting out of deep love and self-giving, the action would make the essence of the one who acts really known in itself. To take this to God, we can say that God's act of revelation *is* a display of God's essence in its deep reality and nature, even if this act is done in interaction with another who is different.

The previous concept of "action" helps in showing that God is relational and personal in nature without reducing his essence to a collection of actions as such. However, Pannenberg still believes that this "actor-action" framework of personhood needs protection from anthropomorphic characterization that may turn the talk of a personal God into a claim that God is one of the forming elements of the substance of human personal being.[77] With regard to

---

74. Ibid., 366.

75. Ibid., 367. Pannenberg points to three major problematic theological implementations of the notion of relationality when he says that an idea of regarding the concept of essence vis-à-vis that of relation must not "mean that God's transcendence vanishes panentheistically in the infinity of nature, as in Spinoza, nor that it is simply an element in the divine process of producing and disclosing the world, as in Hegel, nor finally that it is just a correlate of the concept of the world, as in the metaphysics of Whitehead."

76. Ibid., 367–68. "In the case of personal action the essence of the subject may be seen in the choice and achievement of the goal, so that the kind of action characterizes the one who acts" (ibid., 369).

77. Ibid., 370ff.

the human person, the "I" and the "self" are not yet totally identified, for the human is still on the way toward a full awareness and a full acquirement of identity. The human's personal essence is yet to be fully itself, to be fully real and complete. This is not the case with regard to God's triune personhood. The identity of each of the three divine persons is *mediated* and not originated from or constituted by the persons' relations to each other. "By self-giving to the others," Pannenberg says, "each of the [divine] persons is fully identical with itself."[78] Each divine person should be fully his self and not reduced to his relationality if this person is God from God; if, that is, he enjoys all the infinity and perfection of the divine life. Being infinite in nature, the Father, Son, and Spirit are not copies of each other, even if they share each other in divine action in history. If their common action in or relation to creation is constitutive of their personhood and totally exhaustive of it, they will then be totally identified and copies of each other, for how can one action originate different identities? However, because the three persons' identities are not constituted or exhausted by their actions, the concept of action presupposes acting subjects; and the three persons should be direct *subjects* of divine action if action designates self-distinction. This already complete personal identity of God's triune essence is what prevents God's coming into the world from becoming an experience of completion for God in himself.

2. Personhood and Self-Distinction

"Personhood" as an expression of a self-distinct active subject, rather than an expression of mere relational movements, is historically and Christologically manifested in the relationship between the Father and the incarnate Son. The Son in his total, human, and divine being shares the same divine nature with the Father, as both God from God. However, this does not connote for Pannenberg, as Herbert Neie correctly notes, a form of participation that makes Jesus' deity an "undifferentiated identity with the divine nature," as if "in Jesus God the Father himself had appeared in human form and had suffered on the cross."[79] For Pannenberg, this rather means that the participation in God's divinity lies in the Son's and the Father's self-distinction from each other; not as two forms of relations, but as two self-conscious centers of actions. This is why the relation between the Father and the Son for Pannenberg is expressive of the relation between God and the human Jesus Christ; the

---

78. Ibid., 377.

79. Herbert Neie, *The Doctrine of the Atonement in the Theology of Wolfhart Pannenberg* (Berlin and New York: Walter de Gruyter, 1979), 61.

relation, that is, that takes place between two closely related, yet also distinct and nonconfused subjects. Pannenberg concedes that the classical *logos*-Christology, which he is principally critical about, has after all something crucially correct in emphasizing the unity, but also the differentiation, between the Son and the Father, and in showing that this distinction in the trinitarian being of God points to a necessary distinction in number, and not to a dangerous division in essence.

The Christological understanding of the relation of self-differentiation between Jesus and God has, therefore, anthropological and trinitarian implications. Anthropologically, it shows that the participation that happens between the human and God should not entail that creation is part of God or just a modalist image of his being. Participation in God's actions must not deny that God is the free origin of the contingent world, whose interrelations with God or within itself are "contingent and constitute no eternal order."[80] The concern about evading any panentheistic notion of participation between the human and the divine is what may also explicate Pannenberg's choice of understanding the relation between the incarnate Son and the Father in the form of "obedience." Obedience assumes that the Son as a self-conscious subject is related to another distinct, self-conscious subject, the Father. They are two self-differentiated subjects, not two images of a relational confusion of the human with the divine.

From this anthropological qualification of the notion of "participation," one can glean a salient understanding expressive of the depth of Pannenberg's profound hermeneutics of the Trinity. For Pannenberg, the Father and the Son (even in his eternity) should maintain their distinction as self-conscious, distinct subjects. Turning them into mere relations would be: 1) a retreat toward modalism, as well as 2) a shedding of suspicious light on the reality of the human subjective reality of Jesus of Nazareth. If Jesus is just the Father appearing in human form, he is not then a real self-conscious human. If self-consciousness is an inescapable prerequisite of personhood, the union of the Son and the Father, as well as the unity of God and the human, must be in a form of a relation between two distinct subjects with equally free and autonomous self-consciousnesses. Personhood in God, according to Pannenberg, is not an "anthropomorphic projection of human personhood upon a divine entity, as Fichte and Feuerbach presuppose."[81] It is, rather, an expression of God's

---

80. Ibid., 62.

81. Ibid., 114. Pannenberg, as Neie shows, associates personal being with the future, claiming that being is to be thought from the side of the future. While this is true, I don't believe that Pannenberg develops here a panentheistic, immanentist ontology, where being is just a processive existence. Being is

relational being that is open to the future and that opens the human's being to the future. It is an expression of the reality of self-distinction and self-consciousness that lies in openness to relationality, not in self-disclosure. Pannenberg points to the importance of understanding "person" in terms of a "self-conscious subject" and to the inappropriateness of reducing God's essence to mere actions when he says:

> The properties of the divine operation, because of its contingency, permit no reflection upon a similarity of the effects with the essence of God, and thus do not allow any statement that would transfer a creaturely perfection to God in a superlative sense . . . the contingent operative biblical God is present in his effects . . . in a "personal mode" i.e. by the choice of his acts he decides about the properties to which he binds himself precisely by his choice.[82]

God can never be such a being unless there is a distinction between God's essence and God's actions, God's personhood and relationality. This is why despite his belief that God's full existence as the power of the world lies in the future, Pannenberg is not a panentheist theologian. Contrary to A. N. Whitehead, Pannenberg does not deduce any ontological conclusions about God's being from analyzing God's dynamic, possible, and mutable existence in history.[83]

3. Personhood Immanent and Economic

Pannenberg's understanding of relationality, and of God's and the human's personal nature within the context of their relation to each other, is founded, finally, and most fundamentally, on his hermeneutics of the unity and the distinction between the immanent and the economic Trinities. F. LeRon Shults correctly realizes Pannenberg's belief:

> The biblical trinitarian God is the best explanation for the human experience of being in a historical relation to the true infinite . . . the relation of the immanent and the economic Trinity, their distinction

---

a futural notion for him because this notion alone shows humanity that its freedom is not actual unless it allows humanity to go beyond what is presently existent. Being that lies in the future is thus a call for an "exocentric anthropology," not for an immanentist, panentheistic onto-theology.

82. Pannenberg, *Basic Questions in Theology* (London: SCM, 1970), 3:171–72.

83. Neie, *The Doctrine of Atonement in the Theology of Wolfhart Pannenberg*, 127. On the difference between Pannenberg and Whitehead's panentheism, see 122–28.

and unity as a comprehensive explanation of the relation of all finite things to the infinite God (*sub ratione Dei*) is the key to Christian theology's claim of truth.[84]

This means that every theological understanding of the personal being of God or of the human in the context of their relation stems from the relations of self-differentiation between the three distinct centers of actions of the triune Godhead, which are revealed in the relation of self-distinction between the sending Father and the sent incarnate Son in the power and work of the Spirit. The foundation of the knowledge of the personhood of the Father and the Son lies in Jesus' differentiation of his person from the person of the Father (i.e., John 8:18, 50; 14: 24, 28; Mark 10:18; 13:32; Matt. 20:23).[85] Far from being evidence of the Son's subordination to the Father in nature, such biblical texts points to the subjective self-differentiation between the persons of the Trinity. Moreover, it shows that the relationship of the persons stems from their personal self-distinction. Their relations do not produce or constitute their personhood as an outcome of the network of communion between God's fatherhood, sonship, and spirithood. The relations between the persons *reveal* that the subjects who are related to each other by these relations are self-distinct persons already. "Jesus *shows* himself to be the Son of God precisely in his self-distinction from God."[86] He shows the reality of his personal distinction from the person of the Father vis-à-vis his relation with the Father. He does not acquire his divine personhood by virtue of the relation. If the second meaning is the case, then adoptionism is correct in claiming that by his relation with the Father, Jesus *became* the divine Son; became, that is, what he was not before. It is, rather:

> Precisely by distinguishing himself from the Father, by subjecting himself to his will as his creature, by thus giving place to the Father's claim to deity . . . [Jesus] showed himself to be the Son of God and one with the Father who sent him (John 10:30).[87]

It is precisely by this distinction that Jesus reveals his oneness with the Father, because he shows that his divine person is not an outcome of a divine

---

84. Shults, *The Postfoundationalist Task of Theology*, 104–5.
85. Pannenberg, *Systematic Theology*, 1:309.
86. Ibid., 1:301. My italic.
87. Ibid., 1:310.

relational action from God toward him. His divine person *is* the foundation of his revealed relation with the Father, for, like the Father, his personhood does not primarily lie in the fatherly relation of the Father to him, but in the fact that his personhood, as the Son of the Father, stems from being God from God, from being of the divine essence. The fatherly and filial relations distinguish Jesus from other human creatures. In this sense, the relation with his Father is constitutive of the uniqueness of his personal identity in comparison to the personal identity of other human beings. However, between the Father and the Son, the personal distinction does not only lie in the relations of origin. It also exceeds these forms of relations, because the personhood of the Father and the Son and the Spirit is primarily characterized by infinity, freedom, and mystery. This means that their personhood is always in, yet also beyond, any static forms of relationship, and their personhood is, from eternity to eternity, complete and not the total sum of the persons' relational actions.

Pannenberg endeavors to show that the self-differentiation of the personal identity of the three persons of the Trinity lies not merely in their relations of origin. He pursues this goal by arguing that even the mutual correspondence between Jesus and his God, with regard to the salvific establishment of God's kingdom, should also be considered a manifestation of an ontological form of interrelational self-differentiation between the Father and the Son in the eternal Trinity:

> The handing over of the power and rule of the Father to the Son is then to be seen also as a defining of the intertrinitarian relations between the two, as is their handing back by the Son to the Father.[88]

By expanding the interpenetration spectrum of the three persons beyond the relations of origin, Pannenberg paves the way for an ontologically necessary link between the immanent and the economic Trinities. Yet he also opens up the way, in my opinion, for a crucial ontological and conceptual distinction between personhood and relationality in God's essence. While relationality demonstrates dynamic acknowledgment of the other in his self-distinction, personhood shows the infinite nature of this other, which from the beginning of the relation to its eternal end is totally itself. This distinction between infinity in terms of personhood and self-distinction in terms of relationality allows for an incorporation of the interrelation between God and the human Jesus into the

---

88. Ibid., 1:312–13. "Relations among the three persons that are defined as mutual self-distinction cannot be reduced to relations of origins in the traditional sense" (1:320ff.).

intra-trinitarian relations between the Father and the Son in eternity, without turning such interrelation into a process by which the Father and the Son and the Spirit come to terms fully with their divine being. It is, in other words, the only way to avoid taking panentheism from the God-human realm into the realm of the eternal being of God. Instead of the interaction process in which God and humanity acquire their full being at the end of the process, in this new form of panentheism we have an interaction in which the Father, Son, and Spirit acquire something new or additional they haven't substantially had before, as if God experiences an eternally continuous process of self-recreation or self-personification in his Trinity. This would entail that God is no longer a personal subject with a dynamic, relational nature, but an eternal form of relationality in a pure progressive sense.

Pannenberg avoids the previous ontological distortion of God's being by emphasizing that the act of self-distinction is the evidence that each person in the Trinity is a particular person who is both different from the other two, and related to and united with them both. Pannenberg believes that the most famous undermining of the distinction of personhood and relationality is the Augustinian reduction of the Spirit to the "we" of the communion of the Father and the Son, by means of making the Spirit the eternal communion of love that unites them.[89] And he argues that in this well-known and criticized collapsing of the Spirit's person into a form of communion, there would not be any acknowledgment of a personal self-distinction of the Spirit if he is merely a form of a relation.[90] Reducing any divine person to a form of communion would, then, deny the self-distinction dynamic the Scripture depicts by speaking about three centers of divine action who freely glorify each other. Scripture speaks about three relational agents who freely point to each other by self-differentiation from the other two. For Pannenberg, this biblical standpoint is the way for evading the Western traditional habit of reducing the three persons to individual relations. Claiming that the divine persons are really what they are in their relations means that these relations are complex to an extent that shows the infinite nature of the persons who enjoy the communion. Pannenberg concedes the validity of stressing with Augustine that the total sum of the being of the persons is not greater than each of the relations they make, because in their relations the persons are fully who they are.[91] Yet, this should not in turn negate that their self-distinction as separate centers

---

89. St. Augustine, *The Trinity*, trans. Edmund Hill, ed. E. Rotelle (Brooklyn, NY: New City Press, 1991), 6.5.7.

90. Pannenberg, *Systematic Theology*, 1:316.

91. Augustine, *Trinity*, 6.7.9.

of action is, as Pannenberg says, "so great that they cannot be adduced as comparable examples"[92] or mere communion. This caution to the distinction between personhood and relationality can properly be deemed evidence that Pannenberg, as Bradshaw eloquently says, "wishes to elucidate a doctrine of 'person' which retains the modern experience of creative subjectivity, includes it, but does not absolutize it."[93]

The previous exposition of the threefold foundation of the notion of personhood shows the inevitability and essentiality of Pannenberg's defense of the notion of "self-as-subject" in his anthropology. Jacqui Stewart already realizes that this is Pannenberg's strategy for preserving the integrity of human personhood against "socially determinist arguments."[94] In my opinion, this defense of the integrity of personhood in a way that exceeds social communion is important because the socially determinist and relativist arguments that characterize postmodernity drift easily into an extreme equation of personhood and relationality in a way that negates the person's self-distinction as an existing, free "someone."

Accusing Pannenberg with failure in applying important postmodern notions related to human identity to his own analysis[95] is not a fair assessment—as this defense indicates. Pannenberg, in fact, is showing a conscious, free abstinence from such application. If Pannenberg's understanding of personhood takes into consideration, as I showed, subjective self-differentiation as characteristic of any existing center of action, his avoidance of a postmodernist rejection of subject-hood in a way that turns personhood into a collection of fragmented relations must, therefore, be necessary and required. It makes his anthropology far from reflective of extremely individualist and ideally rationalist presumptions, as Jacqui Stewart inaccurately thinks.[96] His anthropology is rather based on a balanced marrying of "self" with "other." Instead of either reducing the self to a momentary existence produced by

---

92. Pannenberg, *Systematic Theology*, 1:321.

93. Timothy Bradshaw, *Trinity and Ontology: A Comparative Study of the Theologies of Karl Barth and Wolfhart Pannenberg* (Edinburgh: T. & T. Clark, 1988), 223. Because Pannenberg does not want to absolutize subjectivity, Roger Olson is not correct in claiming that all those who are sympathetic to Pannenberg's emphasis on the self-distinction of each of the divine persons are necessarily and evidently supportive of the social analogy of the Trinity. See Olson, "Pannenberg's Doctrine of Trinity," 202. The sympathy stems from the fact that Pannenberg's trinitarian approach is balanced with regard to the ontology of personhood and of being, and not from any sort of eagerness to support a form of "I-we" relationality.

94. Stewart, *Reconstructing Science and Theology in Postmodernity*, 76.

95. Ibid., 77.

96. Ibid., 103.

social, existential actions, or making the self a permanent, unchanging ego that underlies existential consciousness, Pannenberg calls for a self that becomes familiar with itself by means of a dynamic interaction with its surrounding existence; without turning the self into a temporary nonidentified reality. "Familiarity with 'one self,'" says Pannenberg, "is *mediated* through trust in a sheltering and supporting context."[97] The mediated here is the familiarity with, and the awareness of, the self by means of a context. Again, the point here is epistemological and not ontological in nature. It concurs with Pannenberg's understanding of the concept of "knowledge" on the basis of the idea of "self-differentiation." For Pannenberg, "self-differentiation" mediates an awareness of a certain nature; it does not create this nature as such. It just points to the fact that the awareness of the whole self lies in the future, without implying any ontological conclusion such as the self as a temporary outcome of a specific social condition. Pannenberg's account of dialogical personhood stresses self-consciousness on the basis of interrelationality with the external world as primarily a "form of knowing," as Stewart correctly says,[98] not as a form of ontological origination. This eventuates in the conviction that the identification of the self is not totally explained in terms of external social factors.[99] The self is free and not totally relationally determined. "Personality," according to Pannenberg, "is grounded in the destiny that transcends our empirical reality."[100] Personality is transcendent because it lies in the personhood of God, where relationality, freedom, and infinity are intercomplementary and co-constitutive of the totality of personal, subjective being. Neither is collapsed into the other.

This is, in my conviction, where the person of the Holy Spirit plays a crucial role with regard to the meaning of personhood. As the Spirit's hypostatic identity lies in his role of engaging the human with God, it also lies in the freedom and the infinite nature that release the Spirit's personhood from any static, conditional communality. By virtue of the Spirit's mediation of the *imago Dei* personhood to us, we realize that our personhood is not yet complete as long as we are still in the process of history. Yet the ultimate identity of this personhood is not something permanently deferred to the unknown. It is anticipated because it is based on a revealed image of personhood that lies in the three divine persons of God.

---

97. Pannenberg, *Anthropology in Theological Perspective*, 221. Italic is mine.
98. Stewart, *Reconstructing Science and Theology in Postmodernity*, 83.
99. Pannenberg, *Anthropology in Theological Perspective*, 84.
100. Pannenberg, *Systematic Theology*, 3:198.

IV. Toward a Trinitarian Correction

In this chapter, I have pointed to a theological alternative that takes the theology of personhood beyond both the modernist overemphasis on subjectivity and self-enclosed subjectivity, and the postmodernist overemphasis on relationality and dynamic activity. I have pointed to the trinitarian theologies of J. Moltmann and W. Pannenberg, with a relative emphasis on the theology of the latter, in an attempt to show that there are trinitarian theologies that can properly and accurately use the doctrine of God in a debate on general intellectual notions, like "person" and "relation," and show the following:

1. It is true that the notion of "particularity" is ontologically ultimate in God and that identifying a particular thing demands making it part of a relationship and not isolating it individualistically.[101] Yet one needs to push this confession further and argue that it is also equally true that avoiding individualism should not reduce particularity to a reflection of a certain form of relationality. It is crucial to maintain an awareness of the ontological necessity of the person's being a free particular who is not captured by any single form of relationality.

2. It is the responsibility of those who call for adopting trinitarian language for understanding personhood—and who acknowledge the foundational importance of a Trinity-like hermeneutics of God for understanding human personhood—to show in a clear and coherent way that: a) the very dependence of the person on her relations with others to acquire an identity, and that b) this acquiring process involves in its very own existence a possibility of independence from this relation, which allows this person to be undetermined from outside. Only this "dependence-independence" paradigm, which I argue in this chapter is fully manifested in the "communion-in-self-differentiation" life of the three divine persons of the Godhead, can offer an understanding of personhood that maintains communality and freedom side by side. It is alone what shows us that

> [a]s persons we are identical in the midst of change, and on account of our identity we are potentially infinite; for we can progressively appropriate the things and influences outside us, and so transform them, from being limits, into manifestations of ourselves.[102]

---

101. This is Gunton's correct critique of modernity. Gunton, *The Promise of Trinitarian Theology*, 95–96, quoting here John Zizioulas's words on page 9 of a paper titled "Ontology of Personhood," which was prepared for the British Council of Church's Study Commission on Trinitarian Doctrine Today, 1985.

102. John R. Illingworth, *Personality Human and Divine* (London and New York: Macmillan, 1894), 91.

We can only be these infinite characters when our personhood is no longer narrowed down to the relations we make, and when our personhood—as made in the image of the triune God—is predisposed by the Son's grace and directed by the Spirit toward a state of beyond-ness that surpasses any static form of relationality. Personhood can only be an *imago Dei* when the person's being does not melt away into the relations she experiences or the interaction she executes with others from outside. What basically prevents the postmodern mind from conceding this ontological distinction between the person's being and the relational movements in which this person is involved is that the postmodern philosophical, and increasingly the theological, mind is no longer keen on conceiving the doctrinal belief in a God who is the image of an infinite personal Being, whose "only limits is Himself, and who is, therefore, self-determined, self-dependent, self-identical," and most importantly, who has the finite other as "a free manifestation of Himself, and thus, while constituting [the finite's] reality, [this infinite person is] unaffected by [the finite's] change."[103]

What I glean from this Trinity-based understanding of personhood and relationality in God is that one need not escape from the extreme modernist prioritization of subject and self-centered individualism by adopting the dominantly extreme postmodernist prioritization of the concept of "relation" and dynamic openness to the other. In the triune being of God, we have personal subjective being and relational, reciprocal existence side by side without contradiction, confusion, or conflict. God is three self-distinct persons who exist together and are united to each other by means of mutual openness and interrelationality. They are relational persons who act and interact reciprocally with each other and with the human. In the triune God, both "person" and "relation" are original and foundational. Neither is exhaustive of the other, nor is subordinate to or produced as the sum total of the other.

Because this balanced "unity-in-distinction" is inherent in God's nature, God's relation with humanity reflects the same balanced "unity-in-distinction." God's infinite personhood exceeds any form of relationality (as the personhood of the three divine persons exceeds their relations of origin) and is the ground of the personhood that humanity is in the process of acquiring eschatologically. It is the ground that opens up the human self beyond any limited, static form of relationality by means of giving the human her freedom and reconciling her with her existence and with her real being.

It is now time to take the argument on the ontology of personhood back to the main discussion framework that I started with: the relation between

103. Ibid., 92.

theology and other scientific disciplines and surrounding intellectual conditions. The question is now: How can the trinitarian theology of personhood that balances the relationship between "person" and "relation" help us find a model for an interaction between theology and the contemporary postmodern condition; a model, that is, that unites them, yet also maintains their self-distinction? This question will be the subject of the last chapter.

8

Correlation as Relationship Model in/ with the World

I. Relationality as a Reflection of "Unity-in-Self-Differentiation"

In the previous two chapters, I showed that contemporary theology offers a co-relational model representing a balanced interaction between theology and forms of epistemological inquiry that can maintain the integrity and particularity of both. This form of correlation says that: 1) theology should acknowledge the importance of interacting with other disciplines in a way that maintains its own distinctive identity. And, 2) this interaction should not be limited to exclusive self-communication, but should reach an interdisciplinary level, in which both disciplines follow a "unity-in-distinction" form of correspondence. In this final chapter, I will apply this correlational model to the case study discussed in the previous chapter around the trinitarian work of W. Pannenberg and J. Moltmann. The logic that underlies the interdisciplinary correlation between theology and the secular condition, which I traced in F. Watson and H. Frei in chapter six, is similar to the logic that underlies the "unity-in-differentiation" paradigm of the trinitarian ontology of personhood, as seen in the discussion of Moltmann and Pannenberg in the previous chapter. This similarity is an obvious support of the conviction that "everything looks different in the light of the Trinity."[1]

I believe that the trinitarian hermeneutics of "person" and "relation" offers to the debate on the proper relationship between theology and other forms of intellectual conditions the following relevant point: the relation between theology and other intellectual conditions is not per se an originator of the theological message. The content, the language, and the thought-form of theological discourse (i.e., the characteristics that are expressive of its identity)

---

1. Colin Gunton, *The Promise of Trinitarian Theology*, 2nd ed. (Edinburgh: T. & T. Clark, 1997), 28.

are not in the first place, or exclusively, the outcome of its interaction with other fields of knowledge. To the contrary, the relation with other disciplines should shed light on the self-distinction of theology and should help maintain its integrity. The identity of theology is grounded in its communal existence with other intellectual discourses. Theology does not become a follower but a partner in the interdisciplinary correlation created with other fields of knowledge. As the relationships between the Father, the Son, and the Spirit do not dissolve their distinct personhood, but reflect their distinction instead, the relation between God and the human (and, therefore, between the knowledge of God [theo-logy] and human knowledge of the self) does not dissolve their distinct personhood and does not reduce any of them to mere expressions of interactivity. And, as the relation with humanity cannot be the originator of God's being, the relation between the study of God and secular theories of knowledge should not deny theology's self-differentiation and integrity, which derives from the subject matter itself. If the triune God is the theological criterion of the real meaning of relationality and otherness, the distinction between "being" and "action" in the Godhead should be criterial of the right relation between: 1) human personhood and relational actions, and 2) most importantly, between theology and other intellectual conditions expressive of postmodernity.

In this chapter, I will end my study with a further examination of J. Moltmann and W. Pannenberg. After discussing their trinitarian thinking in the light of the "unity-in-differentiation" model of correlationality, I will look at their understanding of the correlation between theology and other forms of intellectual inquiry. In their understanding of this correlation, I see a valid application of what H. Frei and F. Watson call for in their interdisciplinary approach to theological knowledge. In the work of Moltmann and Pannenberg, I see a valid and tenable proposal for rethinking the relationship between theology and postmodernity, not only with regard to the implementation of the notions of "personhood" and "relationality" for understanding God's nature and human nature, but also with regard to all other common subjects and concerns that may relate theology to our contemporary intellectual condition(s).

II. Standing Firmly, Yet Openly before the World

In his doctrine of the Trinity, Moltmann states that the foundational framework of his trinitarian project is an endeavor to develop a social doctrine of the Trinity in opposition to models of the Trinity based upon notions of "substance" and "subject." He justifies this by arguing that thinking about the

Trinity in terms other than those that consider the social patterns of existence characteristic of human life is no longer relevant in the contemporary world. Moltmann prefers, therefore, to speak about the Trinity in language shaped by forms of relationality and communal life, even if this language sounds panentheistic in tone. Moltmann believes that only this language offers a trinitarian theology that accords more with contemporary intellectual conditions.[2] Moltmann's social doctrine of the Trinity also comports with the postmodernist rejection of modernist patterns of thought marked by domination and power, which often resulted in an absolute monism.[3] The absence of a social form of trinitarian thinking, Moltmann concedes, is primarily signified by the modernist supposition that social life and relationality are less primal than the personal self.[4] Against the individualism inherent to most modern theology, Moltmann counteroffers a relational and social model of the Trinity, in which "personal socialism" and "social personalism" are equally and interpenetratingly related and emphasized.[5]

With this, Moltmann sets before theology a real challenge. Despite his call for centralizing sociality and communalism, Moltmann maintains a belief that theology should not undermine its responsibility of standing before the world and enjoying communion with it without "handing itself over to particular social ideologies" that might be popular or dominant in today's social context.[6] Moltmann believes that the theological discourse on the intimate relationship between God and humanity in general demonstrates that theology has the task of responding to, and serving, human society because its subject matter (i.e., the triune God) is strongly related to the world in a mutual correlation, not in any form of domination.

In his stress on the correlational interaction between God and the human, and the duty of theology that stems from it, Moltmann seems to be developing to a certain extent a panentheistic form of correlation between personalism and socialism. Moltmann personally constructs his correlational model on John 17:21, specifically the words "that [the human] also may be in us." Accordingly, he claims that it is possible to speak about the triune God who indwells the

---

2. Jürgen Moltmann, *The Trinity and the Kingdom of God: The Doctrine of God* (London: SCM, 1998), 19–20.

3. Ibid., 192ff., where Moltmann shows how his trinitarian proposal concurs with the surrounding phenomena of rejecting the modernity that characterizes this age, especially political theory.

4. Ibid., 199.

5. Ibid., 200ff.

6. Jürgen Moltmann, *Theology Today: Two Contributions towards Making Theology Present* (London: SCM, 1988), 25.

world in a divine way, and about the world that indwells God in a *creaturely* way.[7] Moltmann believes that a social doctrine of the Trinity is the best theological discourse for relating humanity to the world in a manner that is ultimately grounded in the form of unity between "person" and "communion" as it is in God's own triune life. The "equilibrium between personal freedom and a just society" is now possible in the light of the triune God, with whom the world corresponds and in whom the world even lives.[8] For Moltmann, this possibility is evidence of the public relevance of "the trinitarian experience of community for the development of a new society."[9] Moltmann's implementation of *perichoresis* (the trinitarian technical term that connotes "interpenetration") in his understanding of God, of creation, and of God-human relationships aims at explaining the dynamic being of God and emphasizing the interconnection of God's eternal being and historical existence. But it also aims at inviting the human person to realize that the divine interpenetration is the foundation of a similar interpenetration and interconnection in human existence between individual personhood, on one side, and communal life, on another. For Moltmann, discerning this organic relation between our reasoning on God and our reasoning on the human self ultimately paves the way for conceiving a reciprocal interaction between theology (the discourse on God) and the surrounding intellectual conditions (discourses on human existence), as well as inviting us to consider a possible open interaction and penetration between theology and these conditions—the things that liberate each side from succumbing to a narrow state of self-enclosure.

Having said that, one should again be careful when speaking about this *perichoresis* by means of panentheistic logic. Such a logic obscures the balanced expression in the term "*perichoresis*" of both unity and self-differentiation side-by-side. The value of the understanding of "personhood" and "relationality" from the perspective of "*perichoresis*" should not be ignored. However, using it in an unbalanced way in the service of imagining a relationship between theology and other forms of intellectual inquiry may just lead to a preconditioning of theology by forcing it to adopt without reservation nontheological notions and rules of reasoning that are constitutive of external, surrounding constraints and not inherent to theological reasoning itself. Moltmann, as demonstrated in the previous chapter, adopts Rahner's trinitarian

---

7. Jürgen Moltmann, *Experiences in Theology: Ways and Forms of Christian Theology*, trans. Margaret Kohl (London: SCM, 2000), 311, and *The Trinity and the Kingdom of God*, 99–128.

8. Moltmann, *Experiences in Theology*, 332.

9. Ibid., 333.

rule and attempts to overcome the potential danger of the identification of God *with* humanity. He does not want belief in God's immanent presence in the world or his intimacy with us to become a means for subjecting theology to other forms of inquiry. One cannot but warn that a panentheistic-like conclusion can possibly be gleaned from a hermeneutical emphasis on theology's indebtedness to its historical surrounding context.

One recent theologian who warns about potential dangers in Moltmann's approach (one who believes that Moltmann even invites this reading) is Paul Molnar. Molnar argues that Moltmann's application of the Trinity to understanding the relation between God and creation fails to recognize and maintain God's freedom.[10] Moltmann's emphasis on *perichoresis* without a comparatively equal attention to self-differentiation renders his theological project, for Molnar, crudely panentheistic and one-sidedly processive. Molnar goes so far as to claim that despite his clear attempt at exceeding the limitations of Rahner's Rule, Moltmann fails to take this rule beyond its problematic frontiers, in that he "uncritically uses the principle of mutual conditioning and eliminates any need to conceptualize a God truly independent of creatures."[11]

If the above is an accurate reading of Moltmann, then Molnar is correct in his conviction that Moltmann's panentheism confuses God and humanity and renders the criterial distinction and importance of Christ—as a key distinguishing factor of theology from any other intellectual discipline—futile and unrealistic.[12] And, if Molnar's claim that Moltmann's starting point from experience means that "*we can* explain the *how* of the trinitarian self-revelation by perceiving that God *needs* to suffer in order to love"[13] is also correct,

---

10. Paul D. Molnar, *Divine Freedom and the Doctrine of the Immanent Trinity: In Dialogue with Karl Barth and Contemporary Theology* (London and New York: T. & T. Clark/Continuum, 2002), 198ff.

11. Ibid., 199. See also Alan Torrance's criticism of Moltmann's trinitarian theology. Torrance also believes that Moltmann adopts a form of panentheism that fails to distinguish adequately between God's time and created temporality. Alan Torrance, *Persons in Communion: Trinitarian Description and Human Participation* (Edinburgh: T. & T. Clark, 1996), 311–12ff.

12. Molnar, *Divine Freedom and the Doctrine of the Immanent Trinity*, 199. Roger Olson has made a critique of Moltmann similar to that of Molnar, yet he concedes that Moltmann's approach can be read in more than one way. He initially places Moltmann within the group of theologians, like R. Jenson and E. Jüngel, who interpret Rahner's Rule with a strong tendency to identify the immanent and the transcendent Trinities. See Roger E. Olson, "Wolfhart Pannenberg's Doctrine of the Trinity," *Scottish Journal of Theology* 43 (1990): 197. However, in another place, Olson proposes another view by arguing that Moltmann distinguishes the eternal life of the triune God and the constitution of the historical life of the Trinity. Olson, "Trinity and Eschatology: The Historical Being of God in Jürgen Moltmann and Wolfhart Pannenberg," *Scottish Journal of Theology* 36 (1983): 213–27. Olson personally concedes this difference in his views in footnote 70 of "Wolfhart Pannenberg's Doctrine of the Trinity," 197.

then Moltmann's project entails that theology succumbs subjectively to the constraints of the surrounding intellectual culture in order to be recognized and accepted. However, I do not think that Moltmann would concede that this ultimate, passive, and extreme demand is what he means in his theological hermeneutics. When one compares, with Molnar, Moltmann's stance on Rahner's Rule to Karl Barth's distinction from Rahner in understanding the immanent Trinity, and when one departs from presumed support of Barth and a premeditated acknowledgment of his referentiality, as Molnar does, one would inevitably limit and underrate Moltmann's emphasis on *perichoresis*, for this underrating would sharpen and pinpoint the panentheistic elements in Moltmann's approach. But, despite the existence of such a panentheistic tendency in his theology, throughout his long theological career, Moltmann does not merely point to the necessary distinction between "person" and "relation," or to theology's distinction from secular knowledge. He also departs from a clear and emphatic declaration of God's uniqueness and wholly otherness, though he also stresses that this otherness takes perfect shape and reality in God's intimate relation with creation.

It may be the case that Moltmann's consistent zeal for the perichoretic model of relationality drives his language into panentheistic territory on some occasions. His stress on *perichoresis*, nevertheless, serves the attempt to demonstrate the importance of the openness of theology and of secular intellectual conditions toward each other. It shows that as the cultural enterprise needs theology's contributions for its intellectual activity, theology also needs to execute its activity by the help of the available intellectual means and disciplines. Mutual influence and fellowship are at the core of the notion of "interpenetration" as he uses it in his theological reasoning. One should add that it is equally important to show that *perichoresis* not only points to the relational, reciprocal necessity of each side of the relation to the other. It is also indicative of the self-distinction of each side *in*, and not outside, the realms of this relation. Because Moltmann spends so much time explicating the importance of relationality, more so than the importance of distinction, it is sometimes possible to read his approach as a trinitarian reflection based on human experience, rather than on God's revelation of himself as an "Other" from without.[14] Despite the panentheistic possibility that lingers on the horizon,

---

13. Ibid., 200.

14. Molnar throws trinitarian theologians like Ted Peters, Wolfhart Pannenberg, and Robert Jenson, along with Moltmann, into the same process/panentheist corner (ibid., 141ff.). But Molnar's view is a sign of an overgeneralization. Each one of these theologians departs from a specific hermeneutic of personhood that is not necessarily panentheistic or immanentist in foundation, even if it has immanentist

I still say that Moltmann's theological axiom is a helpful and appropriate contribution to the subject of the proper relation between theology and other intellectual conditions, although it is not fully sufficient in itself and needs another supporting axiom to maintain a dimension of self-differentiation in the perichoretic equation of unity. This axiom takes me once more to Wolfhart Pannenberg's theology.

III. The Theological Criterion of Self-Differentiation Relationality

In the previous chapter, I analyzed Pannenberg's ontology of personhood and his view of "relationality-in-self-differentiation," which he grounds in the trinitarian doctrine of God. I end this study by proposing that Pannenberg's theology presents a criterion of relationality that is far more doctrinally appropriate than any other found in the postmodernist theological proposals discussed in this study.

It is my belief that the superiority of Pannenberg's thought in relation to the subject of this study lies in the fact that, as F. LeRon Shults states:

> He is careful throughout his writings to distinguish his views from relational conceptualizations that dissolve the idea of substance or essence completely, and from theological approaches (like some forms of process theology) that so emphasize the God-world connection that their distinction is blurred.[15]

For Pannenberg, relationality is always located within the thematized concepts that are related to methodological forms of understanding. It is not rigorously used as a redefining notion for being or for essence.

Aware of the rigorous turn in philosophy to the concept of "relation," which, as he argues, made Kant subordinate substance to the category of "relation" and Hegel structure the concept of "essence" as a relational process, Pannenberg counters this approach by implementing the concept of "relation" in order to show *real* and substantial communion between humanity and God, without turning God into either a finite reality or into a correlate expression

---

implications and language. This applies so clearly to Pannenberg, whose theology is far from immanentist and process theology.

15. F. LeRon Shults, *The Postfoundationalist Task of Theology: Wolfhart Pannenberg and the New Theological Rationality* (Grand Rapids: Eerdmans, 1999), 97.

of finitude. The concept of "relation" for him helps show that the notions of "finite" and "infinite," "eternal" and "temporal," are not necessarily opposed to each other.[16] It is never a concept that is used to demonstrate that in relating to the finite, the infinite loses his being or becomes just the self-actualization process of the finite. In his relation to humanity, God does not dissolve his personhood in relationality. Rather, he "gives existence to the [finite's self] as that which is different from himself, so that his holiness does not mean the abolition of the distinction between the finite and the infinite."[17] In other words, the relation does not abolish the distinction between the subjects on its two ends, nor does it abolish them as such. This cannot be at all the case in the God-human realm of connection unless one of the sides of the relation is infinite and is not exhaustively defined or characterized by mere relation to creation.

A similar correlational logic characterizes Pannenberg's view of the relation between theology and other theories of knowledge. Principally, Pannenberg does not invest in a radical difference between theology and other fields of inquiry in the same manner he invests such radical differentiation into the doctrine of creation. Nevertheless, he maintains a qualified view of the relation between theology and other disciplines, in which the relation is not as constitutive of the nature of theology as it is actually an evidence of theology's necessity for providing, *together with* other theories of knowledge, the basis for "the understanding of the perception of meaning, the historical roots of intellectual life."[18] Pannenberg takes over Barth's conviction that theology should regard itself a "practical science" *because* sciences are not all inspired by theology's foundational truth (i.e., faith in the revelation of God in Jesus Christ). For Pannenberg, nevertheless, this particularity does not stand in contrast with looking for a common notion of knowledge that transcends specific particularity and unifies theology and other disciplines.[19] On this notional unifying ground, theology is likely to be a particular *practical* study that includes by nature the human who asks about God and his ultimate goodwill as part of its discourse.[20] Pannenberg believes that this is one of the indicators that

---

16. Ibid., 99.

17. Wolfhart Pannenberg, *Systematic Theology*, trans. Geoffrey W. Bromiley (Edinburgh: T. & T. Clark, 1991), 1:400.

18. Wolfhart Pannenberg, *Theology and the Philosophy of Science*, trans. Francis McDonagh (Philadelphia: Westminster, 1976), 13.

19. Ibid., 18–19. The logic behind such a belief for Pannenberg is that "what is true is that it is possible to argue about truth only where the unity of truth is presupposed." This is what allows theology to "defend its claim to be a science in argument with other views of sciences."

Christianity is not an outdated tradition from the past, but a discipline that is open to the future and holds responsibilities in the present. This, in other words, does not say that theology is the core meaning that underpins every human quest for the good, even if God is the ground of every good. This is a qualification to the theological tradition that considers theology "a positive science" about fixed and absolute truth given from outside. "Christianity," Pannenberg affirms, "goes beyond the scope of the theology regarded as the positive science of Christianity,"[21] because the inquiry about the truth of Christian faith cannot take place in segregation from the inquiring activities of other scientific disciplines on the truth of all the areas of human experience. The task of theology is primarily to interpret and describe Christianity. But, in order to do this, theology "must constantly go *beyond* Christianity."[22]

By this logic, Pannenberg moves noticeably beyond Barth's and Schleiermacher's distinct views of "positive science." He sets, instead, a form of relationality between theology and secular disciplines in which theology maintains its positive distinction as a "science of God" rather than a mere "science of Christianity," taking at the same time the surrounding human historical situation into serious consideration. The core point here lies in showing the validity of theology and its equal credibility and rational authenticity by means of maintaining theology's self-distinction as well as its similarity to other fields of investigations.

By shifting from understanding theology as a science of Christianity to understanding it as a science of God, Pannenberg invites us to move theology away from the limiting boundaries of a modernist privatization of God-talk that reduces it to a mere ethical discourse on the human's individual existence in relation to God's redemption.[23] Contrary to the restriction of the relation

---

20. Ibid., 134 (131–41). According to Pannenberg, the strongest emphasis on the practical and nontheoretical nature of theology characterized Protestant theology in the sixteenth and seventeenth centuries, starting with Luther, Melanchthon, Flacius, Heerbrand, and others (ibid., 235ff.). This emphasis can be generally traced, in my opinion, in the central Protestant concern about the work of Jesus Christ at the expense of his nature or being; and about the doctrine of salvation as the foundation of Christology. The first shows that theology is about *how* God acts, and the second applies this action-centered perspective to humanity by showing how humanity lives in the light of God's providential activity. Both trends present a theology that is basically an ethical discourse related to humanity's good being. In this, I partially differ from Pannenberg's claim that the emphasis on the practical nature of theology has an ontological or anthropological rather than an ethical background (ibid., 239). The anthropological dimension cannot be distinct from the ethical if the presumed view of the theology that combines them is practical only.

21. Ibid., 263 (242ff.).

22. Ibid., 265.

of theology with philosophy to the realm of the individual's ethical-pietistic life, Pannenberg extends the frontiers of the relation between theology and philosophy by first extending the limits of the theology of revelation beyond particular religiosity, such as that of neo-orthodoxy; and, secondly, by extending the boundaries of philosophical inquiry beyond the question of humans' being and purpose, and then placing this question as such in the wider framework on the meaning of existence as a whole.[24] Pannenberg does this neither to show that theology by nature is a philosophical condition, nor to show that philosophy by nature is a theological condition (*theologia naturalis*). He rather wants to show that the possibility of the occurrence of conflict between theology and other intellectual disciplines throughout history "cannot be resolved by [merely] according to each other their own particular and *separate* field of operation."[25] Division is not the solution. Yet, Pannenberg continues, conflation and subsummation are not options either. For, "neither are philosophy and theology able to treat each other as different perspectives of a single truth, *because* the question of the way these two distinct perspectives are to be coordinated into the one truth [i.e., the question of their relationship] is an inevitable one."[26] This question becomes more inevitable in light of the challenging reduction of the subject matter of theology into mere language or a form of textual discourse among many others in postmodernity. In such a situation, even theological language per se is strictly discerned from narrow metaphorical, figurative, and literary angles. Pannenberg is as worried about such a postmodern reductionist imposition as Philip Clayton, who accurately notes that

---

23. Wolfhart Pannenberg, "Christian Theology and Philosophical Criticism," in *The Idea of God and Human Freedom* (Louisville: Westminster John Knox, 1973), 116–43. This ethical approach may just be an alternative to the medieval philosophical approach. Luther, for instance, strictly rejects the medieval overpassive subordination to philosophy. Against the Scholastic belief that one cannot become a theologian without Aristotle, Luther states: "to state that a theologian who is not a logician is a monstrous heretic—this is a monstrous and heretical statement." Martin Luther, "Disputations against Scholastic Theology," trans. H. J. Grimm, in *Luther's Works: Career of the Reformer*, ed. L. H. T. Lehmann (Philadelphia: Muhlenberg, 1957), 12:45. Luther goes further in his language to the extent of saying even "indeed, no one can become a theologian unless he becomes one without Aristotle." This extreme reaction is not my personal view, although I agree with Luther's rejection of the collapsing of theology into philosophy.

24. Pannenberg, "Christian Theology and Philosophical Criticism," 120, 126.

25. Ibid., 128. Italics are mine.

26. Ibid., 128–29.

[t]he biggest threat to conversations [between theology and other intellectual conditions] such as ours is not that we might become metaphysical or political, but that we might have no more to offer than poets or literary critics. If what is needed is poetic reflection on science, surely others can do it better than we![27]

It is because of such a threatening limitation of theological scholarship that Pannenberg develops a critical standpoint against the common tendency among Christian believers to surrender the Christian doctrinal faith to a nonepistemic foundation that lies only in the subjectivist will, feeling, or practice of the community.[28] Theology, Pannenberg suggests, should rather engage with other disciplines' epistemological scholarship, and it should be pursued in a rational manner that reflects real and serious interaction with the historical intellectual condition at hand. Yet what is here importantly and valuably relevant in his conviction for the models of "unity-in-differentiation" or "encounter-in-resistance" is Pannenberg's insistence that this interaction be pursued with a complete awareness of theology's unique and unequal hermeneutics that can make certain epistemic data fully comprehensible.[29]

Pannenberg's previous view is valuable because it prioritizes the holistic dimension of meaning over relativism and partiality by freeing the notion of "meaning" from any reductionism to individualist, partial human dimensions of activity. "Meaning," Pannenberg states, "is not dependent on and created by human (purposive) action, but human action shares in the spiritual reality of meaning that is based on the priority of wholes over parts."[30] This, in my opinion, presses upon us the issue of the ontology of personhood. If "person" connotes the totality of being, and if "relation" connotes the particulars expressive of this being, then personhood as the whole is prior to the relations as parts, and not reduced to or subsumed into them. It is the supra-individual

---

27. Philip Clayton, "From Methodology to Metaphysics: The Problem of Control in the Science-Theology Dialogue," in *Beginning with the End: God, Science and Wolfhart Pannenberg*, ed. C. R. Albright and J. Haugen (Chicago and Lasalle, IL: Open Court, 1997), 396–408, 387.

28. Ibid., 398. Clayton describes such a tendency "a retreat to commitment." I do not, though, think that such a form of theorization may apply to Barth's theology as it may apply, if ever, to Schleiermacher and the Kantian trends of religiosity. Barth would *depart* methodologically from a commitment to faith that itself is based on a trans-subjective reality. He would not really *retreat* to commitment as the context and the content of faith.

29. Ibid., 406.

30. Wolfhart Pannenberg, "Theological Appropriation of Scientific Understandings: Responses to Hefner, Wicken, Eaves and Tipler," in *Beginning with the End*, 432.

meaning that constitutes the meaning of the relational actions of the being of the person.

This equally applies to the "theology-secular cognitive conditions" relationship. It demonstrates that within the realm of human understanding of reality in its totality, neither theology nor any other secular form of cognitive inquiry is per se the conditioning, constitutive foundation of the meaning of this reality, because each one of them is just a part that is dependent on a more original supra-individual whole—that is, the reality of the triune God. In other words, neither the secular cognitive conditions can condition theology as if it is the holistic condition. Nor can theology condition any external cognitive form of inquiry as a holistic meaning. There are even some discussions where theology should not interfere in the details.[31]

Be that as it may, Philip Hefner is right in claiming that the theological thought-form of Pannenberg is the one that should underlie any theological thinking about the Christian understanding of God and of faith in relation to the prevalent intellectual conditions. It is the appropriate one, Hefner correctly continues, because it trades away from any possibility of one-sidedness or subordinationism in theology's and the surrounding contemporary intellectual condition's understanding of each other. Such a thought-form relies on a "dual falsification" hermeneutics, in that while theology opens itself to falsification by means of scientific epistemology, this latter also assimilates itself fully to the theological tradition.[32]

---

31. Ibid., 435–36.

32. Philip Hefner, "The Role of Science in Pannenberg's Theological Thinking," in *Beginning with the End*, 97–115, 111. Hefner goes further to state that this makes Pannenberg's theological researching program unsurpassable by any other program on theology (ibid., 112).

Conclusion: When Theology Stands in History

With regard to the relation between theology and other forms of cognitive inquiry, I proposed that the correlation between theology and the contemporary intellectual conditions should not be a one-direction track. A correlation wherein postmodernity asks the questions and theology provides the satisfactory appealing answers is insufficient. I also argued against any correlation that aims to make theology *alone* raise the questions, and the postmodern discourses *alone* provide appealing and conforming answers to those questions—as if postmodernity is from beginning to end contextualized according to a theological condition. I tried to show that my chief concern lies with the latter option, without understating the seriousness and the danger of the former. In response to those among today's theologians who are eager to show that postmodernity is in itself "a theological condition," I tried to echo what Ingolf Dalferth very eloquently and bravely says to challenge this attitude:

> Theology is not important because it is able to say something about *all* possible topics by employing *all* possible methodologies currently in vogue, but rather because it possesses its own theme. Only because of this theme itself do theology's contributions to the themes of other disciplines deserve to be heard.[1]

It is not the task of theology to offer a theological explanation and hermeneutics for every nontheological, or even religiously masqueraded, issue—nor ought theology to gain a distinctive position by doing so. It is incorrect, as Dalferth rightly affirms, to expect this from theology or to force theology to be the serving executor of such an expectation. Further than just preventing it from being a dependent field of knowledge, this denies theology its uniqueness and difference from other disciplines, and it turns theology inevitably into one trendy discourse among many others through an imitation of certain dominant hermeneutical methods.[2]

---

1. Ingolf U. Dalferth, "Time for God's Presence," in *The Future of Theology: Essays in Honor of Jürgen Moltmann*, ed. M. Volf, C. Krieg, and T. Kucharz (Grand Rapids and Cambridge: Eerdmans, 1996), 140.

On the basis of a conviction similar to Ingolf Dalferth's, I pointed out a theological proposal that represents, in my opinion, a two-direction track of correlation. It is a correlation where both theology and postmodernity ask questions and offer answers in a way that pinpoints areas wherein each can uniquely contribute to the development of the other, without each losing its own distinction and unique identity. From this model of correlation, it is valid to argue that postmodernity needs some theological conditioning, without necessarily implying that the next step is to transform every postmodern discourse into a theological proclamation. From the same model of correlation, one can accept the theologians' use of postmodern discourse about notions like language, plurality, relativism, "*différance*," and so on, without this directly making theology subject to all the assumptions of these concepts or the rules of such discourse.

The accurate relation between theology and history lies not in theology's proclaimed and evident sensitivity and expressiveness of its surrounding intellectual and human situation, but in its evident and proclaimed sensitivity and expressiveness of God's presence and action here and now in the face of this situation. The core issue here is that theology avoids misunderstanding itself as a mere sociological, anthropological, or contextual science. Theology is, as Dalferth says, "neither an empirical nor a historical science." It is, rather, as he continues, a guiding critical knowledge of the triune God, and more specifically, knowledge of God "in His multifarious presence in the varied contexts of our own world and of all possible worlds that owe their existence to his presence."[3] Only a correlation of "unity-in-self-differentiation," such as the one Pannenberg offers, between theology and other disciplines can demonstrate this particular identity of theology. Such a correlation avoids the two extremes of subordination and domination. It allows theology to be up to the duty of clarifying what is distinctively theological in its accounts of personhood and relationality, or any other notions. It also enables theology to succeed in finding the right criterion for what is to be deemed authentically Christian and what is not in the theological conception of any human idea or condition.[4]

This is exactly what causes Christian theology to claim that *God* is, by default, the subject matter of theology, and not any notions or conceptions of God. The validity of this claim is decided according to a rational criterion from

2. Ibid., 140–41.

3. Ibid., 133.

4. Christoph Schwöbel, "Editorial Introduction," in *Persons, Divine and Human: King's College Essays in Theological Anthropology*, ed. Colin Gunton and Christoph Schwöbel (Edinburgh: T. & T. Clark, 1999), 9.

outside the realm of faith. This is similarly the cause of theology's disagreement with the postmodern inability to differentiate in a meaningful way between the reality of something and the rational construction we form to interpret it after our own historically generated awareness, or between God's self-revelation and our imaginative notions and images of the divine.[5] Yes, God reveals God's self to us in the context of our human awareness. But God per se is not a context, nor is God an element constitutive of our human consciousness. Therefore, in the discourse about God, "theo-logy" is supposed to take us *beyond* the boundaries of our realm of awareness in order to realize that this Who is different from us, and eventually that this Who makes us different, too.

In defense of the relation between theology and other fields of knowledge (science, in this case), Pope John Paul II once said that religion and science should aspire to a relational unity in which, by means of correlating with each other, not in spite of it, both maintain their autonomy while working together.[6] This interrelational strategy should, most of all, measure today's theological endeavors for developing an up-to-date trinitarian doctrine of God and a coherent theological anthropology. If the investment in the trinitarian concept of personhood for the sake of interpreting the conditions of human life and being aims at showing that theology always has social and anthropological impact, no matter how indirect this impact may be, then this investment is valid and necessary. There is always an interrelationship between theology and the other forms of conception that inform and construct the natural and social sciences. However, and as Christoph Schwöbel affirms, such an investment is disastrous if its goal is to project certain views of desirable human conceptions or relationships on the divine personal being of the triune God.[7]

The core proposal of this book is that the doctrine of the Trinity is by all means the most central theological discourse and fundamental concept in Christian faith. Not primarily because the Trinity represents the original fountain of the terminology that is most efficiently and descriptively expressive of the concepts of "relationality," "communion," "charity," "reciprocity," "interpenetration," and "otherness." More fundamentally, it is because the doctrine of the Trinity is the most articulate confession of God's being, God's

5. Ibid.,135.
6. Pope John Paul II, "Message of His Holiness John Paul II," in *John Paul II on Science and Religion: Reflections on the New View from Rome*, ed. Robert Russell et al. (Vatican City State: Vatican Observatory Publications/Notre Dame: University of Notre Dame Press, 1990), 10.
7. Christoph Schwöbel, "The Renaissance of Trinitarian Theology: Reasons, Problems and Tasks," in *Trinitarian Theology Today: Essays on Divine Being and Act*, ed. C. Schwöbel (Edinburgh: T. & T. Clark, 1995), 11.

personhood, God's nature, and God's life in Christian faith and thought. It is due to this foundational ontological and onto-theological importance that the difference between Christian faith and other religious theisms is more radical—and sometimes more problematic—than being merely a difference in terms of socio-religious linguistic discourse.

When theologians speak about relationality, communion, otherness, reciprocity, and so on, in terms of a *perichoresis* of Father, Son, and Spirit—of three persons in self-differentiation communion—they not only offer the interreligious or religious-secular debates a language more convenient than other linguistic expressions, or language games, for co-articulating a common, unifying human concern or ultimatum. By speaking about Father, Son, and Spirit, theologians point, instead, in the best and clearest way they can, to an eternal, self-existing, and criterial reality that is no less expressive of an ultimate truth and referential source of meaning, and of being, than of God per se. It points, as the church fathers relentlessly affirm, to the Godhead of the deity whose existence and whose eternal triune essence as such is the one and only source and cause of our being and existence. It is, therefore, always a primary requirement that theology interpret and articulate the trinitarian reality of God throughout the flow of history, so that the doctrine of the Trinity can always be *the* Christian proclamation of God's loving lordship and self-giving reality.

It is because of this ontological nature of the discourse on the Trinity, nevertheless, that the doctrine of the Trinity should not be reduced to a mere linguistic form of speech, to a mere linguistic tool for the human intellectual and existential quest for meaning. It should, rather, safeguard God's self-existing, independent, and distinct revealed personal integrity by playing the role of the proclamatory and hermeneutic confession that conveys the God of Jesus Christ to humanity as a wholly distinct, wholly independent, yet wholly relational *Other*. This can only be achieved by maintaining theology's conceptual and disciplinary integrity, which means restraining from succumbing to the constraints and rules of surrounding scientific and philosophical disciplines, no matter how dominant they are. However, it also means preventing theology from falling into the trap of seeking domination, wherein theology is tempted to turn every existing intellectual claim into a crypto-theological message or a component of a general and primal theological worldview. Maintaining such a balanced relationship, and avoiding the previous two extremes, can only be done on the basis of the doctrine of the Trinity when, and only when, the trinitarian language of personhood and relationality is expressive of a triune personal being who is three persons in relationship, and not of a triune form of relational movement—when, that is, the doctrine of the Trinity is about God's life, and not about humanity's journey of self-realization; about "persons *in* communion," and not about "personal communion."

The challenge before theology in the coming decades is to show that a correlation like the one I propose here is possible. It has to show that a correlation of "unity-in-self-differentiation" is not simply a survival strategy theology has to resort to in order to maintain its presence in today's world. This correlation lies before any need of survival or passion for gaining acceptance that Christian theologians may be tempted to seek. It is an expression of God's trinitarian reality per se; thus there is no theology proper apart from speaking it out. Apart from any panentheistic or one-sidedly immanentist view, such a correlation is tenably formed after the openness of God's trinitarian nature to the created reality of the world. It develops a proper theological attitude toward the postmodern condition, in which theological scholarship progresses by way of dialogue with the extra-theological questions and discoveries, as if these two poles are neither adversary nor subordinate to each other, but rather two different inquiries in a necessary, endless exchange.

Bibliography

Ahlers, Rolf. *The Community of Freedom: Barth and the Presuppositionless Theology.* New York: Peter Lang, 1989.

Allen, Diogenes. *Christian Belief in a Postmodern World: The Full Wealth of Conviction.* Louisville: Westminster John Knox, 1989.

Allison, C. FitzSimons. *The Cruelty of Heresy: An Affirmation of Christian Orthodoxy.* New York: Morehouse, 1992.

Altizer, Thomas. *The Descent into Hell: A Study of Radical Reversal of the Christian Consciousness.* New York: Seabury, 1979.

Antognazza, Maria Rosa. "Revealed Religion: The Continental European Debate," in *The Cambridge History of Eighteenth-Century Philosophy*, edited by Knud Haakonssen. New York: Cambridge University Press, 2006, II: 666–82.

Aquinas, Thomas. *The Summa Theologica.* Translated by Laurence Shapcote, in *Great Books of the Western World*, edited by Mortimer J. Adler. Chicago: Encyclopedia Britannica, 1990, 1.

_____. *Summa Contra Gentiles*, Notre Dame: University of Notre Dame Press, 1975.

Aristotle. *Aristotle's "Categories" and "De Interpretatione."* Translated by J. L. Ackrill. Oxford: Clarendon, 1963.

_____. *Metaphysics, I–IX.* Translated by Hugh Tredennick. Cambridge, MA: Harvard University Press/London: Heinemann, 1975.

Arendt, Hannah. "Thinking and Moral Consideration," *Social Research* 38 (1971): 411–25.

Augustine, St. *The Trinity.* Translated by Edmund Hill, O.P. Edited by John E. Rotelle, O.S.A. Brooklyn, NY: New City Press, 1991.

Awad, Najib G. *God without a Face? On the Personal Individuation of the Holy Spirit.* Tübingen: Mohr Siebeck, 2011.

_____. "Revelation, History and Idealism: Re-examining the Conceptual Roots of Wolfhart Pannenberg's Theology," *Theological Review* 1, no. 26 (2005): 91–110.

_____. "Futural Ousia or Eschatological Disclosure? A Systematic Analysis of Pannenberg's Trinitarian Theology," *Kerygma und Dogma*, 1, no. 54 (2008): 37–52.

———. "Thomas Aquinas' Metaphysics of 'Relation' and 'Participation' and Contemporary Trinitarian Theology," *New Blackfriars Review* 93, no. 1048 (2012): 652–70.

———. "At the Dawn of 'Practice' or Re-thinking the Nature and Role of Theology and Doctrine in the Church," *Journal of Reformed Theology* 8 (2014): 1–32.

Ayers, Lewis. *The Trinity: Classic and Contemporary Readings*. New York: Blackwell, 2000.

Balke, Willem. "Revelation and Experience in Calvin's Theology," in *Toward the Future of Reformed Theology: Tasks, Topics, Traditions*, edited by David Willis and Michael Welker. Grand Rapids and Cambridge: Eerdmans, 1999, 346–65.

Barbour, Ian G. *Myths, Models and Paradigms: A Comparative Study in Science and Religion*. New York: Harper & Row, 1974.

Barth, Karl. *Church Dogmatics*. Edited and translated by G. W. Bromiley and T. F. Torrance. Edinburgh: T. & T. Clark, 1936–77.

———. *The Göttingen Dogmatics: Instruction in the Christian Religion*. Grand Rapids: Eerdmans, 1991.

———. *Protestant Theology in the 19th Century: From Rousseau to Ritschl*. London: SCM, 1959.

Beardslee, William A., et al. *Varieties of Postmodern Theology*. Albany: State University of New York Press, 1989.

Beck, James R., and Bruce Demarest. *The Human Person in Theology and Psychology: A Biblical Anthropology for the Twenty-First Century*. Grand Rapids: Kregel, 2005.

Bella, Robert, et al. *Habits of the Heart*. Berkeley: University of California Press, 1985.

Bernet, Rudolf, Iso Kern, and Eduard Marbach. *An Introduction to Husserlian Phenomenology*. Evanston, IL: Northwestern University Press, 1999.

Bevans, Stephen B., SVD. *Models of Contextual Theology*. Maryknoll, NY: Orbis, 2003.

Blackwell, Albert L. *Schleiermacher's Early Philosophy of Life: Determinism, Freedom and Phantasy*. Chico, CA: Scholars, 1982.

Blocher, Henri A. G. "Karl Barth's Christocentric Method," in *Engaging with Barth, Contemporary Evangelical Critiques*, edited by David Gibson and Daniel Strange. Nottingham: Apollos/InterVarsity, 2008, 21–54.

_____. "Karl Barth's Anthropology," in *Karl Barth and Evangelical Theology: Convergences and Divergences*, edited by Sang Wook Chung. Milton Keynes, UK/Tyrone, GA: Paternoster/Grand Rapids: Baker Academic, 2006, 96–135.

Boethius. "A Treatise Against Eutyches and Nestorius," in *Boethius, The Theological Tractates, The Consolation of Philosophy*, edited by H. F. Stewart, E. K. Rand, and S. J. Tester. Cambridge, MA: Harvard University Press/ London: Heinemann, 1973.

Booth, Edward, O.P. "τό ὑπερεῖναι of Pseudo-Dionysius and Schelling," *Studia Patristica* 23 (1989): 215–25.

Bradshaw, Timothy. *Trinity and Ontology: A Comparative Study of the Theologies of Karl Barth and Wolfhart Pannenberg*. Edinburgh: T. & T. Clark, 1988.

Bracken, Joseph A., S.J., and Marjorie Hewitt Suchocki. *Trinity in Process: Relational Theology of God*. New York: Continuum, 1997.

Braley, Joshua. "A Critique of Gordon Kaufman's Theological Method, with Special Reference to His Theory of Religion," *The Journal of Religion* 1, no. 88 (2008): 29–52.

Brooke, John Hedley. "Science and the Self: What Difference Did Darwin Make?" in *The Evolution of Rationality: Interdisciplinary Essays in Honor of J. Wentzel van Huyssteen*, edited by F. LeRon Shults. Grand Rapids and Cambridge: Eerdmans, 2006, 253–73.

Brown, David. "Trinitarian Personhood and Individuality," in *Trinity, Incarnation and Atonement: Philosophical and Theological Essays*, edited by Ronald J. Feenstra and Cornelius Plantinga Jr. Notre Dame: University of Notre Dame Press, 1989, 48–78.

_____. *The Divine Trinity*. La Salle, IL: Open Court, 1985.

Buller, Cornelius A. *The Unity of Nature and History in Pannenberg's Theology*. London: Littlefield Adams, 1996.

Burhenn, Herbert. "Pannenberg's Doctrine of God," *Scottish Journal of Theology* 6, no. 18 (1975): 535–49.

Busch, Eberhard. *Karl Barth & the Pietists: The Young Karl Barth's Critique of Pietism and Its Response*. Translated by Daniel W. Bloesch. Downers Grove, IL: InterVarsity, 2004.

Calvin, John. *Institutes of the Christian Religion*. Translated by H. Beveridge. Grand Rapids: Eerdmans, 1993.

Capetz, Paul E. *Christian Faith as Religion: A Study in the Theologies of Calvin and Schleiermacher*. London, New York, and Oxford: University Press of America. 1998.

Caputo, John D. *What Would Jesus Deconstruct: The Good News of Postmodernity for the Church*. Grand Rapids: Baker Academic, 2007.

_____, and Michael J. Scanlon. *Transcendence and Beyond: A Postmodern Inquiry*. Bloomington and Indianapolis: Indiana University Press, 2007.

Carlson, Thomas A. "Postmetaphysical Theology," in *The Cambridge Companion of Postmodern Theology*, edited by K. J. Vanhoozer. Cambridge: Cambridge University Press, 2003, 58–75.

Chapman, M. *Ernst Tröltsch and Liberal Theology: Religion and Cultural Synthesis in Wilhelmine Germany*. Oxford: Oxford University Press, 2001.

Chesnut, Roberta C. *Three Monophysite Christologies: Severus of Antioch, Philoxenus of Mabbug and Jacob of Sarug*. London: Oxford University Press, 1976.

Chung, Sang Wook. *Karl Barth and Evangelical Theology: Convergences and Divergences*. Milton Keynes, UK/Tyrone, GA: Paternoster/Grand Rapids: Baker Academic, 2006.

Clayton, Philip. "From Methodology to Metaphysics: The Problem of Control in the Science-Theology Dialogue," in *Beginning with the End: God, Science and Wolfhart Pannenberg*, edited by C. R. Albright and J. Haugen. Chicago and Lasalle, IL: Open Court, 1997, 396–408.

_____, Arthur Peacocke, et al. *In Whom We Live and Move and Have Our Being: Panentheistic Reflections on God's Presence in a Scientific World*. Grand Rapids and Cambridge: Eerdmans, 2004.

Coakley, Sarah A. "The Trinity and Gender Reconsidered," in *God's Life in Trinity*, edited by Miroslav Volf and Michael Welker. Minneapolis: Fortress Press, 2006, 133–42.

Coffey, David. *Deus Trinitas: The Doctrine of the Triune God*. New York: Oxford University Press, 1999.

Collins, Paul M. *Trinitarian Theology: West and East, Karl Barth, the Cappadocian Fathers and John Zizioulas*. Oxford: Oxford University Press, 2001.

Compier, Don H. *John Calvin's Rhetorical Doctrine of Sin*. Lewiston, Queenston, and Lampeter: Edwin Mellen, 2001.

Congar, Yves. *I Believe in the Holy Spirit*. Translated by David Smith. London: Geoffrey Chapman, 1983, 1–3.

Cooper, John Charles. *The "Spiritual Presence" in the Theology of Paul Tillich: Tillich's Use of St. Paul*. Macon, GA; Mercer University Press, 1997.

Copleston, Frederick. *A History of Philosophy: Fichte to Nietzsche*. London: Burns & Oates, 1963.

Crosby, John F. *The Selfhood of the Human Person*. Washington, DC: Catholic University of America Press, 1996.

Cupitt, Don. *Taking Leave of God*. London: SCM, 1980.

Dalferth, Ingolf U. "Time for God's Presence," in *The Future of Theology: Essays in Honor of Jürgen Moltmann*, edited by M. Volf, C. Krieg, and T. Kucharz. Grand Rapids and Cambridge: Eerdmans, 1996, 127–41.

Dallavalle, Nancy A. "Revisiting Rahner: On the Theological Status of Trinitarian Theology," *Irish Theological Quarterly* 2, no. 63 (1998): 133–50.

Danaher, William J. Jr. *The Trinitarian Ethics of Jonathan Edwards*, in *Columbia Series in Reformed Theology*, group of eds. Louisville and London: Westminster John Knox, 2004.

Darwin, Charles. *The Descent of Man and Selection in Relation to Sex*. London: Murray, 1906.

Davis, Leo Donald, S.J. *The First Seven Ecumenical Councils (325-787): Their History and Theology*. Collegeville, MN: Liturgical/Michael Glazier, 1983.

Davis, Stephen T., et al. *The Trinity: An Interdisciplinary Symposium on the Trinity*. New York: Oxford University Press, 2000.

Davies, Oliver. *The Creativity of God: World, Eucharist and Reason*. New York: Cambridge University Press, 2004.

De Muralt, André. *Idea of Phenomenology: Husserlian Exemplarism*. Translated by Garry L. Breckon. Evanston, IL: Northwestern University Press, 1988.

Derrida, Jacques. "The Ends of Man," in *Margins of Philosophy*, translated by Alan Bass. Brighton, UK: Harvester, 1982.

———. "How to Avoid Speaking: Denials," translated by Ken Frieden, in *Derrida and Negative Theology*, edited by Harold Coward and Toby Foshay. Albany: State University of New York Press, 1992, 73–143.

———. "Secrets of European Responsibility," in *The Gift of Death*, translated by David Wills. Chicago and London: University of Chicago Press, 1995, 1–34.

Descartes, René. *Philosophical Writings*. Edited by John Cunningham and Robert Stoothoff, translated by Dugald Murdoch. Cambridge: Cambridge University Press, 1984.

De Vries, Dawn. "Schleiermacher's *Christmas Eve Dialogue*: Bourgeois Ideology or Feminist Theology?," *The Journal of Religion* 69, no. 2 (1989): 169–82.

Dockery, David S. *The Challenge of Postmodernism: An Evangelical Engagement*, 2nd ed. Grand Rapids: Baker Academic, 1995.

———. "So What Happened after Modernity? A Postmodern Agenda for Evangelical Theology," in *The Challenge of Postmodernism: An Evangelical*

Engagement, 2nd ed., edited by David S. Dockery. Grand Rapids: Baker Academic, 1995, 184–98.

Dole, Andrew. "The Case of the Disappearing Discourse: Schleiermacher's Fourth Speech and the Field of Religious Studies," *The Journal of Religion* 1, no. 88 (2008): 1–28.

Dulles, Avery, S.J. *Models of Revelation*. New York: Doubleday, 1983.

Feenstra, Ronald J., and Cornelius Plantinga Jr. *Trinity, Incarnation and Atonement: Philosophical and Theological Essays*. Notre Dame: University of Notre Dame Press, 1989.

Feuerbach, Ludwig. *The Essence of Christianity*. Translated by George Eliot. Buffalo, NY: Prometheus, 1989.

Fichte, J. G. *Attempt to a Critique of All Revelations*. Cambridge: Cambridge University Press, 1979.

———. "Public Religion of the Present Age," in *The Popular Works of Johann Gottlieb Fichte*, translated by William Smith, 4th ed. London: Tuebner, 1889, 257–70.

The Forgotten Trinity: the Report of the BCC Study Commission on Trinitarian Doctrine Today. London: The British Council of Churches, 1989.

Fiddes, Paul. *Participating in God: A Pastoral Doctrine of the Trinity*. London: Darton, Longman & Todd, 2000.

———. *The Creative Suffering of God*. Oxford: Clarendon, 1988.

Phillips, Timothy R., et al. *The Nature of Confession: Evangelicals and Postliberals in Conversation*. Downers Grove, IL: InterVarsity, 1996.

Ford, Lewis. "Contingent Trinitarianism," in *Trinity in Process: A Relational Theology of God*, edited by Joseph A. Bracken, S.J. and Marjorie Hewitt Suchocki. New York: Continuum, 1997, 41–68.

Foucault, Michel. *The Order of Things: An Archaeology of the Human Sciences*. London and New York: Routledge, 2002.

———. *The Archaeology of Knowledge and the Discourse on Language*. Translated by A. M. Sheridan Smith. New York: Pantheon, 1971.

Fox, Patricia A. *God as Communion: John Zizioulas, Elizabeth Johnson, and the Retrieval of the Symbol of the Triune God*. Collegeville, MN: Michael Glazier/Liturgical, 2001.

Frei, Hans W. *Types of Christian Theology*. Edited by G. Hunsinger and W. C. Placher. New Haven and London: Yale University Press, 1992.

———. *Theology and Narrative: Selected Papers*. Edited by G. Hunsinger and W. C. Placher. Oxford and New York: Oxford University Press, 1993.

Frend, W. H. C. *The Rise of the Monophysite Movement: Chapters in the History of the Church in the Fifth and Sixth Centuries*. Cambridge: Cambridge University Press, 1972.

Gadamer, Hans-Georg. *Truth and Method*. London: Sheed & Ward, 1975.

Gallup, C. G. Jr. "Chimpanzees: Self-Recognition," *Science*, June 6, 1983, 86–87.

Gamwell, Franklin I. *The Divine Good: Moral Theory and the Necessity of God*. San Francisco: HarperCollins, 1990.

Garber, Daniel, and Michael Ayers. *The Cambridge History of Seventeenth-Century Philosophy*. Cambridge: Cambridge University Press, 1997–98, 1–2.

Garrett, Aaron. "Human Nature," in *The Cambridge Companion to Eighteenth Century Philosophy*, edited by Knud Haakonssen. New York: Cambridge University Press, 2006, 1:161–77.

Garrett, Brian. "Person," in *Routledge Encyclopedia of Philosophy*, edited by Edward Craig. London and New York: Routledge, 1998, 7:319.

———. "Personal Identity," in *Routledge Encyclopedia of Philosophy*, edited by Edward Craig. London and New York: Routledge, 1998, 7:307–8.

Gasché, Rodolph. *Of Minimal Things: Studies on the Notion of Relation*. Stanford: Stanford University Press, 1999

Gestrich, Christof. *The Return of Splendor in the World: The Christian Doctrine of Sin and Forgiveness*. Translated by Daniel W. Bloesch. Grand Rapids and Cambridge: Eerdmans, 1997.

Gibson, David, and Daniel Strange. *Engaging with Barth: Contemporary Evangelical Critiques*. Nottingham: Apollos/InterVarsity, 2008.

Gilkey, Langdon. *Gilkey on Tillich*. New York: Crossroad, 1990.

Gregersen, Niels H. "Varieties of Personhood: Mapping the Issues," in *The Human Person in Science and Theology*, edited by N. H. Gregersen, W. B. Drees, and U. Görman. Grand Rapids: Eerdmans, 2000, 1–17.

———. "Three Varieties of Panentheism," in *In Whom We Live and Move and Have Our Being: Panentheistic Reflections on God's Presence in a Scientific World*, edited by Philip Clayton and Arthur Peacocke. Grand Rapids and Cambridge: Eerdmans, 2004, 36–47.

Grenz, Stanley J. *The Social God and the Relational Self: A Trinitarian Theology of the Imago Dei*. Louisville and London: Westminster John Knox, 2001.

———, and John R. Franke. *Beyond Foundationalism: Shaping Theology in a Postmodern Context*. Louisville: Westminster John Knox, 2001.

Griffin, David Ray. *God and Religion in the Postmodern World: Essays in Postmodern Theology*. Albany: State University of New York Press, 1989.

———. "Postmodern Theology and A/Theology: A Response to Mark C. Taylor," in *Varieties of Postmodern Theology*, edited by David Ray Griffin et al. Albany: State University of New York Press, 1989, 29–62.

———. "A Naturalistic Trinity," in *Trinity in Process: A Relational Theology of God*, edited by Joseph A. Bracken, S.J. and Marjorie Hewitt Suchocki. New York: Continuum, 1997, 23–40.

———. "Panentheism: A Postmodern Revelation," in *In Whom We Live and Move and Have Our Being: Panentheistic Reflections on God's Presence in a Scientific World*, edited by Philip Clayton and Arthur Peacocke. Grand Rapids and Cambridge: Eerdmans, 2004, 36–47.

Grillmeier, Aloys. *Christ in Christian Tradition: From the Apostolic Age to Chalcedon (451)*. Louisville: Westminster John Knox, 1988, vol. 1.

Guarino, Thomas G. *Foundations of Systematic Theology*. London and New York: T. & T. Clark/Continuum, 2005.

Gunton, Colin E. *The Actuality of the Atonement: A Study of Metaphor, Rationality and the Christian Tradition*. Edinburgh: T. & T. Clark, 2000.

———. *The One, the Three and the Many: God, Creation and the Culture of Modernity*. Cambridge: Cambridge University Press, 1998.

———. *The Promise of Trinitarian Theology*, 2nd ed. Edinburgh: T. & T. Clark, 1997.

———. "The Triune God and the Freedom of the Creature," in *Karl Barth: Centenary Essays*, edited by S. W. Sykes. Cambridge: Cambridge University Press, 1989.

———. *The Barth Lectures*. Edited by Paul H. Brazier. London: T. & T. Clark/Continuum, 2007.

Habermas, Jürgen. *The Divided West*. Edited and translated by Ciaran Cronin. Cambridge, UK and Malden, MA: Polity, 2006.

———. *The Philosophical Discourse of Modernity: Twelve Lectures*. Translated by Frederick Lawrence. Cambridge: Polity, 1987.

———. *Postmetaphysical Thinking: Philosophical Essays*. Translated by William M. Hohengarten. Cambridge, MA and London: MIT Press, 1992.

———. *The Theory of Communicative Action*. Translated by Thomas McCarthy. Cambridge: Polity, 1987.

———. "Remarks on the Concept of Communicative Action," in *Social Action*, edited by G. Seebass and R. Tuomela. Boston and Dordrecht: Kluwer, 1985, 151–78.

Hägglund, Bengt. *History of Theology*. Translated by Gene J. Lund, 3rd ed. St. Louis: Concordia, 1968.

Hanninger, Mark G., S.J. *Relations: Medieval Theories 1250-1325*. Oxford: Clarendon, 1989.

Hastings, Adrian, et al. *Oxford Companion to Christian Thought*. Oxford and New York: Oxford University Press, 2000.

Hauerwas, Stanley. *Wilderness Wanderings: Probing Twentieth-Century Theology and Philosophy*. Boulder, CO: Westview, 1997.

Hefner, Philip. "The Role of Science in Pannenberg's Theological Thinking," in *Beginning with the End: God, Science and Wolfhart Pannenberg*, edited by C. R. Albright and J. Haugen. Chicago and Lasalle, IL: Open Court, 1997, 97–115.

———. "*Imago Dei*: The Possibility and Necessity of the Human Person," in *The Human Person in Science and Theology*, edited by Niels Henrik Gregersen et al. Grand Rapids: Eerdmans, 2000, 73–94.

Hegel, W. G. F. *Early Theological Writings*. Translated by T. M. Knox. Philadelphia: University of Pennsylvania Press, 1971.

———. *Lectures on the Philosophy of Religion*. Translated by E. P. Spiers and J. B. Sanderson. New York: Humanities Press, 1968.

———. *The Difference between Fichte's and Schelling's System of Philosophy*, translated by H. S. Harries and Walter Cerf. Albany: State University of New York Press, 1977.

Heidegger, Martin. *Being and Time*. Translated by John Macquarrie and E. Robinson. New York: Harper & Row, 1962.

Heim, Mark S. *The Depth of the Riches: A Trinitarian Theology of Religious Ends*. Grand Rapids: Eerdmans, 2001.

———. "Salvation as Communion: Partakers of the Divine Nature," in *Theology Today* 3, no. 61: 322–33.

Hemming, Laurence Paul. "*Analogia non Entis Sed Entitatis*: The Ontological Consequences of the Doctrine of Analogy," *International Journal of Systematic Theology* 2, no. 6 (2004): 118–29.

Henriksen, Jan-Olav. "Creation and Construction: On the Theological Appropriation of Postmodern Theory," in *Modern Theology* 2, no. 18 (2002): 153–69.

Heym, Stefan. *The Wandering Jew*. Evanston, IL: Northwestern University Press, 1981.

Hick, Peter. "One or Two? A Historical Survey of an Aspect of Personhood," *Evangelical Quarterly* 1, no. 77 (2005): 35–45.

Hill, William J., O.P. *The Three-Personed God: The Trinity as a Mystery of Salvation*. Washington, DC: Catholic University of America Press, 1982.

Hipp, Stephen A. *"Person" in Christian Tradition and the Conception of Saint Albert the Great*. Münster: Druckhaus Aschendorff, 2001.

Hobbes, Thomas. *Leviathan*. Edited by Richard Tuck. Cambridge and New York: Cambridge University Press, 1996.

Howell, Nancy R. "The Importance of Being Chimpanzee," *Theology and Science* 1, no. 2 (2003): 179–91.

Hunsinger, George. "Postliberal Theology," in *The Cambridge Companion to Postmodern Theology*, edited by K. J. Vanhoozer. Cambridge: Cambridge University Press, 2003, 42–57.

———. "*Mysterium Trinitatis*: Barth's Conception of Eternity," in *For the Sake of the World: Karl Barth and the Future of Ecclesial Theology*, edited by George Hunsinger. Grand Rapids and Cambridge: Eerdmans, 2004, 165–90.

———. "Karl Barth's Christology: Its Basic Chalcedonian Character," in *The Cambridge Companion to Karl Barth*, ed. John Webster. Cambridge and New York: Cambridge University Press, 2007, 127–42.

Hunt, Anne. *Trinity: Nexus of the Mysteries of Christian Faith*. Maryknoll, NY: Orbis, n2005.

Hyman, Gavin. *The Predicament of Postmodern Theology: Radical Orthodoxy or Nihilist Textualism?* Louisville and London: Westminster John Knox, 2001.

Illingworth, John R. *Personality Human and Divine*. London and New York: Macmillan, 1894.

Jaspers, Karl. *Philosophical Faith and Revelation*. London: Collins, 1967.

———. *Reason and Existenz*. Translated by William Earle. London: Routledge & Kegan Paul, 1956.

Jenson, Robert. *The Triune Identity: God According to the Gospel*. Philadelphia: Fortress Press, 1982.

———. *Systematic Theology*. Oxford and New York: Oxford University Press, 1997, 1–2.

———. "The Logic of the Doctrine of the Trinity," in *Dialog* 26, no. 4 (1987): 245–49.

———. "What Is the Point of Trinitarian Theology?," in *Trinitarian Theology Today: Essays on Divine Being and Act*. Edited by Christoph Schwöbel. Edinburgh: T. & T. Clark, 1995, 31–43.

John Paul II, Pope. "Message of His Holiness John Paul II," in *John Paul II on Science and Religion: Reflections on the New View from Rome*, edited by Robert

Russell et al. Vatican City State: Vatican Observatory Publications/Notre Dame: University of Notre Dame Press, 1990.

Johnson, Elizabeth A. *She Who Is: The Mystery of God in Feminist Theological Discourse*. New York: Crossroad, 1992.

Johnson, William Alexander. *On Religion: A Study of Theological Method in Schleiermacher and Nygren*. Leiden: E. J. Brill, 1964.

Jones, Serene, and Clark M. Williamson. "What's Wrong with Us? Human Nature and Human Sin," in *Essentials of Christian Theology*, edited by William C. Placher. Louisville and London: Westminster John Knox, 2003, 133–57.

Jüngel, Eberhard. *God as the Mystery of the World: On the Foundation of the Theology of the Crucified One in the Dispute between Theism and Atheism*. Translated by Darrell L. Guder. Grand Rapids: Eerdmans, 1991.

———. "On Becoming Truly Human: The Significance of the Reformation Distinction between Person and Works for the Self-Understanding of Modern Humanity," in *Theological Essays II*, edited by J. B. Webster, translated by A. Neufeldt-Fast and J. B. Webster. Edinburgh: T. & T. Clark, 1995.

Kalwaitis, Carl. "The Meaning of Original Consciousness: A Philosophical Study of Schleiermacher's Second 'Speech,'" in *The State of Schleiermacher Scholarship Today: Selected Essays*, edited by Edwina Lawler et al. Lewiston, Queenston, and Lampeter: Edwin Mellen, 2006, 81–110.

Kant, Immanuel. *Religion within the Limits of Reason Alone*. Translated by T. M. Green and H. H. Hudson. New York: Harper & Row, 1960.

———. *Lectures on Philosophical Theology*. Ithaca, NY: Cornell University Press, 1978.

———. *The One Possible Basis for a Demonstration of the Existence of God*. Translated by Gordon Treash. Lincoln: University of Nebraska Press, 1994.

Kaufman, Gordon. "Doing Theology from a Liberal Christian Point of View," in *Doing Theology in Today's World*, edited by John D. Woodbridge and Thomas E. McComiskey. Grand Rapids: Zondervan, 1991, 397–415.

———. *God, Mystery, Diversity: Christian Theology in a Pluralistic World*. Minneapolis: Fortress Press, 1996.

———. "Critical Theology as a University Discipline," in *Theology and the University*, edited by David R. Griffin and Joseph C. Haugh Jr. Albany: State University of New York Press, 1991, 35–50.

———. *An Essay on Theological Method*. Missoula, MT: Scholars, 1979.

———. *God the Problem*. Cambridge, MA: Harvard University Press, 1972.

Kärkkäinen, Veli-Matti. *The Trinity: Global Perspectives*. Louisville and London: Westminster John Knox, 2007.

Kelsey, David H. *The Fabric of Paul Tillich's Theology*. New Haven and London: Yale University Press, 1967.

Khan, Charles H. "Questions and Categories: Aristotle's Doctrine of Categories in the Light of Modern Research," in *Questions*, translated by Henry Hiz. Dordrecht: Reidel, 1978, 227–78.

Kierkegaard, Søren. *The Sickness Unto Death*. Translated by Walter Lowrie. Garden City, NY: Doubleday, 1954.

Kilby, Karen. "Aquinas, the Trinity and the Limits of Understanding," *International Journal of Systematic Theology* 4, no. 7 (2005): 414–27.

———. "Perichoresis and Projection: Problems with Social Doctrines of the Trinity," *New Blackfriars* 81, no. 956 (2000): 432–45.

Killen, R. Allen. *The Ontological Theology of Paul Tillich*. Kampen: Kok, 1956.

Kim, Sung Chel. "Schleiermacher's Secret in the *Speeches*," in *The State of Schleiermacher Scholarship Today: Selected Essays*, edited by Edwina Lawler et al. Lewiston, Queenston, and Lampeter: Edwin Mellen, 2006, 59–80.

Knight, Gordon. "The Theological Significance of Subjectivity," *The Heythrop Journal* 1, no. 46 (2005): 1–10.

Kunnuthara, Abraham Varghese. *Schleiermacher on Christian Consciousness of God's Work in History*. Eugene, OR: Pickwick, 2008.

Lawler, Edwina, et al. *The State of Schleiermacher Scholarship Today: Selected Essays*.
Lewiston, Queenston, and Lampeter: Edwin Mellen, 2006.

Layman, Stephen C. "Tritheism and the Trinity," *Faith and Philosophy* 3, no. 5 (1988): 291–98.

Lee, Sang Hyun. "Jonathan Edwards's Dispositional Conception of the Trinity: A Resource for Contemporary Reformed Theology," in *Toward the Future of Reformed Theology: Tasks, Topics, Traditions*, edited by David Willis and Michael Welker. Grand Rapids and Cambridge: Eerdmans, 1999, 444–55.

Letham, Robert. *The Holy Trinity: In Scripture, History, Theology and Worship*. Phillipsburg, NJ: R. & R., 2004.

Levinas, Emmanuel. *Humanism of the Other*. Translated by Nidra Poller. Urbana and Chicago: University of Illinois Press, 2006.

———. *Of God Who Comes to Mind*. Translated by Bettina Bergo. Stanford: Stanford University Press, 1998.

———. *Otherwise Than Being, or Beyond Essence*. Translated by Alphonso Lingins. Pittsburgh: Duquesne University Press, 1998.

Lindbeck, George. *The Nature of Doctrine: Religion and Theology in a Postliberal Age*. Philadelphia: Westminster, 1984.
Little, Joyce A. *Toward a Thomist Methodology*, in Toronto Studies in Theology Lewiston/Queenston: Edwin Mellen, 34 (1988): 34–35.
Locke, John. *Two Treatises of Government and a Letter Concerning Toleration*. Edited by Ian Shapiro. New Haven: Yale University Press, 2003.
Long, Stephen D. "Radical Orthodoxy," in *The Cambridge Companion to Postmodern Theology*, edited by K. J. Vanhoozer. Cambridge: Cambridge University Press, 2003, 126–45.
Lowe, Walter. "Prospects for a Postmodern Christian Theology: Apocalyptic Without Reserve," *Modern Theology* 1, no. 15 (1999): 17–24.
Lukes, Steven. *Individualism*. Oxford: Basil Blackwell, 1973.
Luther, Martin. "Disputations Against Scholastic Theology," translated by H. J. Grimm in *Luther's Works: Career of the Reformer*, edited by L. H. T. Lehmann. Philadelphia: Muhlenberg, 1957, 31.
———. "The Freedom of a Christian," translated by W. A. Lambert, in *Luther's Works*, 31:329–77.
———. "Letters to George Spalatin: Wittenberg, 19, 1516," *Luther's Works: Letters I*, edited by H. T. Lehmann. Philadelphia: Fortress Press, 1963, 48:23–26.
Lyotard, Jean-François. *The Postmodern Condition: A Report on Knowledge*. Manchester: Manchester University Press, 1984.
MacIntyre, Alasdair. *After Virtue: A Study in Moral Theory*. Notre Dame: University of Notre Dame Press, 1981.
Macken, J. *Themes in the Church Dogmatics*. Cambridge: Cambridge University Press, 1990.
Macmurray, John. *Persons in Relation*. London: Faber & Faber, 1961.
Mariña, Jacqueline. *Transformation of the Self in the Thought of Friedrich Schleiermacher*. Oxford and New York: Oxford University Press, 2008.
Marion, Jean-Luc. "The Idea of God," in *The Cambridge History of Seventeenth-Century Philosophy*, edited by Daniel Garber and Michael Ayers. Cambridge: Cambridge University Press, 1997–98, 1.
———. *On Descartes' Metaphysical Prism*. Translated by Jeffrey L. Kosky. Chicago: University of Chicago Press, 1999.
———. "The Essential Incoherence of Descartes' Definition of Divinity," in *Essays on Descartes' Meditations*, edited by Amelie Oksenberg Rorty. Berkeley: University of California Press, 1986, 317–30.

Marshall, Bruce. *The Trinity and Truth*. Cambridge: Cambridge University Press, 2002.
Martin, Bernard. *Tillich's Doctrine of Man*. Digswell Place, UK: James Nisbet, 1966.
McDowell, John C., and Mike Higton. *Conversing with Barth*. Aldershot, UK and Burlington, VT: Ashgate, 2004.
McFadyen, Alistair I. *The Call to Personhood: A Christian Theory of the Individual in Social Relationships*. Cambridge: Cambridge University Press, 1990.
McFague, Sallie. *Metaphorical Theology: Models of God in Religious Language*. Philadelphia: Fortress Press, 1982.
———. *Models of God: Theology for an Ecological, Nuclear Age*. Philadelphia: Fortress Press, 1987.
McKim, Donald K. *Introducing the Reformed Faith: Biblical Revelation, Christian Tradition, Contemporary Significance*. Louisville and London: Westminster John Knox, 2001.
Metga, Norbert W. *Analogy and Theological Language in the Summa Contra Gentiles: A Textual Survey of the Concept of Analogy and Its Theological Application by St. Thomas Aquinas*. Frankfurt am Main: Peter Lang, 1984.
Meyer, Hans. *The Philosophy of St. Thomas Aquinas*. Translated by Fredric Eckhoff. St. Louis and London: Herder, 1954.
Milbank, John. *Theology and Social Theory: Beyond Secular Reason*. Oxford, UK and Cambridge, MA: Blackwell, 1994.
Molnar, Paul D. *Divine Freedom and the Doctrine of the Immanent Trinity: In Dialogue with Karl Barth and Contemporary Theology*. London and New York: T. & T. Clark/Continuum, 2002.
———. "The Trinity, Election and God's Ontological Freedom: A Response to Kevin W. Hector," *International Journal of Systematic Theology* 3, no. 8 (2008): 294–306.
Moltmann, Jürgen. *Experiences in Theology: Ways and Forms of Christian Theology*, translated by Margaret Kohl. London: SCM, 2000.
———. *History and the Triune God: Contributions to Trinitarian Theology*. New York: Crossroad, 1991.
———. *The Trinity and the Kingdom of God: The Doctrine of God*. London: SCM, 1998.
———. *Theology Today: Two Contributions towards Making Theology Present*. London: SCM, 1988.
Moltmann-Wendel, Elisabeth, and J. Moltmann. *Humanity in God*. London: SCM, 1984.

_____. *God—His and Hers*. New York: Crossroad, 1991
Mondin, Battista, S.X. *St Thomas Aquinas' Philosophy: In the Commentary on the Sentences*. The Hague: Martinus Nijhoff, 1975.
Morales, Fabio. "Relational Attributes in Aristotle," *Phronesis* 3, no. 39 (1994): 55–274.
Mostert, Christiaan. "Barth and Pannenberg on Method, Revelation and Trinity," in *Karl Barth: A Future for Postmodern Theology?*, edited by Geoff Thompson and Christiaan Mostert. Hindmarsh: The Australian Theological Forum, 2000.
Nagel, Thomas. "What Is It Like to Be a Bat?," *The Philosophical Review* 83 (1974): 435–50.
Neie, Herbert. *The Doctrine of the Atonement in the Theology of Wolfhart Pannenberg*. Berlin and New York: Walter de Gruyter, 1979
New and Enlarged Handbook of Christian Theology. Edited by Donald W. Musser and Joseph L. Price. Nashville: Abingdon, 2003.
New Catholic Encyclopedia, group of editors, 2nd ed. Washington, DC: Catholic University of America Press/Gale and Thomson Learning, 2003, "Relation," 12:40–44.
New Dictionary of Theology. Edited by Joseph A. Komonchak et al. Wilmington, DE: Michael Glazier, 1987.
Newton, Sir Isaac. *Principia*. Translated by Andrew Motte and Florian Cajori. Berkeley: University of California Press, 1960.
Nietzsche, Friedrich. *Thus Spoke Zarathustra*. Translated by R. J. Hollindale. London: Penguin, 1969.
_____. *The Antichrist: An Essay Towards a Criticism of Christianity*. Translated by Thomas Common, Mineola, NY: Dover, 2004.
_____. *The Twilight of Idols, or How to Philosophize with a Hammer*. Translated by Duncan Large. Oxford and New York: Oxford University Press, 1998.
_____. *The Gay Science, with a Prelude in Rhymes and an Appendix of Songs*, translated by Walter Kaufmann. New York: Vintage Books, 1974.
Nimmo, Paul T. "The Mediation of Redemption in Schleiermacher's *Glaubenslehre*," *International Journal of Systematic Theology* 2, no. 5 (2003): 187–99.
Oden, Thomas C. *After Modernity . . . What? Agenda for Theology*. Grand Rapids: Zondervan, 1990.
_____. "The Death of Modernity and Postmodern Evangelical Spirituality," in *The Challenge of Postmodernism: An Evangelical Engagement*, 2nd ed., edited by David S. Dockery (Grand Rapids: Baker Academic, 2001).

Oliver, Harold. *A Relational Metaphysics*. The Hague, Boston, and London: Martinus Nijhoff, 1981.

Olson, Roger E. "Wolfhart Pannenberg's Doctrine of the Trinity," *Scottish Journal of Theology* 43 (1990): 175–206.

_____. "Trinity and Eschatology: The Historical Being of God in Jürgen Moltmann and Wolfhart Pannenberg," *Scottish Journal of Theology* 36 (1983): 213–27.

_____, Christopher A. Hill, et al. *The Trinity*. Grand Rapids and Cambridge: Eerdmans, 2002.

Ormerod, Neil. "Wrestling with Rahner on the Trinity," *Irish Theological Quarterly* 3, no. 68 (2003): 213–27.

Ovey, M. J. "A Private Love? Karl Barth and the Triune God," in *Engaging with Barth: Contemporary Evangelical Critiques*, edited by David Gibson and Daniel Strange. Nottingham: Apollos/InterVarsity, 2008, 198–231.

Pannenberg, Wolfhart. *Anthropology in Theological Perspective*. Translated by Matthew J. O'Connell. Edinburgh: T. & T. Clark, 1985.

_____. *An Introduction to Systematic Theology*. Grand Rapids: Eerdmans, 1991.

_____. *Basic Questions in Theology*. London: SCM, 1970, 1.

_____. *Christian Spirituality*. Philadelphia: Westminster, 1983.

_____. "Kerygma and History," *BQT* 1, no. 88.

_____. *Jesus—God and Man*. Translated by Lewis L. Wilkins and Duane A. Priehe. London: SCM, 1968. *The Idea of God and Human Freedom*. Louisville: Westminster John Knox, 1973.

_____. *Theology and the Philosophy of Science*. Translated by Francis McDonagh. Philadelphia: Westminster, 1976.

_____. *Systematic Theology*. Translated by Geoffrey W. Bromiley. Edinburgh: T. & T. Clark, 1991, 1.

_____. "Theological Appropriation of Scientific Understandings: Responses to Hefner, Wicken, Eaves and Tipler," in *Beginning with the End: God, Science and Wolfhart Pannenberg*, edited by C. R. Albright and J. Haugen. Chicago and Lasalle, IL: Open Court, 1997, 427–43

_____. "Problems of a Trinitarian Doctrine of God," *Dialog* 4, no. 26 (1987): 250–57.

_____. "The God of History: The Trinitarian God and the Truth of History," *Kerygma und Dogma* 23 (1977): 76–92.

Parfit, Derek. *Reasons and Persons*. Oxford: Oxford University Press, 1984.

Patočka, Jan. "La Civilisation Technique est-elle Civilisation de Déclin, et Pourquoi?," in *Essais Hérétiques sur la Philosophie de l'Histoire*. Lagrasse: Verdier, 1981

(Eng. J. Patočka, "Is Technological Civilization a Civilization in Decline, and If So, Why?," in *Heretical Essays on the Philosophy of History*, translated by Erika Abrams. Prague: Peltice, 1975.

Pearse, Meic. "Problem? What Problem? Personhood, Late Modern/ Postmodern Rootlessness and Contemporary Identity Crises," *Evangelical Quarterly* 1, no. 77 (2005): 5–11.

Percival, H. M. *The Seven Ecumenical Councils*, from *A Select Library of Nicene and Post-Nicene Fathers*. Grand Rapids: Eerdmans, 1979, 14.

Peters, Ted. *God the World's Future: Systematic Theology for a New Era*, 2nd ed. Minneapolis: Fortress Press, 2000.

———. *God as Trinity: Relationality and Temporality in Divine Life*. Louisville: Westminster John Knox, 1993.

Pfleiderer, Otto. *The Development of Theology in Germany Since Kant and Its Progress in Great Britain Since 1825*. Translated by J. F. Smith. London: Swan Sonnenschein, 1890.

Pieper, Josef. *The Concept of Sin*. Translated by Edward T. Oakes, S.J. South Bend, IN: St. Augustine's, 2001.

Pippin, Robert B. *Modernism as a Philosophical Problem*. Oxford and New York: Blackwell, 1990.

Pitkin, Barbara. "The Protestant Zeno: Calvin and the Development of Melanchthon's Anthropology," *Journal of Religion* 3, no. 84 (2004): 345–78.

Placher, William C. *The Triune God: An Essay in Postliberal Theology*. Louisville and London: Westminster John Knox, 2007.

———. *Unapologetic Theology: A Christian Voice in a Pluralistic Conversation*. Louisville: Westminster John Knox, 1989.

Plato. *The Republic*. Translated by Melissa Lane and H. D. P. Lee. 3rd ed. London: Penguin Classics, 2007.

Powell, Samuel M. *The Trinity in German Thought*. Cambridge: Cambridge University Press, 2001.

Prestige, G. L. *God in Patristic Thought*. London: SPCK, 1981.

Price, Daniel J. *Karl Barth's Anthropology in Light of Modern Thought*. Grand Rapids and Cambridge: Eerdmans, 2002.

Pugliese, Marc A. "Is Karl Rahner a Modalist?" *Irish Theological Quarterly* 2, no. 28 (2003): 229–49.

Rahner, Karl. *Foundations of Christian Faith: An Introduction to the Idea of Christianity*. Translated by William V. Dych. New York: Crossroad, 1989.

_____. *Theological Investigations*. Translated by Kevin Smith. Baltimore: Helicon, 1966, 4.

_____. *Theological Investigations*. Translated by Edward Quinn. New York: Crossroad, 1983, 18.

_____. *Theological Investigations*. Translated by Hugh M. Riley. New York: Crossroad, 1988, 21.

_____. *The Trinity*. Translated by Joseph Donceel. New York: Crossroad, 1997.

_____. "Der dreifaltige Gott als transzendenter Urgrund der Heilsgeschichte," in *Mysterium Salutis, Grundriss heilsgeschichtlicher Dogmatik*, 2, hrsg. J. Feiner u. M. Löhrer. Einsiedeln: Benziger, 1974.

Ratzinger, Cardinal Joseph. *Dogma and Preaching*. Chicago: Franciscan Herald, 1989.

Rauser, Randal. "Rahner's Rule: An Emperor Without Clothes?," *International Journal of Systematic Theology*, 1, no. 7.1 (2005): 81–94.

Redeker, Martin. *Schleiermacher: Life and Thought*. Translated by J. Wallhausser. Philadelphia: Fortress Press, 1973.

Richard St. Victor. *De Trinitate*, in *Sources Chrétiennes*. Edited by G. Salet. Paris: Cerf, 1959, 63.

Richards, Robert L., S.J. *The Problem of an Apologetical Perspective in the Trinitarian Theology of St. Thomas Aquinas*, in *Andecta Gregoriana*, 131.

Ricoeur, Paul. *Oneself as Another*. Translated by Kathleen Blamey. Chicago and London: University of Chicago Press, 1994.

_____. *Freud and Philosophy: An Essay on Interpretation*. Translated by D. Savage. New Haven: Yale University Press, 1970.

_____. *History and Truth*. Translated by Charles A. Kelbley. Evanston, IL: Northwestern University Press, 1977.

_____. *The Symbolism of Evil*. Translated by Emerson Buchan. Boston: Beacon, 1969.

Riggs, John W. *Postmodern Christianity*. Harrisburg, London, and New York: Trinity Press International/Continuum, 2003.

Ring, Nancy C. *Doctrine within the Dialectic of Subjectivity and Objectivity: A Critical Study of the Positions of Paul Tillich and Bernard Lonergan*. San Francisco: Mellen Research University Press, 1991.

Rise, Svein. *The Academic and the Spiritual in Karl Rahner's Theology*. Frankfurt am Main: Peter Lang, 2000.

Robert, Richard. "Barth on Time," in *Karl Barth—Studies in His Theological Method*, edited by Stephen Sykes. Oxford: Oxford University Press, 1979, ch. 4.

Rohls, J. *Protestantische Theologie de Neuzeit I: Die Voraussetzungen und das 19 Jahrhundert.* Tübingen: Mohr, 1997.

Rorty, Amélie Oksenberg. *Essays on Descartes' Meditations.* Berkeley: University of California Press, 1986

Routledge Encyclopedia of Philosophy. Edited by Edward Craig. London and New York: Routledge, 1998, 7.

Said, Edward. *Beginnings: Intentions and Methods.* New York: Basic Books, 1975.

Selander, Sven-Ake. "Human Language between Christian and Secular," in *The Human Image of God*, edited by Hans-Georg Ziebertz et al. Leiden, Boston, and Köln: Brill, 2001.

Scanlon, Michael J. "Trinity and Transcendence," in *Transcendence and Beyond: A Postmodern Inquiry*, edited by J. D. Caputo and M. J. Scanlon. Bloomington: Indiana University Press, 2007, 66–81.

Schleiermacher, Friedrich. "Toward a Theory of Sociable Conduct," translated by Jeffrey Hoover, in *Friedrich Schleiermacher's "Toward a Theory of Sociable Conduct" and Essays on Its Intellectual-Cultural Context*, edited by Ruth D. Richardson. Lewiston, Queenston, and Lampeter: Edwin Mellen, 1995.

———. *On Religion: Speeches to Its Cultural Despisers.* Translated by John Oman. New York: Harper & Row, 1958.

———. *The Christian Faith*, edited by H. R. Mackintosh and J. S. Stewart. Philadelphia: Fortress Press, 1976.

Schonnenberg, Piet, S.J. *Man and Sin: A Theological Review.* Translated by Jospeh Donceel, S.J. Notre Dame: University of Notre Dame Press, 1965.

Schrag, Calvin O. *The Self after Postmodernity.* New Haven and London: Yale University Press, 1997.

Schröder, Caroline. "'I See Something You Don't See': Karl Barth's Doctrine of Providence," in *For the Sake of the World: Karl Barth and the Future of Ecclesial Theology*, edited by George Hunsinger. Grand Rapids and Cambridge: Eerdmans, 2004, 115–35.

Schwöbel, Christoph. "The Renaissance of Trinitarian Theology: Reasons, Problems and Tasks," in *Trinitarian Theology Today: Essays on Divine Being and Act*, edited by C. Schwöbel. Edinburgh: T. & T. Clark, 1995, 1–30.

———. "Editorial Introduction," *Persons, Divine and Human: King's College Essays in Theological Anthropology*, edited by Colin Gunton and Christoph Schwöbel. Edinburgh: T. & T. Clark, 1999.

―――. "Rational Theology in Trinitarian Perspective: Wolfhart Pannenberg's *Systematic Theology*," *Journal of Theological Studies* 2, no. 47 (1996): 498–527.

Sherman, Robert. *The Shift to Modernity: Christ and the Doctrine of Creation in the Theologies of Schleiermacher and Barth*. London and New York: T. & T. Clark/Continuum, 2005.

Shults, F. LeRon. *The Postfoundationalist Task of Theology: Wolfhart Pannenberg and the New Theological Rationality*. Grand Rapids: Eerdmans, 1999.

―――. *Reforming Theological Anthropology: After the Philosophical Turn to Relationality*. Grand Rapids and Cambridge: Eerdmans, 2003.

Sikka, Sonia. "Questioning the Sacred: Heidegger and Levinas on the Locus of Divinity," *Modern Theology* 3, no. 14 (1998): 299–323.

Smith, Huston. "Can Modernity Accommodate Transcendence?" in *Modernity and Religion*, edited by W. Nicholls. Waterloo, ON; Wilfrid Laurier University Press, 1988, 157–66.

Smith, Timothy L. *Thomas Aquinas' Trinitarian Theology: A Study in Theological Method*. Washington, DC: Catholic University of America Press, 2003.

Solomon, Robert C. *Continental Philosophy Since 1750: The Rise and Fall of the Self*, in *A History of Western Philosophy*. Oxford: Oxford University Press, 1988, 7.

Spinks, Bryan D. "Trinitarian Belief and Worship: A Historical Case," in *God's Life in Trinity*, edited by M. Volf and M. Welker. Minneapolis: Fortress Press, 2006, 211–22.

Stiver, Dan R. "Theological Method," in *The Cambridge Companion to Postmodern Theology*, edited by K. J. Vanhoozer. Cambridge: Cambridge University Press, 2003, 170–85.

Stewart, Jacqui A. *Reconstructing Science and Theology in Postmodernity: Pannenberg, Ethics and the Human Sciences*. Aldershot, UK and Burlington, VT: Ashgate, 2000.

Stewart, Melville Y. *The Trinity, East/West Dialogue*. Dordrecht, Boston, and London: Kluwer, 2003.

Tanner, Kathryn. *Theories of Culture: A New Agenda for Theology*. Minneapolis: Fortress Press, 1997.

Taylor, Charles. *Sources of the Self: The Making of the Modern Identity*. Cambridge, MA: Harvard University Press, 1989.

―――. "Understanding and Human Science," *Review of Metaphysics* 34 (1980): 25–38.

Taylor, Mark C. *Deconstructing Theology*. New York: Crossroad/Chico, CA: Scholars, 1982.
_____. *Journeys to Selfhood: Hegel and Kierkegaard*. Berkeley: University of California Press, 1980.
_____. *Erring: A Postmodern A/theology*. Chicago and London: University of Chicago Press, 1984.
Te Velde, Rudi A. *Participation and Substantiality in Thomas Aquinas*. Leiden, New York, Köln: Brill, 1995.
Thompson, Geoff, and Christiaan Mostert. *Karl Barth: A Future for Postmodern Theology?* Hindmarsh: Australian Theological Forum, 2000.
Tice, Terrance N. *Schleiermacher*. Nashville: Abingdon, 2006.
Tillich, Paul. *The Construction of the History of Religion in Schelling's Positive Theology: Its Presuppositions and Principles*. Translated by Victor Nuovo. London: Associated University Press, 1974.
_____. *The Courage to Be*. New Haven and London: Yale University Press, 1952.
_____. *The Dynamics of Faith*. New York: Harper & Brothers, 1957.
_____. *Systematic Theology*. Chicago: University of Chicago Press, 1967, 1–3.
Torrance, Alan. *Persons in Communion: Trinitarian Description and Human Participation*. Edinburgh: T. & T. Clark, 1996.
Torrance, Iain R. *Christology after Chalcedon*. Eugene, OR: Wipf & Stock, 1998.
Tracy, David. *Plurality and Ambiguity: Hermeneutics, Religion, Hope*. New York: Harper & Row, 1987.
_____. *Blessed Rage for Order: The New Pluralism of Theology*. Chicago and London: University of Chicago Press, 1996
Turcescu, Lucian. *Gregory of Nyssa and the Concept of Persons*. Oxford: Oxford Press, 2005.
Van Driel, Edwin Chr. "Karl Barth on the Eternal Existence of Jesus Christ," *Scottish Journal of Theology* 1, no. 60 (2007): 45–61.
_____. *Incarnation Anyway: Arguments for Supralapsarian Christology*. Oxford and New York: Oxford University Press, 2008.
Vanhoozer, Kevin J. "Theology and the Condition of Postmodernity: A Report on Knowledge (of God)," in *The Cambridge Companion to Postmodern Theology*, edited by K. J. Vanhoozer. Cambridge: Cambridge University Press, 2003, 3–25.
_____. *The Drama of Doctrine: A Canonical-Linguistic Approach to Christian Theology*. Louisville: Westminster John Knox, 2005.

Volf, Miroslav. *After Our Likeness: The Church as the Image of the Trinity*. Grand Rapids and Cambridge: Eerdmans, 1998.

———. "Theology, Meaning and Power: A Conversation with George Lindbeck on Theology and the Nature of Christian Difference," in *The Nature of Confession: Evangelicals and Postliberals in Conversation*, edited by Timothy R. Phillips and Dennis L. Okholm. Downers Grove, IL: InterVarsity, 1996.

———, Cameron Krieg, and Thomas Kucharz. *The Future of Theology: Essays in Honor of Jürgen Moltmann*. Grand Rapids and Cambridge: Eerdmans, 1996.

———, and Michael Welker, *God's Life in the Trinity*. Minneapolis: Fortress Press, 2006.

———. "'The Trinity Is Our Social Program': The Doctrine of the Trinity and the Shape of Social Engagement," *Modern Theology* 3, no. 14 (1998): 403–23.

Ward, Graham. "Barth, Hegel and the Possibility of Christian Apologetics," in *Conversing with Barth*, edited by John C. McDowell and Mike Higton. Aldershot, UK and Burlington, VT: Ashgate, 2004, 53–67.

Ward, Keith. *Holding Fast to God*. London: SPCK, 1982.

———. "Deconstructive Theology," in *The Cambridge Companion to Postmodern Theology*, edited by K. J. Vanhoozer. Cambridge: Cambridge University Press, 2003, 76–91.

Ware, Kallistos. "The Holy Trinity: Paradigm of the Human Person," in *The Trinity, East/West Dialogue*, edited by Melville Y. Stewart. Dordrecht, Boston, and London: Kluwer, 2003, 227–43.

Watson, Francis. "The Scope of Hermeneutics," in *The Cambridge Companion to Christian Doctrine*, edited by Colin E. Gunton. Cambridge: Cambridge University Press, 1997, 65–80.

———. *Text, Church and World: Biblical Interpretation in Theological Perspective*. Edinburgh: T. & T. Clark, 1994.

Webb, C. C. J. *God and Personality*. London: Allen & Unwin, 1919.

Webster, John. "Barth and Postmodern Theology: A Fruitful Confrontation?," in *Karl Barth: A Future for Postmodern Theology?*, edited by Geoff Thompson and Christiaan Mostert. Hindmarsh: Australian Theological Press, 2000, 1–72.

———. *Barth's Moral Theology: Human Action in Barth's Thought*. Edinburgh: T. & T. Clark, 1998.

_____. "'There Is No Past in the Church, So There Is No Past in Theology': Barth on the History of Modern Protestant Theology," in *Conversing with Barth*, edited by John C. McDowell and Mike Higton. Aldershot, UK and Burlington, VT: Ashgate, 2004, 14–39.

_____. *The Cambridge Companion to Karl Barth*. Cambridge and New York: Cambridge University Press, 2007.

Weinberg, Julius R. *A Short History of Medieval Philosophy*. Princeton: Princeton University Press, 1966.

Welch, Claude. *In This Name: The Trinity in Contemporary Theology*. New York: Charles Scribner's Sons, 1952.

_____. *Protestant Thought in the Nineteenth Century: 1799-1870*. New Haven: Yale University Press, 1972.

Welker, Michael. "Is the Autonomous Person of European Modernity a Sustainable Model of Human Personhood?," in *The Human Person in Science and Theology*, edited by Niels Henrik Gregersen et al. Grand Rapids: Eerdmans, 2000, 95–114.

West, David. *An Introduction to Continental Philosophy*. Cambridge: Polity, 1982.

Williams, Rowan D. *Lost Icons: Reflections on Cultural Bereavement*. Edinburgh: T. & T. Clark, 2000.

_____. "Barth on the Triune God," in *Karl Barth: Studies of His Theological Method*, edited by S. W. Sykes. Oxford: Oxford University Press, 1979.

Willis, David, and Michael Welker, eds. *Toward the Future of Reformed Theology: Tasks, Topics, Traditions*. Grand Rapids and Cambridge: Eerdmans, 1999.

Wilson, John E. *Introduction to Modern Theology: Trajectories in the German Tradition*. Louisville and London: Westminster John Knox, 2007.

Wilson, John F. "Modernity and Religion: A Problem of Perspective," in *Modernity and Religion*, edited by William Nicholls. Waterloo, ON: Wilfrid Laurier University Press, 1988, 9–18.

Wippel, John F. "Metaphysics," *The Cambridge Companion to Aquinas*, edited by Norman Kretzmann and Eleonore Stump. Cambridge: Cambridge University Press, 1993, 85–127.

Wojtyla, Karol. "Human Nature as the Basis of Ethical Formation," in *Person and Community: Selected Essays*, edited by Karol Wojtyla, translated by Theresa Sandok. New York: Peter Lang, 1993, 95–100.

Young, William W. III. "From Describing to Naming God: Correlating the Five Ways with Aquinas' Doctrine of the Trinity," *New Blackfriars Review* 999, no. 85 (2004): 527–41.

Zahavi, Dan. *Husserl's Phenomenology*. Redwood, CA: Stanford University Press, 2003.

Zizioulas, John D. *Being as Communion: Studies in Personhood and the Church*. Crestwood, NY: St. Vladimir's Seminary Press, 1993.

———. "On Being a Person: Toward an Ontology of Personhood," in *Persons, Divine and Human*, edited by C. Schwöbel and C. Gunton. Edinburgh: T. & T. Clark, 1999, 33–46.

Index of Names

Allen, D., 4, 102
Altizer, T., 222–223, 226, 228, 229
Anselm, 67 n.97, 89 n.148
Antognazza, M. R., 36 n.2
Aquinas, see Thomas Aquinas
Arendt, H., 110–111
Aristotle, 2, 25, 26, 28–30, 67 n.97, 171, 172–175, 180, 189, 191, 300 n.23
Arius, 177
Augustine, 34, 85, 106–107, 130 n.118, 162, 271, 284

Barth, K., 11–12, 55, 56–91, 138, 142, 147 n.16, 188, 203 n.1, 222, 224, 245, 248, 259, 270, 271, 274, 296, 298, 299, 301 n.28
Benedict XVI, 142
Bevans, S., 98 n.6
Blocher, H., 79 n.125
Boehme, J., 129 n.113
Boethius, 11, 24–32, 33, 34, 170, 182
Boff, L., 161
Bradshaw, T., 285
Brooke, J. H., 20
Brown, D., 194–195
Brunner, E., 56
Buber, M., 275
Busch, E., 66 n.94

Calvin, J., 209 n.19
Cappadocian fathers, 25, 154, 170, 188
Chapman, M., 58 n.70
Cicero, 24, 30
Clayton, P., 300–301
Coakley, S., 135 n.130
Cobb, J., 210 n.22
Coffey, D., 40
Coleridge, S. T., 11 n.10

Congar, Y., 146
Coplestone, F. C., 37
Cupitt, D., 101–102 n.10
Cyril of Alexandria, 80 n.126

Dalferth, I. U., 4, 303, 304
Dallavalle, N. A., 261
Darwin, C., 20, 21–22
Derrida, J., 115–117, 118, 231, 253 n.44
Descartes, R., 34, 35, 36, 53–54 nn.61–62, 67 n.97
Diderot, D., 21
Dulles, A., 99 n.6
Dun Scotus, 172

Eutyches, 26, 27

Feuerbach, L., 64, 131 n.118, 280
Fichte, J. G., 32, 36–40, 48, 90, 119, 280
Fiddes, P., 164–170, 172, 179, 186–187
Flacius, M., 299 n.20
Ford, L., 144
Foucault, M., 98 n.5, 113–115, 116 n.64, 118, 129
Fox, P. A., 135–136
Frei, H., 13, 14, 100, 203 nn.1–2, 205, 237, 239, 244–248, 251, 252, 255, 257, 291, 292

Garrett, A., 24
Gasché, R., 181
Gilkey, L., 240, 241
Girard, R., 107 n.27
Gregersen, N. H., 20 n.3, 24, 25
Gregory of Nyssa, 155, 162
Gregory Palamas, 277 n.72
Grenz, S. J., 113, 134–135, 199, 203 n.1
Griffin, D. R., 112, 143

333

Guarino, T. G., 235, 243, 255
Gunton, C. E., 10, 58–59, 78–79 n.125, 88, 101 n.10, 102, 127 n.106, 130–131 n.118, 138–139, 195, 198 n.182, 266 n.25, 271 n.46, 287 n.101

Habermas, J., 128–129, 130, 131
Hartshorne, C., 210 n.22
Heerbrand, J., 299 n.20
Hefner, P., 120–121 n.81, 302
Hegel, G. W. F., 54, 57 n.67, 67–69, 90, 106 n.25, 129, 223, 224, 227, 231, 277, 278 n.75, 297
Heidegger, M., 117 n.69, 119, 129
Heim, M. S., 192
Herder, J. G., 21
Heym, S., 121, 191 n.164
Hick, P., 21, 32 n.36, 182 n.145
Hipp, S. A., 24–25, 28, 31–32
Hobbes, T., 63
Homer, 33 n.38
Howell, N. R., 21 n.6
Hume, D., 21, 35, 67 n.97
Hunsinger, G., 80 n.126, 88 n.148, 187–188, 203–204, 251 n.38
Hyman, G., 107 n.28

Illingworth, J. R., 8 n.7, 287

Jaspers, K., 41 n.18, 91–92, 93
Jenson, R., 142, 148–156, 158, 160, 161, 170, 172, 179, 186–187, 189 n.161, 255, 295 n.12, 296 n.14
Joachim of Fiore, 148 n.17
John Paul II, 305
Johnson, E., 135, 136
Jones, S., 127
Jüngel, E., 40 n.13, 160, 189 n.161, 295 n.12

Kant, I., 21, 35, 36, 37, 39, 54, 58, 67 n.97, 68, 90, 119, 129, 219, 220, 247 n.22, 277, 297

Kaufman, G., 13, 100, 205, 213–222, 235–236, 239, 242
Kelsey, D. H., 46
Kierkegaard, S., 68–69, 231
Kilby, K., 184, 194 n.171

LaCugna, C. M., 161
Leibniz, G. W., 131 n.119
Lessing, G. E., 36–37 n.2
Levinas, E., 118–125, 132
Lindbeck, G., 104–105, 203 n.1, 245 n.17, 248 n.29
Locke, J., 35, 63
Lonergan, B., 56
Long, S. D., 251 n.37
Luther, M., 153, 299 n.20, 300 n.23

Macmurray, J., 11 n.10, 130, 131
Marion, J.-L., 254 n.44
Martin, B., 41
Marx, K., 106 n.25, 129 n.113
Mattingly, B., 180
McFadyen, A., 19
Melanchthon, P., 299 n.20
Metga, N. W., 183
Meyer, H., 175
Milbank, J., 105–107
Molnar, P. D., 295–296
Moltmann, J., 13, 14, 135 n.130, 160, 161, 195, 237, 244, 266–272, 273, 287, 291, 292–297
Moltmann-Wendel, E., 135 n.130

Nagel, T., 196
Neie, H., 279, 280 n.81
Newton, I., 53 n.60
Nietzsche, F. W., 35, 67 n.97, 70 n.104, 106 n.25, 108–112, 113–114, 115, 116, 129 n.113, 231

Oden, T., 100 n.7
Oliver, H., 131
Olson, R. E., 273, 285 n.93, 295 n.12
Origen, 2, 249

Ovey, M. J., 88–89 n.148

Pannenberg, W., 13–14, 161, 169 n.98, 188–189, 237, 244, 265 n.22, 266–267, 272 n.49, 273–286, 287, 291, 292, 296 n.14, 297–302, 304
Parfit, D., 127
Patočka, J., 117 n.67
Peters, T., 126, 148, 156–164, 170, 172, 179, 186–187, 264, 296 n.14
Phan, C., 180
Placher, W. C., 104 n.17, 245 n.17
Plantinga, A., 67 n.97
Plato, 2, 21 n.7, 30, 33, 34, 67 n.97, 109 n.36, 110
Pseudo-Dionysius, 254 n.44

Rahner, K., 56, 142, 145–147, 159–160, 259–264, 265, 266, 267, 268, 270, 271, 273, 294–295
Ratzinger, J., see Pope Benedict XVI
Richard of St. Victor, 130–131 n.118
Richards, R. L., 179 n.136
Ricoeur, P., 20 n.4, 112 n.46
Rise, S., 263
Rohls, J., 58 n.70
Rousseau, J.-J., 276 n.64

Sabellius, 177
Said, E., 114 n.53
Sartre, J.-P., 92 n.157
Scanlon, M., 145–148
Schleiermacher, F. D. E., 55, 56, 299, 301 n.28
Schoonenberg, P., 1
Schrag, C. O., 52, 92, 127
Schröder, C., 74 n.116
Schwöbel, C., 7, 8, 59 n.74, 262–263, 273–274, 305
Selander, S.-A., 137 n.135
Shults, F. L., 281–282, 297
Sikka, S., 124
Smith, T. L., 179
Spinoza, B., 278 n.75

Stewart, J. A., 275, 285, 286
Stiver, D. R., 245 n.15
Swinburne, R., 67 n.97

Tanner, K., 1 n.1
Taylor, C., 21 n.6, 33–34, 53–53 n.61
Taylor, M. C., 13, 54, 67–68, 100, 111–112, 205, 222–234, 235–236, 239, 242
Thomas Aquinas, 2, 12, 67 n.97, 168, 170, 171, 172–173, 175–186, 188, 190, 191, 209 n.19, 272 n.48, 277 n.72
Tillich, P., 11–12, 38 n.7, 41–51, 52, 55, 56, 61, 89–91, 222, 239–242
Torrance, A. J., 295 n.11
Tracy, D., 13, 100, 205–213, 221, 235–236, 239, 242
Turcescu, L., 173–175

Van Driel, E. C., 81 n.130
Vanhoozer, K. J., 100–104
Volf, M., 142 n.3, 161 n.67, 183 n.150, 193–194, 255–257

Ward, G., 1 n.2, 69 n.101, 204–205
Ward, K., 101 n.10, 205
Ware, K., 192–193
Watson, F., 13, 14, 100, 205, 237, 239, 244, 249–254, 255, 257, 291, 292
Webb, C., 32 n.36
Webster, J. B., 57 n.68, 58 n.72, 59–60, 84, 86–87, 94 n.160
Weinberg, J., 182–183
Welch, C., 58 n.71
Welker, M., 90, 121 n.82
West, D., 97 n.1, 116 n.64
Whitehead, A. N., 131 n.119, 278 n.75, 281
William of Occam, 172
Williams, R. D., 195
Young, W. W. III, 176 n.120, 179
Zizioulas, J. D., 135, 136, 142, 287 n.101

Index of Subjects

action, 27, 40, 151–153, 155, 160, 170, 195, 247, 266, 270, 277, 278, 279, 281, 301
analogy, 183–184, 185
anhypostasis, 264–265
anthropocentricism, 51–52, 53, 56, 59, 60–89, 98, 109–110, 134
anthropodicy, 64
anthropology, 54, 55, 75, 84, 86–87, 88, 114–115, 125–126, 128, 134, 135, 137, 193, 246, 267, 275, 276, 280, 285–286, 304, 305
anthropomorphism, 40, 133, 269, 278, 280
apologetics, 1 n.2
a/theology, 228–234
attributes, 276–277

being, 9, 13, 25, 30, 32, 36, 37, 43, 48, 65, 85, 89, 91, 92–93, 115, 118, 122, 123–124, 130, 132, 137, 139, 142, 143, 163, 164–171, 175, 176, 177, 178, 179, 181, 185, 186, 188, 191, 192, 215, 218–219, 229, 250–251, 256, 259, 262, 263, 267, 268, 270, 275–276, 280–281, 282, 284, 286, 288, 292, 294, 301–302, 305, 306
bodies, 27, 127
British Council of Churches, 133–134

cause, 176, 182, 183, 186, 195
Christ, see Jesus Christ
Christology, 9, 26–28, 76–83, 86, 144, 246, 247, 275, 276, 279–280; Chalcedonian Christology, 80 n.126, 81 n.130

church, 1–4, 5, 42, 57, 106, 133, 151, 164, 166, 169, 194, 199, 222–223, 236, 249, 260
collectivism, 194
communion, 25, 56, 67, 71, 85, 92, 93, 94, 132, 134, 136, 137, 139, 142, 157, 166, 168, 178, 187, 282, 284–285, 287, 293, 294, 297, 305, 306, 307
contingency, 68, 69, 93, 141, 144, 158, 181, 215, 280
conversation, 207–208, 210, 221
Copernican Revolution, 62–63
correlation, 13–15, 41–44, 45, 47–48, 49, 50, 51, 52, 89, 90–91, 99–100, 203–237, 239–257, 291–307
cosmological argument, 68
creation, doctrine of, 275, 298

deconstruction, 116, 204–205, 223, 230, 231, 233, 236, 251, 252, 253
dialogical personalism, 275, 286
différance, 106, 204, 211, 228, 229, 251, 253
disciplinary boundaries, 249–254
dualism, 2; Platonic dualism, 2
ecclesiology, 9, 183 n.150
election, 73–79, 81, 82, 83, 86, 87
epistemology, 2, 5, 9, 28, 36–37, 41, 44, 46, 48, 99, 114, 125, 128, 132, 136, 138, 165, 166, 168–170, 179, 180, 184, 207, 215, 219, 224, 225, 227, 236, 244, 246, 247, 259, 275, 286, 291, 301, 302
erring, 230–231
eschatology, 9, 61, 78, 81, 84, 94, 144, 149–150, 153, 156–164, 264, 268, 273, 281, 288

essence, 2, 31–32, 37, 39, 49, 94, 191, 115, 118, 123, 128, 167, 168, 176–178, 179, 181, 182, 184, 189, 199, 259, 262, 263–264, 269, 270, 276–279, 280, 281, 283, 297, 306
eternity, 148–164, 273, 298
existence, 9, 13, 24, 26, 27, 28, 30, 32, 36, 37, 39, 41, 43, 45, 46, 48, 49, 65, 69, 82, 85, 91, 92–93, 94, 107, 109, 110, 127, 130, 132, 164, 168, 170, 175, 176, 177, 178, 179, 180, 181, 182, 185, 192, 211, 216, 219, 225, 226, 229, 240, 241, 247, 256, 268, 269, 273, 275–276, 288, 293, 294, 300, 306

falsehood, 69–72, 78
finitude (the finite), 48–49, 51, 56, 68–69, 115, 123, 164, 176, 181, 192, 224, 225, 229, 234, 240, 264, 274–275, 282, 297–298
first principles, 28–29
forms, 28

gift, 117
God, 36–40, 44–51, 61–66, 73–76, 90, 93, 101, 108–112, 113, 116, 122–125, 132–139, 143–148, 149–171, 175–177, 186–192, 197, 199, 209–212, 213, 215, 217–220, 224–226, 227–228, 229–230, 231–234, 235, 236, 240–241, 250–251, 252–253, 254, 255, 256, 257, 259–272, 276, 278–284, 287–288, 293–295, 298, 302, 304, 305–306; as absolute subject, 40, 111, 269, 271; as Creator, 62–63, 181–183, 186, 187, 197, 232, 250, 280, 306; doctrine of, 3, 8, 24, 35, 56, 91, 141, 158, 188, 189–190, 198, 263, 264, 265, 266, 267, 278, 287, 305; as elector, 73–79, 81, 82, 83, 87; and gender, 135; as Ground of Being, 49–50, 241; and history, 268–269, 294; as originating Cause, 49; personhood of, 3, 15, 23, 40, 45, 49, 50, 52, 55, 59, 75, 82, 84–86, 87, 88, 89, 91, 92, 94, 133, 134, 141–171, 172, 178, 179, 184, 186, 187, 190, 191, 192, 193, 195, 198, 230, 259, 261, 264–266, 267, 270, 271, 272, 273, 275, 279, 280, 282, 283, 284, 286, 287–288, 291, 292, 298, 305–306; as projection, 64, 75–76, 137, 195, 280; self-communication of, 260–262, 270, 271; simplicity of, 177, 178, 189; as 'watchmaker,' 53; as wholly other, 55–89, 90, 123, 137, 195, 211, 215, 251, 257, 296, 306
God the Father, 23, 49–50, 51, 53, 61, 87, 88, 89, 138, 142, 146, 149, 150, 151–152, 154, 155, 156, 163, 165, 167, 168, 169, 177, 178, 180, 182, 193, 259, 266, 270, 271, 275, 279–280, 282–284, 292, 306
God the Holy Spirit, see Holy Spirit
God the Son, 23, 49–50, 53, 61, 77, 78, 87, 88, 89, 138, 142, 144, 148, 150, 151–152, 154, 155, 156, 160, 163, 165, 166, 167, 168, 169, 177, 178, 180, 182, 193, 226, 259, 266, 270, 272, 275, 279–280, 282–284, 288, 292, 306
see also Jesus Christ

hierarchy (hierarchism), 2, 13, 14, 15, 99, 185, 204, 233, 254, 256
Holy Spirit, 23, 49–50, 51, 53, 61, 87, 88, 89, 138, 142, 143, 146, 148, 149, 150, 151–152, 154, 155, 158, 160, 163, 165, 166, 167, 168, 169, 177, 178, 182, 259, 266, 270, 271, 275, 279, 282, 284, 286, 288, 292, 306
human (humanity): continuity with animals, 20–22; and sin, 70, 77–79, 80, 82, 94, 261; as subject, 40

Index of Subjects | 339

hypostasis, 30, 32, 52, 85 n.141, 141, 151, 167, 178, 259, 263, 270, 271–272

immanence, 122–125, 139, 160, 163, 247, 251, 295
incarnation, 23, 26–28, 66–67, 77–83, 89, 133, 143, 144, 146, 151, 153, 154, 157, 163, 187, 260, 268, 279
individualism (individuality), 11, 12, 25, 29, 30, 31, 32, 33, 34, 35, 48, 50, 52, 55, 56, 65, 66, 67, 79, 83, 84, 87, 90, 93, 94, 114–115, 125, 126, 133, 141, 157, 167, 178, 194, 195, 228, 263, 270, 275, 285, 287, 288, 293
individuation, 31, 32, 33, 34, 52, 132, 178, 301
infinity (the infinite), 36, 38, 39, 48, 49, 51, 52, 53, 54, 55, 56, 64, 68–69, 88, 92–93, 118–125, 141, 164, 176, 181, 186, 192, 215, 224, 228, 230, 234, 236, 240, 257, 264, 274–275, 279, 282, 283, 284, 286, 288, 298

Jesus Christ, 23, 61, 66–67, 69–70, 72, 73, 76–83, 86, 87–88, 94, 143, 144, 146, 149, 151, 152–153, 154, 156, 158, 160, 163, 165, 186, 187, 193, 199, 215, 222, 232, 235, 246, 262, 268, 269–270, 275, 279–280, 282–284, 295, 298, 306; two natures of, 26–28, 51, 80–82, 279
see also Christology, God the Son

liberal theology, 213–222
Logos, 26, 78 n.124, 80, 82, 151, 153, 154; *logos asarkos*, 78 n.124; *logos ensarkos*, 78 n.124

metaphysics, 36, 92, 101–102, 106, 115–116, 119, 131, 138, 145, 158, 159, 160, 180–186, 188, 208, 209–211, 251, 269, 301

modernism (modernity), 2–4, 5, 6, 7, 9, 10–11, 12, 13, 19–40, 52, 53, 55, 56, 58, 59–69, 72–73, 75, 76, 79, 82, 83, 84, 87, 88, 89–91, 92, 93–94, 97, 99, 102, 103–104, 106, 112, 114, 115, 116, 119, 125–126, 127, 129, 130, 131, 132, 133, 134, 135, 138, 157, 194, 196, 197, 198, 199, 203, 205–207, 211, 224, 227, 244, 249, 251, 254, 265, 266, 272, 277, 287, 288, 293, 299; modernist theologies, 10, 92, 103–104, 254, 264, 293
morality, 65, 86–87, 109, 110, 119
mystery, 36, 146, 158, 215, 260–261, 270, 283

nature, 25–28, 29, 46, 50, 52, 92, 101, 141, 142, 177, 178, 182, 184–185, 186, 199, 210, 215, 256, 268, 271, 272, 276, 282, 283, 284, 286, 292, 306, 307
necessity, 68, 144, 181, 287
negative theology, 253
nihilism, 106

ontology, 2, 9, 10, 11, 12, 20, 28, 41, 46, 48, 85, 89, 91, 93, 101–102, 106, 114, 120, 137, 143, 151, 155, 163, 168–170, 172, 176, 179, 180, 181, 182, 188, 192, 194, 195, 199, 224–225, 235, 240, 251, 253, 259, 260–261, 262, 264, 265, 266, 267, 268, 270, 274, 276, 277, 281, 283, 284, 286, 287, 288, 291, 297, 301, 306
opera ad intra/extra trinitatis, 270
otherness (the other), 9, 10, 12–13, 14, 25, 30, 40, 41, 64, 65, 66, 67, 82, 89, 92, 111, 115, 116, 118–132, 136, 139, 141, 143–148, 167, 186–196, 197, 215, 224, 226–227, 229, 235, 241–242, 269, 270, 275, 276, 283, 285–286, 292, 296, 305
ousia, 141, 167, 168

panentheism, 192–193, 195, 280, 281, 284, 293–294, 295, 296–297
participation, 12, 84, 100, 139, 143–148, 164–171, 180–186, 190–191, 192, 196, 265, 268, 269, 270, 280; mutual participation, 128–132, 137, 265
particularity (particulars), 13, 25, 28, 29, 30–31, 32, 36, 50, 52, 54, 56, 92–93, 132, 160, 178, 184, 194, 205, 240, 241–242, 243, 251, 255, 256, 287, 298
perichoresis, 85, 157, 163, 164, 167, 170, 226, 237, 255–256, 259–289, 294, 295, 296, 305, 306
person (personhood), 2–3, 7–11, 13, 14, 19–27, 30–34, 35, 40, 41–55, 56, 59, 73, 84–88, 89–94, 108–140, 141–171, 172, 178, 179, 184–185, 187, 189, 190, 192–195, 237, 256, 259–289, 291, 292, 294, 297, 301–302, 304, 306
pluralism, 213, 217–218, 221–222, 306
pneumatology, 9, 247, 284, 286
see also Holy Spirit
postmodernism (postmodernity), 3–6, 8–9, 10–11, 12, 13, 21, 35, 92, 94, 97–140, 141, 142–143, 170, 194, 195, 196, 197, 198–199, 203–213, 219, 223, 227, 228, 235, 236, 242, 244, 249, 250–251, 252, 253–254, 265, 267, 272, 285, 288, 289, 292, 293, 300, 303–307; postmodernist theologies, 5–7, 10, 11, 92, 94, 97, 103–104, 133, 134, 137, 138, 172, 180, 184, 190, 195, 197–199, 223, 235, 239, 254, 264, 297
premodernity, 63, 222

Rahner's Rule, 142, 145–147, 155, 158–161, 259–267, 273–274, 281, 283, 294–296

reason (rationality), 24, 25, 31, 32, 33–34, 35, 37, 57–58, 92, 119, 128, 134, 180, 184–185, 285
relatio, 171–180
relation (relationality, relationship), 2, 3, 7–11, 12–13, 14, 25, 35, 41–55, 56, 67, 77, 79, 82, 83, 85, 86, 87, 88, 89, 90, 91, 92, 93, 94, 99–100, 114–115, 118, 119, 121, 123, 125, 126–127, 128, 129, 130–140, 141–195, 196, 223, 225, 234, 237, 240, 244, 255, 259–289, 291–302, 304, 305, 306
revelation, 24, 38, 39–40, 46–48, 52, 56, 81, 84, 85, 88, 90, 101, 149, 160, 218, 224, 230, 233, 235, 242, 247, 259, 262, 267, 269, 274, 277, 278, 282, 295, 296, 298, 300, 305
revisionist theology, 205–213

Seinsweise, 84–85, 87, 88, 89, 142, 266, 269, 274
self (selfhood), 2, 3, 8, 10, 11, 14, 19–24, 31, 32, 33, 34, 35–94, 108–140, 143, 167, 191, 194, 195, 199, 206, 223, 226, 228, 229, 230, 231, 233, 236, 237, 241–242, 261–262, 269, 275, 276, 279, 285–286, 288, 293, 305
self-assertion, 72, 74, 79, 82, 84
self-awareness, 48–49, 50, 51, 52, 63, 64, 65–66, 67, 71, 91
self-centeredness, 12, 48, 50, 125, 133
self-denial, 72
self-differentiation, 267, 269, 270, 273–286, 291–292, 294, 295, 297–302, 306, 307
self-distinction, 53, 93, 132, 139, 198, 256, 265, 266, 275, 276, 279–281, 282, 283, 284–285, 288, 289, 292, 296, 299
self-fulfillment, 49, 52, 57, 62, 63, 65, 67, 72, 74, 79, 82–83, 87, 93, 109, 112, 115, 120, 123, 133, 150, 225, 268

self-sufficiency, 74, 79, 89, 114, 115, 118, 126, 132, 141, 142, 206, 273
sociality, 143–148, 150, 164–171, 256, 275, 285, 286, 293
soteriology, 9, 191, 260–263, 268–269
subject, subjectivity, 3, 11, 40, 41, 53, 87, 88, 93, 94, 116, 118, 121, 122, 123, 126, 127, 129, 134, 181, 182, 199, 263, 265, 267, 269, 270, 276, 285, 286, 287, 288, 292
subordination, 13, 15, 90, 102, 203–205, 229, 247, 262, 282, 302, 304
subsistence, 2, 9, 26–28, 30, 31, 32, 33, 34, 168, 170, 171, 172, 178, 179, 180, 182, 184, 185, 186, 190, 193, 259, 264, 270
substance, 2, 9, 25, 26, 27, 28, 30–32, 34, 134, 166, 167, 170, 172–175, 176, 177, 178, 179, 180, 182, 183, 186, 189, 269, 271, 277–278, 292, 297
substratum, 30

τὰ πρός τι, 171, 173, 181
temporality, 148–164, 273, 298
theodicy, 64
theology, 12, 56–62, 64–66, 67, 89–91, 132, 133, 136, 138, 199, 207, 208–209, 213–234, 239, 240–241, 243, 244–254, 255, 256, 257, 288, 298–307; as authoritarian, 215–216, 221; and biblical studies, 251–253; and culture, 2, 3–4, 10; as event, 42; and historical context, 1–4, 5, 8, 62; and intellectual context, 2, 3, 4–7, 8, 10, 12, 14, 57, 59, 60, 90, 94, 97–107, 108, 134, 195, 196–197, 203–205, 207, 212–213, 214–222, 234, 235, 237, 239, 243, 244, 246, 247–248, 250, 252, 255, 257, 266–267, 288–289, 291–307; as philosophical reflection, 208–209, 211–212; as pietism, 66–67; role of theologians, 1–3
transcendence, 35, 36, 37, 38–39, 46, 90, 91–92, 93, 94, 114, 119, 122–123, 125, 127, 128, 134, 137, 138–139, 143–156, 158, 186, 192, 196, 199, 206–207, 208, 210–212, 219, 232, 233, 236, 247, 250, 251, 254, 257, 259, 267, 276, 278, 286
Trinity, doctrine of, 7, 8, 9, 10, 11, 13, 14, 15, 22–23, 49–51, 52–53, 54–55, 61, 84–85, 87–88, 89–94, 133–140, 141–199, 222, 237, 256–257, 259–289, 292–293, 305–307; as event, 153, 155, 168–170; relations of origin, 93, 166, 167, 177, 283, 288; Trinity as 'symbol', 135–137

'ultimate concern,' 40, 41–51, 52
unity, 13, 30, 184, 205, 255, 280, 281–282, 288, 289, 291–292, 294, 297, 301, 304, 305, 307
universality (universals), 29, 30, 31, 50, 54, 56, 185, 267–268

wholeness, 162–164

CPSIA information can be obtained
at www.ICGtesting.com
Printed in the USA
FFOW03n1653130314
4200FF